Environmental Problems/
Behavioral Solutions

THE BROOKS/COLE BASIC CONCEPTS IN ENVIRONMENT AND BEHAVIOR SERIES

Series Editors:

Irwin Altman, The University of Utah
Daniel Stokols, University of California, Irvine
Lawrence S. Wrightsman, The University of Kansas

AN INTRODUCTION TO ECOLOGICAL PSYCHOLOGY
Allan W. Wicker, Claremont Graduate School

CULTURE AND ENVIRONMENT
Irwin Altman, The University of Utah
Martin Chemers, The University of Utah

INQUIRY BY DESIGN:
TOOLS FOR ENVIRONMENT-BEHAVIOR RESEARCH
John Zeisel, Harvard University

ENVIRONMENTAL EVALUATION:
PERCEPTION AND PUBLIC POLICY
Ervin H. Zube, University of Arizona

ENVIRONMENTAL PROBLEMS/BEHAVIORAL SOLUTIONS
John D. Cone, West Virginia University
Steven C. Hayes, University of North Carolina

Environmental Problems/ Behavioral Solutions

JOHN D. CONE
West Virginia University

STEVEN C. HAYES
University of North Carolina

BROOKS/COLE PUBLISHING COMPANY
MONTEREY, CALIFORNIA

Published by the Press Syndicate of the University of Cambridge
The Pitt Building, Trumpington Street, Cambridge CB2 1RP
32 East 57th Street, New York, NY 10022, USA
296 Beaconsfield Parade, Middle Park, Melbourne 3206, Australia

© 1980 by Wadsworth, Inc., Belmont, California 94002
© Cambridge University Press 1984

First published 1980 by Wadsworth, Inc.
First published by Cambridge University Press 1984

Printed in the United States of America

ISBN 0 521 31973 0

Library of Congress Cataloging in Publication Data

Cone, John D   1942-
    Environmental problems/behavioral solutions.

    (Brooks/Cole series in environment and behavior)
    Bibliography: p.
    Includes index.
        1.   Environmental psychology.   2.   Behavior modifica-
tion.   I.   Hayes, Steven C., joint author.   II.   Title.
III.   Series.
BF353.C66   363.7'001'9   80-12471
ISBN 0-8185-0392-0

Front cover photo © *Stanley Rice. Back cover photo* © *Elizabeth Crews, Icon.*

Acquisition Editor: *William H. Hicks*
Project Development Editor: *Claire Verduin*
Manuscript Editor: *Grace Holloway*
Production Editor: *Patricia E. Cain*
Interior and Cover Design: *Jamie Sue Brooks*
Illustrations: *Ayxa Art*
Typesetting: *Graphic Typesetting Service, Los Angeles, California*

To
Laura Churchill Cone and Ruth D. Hayes
and to the memory of
Jack Cone, Charles A. Hayes, Jr., and Edwin Koupal

SERIES FOREWORD

The study of environment and behavior has shown a rapid development in recent decades; we expect that interest in this field will continue at a high level in the future. As a young and informative area, it has many exciting qualities. For example, the analysis of the relationship between human behavior and the physical environment has attracted researchers from many fields in the *social sciences,* such as psychology, sociology, geography, and anthropology, and from the *environmental design* fields, such as architecture, urban and regional planning, and interior design. The multidisciplinary character of this field has led to an atmosphere of stimulation, cross-fertilization, and, yes, even confusion and difficulty in communication. Furthermore, because of the diversity in intellectual styles and goals of its participants, research on environment and behavior has as often dealt with applied, real-world problems of environmental design as it has treated basic and theoretical issues.

These factors, coupled with the relatively young stage of development of the field, led us to believe that a series of short books on different areas of the environment and behavior field would be useful to students, researchers, and practitioners. Our view was that the study of environment and behavior had not yet firmed up to the point that a single volume would do justice to the wide range of topics now being studied or to the variety of audiences interested in the field. Furthermore, it became clear to us that new topical areas have emerged over the past decade and that some vehicle is necessary to facilitate the evolutionary growth of the field.

For these reasons, Brooks/Cole established the present series of books on environment and behavior with the following goals in mind: first, we endeavored to develop a series of short volumes on areas of research and knowledge that are relatively well established and are characterized by a reasonably substantial body of knowledge. Second, we have recruited authors from a diversity of disciplines who bring to bear a variety of perspectives on various subjects in the field. Third, we asked authors not only to summarize research and knowledge on their topic but also to set forth a "point of view," if not a theoretical orientation, in their book. It was our intention, therefore, that these volumes be more than textbooks in the usual sense of the term—that they not only summarize existing knowledge in an understandable way but also, we hope, advance the field intellectually. Fourth, we wanted the books in the series to be useful to a broad range of students and readers. We planned for the volumes to be educationally valuable to students and professionals from different fields in the social sciences and environmental-design fields and to be of interest to readers with different levels of formal professional training. As part of our broad and flexible strategy, the series will allow instructors in a variety of fields teaching a variety of courses to select different combinations of volumes to meet their particular course needs. In so doing, an instructor might select several books for a course or use a small number of volumes as supplementary reading material.

Because the series is open-ended and not restricted to a particular body of content, we hope that it will not only serve to summarize knowledge in the field of environment and behavior but also contribute to the growth and development of this exciting area of study.

Irwin Altman
Daniel Stokols
Lawrence S. Wrightsman

PREFACE

The course of our involvement with environmentally relevant psychology parallels that of the field itself. This book is organized so as to follow that course. In 1972, when we first began working together, both of us had two relatively separate interests: the environment and psychology. One of us (J.D.C.) had an established background in the scientific study of human behavior and a personal commitment to the solution of environmental problems; the other (S.C.H.) had developing scientific interests and was fresh from a year of full-time environmental activism. The mixture of these two interests seemed natural to us. Psychologists are scientists with an interest in the understanding and control of behavior, and many environmental problems seem to be clearly behavioral. This book is about the marriage of these two areas.

Part I describes the differences between physical and behavioral technology and notes that the latter generally has been ignored in the study of environmental problems. When behavior has been studied, it usually has been viewed as a reaction to environmental characteristics rather than as a cause of them. Chapter 1 defines environmentally relevant behavior and distinguishes between protective and destructive types of relevance. The chapter also outlines a conceptual orientation toward the development of a technology for controlling these behaviors. A taxonomy of environmentally protective and destructive behaviors is presented in Chapter 2.

In Part II the basic principles of environmentally relevant behavior are presented (Chapter 3), and the research tactics and designs for studying them are described (Chapter 4). Whereas Part I presents a set of conceptual/philosophical biases, Part II provides the tools with which these biases can be brought to bear on environmental problems.

Directed by its biases and armed by its tools, the first tentative work in environmentally relevant psychology began in the early 1970s. The first area to be investigated with much intensity was environmental aesthetics, particularly litter control and noise control. Part III documents the work on these problems.

Environments can do more than annoy or disgust. They can be depleted; they can be polluted; they can even kill. Thus, emboldened by the early success in aesthetic areas, researchers in the field soon began to attack more serious problems, such as recycling, energy consumption, and transportation. These areas are examined in Part IV.

As the problems have become more complicated, the solutions have become more difficult to find. Researchers throughout the field are heartened by the progress achieved thus far but are sobered by the tasks yet ahead. In Part V we address some of these tasks. We examine the difficult issues of generality and maintenance, and we speculate on the proper role for behavioral scientists to take in solving environmental problems.

The book has been written for upper-division undergraduate or beginning graduate students in any of the behavioral sciences or in fields of study dealing with environmental design. A knowledge of general behavioral-science research procedures is not required, nor is a specific acquaintance with applied behavior analysis. Chapters 3 and 4 have been included particularly for readers without such prior experience and may be skipped by others who find them too repetitious of earlier learning.

To further the book's general applicability to a wide range of audiences, we have included a glossary of terms. In addition, because doing things about environmental problems may have more pedagogic value than merely reading about them, projects have been suggested at the end of many of the chapters. These projects are not merely academic exercises. They are included to foster an interest in the value of empiricism and experimentation, not just as a part of science but as a part of life.

The preparation of this small volume has been assisted by numerous people in whose debt we will long remain. The consulting editors for this Brooks/Cole series—Daniel Stokols, Lawrence Wrightsman, and, especially, Irwin Altman —provided many hours of their time and many useful comments on early drafts of each chapter. It is largely due to Irv's careful editorial suggestions and his skillful blend of positive reinforcement and criticism that the book has finally been completed. Many other colleagues have helped, but E. Scott Geller deserves special mention for his continued, unselfish provision of early copies of his own prolific writings in this area.

Writing a book is challenge enough without having numerous hassles with the technical preparation of the manuscript. We are sincerely grateful to Beverly Ruf and Genene Sharp, who, by their competent handling of the manuscript's typing and proofing, gave us the "space" to be more concerned with the substance of our message. In this regard we want also to acknowledge the tremendous support given us by the staff at Brooks/Cole. William Hicks and Claire Verduin guided us from the beginning in managing the overall flow of the manuscript. Along the way, Loraine Brownlee, Vena Dyer, Karen List, and Bob Rowland have assisted in various capacities. Thanks must also go to Grace Holloway, whose final editing was exceptionally competent. Not only did she catch all our grammatical *faux pas,* but she also read for content and made numerous useful (if painful!) suggestions for improving the organization and flow of the book. Deborah Windom assisted greatly with the index.

Last, we wish to express special appreciation to our wives and families. Jan Cone was exceptionally patient and supportive, especially during one intensive period of writing in which both of us were living in the same house but writing on juxtaposed schedules (S.C.H., "the mole," worked best between 10 P.M. and 8 A.M.!).

John D. Cone
Steven C. Hayes

CONTENTS

PART I
**THE NATURE OF ENVIRONMENTALLY RELEVANT
BEHAVIORAL SCIENCE   1**

**CHAPTER 1   BEHAVIORAL SCIENCE AND
ENVIRONMENTAL PROBLEMS   3**

Physical versus Behavioral Technology   4
Environmentally Relevant Behaviors   5
A Framework for Examining Behavior   6
Summary   10

**CHAPTER 2   ENVIRONMENTALLY RELEVANT
PSYCHOLOGY   11**

Environmental Relevance: A Matter of Degree   11
A Taxonomy of Environmental Problems and
Relevant Behaviors   15
Environmentally Relevant Psychology:
A Definition   18
Summary   20

PART II
**AN APPLIED BEHAVIOR-ANALYTIC APPROACH TO
ENVIRONMENTALLY RELEVANT BEHAVIORAL
SCIENCE   23**

CHAPTER 3   BASIC PRINCIPLES OF BEHAVIOR   25

Two Types of Behavior   25
Increasing Behavior   26
Decreasing Behavior   28
Stimulus Control   30
Timing the Stimulus Change   30

Scheduling the Stimulus Change   31
Schedules Based on Single Responses of More Than
    One Person   33
Applying the Basic Principles   34
Summary   35

**CHAPTER 4   RESEARCH STRATEGIES AND DESIGNS IN
THE DEVELOPMENT OF BEHAVIORAL SOLUTIONS   36**

The Correlational/Descriptive Strategy   38
Experimental/Manipulative Strategies   41
Measuring the Dependent Variable   50
Summary   50

**PART III
SOLVING PROBLEMS OF ENVIRONMENTAL AESTHETICS   53**

**CHAPTER 5   ENVIRONMENTAL AESTHETICS: LITTER
AND ENVIRONMENTAL DESIGN   55**

Litter   55
Designing Environments to Minimize Litter and
    Perpetuate Their Own Attractiveness   74
Summary   80
Suggested Projects   81

CHAPTER 6   NOISE AND ITS CONTROL   85

Sound and Its Measurement   86
The Definition of Noise   88
The Effects of Noise   90
The Control of Noise   92
Summary   103
Suggested Project   103

**PART IV
SOLVING HEALTH-RELATED AND RESOURCE-RELATED
ENVIRONMENTAL PROBLEMS   105**

CHAPTER 7   POPULATION CONTROL   107

The Ethics of Population Control   108
Views on Population Control   110
Research Issues   114
Family-Planning Programs   116

Summary   125
Suggested Project   125

CHAPTER 8   RECYCLING   127

The Problem of Waste: Why Recycle?   127
The Factors Inhibiting Recycling   130
Methods of Waste Reduction and Resource
    Recovery   133
Summary   148
Suggested Project   148

CHAPTER 9   TRANSPORTATION   149

The Energy Used in Transportation   149
Altering the Use of Mass-Transit Systems   150
Altering the Use of Automobiles   156
Reducing Fuel Usage in Fleet-Operated Trucks   161
Issues in Altering Transportation Behavior   162
Summary   167
Suggested Projects   168

CHAPTER 10   RESIDENTIAL ENERGY CONSERVATION   173

Altering Overall Energy Consumption in
    Individual Residences   175
Altering Specific Energy-Related Behaviors   193
Reducing Energy Consumed in Master-Metered
    Housing   195
Summary   197
Suggested Project   198

CHAPTER 11   RESIDENTIAL WATER CONSERVATION   199

Major Uses of Water in the Home   201
Water-Saving Devices   201
Deterrents to Residential Water Conservation   206
What Can Behavior Analysts Do about Water
    Conservation?   210
Summary   213
Suggested Projects   214

PART V
PROMOTING THE USE OF BEHAVIORAL APPROACHES TO
ENVIRONMENTAL PROBLEMS   219

CHAPTER 12 THE GENERALITY OF BEHAVIORAL SOLUTIONS 221

Types of Generality 222
Evidence for the Generality of Behavioral
Solutions 222
Tactical Considerations in Behavioral
Solutions 228
Contributions of Reactive Research to
Behavioral Solutions 229
Prevention of the Development of Environmentally
Destructive Behavioral Repertoires 231
An Eco-Systems Perspective 232
Summary 232

CHAPTER 13 PROMOTING BEHAVIORAL-SCIENCE IMPACT THROUGH EXPERIMENTAL SOCIAL REFORM 234

Systems-Level Contingencies 234
How Can We Influence Systems? 237
Behavioral Experimentation: How, What,
and Why? 238
What Does the Behavioral Scientist Need? 240
Issues in the Pursuit of Behavioral Solutions 241
The Future of Environmentally Relevant
Psychology 243

Glossary 244
References 250
Author Index 267
Subject Index 273

Environmental Problems/
Behavioral Solutions

PART I

THE NATURE OF
ENVIRONMENTALLY
RELEVANT
BEHAVIORAL SCIENCE

Part I of this book deals with the biases of the authors. Put more gently, the first two chapters establish a context within which to understand the rest of the book by conveying our own perspective on the role of behavioral science in the solution of environmental problems.

As you read Part I, you will encounter a distinction between physical technological solutions and behavioral technological ones. The importance of both and the relative neglect of the second are emphasized. We attempt to remedy some of this neglect by calling attention to the various environmentally relevant behaviors (that is, human activities that influence the nature or extent of physical environmental problems) and by showing ways in which those behaviors can be increased or decreased (behavioral technology).

In Chapter 1 we distinguish between two major classes of environmentally relevant behaviors: protective and destructive. An important problem is to find ways of increasing the first while decreasing the second. A conceptual orientation toward the development of an effective behavioral technology is shown to be very useful, and one based on the principles of the experimental analysis of behavior is suggested in Chapter 1 and elaborated on in Chapter 2. We also describe the advantages of examining environmental problems in terms of the conflict between short-term and long-term effects of behavior. Effective solutions are often the product of a greater congruence between the two.

Chapter 2 provides a more specific listing of environmentally protective and destructive behaviors, together with the major categories of environmental problems (for example, aesthetic, health related, resource related) to which the behaviors apply. We show that although many human activities are relevant to the quality of the physical environment, some are more directly relevant than others. Thus, picking up trash along a highway or in a public park is more directly related to the problem of litter than is a verbal statement on one's feeling or attitude about trash. Our bias toward the more relevant behaviors is clearly evident in Chapter 2.

However, within the general field of environmental psychology our point of view is a minority one. A review of recent literature documents the extent to which the majority view is primarily concerned with the effects of environment on behavior rather than with the effects of behavior on environment. Some reorientation is needed if we are all to develop an adequate understanding of environmental problems and their solutions.

Chapter 1

BEHAVIORAL SCIENCE AND ENVIRONMENTAL PROBLEMS

. . . the "doomsday" predictions of demographers (Ehrlich, 1968; Meadows, Meadows, Randers, & Behrens, 1972), the shrinkage of natural resources . . . and the deterioration of environmental quality prompted widespread concern about the constraints of the ecological environment. Suddenly, psychologists "rediscovered" the large-scale physical environment and, in collaboration with architects and planners, became increasingly involved in studying its impact on behavior [Stokols, 1978, pp. 255–256].

The year 1970 appears to have been a landmark one for the populist environmental movement. It was also the beginning of a clearly definable behavioral-science involvement in problems of the physical environment. On "Earth Day" in that year, demonstrations in nearly every major U.S. city called immediate and alarming attention to the deteriorating condition of our environment. At the same time major position papers emerged (Craik, 1970; Wohlwill, 1970) on the embryonic study of behavior/environment relations from a psychological perspective.

Of course, concern with the physical environment as it affects behavior was not first articulated in 1970. That interest had been around for at least 35 years, especially among early Gestalt psychologists (for example, Koffka, 1935). However, behavioral scientists seriously concerned with human/environment relations (ecological psychologists, for example) were few before the 1970s, with most of the formal investigation of human/environment interaction confined to the work of Barker and his colleagues at the University of Kansas (see Barker, 1963, 1968). With widespread trumpeting of a coming disaster for the ecosphere during the later 1960s and early 1970s, enough behavioral scientists became involved in the study of environment/behavior relationships to produce a burgeoning field of inquiry. The result of this rediscovery is a rather loose collection of books, articles, theoretical statements, and empirical studies all having something to do with behavior/environment interaction.

In spite of increased activity in the area, though, a clear definition of environmental study from a psychological perspective has proved elusive. After all, if you view behaviors as natural phenomena, then they must be the result of both past (for example, evolution, experience) and present conditions in the environment and the organism. In that sense, all of behavioral science is involved in the study of behavior/environment interrelations. But environmental psychology is distinguishable from other areas of behavioral science, as the following analysis will show.

Stokols (1978) has recently differentiated environmental psychology from other areas of behavioral science on the basis of three major dimensions: (1) an ecological perspective, (2) an emphasis on scientific strategies for solving community/environment problems, and (3) an interdisciplinary approach. In an exhaustive review of research characterized by these dimensions, Stokols concluded that the field is "more than an assortment of loosely-defined problem areas but less than a comprehensive, coherent paradigm" (p. 257). He summarized research to date in eight topical areas within the field. These are cognitive representation of the spatial environment, personality and the environment, attitudes toward the environment, environmental assessment, experimental analysis of ecologically relevant behavior, movement of humans through space, impact of the physical environment on behavior, and ecological psychology.

Our book deals with only one of these areas, the experimental analysis of ecologically relevant behavior. We are concerned with human actions as they relate to problems in the physical environment. Simply put, our goal is to encourage the development of a behavioral technology adequate for the solution of environmental problems.

What do you think of when you hear the word *technology?* Most people are reminded of such things as machines, labor-saving devices, or industrialization. Technology includes these, of course, but it has a wider meaning. The root of the word is a Greek term that means "art, craft, or skill"—in other words, knowing how to do something. In this book we will explore the question "What do we need to know how to do in order to solve environmental problems?" Put another way, "What kind of technology do we need to develop?" Because this is a book about behavior, we will direct most of our attention to the kind of technology behavioral scientists can create.

PHYSICAL VERSUS BEHAVIORAL TECHNOLOGY

Attempts to solve environmental problems have followed several distinct courses. One of the most popular tactics has been the development of new *physical* technology. Enormous amounts of money have been spent in such areas as nuclear energy, solar energy, insulation technology, antipollution technology, and so on, with the view that if we only had appropriate physical technology, our environmental problems would disappear. The popularity of this approach to environmental problems does not mean that it is the only, or even potentially the most successful, avenue. Development of new methods of insulating houses is hardly important unless people actually use these methods. Building smaller and more efficient automobiles will not solve our resource or pollution problems if more and more people drive more and more cars more and more often. Under such conditions, having smaller, more efficient cars may delay or prevent more serious problems from developing, but that is not the same as a solution.

The point is that the impact of physical technology on environmental problems always depends on whether and how it is used. Put another way, environmental impact usually depends most directly upon people's *behavior* and only indirectly on physical technology. Social scientists are concerned with the understanding of behavior, and, hopefully, they have something to say about how to influence the proper use of physical technology. Unfortunately, although physical technology (for example, cars, TV, missiles, electricity production) has expanded incredibly during the past century, developments in *behavioral* technology have lagged far behind.

The term *behavioral technology* refers to the science, art, skill, or craft of influencing socially important human behavior. Many institutions in society —for example, politics, religion, advertising, and education—use various forms of behavioral technology. Only quite recently, however, have social scientists begun to study and develop a technology of behavior that has a sound scientific footing. The state of behavioral technology can be compared to the state of physical technology in the early stages of the Industrial Revolution: we are just beginning to approach the subject systematically.

The imbalance of physical and behavioral technology seems to be at the root of many of society's difficulties, and none more so than environmental problems. It is not that physical technology itself is bad or dangerous; it is that without knowing how to control it we are in danger of its controlling us. Behavioral technology can help us put physical technology to appropriate use.

In addition to contributing to the best use of physical technology, behavioral technology can be useful in solving or alleviating environmental problems for which helpful physical technology is not available or effective. For example, litter is a problem that is currently impossible to control fully through physical technology. Throwing trash on the ground is a human behavior, one that is problematic despite the advances made by physical technologists in developing biodegradable trash, efficient street sweepers, and the like. Behavioral techniques are needed (and as we will show in Chapter 5, are largely available) to help solve this problem. Thus, with or without available physical technology, the development of an adequate behavioral technology seems critical to the solution of environmental problems. In many ways, that sums up the message and purpose of this book.

ENVIRONMENTALLY RELEVANT BEHAVIORS

Seeing the potential importance of a behavioral technology is the first step toward an environmentally relevant psychology. The second is to decide what behaviors need to be influenced. Environmentally relevant behaviors are those human activities that influence, in a positive or negative fashion, the nature or extent of physical environmental problems (Cone & Hayes, 1976). There are at least two broad classes of such activities. The first is *environmentally protective* behaviors. These are actions that improve environmental conditions. For example, picking up litter, buying efficient appliances, and recycling glass are environmentally protective. A major goal of environmentally relevant psychology is to establish and strengthen these activities. The second class consists of *environmentally destructive* behaviors. These are actions that worsen environmental conditions. Examples would include throwing down trash, turning up the thermostat on the furnace, and driving a gas-guzzling automobile. A second major goal of environmentally relevant psychology here is to eliminate or decrease the strength of these behaviors.

The distinction between environmentally protective and destructive behaviors is an important one. Litter, for example, is often thought of as a single problem behavior. It is not. Many behaviors influence the amount of trash on the ground. These behaviors are both protective (for example, buying products packaged in recyclable or returnable containers, picking up litter) and destructive (for example, disposing of litter improperly). As will be discussed in Chapter 5, recent evidence shows that programs that lead to a decrease in the environmentally destructive behaviors involved in littering do not lead automatically to an increase in the environmentally protective behaviors involved and vice versa. Thus, it is important to identify both types of behaviors that relate to a given environmental problem.

A FRAMEWORK FOR EXAMINING BEHAVIOR

As indicated by its title, this book is about behavioral solutions to environmental problems. As such, it is not primarily focused on ways in which human behavior is affected by various aspects of the context in which it occurs. Instead, the book is concerned with the reverse—that is, with ways in which behavior affects the physical environment so as to contribute to its future well-being or demise.

Conceptually, we subscribe to the view that most environmentally relevant behavior can be thought of in terms of the three components of an operant paradigm described by B. F. Skinner (1953). This model is symbolized by the terms S^D–R–S^R. In the model a "discriminative stimulus" (symbolized by the letters S^D), or environmental context, sets the occasion for a response (R). You might think of an S^D as a signal that a particular behavior is called for in a particular context. The response itself often acts upon the environment; that is, the world around us sometimes changes as a function of what we do. These changes (symbolized by S^R) can be either positive (S^{R+}) or negative (S^{R-}). We call the change "reinforcing," or positive (S^{R+}), when it is shown that the future likelihood of that behavior (given that situation, or S^D) increases. If the response decreases in frequency in the future, we say the change has been negative, or "punishing" (that is, the response has been followed by a punisher, S^{R-}). We will talk more about these terms in Chapter 3.

To see that this paradigm is a fruitful way to view behavior in relation to the numerous environmental problems presently confronting us, consider the following example. It has long been known that the consequences that are most likely to influence behavior are, other things being equal, those that follow the behavior closely in time (see, for example, Rachlin & Green, 1972). Many environmental problems are seemingly due to this fact about behavior. They often appear to involve conflicts between short-term positive consequences and long-term negative ones. Thus, many environmental problems are the result of what Platt (1973) has referred to as "social traps." In his words, "men or organizations or whole societies get themselves started in some direction or some set of relationships that later prove to be unpleasant or lethal and that they see no easy way to back out of or to avoid" (p. 641).

As an example, Platt describes Hardin's (1968) well-known "tragedy of the commons," in which a grassy square in the center of towns and hamlets would be set aside for the common use. Generally, inhabitants would graze their cows on the grass. Because everyone was free to use the commons, the more cows a person had, the better off he or she would stand to be financially. As might be expected, as individuals increased their herds, more and more grass was consumed until eventually none was left and the cows all perished. What had been individually reinforcing in the short run was collectively punishing in the long run. In terms of the three components of the operant paradigm, we can diagram Platt's notion as follows:

$$S^D - R - S^{R+} \text{ short} \ldots S^{R-} \text{ long.}$$

The diagram shows a discriminative stimulus setting the occasion for a response whose short-term consequence is reinforcing (S^{R+} short). The long-term consequence is punishing (S^{R-} long), however.

The paradigm seems applicable to numerous environmental problems. Consider, for example, the wasteful use of natural gas. Given a cold house (S^D), a person might react by turning the thermostat to 78° (R). The short-term consequence would be increased warmth and comfort (S^{R+} short). The long-term consequences would be likely to be a higher gas bill for the person and depletion of our natural-gas supplies (S^{R-} long) at a faster rate than if a lower thermostat reading had been tolerated. Similarly, consider the hunting and killing of certain species of animals such as the Australian kangaroo. The immediate consequence of killing kangaroos (R) is access to valuable hides that can be exchanged for money (S^{R+} short). Of course, the competitive extermination of kangaroos by numerous individuals for short-term gains leads to the eventual long-term situation in which no more are available to kill (S^{R-} long).

Table 1-1. Environmental Examples of Social Traps Diagrammed Using Three-Term Operant Notation

Activity	Discriminative Stimulus (S^D)	Response (R)	Short-Term Consequence ($S^R \pm$ short)	Long-Term Consequence . . . ($S^R \pm$ long)
Littering	trash	litter	relief from burden of carrying trash "+"	littered environment "−"
Nonlittering	trash	hold	burden of carrying trash "−"	clean environment "+"
Nonlittering	trash	hold	praise or other reward "+"	clean environment "+"
Antilittering	trash	pick up	praise or other reward "+"	clean environment "+"
Water pollution	waste	dump in river	relief from burden of waste "+"	polluted river "−"
Burying wastes	waste	bury	increased cost of production "−"	clean river "+"
Burying wastes	waste	bury	tax incentives "+"	clean river "+"

As a preliminary example of how this analysis can be applied to the solution of environmental problems, consider the general case of pollution. Quigley (1970) has defined environmental pollution as the "movement of objects by human action from places or conditions where they are natural or unobjectionable to places or conditions where they are unnatural, objectionable, and injurious" (p. 1). Littering can be viewed as a specific instance of the general class of pollution behaviors (Cone, Parham, & Feirstein, 1972). Symbolically, a piece of trash in one's hand (S^D) requires holding (R) something that may be mildly unpleasant (S^{R-} short). Littering, or ridding oneself of the trash, is therefore reinforcing, at least in the short run. The alternatives are diagrammed in Table 1–1.

The second row of the table shows that the immediate (short-term) consequence of the alternative to littering is negative; that is, one must remain in contact with (hold) the annoying trash until an appropriate container can be located. Thus, to reduce littering by increasing its alternative will require finding ways of avoiding or overcoming the short-term negative consequences of holding onto trash, an example of which is represented in the third row of the table. Another possibility also exists, that of antilittering, or picking up trash others have discarded. Antilittering is also depicted in Table 1–1. Note from the table that praise has been used to strengthen the response of picking up trash. Other consequences could also be used and indeed have been, as will be shown in Chapter 5.

The present discussion is intended to illustrate the general approach one can take in seeking behavioral solutions to environmental problems. If littering is properly construed as a member of the general class of pollution behaviors, other forms or members of that class can be studied in a similar manner. For example, consider the act of discharging industrial waste into a neighboring river. This form of pollution is also diagrammed in Table 1–1. The alternative to water pollution presented in the table is identical to that in our nonlittering example, and the implications for intervention are the same; that is, ways will be needed to overcome the negative short-term consequences of the alternative. In the case of antilittering, praise was used. For water pollution one suggestion has been that the federal government offer tax incentives to companies that engage in nonpolluting alternatives. This solution is diagrammed in the last row in Table 1–1. If we compare the last row with the immediately preceding one for pollution, it is clear that the effectiveness of the solution hinges in part on the relative magnitude of the short-term consequences; that is, if the tax incentive is to be effective, it must be greater than the increased cost of burying the waste (S^{R-} short).

There are other behavioral principles that may aid us in the development of solutions to environmental problems (see Chapter 3). The point we have been making is that environmental problems take on an entirely different cast when viewed from a psychological perspective. But psychologists are not the only professionals taking this perspective; many other types of behavioral scientists have contributed to the development of environmentally relevant psychology. The nature of that endeavor will be discussed in the next chapter.

SUMMARY

A psychological approach to environmental problems is one that examines the behavioral contribution to these problems. The goal of this approach is the development of a behavioral technology for controlling environmentally protective and destructive behavior. In this book we will approach behavior from the perspective that although it is greatly influenced by its environment it also exerts a reciprocal influence on the environment. Such a perspective leads to the delineation of several aspects of environmental problems as critical—for example, the congruence of short-term and long-term consequences. Behavioral scientists of all varieties can contribute to the generation of solutions to environmental problems within the framework of an environmentally relevant psychology, as later chapters will show.

Chapter 2

ENVIRONMENTALLY RELEVANT PSYCHOLOGY

In the previous chapter we defined environmentally relevant behavior and outlined the general characteristics of a psychological approach to environmental problems. In this chapter we introduce the notion that many human activities are environmentally relevant but that some are more so than others. To make this point, we review recent literature in the field of environment and behavior and classify it in terms of its focus. We note that most of the research emphasis to date has been on the environment as it affects behavior. The result is that most of the literature has only indirect environmental relevance at best.

To facilitate a more direct approach, a taxonomy of environmental problems and of behaviors relevant to their solution is provided. We describe problems of environmental aesthetics, health, and natural resources. The chapter ends with a definition of environmentally relevant psychology and a description of its major characteristics.

ENVIRONMENTAL RELEVANCE: A MATTER OF DEGREE

In Chapter 1 we distinguished between environmentally protective and environmentally destructive behaviors. Within each of these general categories, behaviors will differ in the degree to which they relate directly to environmental difficulties (Cone & Hayes, 1976). Many activities (littering, for example) have a direct, functional impact on problematic environmental conditions; that is, changes in the rate or intensity of the behavior are virtually certain to have a corresponding effect on the environment. Other behaviors are environmentally relevant but in a much less direct fashion. They can be said to be thematically or conceptually related to environmental problems rather than functionally related to them. Voting for a conservation-oriented politician, having a certain attitude toward pollution, or buying an energy-efficient air conditioner are examples of behaviors that are related to environmental problems at a conceptual level but not necessarily at a functional one. Attitudes toward pollution may influence other, more important environmentally related behaviors in oneself or others, or such attitudes may be functionally independent of and irrelevant to the solution of environmental problems. Buying an efficient air conditioner could save energy or could actually lead to increased consumption due to increased use (perhaps now rationalized by the fact that the air conditioner is "efficient").

The issue of directness is important for environmentally relevant psychology because it is possible to err on the side of either too much or too little concern for indirectly relevant behaviors. The general field of environmental psychology has consistently emphasized behaviors with *presumed,* but often not demonstrated, environmental relevance. Documentation for this observation comes from an earlier paper (Cone & Hayes, 1976) in which we reviewed all research studies described in the first five volumes of the major journal in the field, *Environment and Behavior.* We examined all data-based conclusions from those studies and categorized them in terms of their focus. We distinguished two general types of studies: (1) those primarily concerned with the effects of the environment on some aspect of human functioning and (2) those primarily concerned with the effects of behavior on the environment.

Examples of the first type of study are those looking at the effects of airport-noise levels on the psychological well-being of people in nearby housing, investigating the effects of crowding on performance of simple and complex intellectual tasks, and examining the relationship between air pollution indexes and deaths from respiratory ailments. Each study of this type takes the environmental circumstance as more or less given and looks at some human behavioral and/or physiological reaction to it.

Examples of the second type of study are those looking at the effects of rewarding children for picking up litter on the amount of trash in a city park, examining the relationship between tax incentives and corporate pollution of rivers and streams, and investigating the effects of mass-education campaigns on energy conservation in residential dwellings. Each study of this type systematically manipulates some aspect of behavior and then examines its effects on the environment.

Of the studies we reviewed, the vast majority were of the first type. In fact, when the conclusions of all 128 studies were classified, 97.7% of them were found to have a human-behavior focus; that is, environmental variables were studied for their *effects on behavior* rather than vice versa. For example, Canter and Thorne (1972) showed that preferences in architectural style were different between groups of college students in Sydney, Australia, and Glasgow, Scotland. Presumably, environmental/geographical differences produced the variation in preference. Studies of attitudes toward noise, smog, litter, and other forms of pollution are additional examples of environmental research having a human-behavior focus.

This approach to environment/behavior studies can be thought of as "reactive" (Cone & Hayes, 1976) because it examines reactions or responses *to* environmental problems rather than the problems themselves. We include in this category any study of the effects of some feature of the physical environment on some type of behavior. The behavior may be a verbal statement, as in the case of attitudes; a physiological response, as in the case of respiratory ailments related to smog; or a movement, as in the case of attempting to escape from crowded, noisy, or smoggy circumstances.

In reactive research, behaviors are often studied that are only indirectly related to the environmental problem. They have thematic or conceptual relevance to the problem but are not functionally related to it. A common rationale for these studies is that research on these reactions will lead to a better understanding of the problem and eventually to its solution. Unfortunately, the route from reactions to an environmental circumstance to changes in it is rather indirect and lengthy. It is one thing to know that people have generally negative attitudes toward a particular problem, for example, and quite another to get them to *do* something about it. We know more about people's perceptions of environmental problems from such research, but the problems themselves continue unabated.

Why is there such a one-sided emphasis on this type of research? There seem to be several explanations. As Craik (1970) has noted, "strategic assumptions and methodological obstacles partially explain the neglect of physical environmental variables" (p. 14). He goes on to suggest greater attention to physical environmental characteristics, a suggestion with which we heartily agree. Rather than confining our research to attitudes *toward,* adaptation *to,* and movement *toward* and *away* from various types of environments, it seems we could benefit greatly from studying aspects of the physical environment itself and ways it is affected by the behavior of its inhabitants.

This point of view has not gone unchallenged. With respect to verbal reactions or attitudes, Wohlwill (1975) has noted that when problems have a central cognitive or attitudinal component, then the broad field of attitude study becomes relevant. We would agree—at least partially. Indeed, we have no quarrel with research on what people *say* about the environment and about their reactions to it. Our concern is with the tacit assumption underlying such studies. Their justification on the grounds that changing beliefs is the way to change other types of behavior having a more direct, functional relationship to environmental characteristics is certainly problematic. The difficulty with such an assumption is the repeated demonstration of the independence of verbal and overt motor forms of behavior (see Wicker, 1969, 1972). The psychological literature is replete with studies showing that saying does not lead to doing. Moreover, environmental research that has included measures of both types of behavior has similarly shown either their complete independence or only moderate overlap. For example, Heberlein (1971) observed persons who dropped or retained a handbill given to them by an experimenter. When interviewed later, only 50% of those observed to have littered actually admitted it. In another study, Bickman (1972) observed college students walking past trash that had been deliberately planted in their path. When interviewed, 94% responded "yes" when asked whether it should be "everyone's responsibility to pick up litter when they see it" (p. 324). However, only 1.4% of the students actually picked up the litter!

A few studies (for example, Seligman, Kriss, Darley, Fazio, Becker, & Pryor, 1977) have shown a stronger relationship between saying and doing. But even if they were strongly related in a correlational sense (see Chapter 4), one would still have to demonstrate that by directly changing environmental attitudes, one can influence the environment itself. Thus far, a great deal of time and effort has gone into developing scales designed to measure environmental attitudes (for example, Maloney & Ward, 1973; Tognacci, Weigel, Widenn, & Vernon, 1972) and relating such measures to other variables such as education (for example, Jaggi & Westacott, 1974) or participation in antipollution clubs (Levenson, 1973). But very few studies have actually *changed* attitudes and then examined the effects of this change upon the environment or upon directly relevant behaviors (compare Geller, Bowen, & Chiang, 1978). Until this is done, the importance of environmental attitudes will remain unknown.

As an example of these points, imagine you are interested in reducing the consumption of electricity in a college dorm. You reason that the excessive consumption of energy in the dorm is due to students' beliefs that the energy problem is a myth and that their own life-style has no influence on energy consumption. You devise an energy-attitude measure, administer it, and obtain data showing that students do have these attitudes. Accordingly, you inform the residents of the scope and importance of the problem, and you try to "raise their energy consciousness" by showing them how they waste energy in their day-to-day activities. Now you measure their attitudes again and find that they are greatly changed for the better. Job done, you relax, confident that you have helped solve a critical problem. But wait! The environmental problem you started with was excessive energy consumption. Did your program lead to decreased energy use? As we will show in Chapter 10, several studies have actually tried such educational programs, and in most cases the answer, unfortunately, was "no."

The value of reactive studies, especially those measuring verbal responses to the environment, will be discussed more thoroughly in Chapter 12. Suffice it to say here that we are generally supportive of a bi-directional approach to behavior/environment studies—that is, the study of both the environment as it affects behavior and behavior as it affects the environment (Stokols, 1978)—and certainly see value in measuring attitudes toward environmental features. However, it is important not to divert valuable resources from studying behavior as it directly affects the environment on the assumption that changing attitudes is an important prerequisite to changing behavior. This assumption simply has not received empirical support.

These cautions notwithstanding, however, it is important not to be too cavalier in our rejection of reactive research. In the evolution of concern about various environmental problems, a sequence of events has occurred that you will see appearing again and again throughout this book. First, the problem is recognized. Next, physical technology is developed to solve it. Eventually, it is realized that physical technology alone cannot solve the problem and that its behavioral components must be examined. Early work on the behavioral side of the problem usually deals with indirect features such as attitudes, knowledge, or information. Out of this, educational programs and appeals are developed that attempt to change these attitudes. Finally, as the problem continues, more direct behavior-change technologies are developed.

Since our concern in this book is with behaviors having direct, functional environmental relevance, it might be helpful to outline just what some of these behaviors are. The next section does so.

A TAXONOMY OF ENVIRONMENTAL PROBLEMS AND RELEVANT BEHAVIORS

Because environmentally relevant psychology must deal with human actions bearing on environmental quality, it seems useful to develop a systematic description of those circumstances that are termed environmental problems and the behaviors that may influence them. To accomplish this, environmental concerns can be divided into three major areas: (1) environmental aesthetics and the quality of life, (2) physical health and the survival of the human species on this planet, and (3) concern for the maintenance and efficient use of available non-renewable resources. Such a three-way division allows for the ready categorization of most current environmental problems, as can be seen in Table 2–1. The table also shows some examples of behaviors that are protective or destructive in each area.

Problems of Environmental Aesthetics

Both the natural and the built environment impinge on our senses in ways that can be described as pleasant or unpleasant. A concern for this quality of the environment may exist quite apart from any direct concern for physical health or resource management. For example, the prevention and control of litter seem to be primarily an issue of aesthetics; a littered environment seems unpleasant to most of us. Other problems in this category include the protection and maintenance of natural areas and wildlife (forests, parks, wilderness, endangered species). Issues of forestry practice (for example, clear-cutting trees) or mining procedures (for example, land reclamation) may be, in part, aesthetic. Concern over the decay of urban areas, the proliferation of billboards, the deterioration of buildings, and other aspects of the built environment would be categorized here. Finally, unpleasant nonvisual events such as nonharmful but aversive noise levels, undesirable vibration, and unpleasant odors belong in the aesthetic group.

Health-Related Problems

The second group of environmental problems relates to detrimental effects on physical health. Air pollution, water pollution, land pollution, radiation hazards, collection of toxic substances in the food chain, and extremely high levels of noise fit into this category.

Table 2–1. A Taxonomy of Environmental Problems and Examples of Behaviors Positively or Negatively Influencing Each

	Behavioral Examples	
Environmental Problems	*Environmentally Protective*	*Environmentally Destructive*
Aesthetics		
Litter	Buying deposit bottles Picking up trash from the ground	Buying overpackaged materials Throwing trash on the ground
Natural environment and wildlife	Supporting wilderness legislation Staying on paths in parks	Buying garments made from pelts of endangered species Cutting down forests
Built environment	Refurbishing old buildings Taking down ugly billboards	Throwing rocks through windows of old urban buildings Putting up gaudy billboards
Noise (moderate levels)	Buying plastic trash cans Avoiding needless use of motorized devices	Running chain saws in wilderness areas Taking mufflers off motorcycles
Smells, heat, vibration	Building good sewage plants Lessening vibration from motors	Using foul-smelling chemicals Burning trash
Health		
Air	Buying cars with clean-burning engines Passing laws to control industrial stacks	Disconnecting antipollution devices on cars Burning trash
Land	Fighting dams that will allow salt water to spoil farmland Recycling materials that might go to the dump	Overusing fertilizer Using toxic insecticides
Water	Building sewage-treatment facilities Reusing industrial effluent	Dumping used oil in storm drains Putting raw sewage in streams
Food	Buying organic food Using biological pest controls	Putting toxic chemicals in food Using DDT

Noise (high levels)	Supporting noise legislation Wearing earplugs	Flying planes at supersonic speeds over land Exposing factory workers to excessive noise
Radiation	Avoiding aerosol sprays to protect the ozone layer Slowing the premature development of nuclear power	Storing radioactive wastes in unsafe containers Overusing X rays
Thermal	Putting cooling towers in factories	Dumping hot water from power plants into streams
Resources Energy	Turning off air conditioners Buying efficient appliances	Turning up thermostats in winter
Population	Using birth control Disseminating family-planning information	Having ten children Discouraging birth control
Transportation	Riding buses rather than driving cars Supporting modernization of trains	Raising bus fares excessively
Recycling	Buying recyclable materials Setting up glass-recycling depots	Buying nonrecyclable plastic
Soil	Contour-plowing land Planting winter crops	Strip-mining without reclaiming the land Tearing down windbreaks
Water	Buying composting toilets	Running garden hoses constantly

17

Resource-Related Problems

The last group of problems involves the consumption of nonrenewable resources. These problems often contribute to health-related or aesthetic-related problems such as those already mentioned, but a concern for resource management would exist regardless of the short-term effects on physical health or environmental aesthetics. Examples of these problems include excessive energy consumption; failure to recycle metal, paper, glass, or other products; inadequate water or soil conservation; overpopulation; and inadequate mass transit.

This listing of environmental problems is not exhaustive (for example, *air pollution* is a broad term encompassing many specific problems), nor is it mutually exclusive. Frequently a single behavior or a single environmental problem will have environmental relevance in two or all three of the areas. Excessive use of automobiles, for example, produces pollution, which is aesthetically unpleasant *and* is damaging to health *and* depletes supplies of fossil fuels. The suggested system does draw attention, however, to some of the different ways in which events can be seen as environmental problems.

In each of these areas, it is possible to locate both environmentally protective and destructive behaviors that relate to the problem. In subsequent chapters we will describe in more detail the behavioral nature of many of these problems and the development of programs helpful in the control of these behaviors, but the list of behaviors in Table 2–1 should make a point: the ways in which we influence our environment are diverse and pervasive. It is not an exaggeration to say that virtually everything we do each day has some environmental impact —protective or destructive.

ENVIRONMENTALLY RELEVANT PSYCHOLOGY: A DEFINITION

The subject matter of environmentally relevant psychology has been partially delineated in the preceding sections, but a more formal definition can now be made. Environmentally relevant psychology is the study of ways of increasing behaviors that are environmentally protective and of decreasing those that are environmentally destructive. These behaviors must have been shown to be directly or indirectly related to aesthetic, health-related, or resource-related aspects of the physical environment (Cone & Hayes, 1976).

In addition to having these characteristics, an environmentally relevant psychology is:

1. Analytic. As Baer, Wolf, and Risley (1968) have noted, "An experimenter has achieved an analysis of a behavior when he can exercise control over it" (p. 94). At the most fundamental level this means that the experimenter must demonstrate a systematic and replicated relationship between the experimental manipulations and a meaningful change in the environment. At higher levels of analysis, there may also be a determination of the components of the intervention that are effective, a delineation of the boundary conditions under which the intervention will succeed or fail, and a parametric analysis of the intensity of intervention required. This kind of experimental research may be oriented toward either intersubject designs using groups or intrasubject designs. Issues of design are described in Chapter 4.

2. Technologically precise. Because the purpose of environmentally relevant psychology is to change behaviors of environmental importance, it is critical that the procedures used be stated in such a way that they can be repeated by others who have read the research reports. The important details of any given program must be included, so that other investigators in the field can build upon and systematically replicate previous research.

3. Conceptually systematic. In developing an applied area, there is always the danger that each problem will be approached and answered on its own terms, without necessarily showing any relevance to known psychological principles or to other problem situations. The result is a body of "tricks of the trade," each one unrelated to all the others, so that solving one problem has little or nothing to contribute to the solution of others (Wohlwill & Carson, 1972). By showing the relevance of particular findings to principles of behavior (outlined in the next chapter), the field has a better chance of growing in an orderly fashion, of developing into a discipline rather than a loose collection of specific solutions to specific problems.

4. Systems oriented. A last characteristic of environmentally relevant psychology is that it should consider the overall or long-term impact of environmental programs from a systems point of view (compare Willems, 1974). The environmental movement has emphasized the interrelatedness of environmental characteristics and the importance of taking a comprehensive view. For example, by reducing the number of predators, we may have an increase in pests, leading to decreased crop yields, and so on. Understanding the interrelationships among units of the ecosystem should lead to a similar realization with regard to environmental programs.

This point is of such importance that it deserves some additional exploration. Often technology has been shown to be excessively narrow in its focus; this is true for both physical technology and behavioral technology. Typically, the long-term or overall impact of programs designed to solve specific problems is overlooked or misread. Let us take examples from each type of technology and see whether we can discern the potential overall or long-term impact.

First, consider solar energy. The development of physical technology in this area may someday reach the point that we have a virtually unlimited supply of clean energy. Sound good? Well, it does until you think about what we might do with it. With unlimited energy our standard of living would soar (good), but our consumption of goods and resources would also soar (not so good). We could use this energy to increase food production (good), but we might also see a rise in population and associated pollution (not so good). We might have a great deal more free time as more and more energy-consuming automation occurred (good), but we might use this time in such a way that our parks, wilderness areas, and rural areas would be overrun with campers and tourists (not so good). Thus, from an ecological or systems view, the interrelationships among events are such that a solution of one problem may create many others.

Next, consider recycling. Assume we develop a behavioral technology that is so successful that *all* newspapers are collected and taken to a recycling plant instead of being thrown away. This saves trees (good), but it may also produce water pollution from the ink-removal process (not so good). The recycling saves the energy used to make virgin paper (good), but it also consumes a good deal of energy in the process of collecting the papers and in the recycling process itself (not so good). Thus, without a careful analysis of the overall and long-term impact of changes we make, there is no way to say that they are environmentally desirable.

One way to ensure that the many dimensions of environmental problems (for example, economic, biological, social, psychological, political) are recognized and considered is to approach these problems from a transdisciplinary perspective. Psychologists may have a good deal to say about environmentally relevant behavior, but an understanding of the problem and of the steps needed to solve it often involves a good deal of knowledge about other fields of study as well. We are writing this book from the standpoint of psychologists, but that does not mean that an environmentally relevant psychology will be independent of other areas of knowledge. It cannot be effective without the contribution and interaction of many fields.

SUMMARY

Although the great majority of research in environmental psychology has concerned behaviors only indirectly related to environmental problems themselves, an environmentally relevant psychology focuses on changes in the physical environment produced by human actions or on these actions themselves if their impact upon the environment is obvious. These behaviors and their products are studied experimentally, so that functional relationships can be determined. Reports of these studies are technically precise, enabling other researchers to replicate the findings and implement them elsewhere. These reports also show the relevance of the studies to principles of behavior. Finally, such research reveals a concern for the overall or long-term impact of developed programs on the environment and generally involves contributions from a variety of scientific disciplines.

We have shown that environmental problems can be grouped into those dealing with aesthetic, health-related, or resource-related aspects of the physical environment. Within each of these broad categories, it is possible to identify both environmentally protective and destructive behaviors.

Though environmentally relevant psychology can be approached from several theoretical positions, by far the greatest amount of research showing the above characteristics has been done from the point of view of the experimental analysis of behavior (B. F. Skinner, 1953). Because this book is based on an understanding of behavioral principles, it is to these that we now turn.

PART II

AN APPLIED BEHAVIOR-ANALYTIC APPROACH TO ENVIRONMENTALLY RELEVANT BEHAVIORAL SCIENCE

Part I has provided an overview of the approaches generally taken in environment/behavior studies. It has also indicated where our point of view diverges from the mainstream. Our biases have been described and supported. Having laid the conceptual/philosophical foundation for the remainder of the book, the first two chapters have set the stage for Part II. Now we turn to providing you with some tools to implement the kind of behavioral-science view of environmental problem solving suggested in Part I.

Chapter 3 provides a brief but reasonably complete description of the basic principles of behavior. It emphasizes that human activities affecting the environment are operant behaviors that can be understood in terms of the principles of the experimental analysis of behavior. Viewed in this way, environmentally relevant behaviors can be changed effectively by the systematic application of procedures developed and verified in both laboratory and field settings. These procedures and their use are also described in Chapter 3.

Armed with generally applicable behavior-change technology, we are now ready to bring these procedures to bear on solving important environmental problems. Because many of the procedures will not have been previously applied to particular environmental problems, however, it will be necessary to evaluate their effectiveness rather carefully. The tools needed for this evaluation are presented in Chapter 4. Here again, the exposition is brief. It is intended more as an introduction to facilitate understanding of the research discussed in later chapters than as a complete preparation in the methodology of evaluation.

Chapter 4 introduces the major research paradigms in behavioral science: correlational and experimental. The potential value of each in building a discipline of environmental-problem solution is described. Because of their more direct relevance to the development of behavioral technology, however, we place more emphasis on experimental/manipulative approaches than on correlational ones. Further, within this general category we stress intrasubject designs in which behavior or environmental conditions are monitored over relatively long periods. Changes in behavior or environment from their baseline conditions are then observed as an experimental variable is manipulated in an intervention phase. Intrasubject designs have been those most widely used by researchers taking an applied behavior-analytic approach to environmental-problem solution.

After completing Part II, you should have some appreciation for both our conceptual/philosophical biases and the tools necessary to put these biases to work in developing an effective behavioral technology.

Chapter 3

BASIC PRINCIPLES
OF BEHAVIOR

In the previous chapter we said that environmental problems have behavioral components inasmuch as human actions are nearly always involved in the origins of the problems and/or their perpetuation. Indeed, it is the thesis of this entire volume that behavior affects the environment and that developing effective solutions to environmental problems requires a thorough understanding of their behavioral components. Consequently, this chapter provides a brief overview of the principles governing behavior, generally, and shows their application to environmentally relevant behavior, specifically.

TWO TYPES OF BEHAVIOR

In what follows you will be introduced to the two major types of behavior most commonly studied by behavioral scientists: respondent and operant. You have already been exposed to the three components of the operant paradigm in Chapter 1. The present chapter provides a more thorough exposition of those components, especially the various types of consequences one can arrange to increase or decrease behavior. In the next few pages you will learn that there are two basic ways to increase the strength of behavior: positive reinforcement and negative reinforcement. You will also learn that there are two basic ways to decrease behavior: punishment and extinction. The effective use of these procedures requires the appropriate timing and scheduling of stimulus events. These events, positive reinforcers, negative reinforcers, and punishers will be defined, and their timing and scheduling described.

Typically, psychologists distinguish between behavior that depends largely on some prior stimulation and behavior that depends mainly on changes in stimulus conditions following it. In the classic example of the former, a dog is shown to salivate when presented with meat powder (Pavlov, 1927). Such behavior is said to be *respondent* in that the organism responds to a stimulus or environmental change presented to it. The likelihood of the behavior's (response's) occurring is greatly dependent upon the magnitude of the antecedent stimulus. In the classic example of the latter, a rat is shown to increase the frequency of bar pressing when that response leads to, or is followed by, the presentation of a food pellet (Skinner, 1938). Such behavior is called *operant* in that the organism operates on its environment, and, when certain effects are produced, the behavior changes. The probability of operant behavior's occurring in a particular situation is said to be a function of consequent-stimulus change. The probability of respondent behavior is a function of antecedent-stimulus change.

All of us manifest a variety of both operant and respondent behaviors in our daily lives. Human examples of respondent behaviors include activities of the autonomic nervous system, smooth muscles, and endocrine glands. Thus, when we produce tears in response to a speck of dirt in our eye, we are responding to the change in our environment. When we startle to a sonic boom, feel our heart rate increase in the presence of a loved one, or jump when stuck with a pin, we are responding to our environment. Such behavior is largely involuntary and occurs rather automatically. Changing it involves altering the stimulus environment preceding it.

Respondent behavior often leads us to define environmental situations as problems. For example, startle-like reactions to loud noise are generally unpleasant, so the production of noise is defined as an environmental problem. The burning sensation in one's eyes caused by airborne pollutants is also unpleasant and leads to the definition of air pollution as a problem. Respondent behaviors of this type are not viewed as environmentally relevant in the sense mentioned in Chapters 1 and 2 because they are not directed toward the solution of environmental problems. Rather, respondent behaviors are important *reactions* to environmental conditions. They, in turn, generate other behavior designed to bring about improvement in the condition. Since it is these operant behaviors that are most environmentally relevant in the sense mentioned earlier, the remainder of this chapter is devoted to the principles of operant behavior. Space limitations do not allow a comprehensive exposition of these principles and their application, but interested readers are referred to Millenson (1967), Reynolds (1975), and Holland and Skinner (1961) for more complete treatments.

To show that behavior is indeed operant behavior, it is necessary to control it in predictable ways. Control can usually be shown by systematic increases and decreases in the frequency of the behavior of interest. In the sections that follow, the principles of operant behavior are organized on the basis of whether they increase behavior or lead to its decrease.

INCREASING BEHAVIOR

Picking up trash in one's yard or neighborhood, riding a mass-transit system to work, taking recyclable materials to a recycling center, and turning out unused lights are all operant behaviors having relevance to environmental problems. Moreover, they are all behaviors that most of us would agree should be increased in the interest of environmental quality. Similarly, installing scrubbers in the smokestacks of coal-burning electrical utilities, catalytic converters on the exhausts of automobiles, and noise reducers on the engines of jet aircraft are environmentally relevant behaviors it would be helpful to increase. Many additional examples were provided in Table 2–1. In the explanation of the basic principles of operant behavior that follows, try to extend the application of such principles from the simple responses we will mention to environmentally relevant ones such as these. Later chapters will provide examples of similar extensions, and it might be instructive to see how closely your ideas parallel those already tried out and published in the literature.

In the classic example mentioned earlier, a laboratory rat is taught to press a bar to produce food pellets. When pellets are forthcoming, pressing increases. In the earliest demonstrations of the effects of consequences on behavior, Thorndike (1898) showed that a variety of animals (for example, dogs, chickens, and kittens) could learn responses (for example, pressing levers, pulling strings, moving latches) that would get them out of a cagelike box. The animals engaged in essentially random, trial-and-error responding at first, and it took quite a while for them to perform the key behavior that permitted escape and gained them access to a small amount of food outside the box. On subsequent trials, however, Thorndike observed the animals to display less and less random, trial-and-error behavior; they restricted their responding more closely to the acts instrumental in producing freedom. This observation led Thorndike to define a *law of effect,* which, stripped to its essentials, states that behavior is affected by the consequences of previous behavior. More commonly, the law of effect holds that behavior followed by a satisfying state of affairs is likely to be repeated, whereas that followed by annoyance is not.

Nearly everyone can verbalize some facsimile of the law of effect and understands that behavior leading to predictable payoffs is more likely to be repeated than that which does not. The phenomenon of increasing responding by manipulating response consequences is known as the principle of *reinforcement.* If, in a particular situation, a behavior occurs, a consequence is presented, and the behavior is then observed to increase in frequency in that situation, the operations involved are referred to as *positive reinforcement,* and the consequence presented after the behavior is a *positive reinforcer.* In the earlier example of the bar-pressing rat, the bar press (response) led to the presentation of a food pellet (consequence), and the pressing was observed to increase in frequency. Since the definition of the consequence requires the observation of its effects on behavior, the food pellet can now be referred to as a positive reinforcer because it was accompanied by a behavioral increase.

It is important to note that the categorization of consequent stimuli is empirical and thus cannot be determined before observing its effect on behavior. For example, the presentation of candy to a child who has just cleaned up his or her room cannot be called the use of a reinforcer until it is noted that future room cleaning is accelerated. Similarly, the presentation of "We are saving oil" decals to energy-conserving fuel-oil customers (Seaver & Patterson, 1976) cannot be referred to as positive reinforcement unless and until actual increases in oil conservation are noted.

Positive reinforcement is not the only procedure that leads to an increase in responding. Increases also occur when behavior results in the *removal* or *avoidance* of certain stimuli. When that occurs, we say the response has been *negatively reinforced*. A popular example is the putting on of warm wraps in the winter. Putting on the wraps removes or avoids the sensation of cold, and we observe that this particular dressing behavior increases when cold weather is encountered in the future. Quickly adjusting the shower from all cold or all hot water is another example of behavior that is strengthened by removing or avoiding certain stimulus conditions (that is, extremes of water temperature).

An example of an environmentally relevant behavior that might be strengthened in this way would be the monitoring of the reclamation activities of an Appalachian strip miner. If it were demonstrated that monitoring resulted in more reclaimed land and that the frequency of monitoring increased, then we would say that the act of monitoring was negatively reinforced. It got rid of the unsightly, unreclaimed land. In a similar way, littering and polluting are frequently behaviors that are negatively reinforced. In each case the behavior gets rid of or avoids some stimulus (trash, acid mine drainage, and so on). Successfully ridding oneself of these stimuli leads to an increase in littering and pollution.

It should be noted that in all of the above examples, just as in those of positive reinforcement, the consequences of the behavior lead to its increase. Any stimulus change following the occurrence of a response is termed reinforcement if it results in an increase in the response. Whether the procedure is positive or negative depends on the operations involved in the stimulus change. If the response leads to the presentation of a stimulus, the procedure is *positive reinforcement,* and the consequent stimulus is called a positive reinforcer. If the response removes and/or avoids a stimulus, the procedure is negative reinforcement, and the consequent stimulus is called a *negative reinforcer*. It is important to emphasize that neither the procedure nor the stimulus can be labeled until their effects on the behavior are noted.

DECREASING BEHAVIOR

Littering, polluting air or water, propagating indiscriminately, wasting energy, and leaving stripped land unreclaimed are all environmentally destructive behaviors that most of us would agree should be decreased. As operant responses, these acts are also affected by their consequences. There are three procedures that lead to responses being weakened. Two of these are labeled *punishment*.

In the most familiar example of punishment, a stimulus is presented following a behavior, and the behavior is observed to decrease in strength. Suppose a baby's crying leads to mother's scolding, and baby's crying decreases. The effect of the crying is to present (or bring about) mother's scolding, and the effect of that scolding is to reduce future crying. Having observed all that, it is possible to label both the procedure as punishment and the consequent stimulus as a punisher. In the case of environmentally destructive behaviors, a verbal reprimand or public outcry might lead to lessened littering, pollution, and energy wastage. If so, we would refer to our procedures as punishment and to our consequent stimuli as punishers.

Another form of punishment involves the *removal* of some stimulus following the occurrence of a behavior. Suppose a baby's crying is followed by mother's leaving the room. Suppose, further, that the effect of mother's departure is a decrease in baby's crying. The procedure in this case is punishment. Just as in our earlier examples of punishment, some stimulus change following behavior led to its decrease. However, in this situation it was the removal of a stimulus that produced the effect rather than its presentation. When the removal or avoidance of an event leads to a decrease in behavior, the procedure is termed punishment, but the stimulus removed is a positive reinforcer.

Everyday examples of this form of punishment are plentiful. Fines imposed for traffic violations, interest charges for late payment of installment loans, and restricting a teenager's hours because of excessive lateness are all instances of punishment through the removal of positive reinforcers. Similarly, fines levied by the Environmental Protection Agency for air, noise, and water pollution, and by other law-enforcement agencies for littering, are examples of this type of punishment.

Behaviors may also be decreased if they are no longer followed by their usual consequences. Thus, if a child's supermarket temper tantrums no longer result in mom's giving her an ice-cream cone "to shut her up," the tantrums may decrease. If simple withholding of a stimulus following a response leads to its decrease in this manner, we refer to the procedure as *extinction* and the stimulus as a positive reinforcer. Again, examples abound in everyday life. A spouse's appearance deteriorates in the absence of positive comments from a mate. People stop working when they are no longer paid. Pupils make more errors when the teacher stops commenting favorably on accurate performance.

Just as there are two types of reinforcement and punishment, there are two types of extinction. In addition to the above type, it is possible for behavior to increase when no longer followed by its customary stimulus change. Thus, if the police stop giving tickets for traffic violations, it is probable that violations will increase. If the Coast Guard stops monitoring waterways and fining polluters, it is likely that illegal marine discharges will increase. When simple withholding of a stimulus following a response leads to its increase in this manner, we refer to the procedure as extinction and to the stimulus as a punisher.

Thus, extinction may lead to decreases in some behaviors and increases in others. On the one hand, if a behavior is being maintained by reinforcing consequences, the elimination of those consequences will lead to its decrease. On the other hand, if a behavior is being suppressed by punishing consequences, the elimination of those will lead to its increase.

STIMULUS CONTROL

When consequences (either reinforcers or punishers) are consistently provided for certain responses, the consequences are usually accompanied by distinct features of the stimulus environment. In Chapter 1 we referred to those features as discriminative stimuli, or S^Ds. For example, when milk is presented to an infant, the milk is often preceded by the soothing voice and smiling face of the mother. When food pellets are presented following a lever press by a rat, they are preceded by the tactile sensations of the bar, the distinct feel of the grid floor, and so on. As a result of the consistent pairing of these environmental attributes with reinforcement (or punishment), the attributes themselves begin to exert some control over the behavior. If these stimulus attributes come to control behavior to the point where that behavior occurs only in their presence, the behavior is said to be under stimulus control.

Behavior-change procedures based on stimulus control have been used with varying success to treat a number of clinical problems (Karen, 1974). Excessive drinking, smoking, and overeating are examples. Have you ever noticed how some things around you cause you to eat? A very common example is eating while watching TV. If you do it often enough, TV eventually becomes a cue to eat. You may sit down to watch a football game and, hungry or not, immediately think of a ham sandwich. This principle has been used with clients given to excessive between-meal snacking. For example, eating has been restricted to certain times of the day and to tables covered with brightly colored tablecloths (Stuart & Davis, 1975). After the client eats consistently in the presence of these cues and not around others, the cues take over the control of eating behavior, and the client becomes less and less likely to associate eating with other stimulus contexts. The range of stimuli associated with eating has been deliberately narrowed in order to control food intake and thus the gaining of weight.

Examples of the use of stimulus-control procedures are available for environmentally relevant behavior. One is much less likely to litter when driving in front of a police car; industrial river polluters are careful not to discharge wastes in the presence of a Coast Guard launch; displays of contraceptives in stores may cue their purchase and use. Later chapters will describe some of the attempts to use signs, letters, and handbills as a form of stimulus control over littering, energy conservation, and recycling.

TIMING THE STIMULUS CHANGE

The preceding discussion of the procedures generally available for increasing and decreasing behavior makes it clear that they are based on changes in the environment immediately following the behavior. It is important that such consequences follow responses as closely in time as possible. In general, the longer the response/consequence interval, the less control the stimulus change will exert. An environmentally relevant example of this principle would be that the longer it takes the courts to fine industrial polluters, the less effective the fines will be in preventing future pollution by those firms.

SCHEDULING THE STIMULUS CHANGE

Another important determinant of the effects of consequences on behavior is the frequency with which they follow it. Consider the case of picking up trash, or antilitter behavior. If you were rewarded every time you picked trash up from the ground, you would be quite likely to pick it up frequently. Your behavior would be under the influence of a *continuous-reinforcement,* or *CRF,* schedule (Ferster & Skinner, 1957). If you were rewarded only some of the times you picked up trash, your behavior would be under the control of an *intermittent-reinforcement* schedule. We say that an intermittent schedule is in effect when some responses are rewarded while others are not.

Intermittent schedules can be divided into those based on time and those based on number of responses. In time-based, or *interval,* scheduling, the first response after the passage of a certain amount of time is consequated.[1] The time interval can be fixed (FI) or variable (VI). Thus, consequating the first response after every two-minute interval would be using an FI–2-min. schedule. Consequating the first response occurring on the average after every two-minute interval, but sometimes after one minute, sometimes after three, would be an example of a variable-interval, or VI–2-min., schedule. If you were rewarded for the first piece of trash picked up after every five minutes had passed, your antilittering behavior would be on an FI–5-min. schedule. Similarly, if you were given the reward for the first piece of trash picked up after five minutes on the average, but sometimes after three minutes, after six minutes, and so on, your behavior would be on a VI–5-min. schedule.

In response-based, or *ratio,* scheduling, the consequence can also be delivered on a fixed or variable basis. If every third response pays off, the schedule being used is a fixed ratio of one consequence for every three responses, or an FR–3. Similarly, if consequences are delivered on the average after every third response, a variable-ratio schedule is in effect, in this case a VR–3. A VR–7 schedule would indicate that on the average every seventh response is consequated, but sometimes the consequence is delivered after the third, tenth, and so on.

Returning to our antilittering example, you would be on an FR–4 schedule if you received a reward of some sort after every fourth piece of trash you collected or after every fourth time you filled a trash barrel. If you received the reward after a variable number of pieces or filled barrels, you would be on a

---

[1] After Karen (1974, p. 52), we prefer the term *consequation* because it is more general and includes both reinforcement and punishment. Of course, *to consequate* is a psychological neologism.

variable-ratio schedule. Which of these schedules do you think would be most likely to work for you? In other words, do you think there would be any difference in the amount of trash collected if you were paid off on a fixed basis or on a less predictable, variable basis?

One last type of schedule is termed *conjugate reinforcement*. Sometimes the level of a particular consequence varies with the level of the behavior. In a sense, the "schedule" is one of intensity rather than time. For example, turning up the thermostat produces a change in the temperature that is proportional to the behavior. The higher the setting is put on the thermostat, the higher the temperature. Similarly, the less trash thrown down, the less littered the landscape; the lower the volume on the stereo, the lower the noise. Conjugate schedules are pervasive. Most such schedules produce behavior that is weak when the conjugate effects are very low or very high. Take noise as an example. Sounds that are too soft may be just as undesirable as sounds that are very loud. Thus (though perhaps for different reasons), we will try to keep the sound levels at some medium range of loudness.

The strength of many behaviors has been shown to be affected by the particular schedule used to maintain them. It is generally accepted that continuous reinforcement is best while teaching a new response. Once the response has been learned, the emphasis changes from teaching it to maintaining it, and schedules are changed accordingly. For maintaining performance of already learned behavior, it has generally been found that intermittent scheduling of the consequences is best.

Whether one uses interval or ratio schedules depends on the type of behavior and the frequency wanted, but variable forms of intermittent scheduling will produce smooth, steady responding. Fixed-ratio and interval schedules tend to be associated with spurts of responding just before the presentation of the consequence. A popular example nicely illustrates these points. Consider the activity involved in playing a slot machine. The owners of the casino want to generate high, steady rates of this type of behavior because every lever pull means money for them. They have also found that making jackpots unpredictable leads to much steadier rates of behavior than would occur if winning was permitted on a fixed, or regular, basis. Finally, they know that variable-interval schedules tend to generate slow, steady rates of responding whereas variable-ratio schedules produce high, steady rates. The reason for this difference is that since a variable amount of time must pass before a response will be consequated on a VI schedule, there is no advantage to rapid responding. However, since only a variable number of responses determines the delivery of consequences on a VR schedule, the more responses produced, the quicker the payoff will appear.

A lot of our behavior is maintained on pretty clearly defined schedules of consequation. People paid for producing a certain number of items are said to be on piecework, which is merely another way of referring to fixed-ratio scheduling. Those of us on salaries are paid on fixed-interval schedules. Preparing meals in some households is obviously maintained on a variable-ratio schedule, exemplified by the "mms," "ahs," and "great meal" comments following occasional dinners. In the environmental area it is easy to find examples of consequence scheduling. Inspections of industrial-discharge sites along inland waterways are made on a random, or variable-interval, basis by the Coast Guard. Air-quality measures, however, are likely to be scheduled on a fixed-interval basis, such as daily at 9 A.M. and 5 P.M. Some of us deposit trash appropriately because punishment for littering is scheduled on a variable basis. Thus, we might get by with throwing trash from our car window six times before being caught on the seventh. The next time we might be caught after only two successful trash throws. The unpredictable nature of the consequence keeps us from littering. For some, however, the scheduling of fines is too thin. They are not encountered frequently enough to have much effect on behavior. Hence the large amount of litter in certain areas.

SCHEDULES BASED ON SINGLE RESPONSES OF MORE THAN ONE PERSON

Up to now our discussion of consequence scheduling has dealt with the behavior of individuals; that is, the stimulus change occurred after the first response following the passage of time (interval schedule) or after the nth response in a series of responses (ratio schedule) performed by an individual. In environmentally relevant psychology it has sometimes proved useful to time the delivery of consequences on the basis of the number of persons engaging in a particular behavior. In one example, Deslauriers and Everett (1977) examined the effects of giving tokens to people for boarding a public bus. The researchers were interested in whether the tokens, good for between 5¢ and 10¢, would increase the number of bus riders. They found that awarding tokens to each passenger resulted in a 33% increase in ridership. More important, however, was their finding that thinning this schedule to every third person (on the average) was just about as effective, yielding an increase in ridership of 30% over baseline. In other words, reducing the number of tokens delivered (and thus their cost) by two-thirds appeared to produce no corresponding decrement in the effectiveness of the consequence. In another example of such *person scheduling* (Cone & Hayes, 1977), Kohlenberg and Phillips (1973) found that deposits in a trash barrel at a public zoo increased dramatically when coupons exchangeable for soft drinks were awarded to every seventh, tenth, or twentieth depositor, on the average.

Person scheduling is different from those schedules discussed previously in that only one response is required and in that the delivery of the consequence is based on the number of persons since the last consequence rather than the number of responses or the passage of time. Just as with ratio and interval schedules, person schedules can be continuous (every person, or EP) or intermittent. Moreover, the latter can be fixed (FP) or variable (VP). Thus, consequences can be delivered after a constant number of persons (for example, FP–3, FP–6, and so on) or after a variable number (for example, VP–3, VP–6, and so on). Various combinations of schedules are also possible. For example, tokens might be awarded the first person boarding a bus after a variable period of time—say, ten minutes on the average. Or the first person depositing trash every ten minutes might be rewarded in some way. More complex combinations are possible, but their discussion is beyond the scope of this text. Suffice it to say that scheduling consequences on a person basis has important implications for behavioral solutions to environmental problems.

APPLYING THE BASIC PRINCIPLES

Although we have discussed the principles of behavior change as somewhat separate phenomena, their effective application requires skillful combination. In most cases we are not concerned with merely increasing or decreasing a single response. When dealing with an objectionable behavior to be reduced or eliminated, for example, there is usually an alternative, incompatible response to be increased. Thus, in trying to reduce litter, one might focus on the act of disposing of trash inappropriately or, instead, on the alternative, incompatible act of picking it up. Indeed, although most legal solutions of the litter problem have concentrated on the former, behavior-analytic approaches have focused on the latter. In practice, the different emphases resolve to punishing an undesirable action and/or reinforcing its alternative.

The most effective behavior-change strategies are those employing both a decelerative and an accelerative emphasis at the same time. Thus, while maintaining an active program of systematic punishment for dumping industrial wastes into nearby streams, enforcement agencies might simultaneously reward those industrial plants found to be disposing of wastes in appropriate ways. For example, the agencies might support public announcements of the environmental benefits produced by the companies' efforts. The goodwill generated by such favorable publicity could be an enormously effective reinforcer for the firms.

It is generally well understood that behavior-control tactics in our society are primarily aversive; that is, they are aimed at *doing away with* deviant or objectionable behavior. But it is a rare deviant act that cannot be defined as both the occurrence of an unsatisfactory behavior *and* the simultaneous absence of a satisfactory one. Many examples of this fact were provided in our comparison of environmentally protective and destructive behaviors in Table 2–1. Littering can be considered as the act of disposing of trash inappropriately or as the absence of appropriate trash-disposal behavior. Obviously, the two behaviors are mutually exclusive in a given individual (at least with respect to the same piece of trash). That the acceptable and unacceptable acts are incompatible can be interpreted to mean that increasing appropriate disposal will decrease littering. If so, solutions to the litter problem might be positively focused, aiming at reinforcing antilitter behavior. Indeed, most of the studies described later have taken just such an approach.

Effective uses of the principles of behavior change have frequently combined accelerative and decelerative approaches rather than relying on only one. For example, McAllister, Stachowiak, Baer, and Conderman (1969) used teacher disapproval and praise for inappropriate and appropriate talking, respectively, in a high school English class. Substantial reductions in inappropriate talking were produced. Similarly, Madsen, Becker, and Thomas (1968) demonstrated that although rules alone had little effect on classroom behavior, the combination of ignoring inappropriate behavior (getting out of seat, making noise, hitting, and so forth) and showing approval of appropriate behavior was very effective in improving the classroom behavior of kindergarten and second-grade children.

To reiterate, behavior-change principles in combination are likely to lead to the most effective intervention strategies. It is a rare unacceptable behavior that cannot be viewed as the absence of an acceptable one. Simultaneously decelerating the first through punishment or extinction while accelerating the second through reinforcement will generally prove effective. Efforts should be made to implement this point of view in behavioral solutions to environmental problems. Indeed, it would be interesting if all law-enforcement agencies were required to balance their use of punishing and reinforcing tactics. Enforcing the law (including environmental regulations) could as easily be interpreted to mean catching people obeying it and praising or rewarding them as catching them breaking it and criticizing or punishing them. Presumably, this more balanced approach would result in more effective enforcement.

SUMMARY

Behavioral scientists are concerned with both respondent and operant behavior. However, scientists dealing with solutions to environmental problems are more apt to emphasize responses affected by their consequences—that is, operant behavior. We have described both positive-reinforcement and negative-reinforcement procedures for increasing behavior. We have also described punishment and extinction procedures for decreasing behavior.

The effective use of these procedures for increasing and decreasing behavior involves the careful timing and scheduling of stimulus events. These events, positive reinforcers, negative reinforcers, and punishers have been defined, and examples of their use have been provided. Finally, we have noted that the behavior-change procedures in most common use in contemporary society involve the application of punishing consequences to do away with or decrease behavior. A more effective overall tactic would involve the combination of positive reinforcement and punishment. Such a combined approach could be used in the solution of environmental problems, as our examples showed.

Chapter 4

RESEARCH STRATEGIES AND DESIGNS IN THE DEVELOPMENT OF BEHAVIORAL SOLUTIONS

> The problem is that most people don't really know how much electricity various appliances use. Before effective conservation programs are possible, it will be necessary to inform the general public about such basic facts.

This statement seems reasonable and basic enough to be accepted at face value. People might be more judicious in their use of electrical energy if they were better informed about how much electricity is used by each of their household appliances. However, at the very foundation of an effective science of human/environment interaction is a basic distrust of the validity of such statements—a general skepticism concerning what might usually be considered common knowledge or common sense.

What if the statement were true? If it were, one reasonable conservation tactic would be to increase the availability of such basic information, to educate people to help them conserve. Mass-education campaigns costing millions of dollars might be (and, indeed, have been) based on such a premise. The result should be less use of electricity. But what if the statement were not true? Then resources should be diverted toward other conservation strategies that have been shown to be more promising. If the statement had been false but no one bothered to test it because it seemed so obviously true, not only would millions of dollars have been wasted, but the environmental damage caused by overconsumption would continue. Moreover, scientific attention to other, more relevant variables might have been diverted, thereby slowing the development of really effective conservation tactics.

It is the truth or falsity of such statements that this chapter is all about. To solve serious environmental problems, common sense must be continually challenged. Environmental problem solvers must be, above all, skeptical. This has always been a vital characteristic of scientists, applied or basic. The skeptic wants proof of the validity of premises such as those contained in our opening statement. Validity is established through a variety of experimental operations that bear upon the basic logic of the premises being tested.

In the next few pages we will discuss these operations in terms of the major research strategies and specific research designs used by behavioral scientists. We will show the need to define researchable problems as a set of premises, the validity of which is testable. Two major research strategies will be described: correlational/descriptive and experimental/manipulative. Independent and dependent variables will be defined, and two general approaches to designing experiments to examine relationships among these will be mentioned: intersubject and intrasubject. Examples of each general approach will be provided.

As a first step toward understanding general behavioral-science research strategies, let us look at the logic involved in a test of our opening statement. To do that, we must identify the premises involved and the conclusion derived from them. One premise is that "most people don't really know how much electricity various appliances use." The conclusion is that effective conservation programs require such knowledge. An unstated premise, needed to complete our syllogism, is that there is a relationship between knowledge and use. Stated formally, the following logic is implied:

Premise 1:   (Unstated.) People use electricity more efficiently (that is, they waste less) when they know how much various appliances use.

Premise 2:   "Most people don't really know how much electricity various appliances use."

Conclusion: "Before effective conservation programs are possible, it will be necessary to inform the general public about such basic facts."

The science of environmental problem solving must be based on the testing of premises such as these. In the remainder of this chapter, we will provide a brief overview of the scientific armamentarium needed to test premises. We will illustrate much of our discussion by reference to our opening statement.

We shall start with the relatively easy task of testing the validity of our second premise. It would be no great problem to develop a test to determine how much knowledge people have about the amount of electricity used by different appliances. Once this were done, the test could be administered, scored, and the premise verified or rejected.

A test of our first premise (that there is a relationship between knowledge and use) is a bit more challenging. However, a number of options are available. Initially, we will have to operationalize, or make measurable, certain elements of the premise: we need a definition or measure of "efficient use" and a measure of knowledge about how much various appliances use. If we have developed the latter in our test of the second premise, we can concentrate now on the former. Our measure of efficient use might take a variety of forms, but it would probably involve some way of gathering data on activities such as ironing clothes in large batches, using whistling teakettles on electric ranges, turning off the electric hot-water heater when away from home on extended vacations, and turning off electric baseboard heaters in unused rooms. Each of these practices is aimed at efficient use of electricity. Having developed both "efficient-use" and "knowledge" measures, we have operationalized the key terms in our premise and are now in a position to test it.

THE CORRELATIONAL/DESCRIPTIVE STRATEGY

Although several approaches could be taken at this point, the simplest and perhaps most widely used would be a *correlational* one. We could get scores on our two measures for a sample of people. These people would be randomly selected from a larger population to which we were interested in generalizing; that is, we would look at a portion of the people in some identifiable group. Suppose we wanted to know about the relationship between energy knowledge and use among residents of North Carolina. We would not study all residents (even if we could, it would be too time consuming), so we would select some of them for study. If we select randomly, so that anyone in North Carolina has just as good a chance of being selected as anyone else, then we can be confident that our sample will be representative of the larger group (that is, North Carolina residents).

The question being asked is merely whether a relationship exists between knowledge and efficient use. The assumption is that there is a positive correlation between these two variables such that the more knowledge a person has about the wattage ratings of different appliances, the more efficiently he or she uses them. To test this assumption using a correlational strategy, we would take the knowledge and use data we have for our sample group of persons and calculate a *correlation coefficient*. The magnitude of the coefficient is a measure of the strength of the relationship between the two variables. As most readers may know, the maximum range of such values is from -1.0 to $+1.0$, with zero indicating no tendency for the two characteristics to vary together. The larger the coefficient, the stronger the relationship. Space limitations do not permit a discussion of the mechanics of calculating correlation coefficients, but interested readers can find this information in a variety of basic statistics texts (see, for example, Edwards, 1967; Hays, 1963; Nunnally, 1967; Wiggins, 1973).

An important point about correlational/descriptive strategies is that in showing or describing relationships among variables, they are causally neutral; that is, these strategies merely show whether and how closely two variables are associated. It is not possible to infer that one of the variables *caused* changes in the other. Science is concerned with the study of relationships among variables of two general classes: dependent and independent. In the experimental strategies to be discussed later, some variables are deliberately manipulated (changed, varied), and the effects of the manipulations are noted on other variables. Things that are systematically changed are known as *independent variables*. The things affected by their change are known as *dependent variables;* that is, changes in some characteristics are shown to be dependent on, or caused by, changes in others. Correlational studies do not involve the systematic manipulation of some variables in order to observe their effects on others. The relationships among different characteristics are examined to see whether they vary together. Since nothing is systematically altered, we speak of correlational studies as involving the relationships among different dependent variables, with no causality shown.

In *experimental* studies, however, we have both types of variable. A popular toothpaste advertisement depicts one group of children brushing with a brand containing fluoride and another using a brand without fluoride. After a long period of time, the numbers of cavities for both groups of children are determined. Which are the dependent and independent variables in this study? You can figure it out by asking yourself what was manipulated (independent variable) and what was affected by this manipulation (dependent variable). We will come back to experimental studies later in the chapter.

With a correlational approach to our electricity example, we might be able to show that knowledge of wattage ratings and efficient use of appliances are positively correlated—that is, that persons with high knowledge scores also tend to have high efficient-use scores. But we would not be able to say that more knowledge *caused* more efficient use because we have not manipulated either of our two variables in any systematic way. Indeed, we merely took the variables as they came to us naturally and examined the relationship existing between them. The correlational strategy is often termed descriptive because it is used for indexing (or describing) relationships among things.

It is intuitively appealing to suppose that a causal relationship exists between knowledge of wattage ratings and efficient electricity use because we assume that, having gained the wattage information, a person is now in a position to alter appliance use accordingly. In other words, it seems common sense to suggest that the improvement in information *caused* the person to be able to use electricity more efficiently. Such causal inferences from correlational designs are improper, however, because of the basically uncontrolled nature of the investigation. Both characteristics being correlated are free to vary. Neither is systematically manipulated in a controlled way.

It is possible that a third variable is actually responsible for any relationship between the other two. In our illustration, for example, it may be that more intelligent or better educated people tend to use electricity more efficiently. It is even possible that they were taught efficient uses of appliances at some time during their educational careers. It is also quite likely that these people have learned something about appliance wattage ratings. However, one would not *need* to know these ratings to learn efficient appliance use. Thus, we would be in error concluding that knowledge of wattage ratings produced greater efficiency. A third factor, in this case general education, may have actually been the cause of both of the measured variables.

Before conclusions about cause/effect relationships between variables are warranted, it is necessary to control all the variables that may influence the relationship. It is then possible to manipulate one (the independent variable) systematically and note corresponding changes in the others (the dependent variables).

If a major aim of the science of environment/behavior relationships is the discovery of causal relationships, then what good are correlational/descriptive strategies, which do not provide this information? The answer is that any science needs a combination of research designs and strategies to develop most effectively. The conduct of carefully controlled experimental studies is an expensive, difficult undertaking. Before they are carried out, investigators will want some information suggesting the possibility of a relationship between the variables of interest to them. In well-established sciences the important variables and likely relationships among them are already known. In new areas of research, however, this is not the case. It is necessary to map out the field, to delineate important variables and establish tentative relationships among them. This mapping function is most economically accomplished with correlational studies. It is relatively easy to get data on a large number of variables and calculate correlation coefficients among them. Indeed, the use of high-speed data-processing equipment and correlational procedures such as factor analysis (see Horst, 1965) allow the rapid and meaningful reduction of large amounts of data and the highlighting of relationships among many variables considered simultaneously. Once such relationships have been discovered and documented using correlational procedures, more specific questions, such as their causal nature, can be investigated in tightly controlled experimental studies.

In addition to this important function, correlational studies are necessary when looking at relationships among variables that cannot be controlled and manipulated systematically. The entire science of astronomy is built on such relationships, since the systematic manipulation of stars and planets has thus far eluded us. In environmental studies it is conceivable that certain factors will not be sufficiently controllable for experimental designs. For example, studies of the interaction of particular atmospheric conditions and exhaust emissions in the Los Angeles Basin may have to be correlational because of the impossibility of manipulating the atmospheric conditions. Of course, analogues of these could be studied in simulated laboratory experiments, but the multiplicity of "real-world" variables not duplicated in the laboratory might seriously limit the generality of the conclusions.

It should be emphasized that the development of any science is best accomplished using a balanced diversity of research strategies and designs. Though the benefits of a correlational/descriptive approach, especially in the early development of a field of inquiry, have been highlighted here, the importance of balance must not be overlooked. In Chapter 1 we noted that the study of behavior/environment relationships has thus far overemphasized correlational approaches. In the application of behavioral principles to the solution of environmental problems, it will not be enough to know how particular individuals' or corporations' attitudes toward environmental protection are correlated with their waste-disposal activities. It will be necessary to manipulate variables to effect changes in waste disposal. The identification of the most powerful of these variables must occur in relatively well-controlled studies of the type discussed in the next section.

EXPERIMENTAL/MANIPULATIVE STRATEGIES

As was just mentioned, once correlations among numerous variables have been calculated, it is possible to examine them for plausible controlling relationships. Assume, for example, that a negative correlation has been found between severity of pollution readings and number of Coast Guard inspectors on a certain major waterway; that is, the more inspectors, the less the pollution. Suppose, further, that this relationship was based on pollution readings and inspector counts across a large number of waterways. The commonsense interpretation would be something like "Of course, if you want more compliance with EPA regulations on discharges, you'll have to increase the number of inspectors." Such a view seems reasonable enough until we remember that it is based on correlational evidence and must therefore be considered tentative. Suppose the reverse had been found; that is, the more inspectors, the worse the pollution. Would you conclude from this positive correlation that increasing the number of inspectors increases the amount of pollution? Probably not, since the number of inspectors was not systematically varied, and it is conceivable that they were merely assigned in numbers consistent with the severity of the pollution in the various waterways to begin with. In other words, the more seriously polluted waterways may have had a larger number of inspectors assigned to them.

To determine what effect, if any, the number of inspectors has on pollution, it will be necessary to employ a research design that adequately controls for the effects of other variables. Although a variety of possibilities exists, only a few designs basic to the remaining chapters of the book will be discussed here.

Let us return to our earlier example of the relationship between knowledge of wattage ratings and efficient use of appliances. Recall that we were concerned primarily with the validity of the premise that "people use electricity more efficiently when they know how much various appliances use." Having operationalized, or made measurable, both "knowledge" and "efficiency," we might have examined the correlation between these variables in an initial descriptive study designed to map the variables in the general area of efficient electricity use. In other words, we might have gathered data on a variety of characteristics in addition to knowledge and use and then employed sophisticated correlational procedures to determine promising avenues for more careful analysis. For example, we might have included age, intelligence, level of education, occupation, number of children, size of dwelling, and so on in our analysis. The basis for the assumption in our initial premise might have been the finding that, of all these variables, the most closely associated with efficiency was our measure of knowledge.

We are now interested in determining the nature of this relationship more precisely. If increased knowledge leads to (causes) greater efficiency, then it would be reasonable to improve conservation by designing programs to educate the public. Before committing large sums of money to such an effort, however, it would be important to show, conclusively, that such a cause/effect relationship exists.

In what follows, we shall describe research designs aimed at unequivocal demonstrations of causal relationships. After Paul (1969), these designs will be oriented along a continuum representing progressively more control. As the degree of control increases, the confidence in the relationship between independent and dependent variables increases. As Paul has noted, "there is really only one principle of design: the experiment should be designed so that the effects of the independent variables can be evaluated unambiguously" (p. 35). To the extent that research errors have been avoided, such unambiguous evaluations will be possible.

It has become commonplace in applied behavior analysis to distinguish two major tactical approaches to research design and the establishment of lawful relationships between dependent and independent variables (see Hersen & Barlow, 1976; Sidman, 1960). One can study these relationships briefly in a large number of subjects who have been divided into groups, some of whom are exposed to the independent variable (or varying levels of it) and some of whom are not. Conclusions from such studies are based on producing differences between groups that were initially comparable and continue to be so except for the application of the independent variable. The most familiar example of this type of design is the classic "true" experiment with experimental and control groups. Such designs are termed *between-subject* or *intersubject* analyses because their results depend on the production of differences between groups of different subjects. We will discuss these designs shortly.

Another major research tactic is the intensive study of one or a few subjects over a relatively long period during which the independent variable is present at certain times and not at others. Conclusions in these studies are based on differences in the same subject or subjects at these different times. Hence the reference to them as *within-subject* or *intrasubject* analyses.

The advantages and liabilities of these two general strategies have been enumerated before (see Hersen & Barlow, 1976; Kazdin, 1973; Paul, 1969; Sidman, 1960) and will not be reiterated here. As Paul (pp. 46–48) has noted, however, both can establish cause/effect relationships when carefully executed. Because of their greater popularity in applied behavior-analytic studies of environmental problems, our discussion will focus on intrasubject analyses. Before describing them, however, a brief discussion of the most common intersubject designs is in order.

Classic True Experiments

If, in our electricity example, we wanted to show that increased knowledge results in, leads to, or causes more efficient appliance use, we could start with a moderately large sample of persons randomly selected from some larger population to which we were interested in generalizing our findings. We would then randomly designate a portion (say, half) of our subjects to receive a blitz course in the wattage ratings of common appliances. These subjects thus constitute our experimental group, of course, since they alone are exposed to the independent variable (blitz course). The remaining subjects make up our control group. After the experimental subjects have been exposed to the course, the appliance use of both groups would be monitored. If systematic differences favoring the experimental subjects were noted, we could conclude that a cause/effect relationship existed between knowledge and efficiency, thus establishing the validity of our initial premise.

To be sure, the above example is a basic, stripped-down model of a classic true experiment. Various options or embellishments would no doubt be added were the study actually conducted. For example, though the initial comparability of our groups on knowledge of wattage ratings can be assumed because we used random assignment, a pretest of all subjects' knowledge would establish this comparability more objectively. Moreover, a posttest of knowledge would document any increase actually produced by the course and provide a firmer basis for concluding a causal relationship. In addition, had we not found differences in efficiency after the course, we would still be in a more enlightened position because we would have precourse and postcourse data showing that gains in knowledge had actually been produced. Without such data we would not really know whether the course had taught our subjects anything about wattage ratings.

The basic two-group true experiment permits gross cause/effect relationships to be established. To reiterate, the design is considered an intersubject one because our conclusions about the effect of the independent variable rely on the production of differences between two groups of subjects who were initially comparable. Had the posttest results shown no differences between our groups, we could not have concluded that our independent variable was causally related to our dependent one.

We say the causal relationship established in classic two-group experiments is gross because about all it demonstrates is an overall effect. In the above example, our course on wattage ratings is obviously a very complex variable composed of many different features. For example, the course may have involved lots of lecture and very little reading or the reverse. It may have been taught by a representative of a local ecology club, an employee of an electric utility, or a college professor of electrical engineering. The course may have run for 15 hours or five or 30. The ratings of only a few major appliances may have been stressed, or those of everything from hot-water heaters to doughnut makers may have been included. The experimental-group/control-group design does not tell us which of these components of the course may have contributed to the observed effect. It merely tells us that the course as a whole made a difference. Some of the components may have mattered; some may not have.

Since science is based on the discovery of specific relationships, more sophisticated research designs have been developed. The next section describes a design that permits the manipulation of more than one variable at a time. This type of design permits a look at the specific components of our gross independent variable and a determination of which are producing some or all of the experimental effect.

Factorial Experiments

Suppose we had conducted the above experiment and showed that the course had had an effect on energy knowledge and efficient use of appliances. Suppose also that the course had covered 20 hours of lecture and group discussion. A very practical question might center around the length of the course. Were all 20 hours needed? Could the same effect have been obtained with a course only half as long? Another question might deal with the basic format of the course. Could programmed, self-teaching materials have been substituted for a lecturer and group discussion?

Although it would take a number of different two-group true experiments to answer these questions, a single, carefully conducted *factorial* experiment would provide many of the answers simultaneously. If we wanted to examine course length and format, we would first define these independent variables more fully. For simplicity, let us compare course lengths of ten and 20 hours and programmed versus lecture formats.

As in our true experiment, we would start with a group of subjects randomly selected from a larger population to which we wish to generalize our findings. We would then randomly assign our subjects to ten-hour and 20-hour course lengths such that half ended up in each. We would next divide these two groups randomly into two others, one representing a programmed and one representing a lecture format. The result is a 2 × 2 factorial design with four groups of subjects. The design is diagrammed in Table 4–1. By using appropriate statistical procedures (analysis of variance; see Hays, 1963), it is possible to examine the effects of length and format separately and in combination with one another.

To determine the effects of course length, posttest data for subjects receiving ten hours of programmed instruction and those receiving ten hours of lectures would be combined and compared with the combined data for the two groups receiving 20 hours of instruction. Similarly, the effects of format would be evaluated by combining the ten-hour and 20-hour groups receiving programmed instruction and comparing them with the combined groups receiving lectures. At this point we would know whether length and format made any difference in our

Table 4–1. A 2 × 2 Factorial Design Evaluating Two Different Course Lengths and Two Different Course Formats

		Course Length	
		10 hours	*20 hours*
Course Format	*Programmed*	$\overline{X} = 75.3\%$	$\overline{X} = 90.2\%$
	Lecture	$\overline{X} = 53.2\%$	$\overline{X} = 93.1\%$

posttest data. This is clearly more specific information than would be gained from the simple two-group experiment discussed earlier.

The beauty of the factorial design, however, is that even more specific questions can be answered. Suppose our two variables interact so that different effects for each are produced depending on which level of the other is used; that is, suppose the effect of programmed instruction depends on the length of the course. It is conceivable, after all, that no difference in format would be evident for courses 20 hours long, but that programmed instruction would be superior to lectures for courses only ten hours in length. If this were the case, we might not see an overall effect for format. Or we might not see as large an effect if course length is disregarded. When length is considered, however, we find format differences. In analysis-of-variance terms, we say there is an interaction between our independent variables such that the effects of one depend on the level of the other. In the example here, we would be saying something like "Generally, it does not matter greatly whether the course is programmed or has a lecture format. However, if you have only ten hours to spend, the programmed format is better." We have included values in Table 4–1 that illustrate this point. If we disregard course length, we find that persons exposed to the programmed format obtain mean scores of 82.75% correct while those receiving traditional lectures get mean scores of 73.15%. The difference between formats when time is disregarded is 9.6%. There is essentially no difference between the groups exposed to 20 hours of instruction. However, when only ten hours are used, the difference between the groups seems rather large (22.1%).

We would need to use appropriate statistical procedures to tell whether this seemingly large difference is great enough to be important scientifically. When scores are obtained for groups of persons, the scores will rarely be exactly the same because of numerous random factors influencing them. Even scores for the same group of persons will fluctuate from one occasion to the next. Statistical tests are used to determine whether differences in scores are due to random fluctuation or to systematic manipulation of one or more independent variables.

If the differences between scores are large enough to be considered nonchance, or nonrandom, we say they are statistically significant. Statistical tests would ordinarily be used to evaluate the size of differences in any intersubject study, including the classic true experiment described earlier.

When intrasubject designs are used in applied behavior analysis, the preference has generally been to avoid tests of statistical significance. Instead, emphasis is placed on the social/practical significance of differences between phases of the design. The application of the criterion of social utility is based on the observation that a particular procedure (independent variable) might produce an effect that is large enough to be statistically significant but is too small to be of much practical value. A reference to the data in Table 4–1 might make this point clearer. Recall that the difference between scores of persons receiving lectures versus those exposed to programmed instruction was 9.6% when averaged over both lengths of instruction. Given enough subjects and carefully controlled conditions, this difference might be enough to be statistically significant. However, before its social significance could be evaluated, it would be necessary to have some additional information. For example, are the scores of the persons receiving programmed instruction higher enough to result in less energy use by this group as a whole? Are they higher enough to offset the added initial cost of programming the course versus presenting it in the usual lecture format?

These questions are different from asking whether the difference is large enough to be the result of nonchance factors. It is very possible that a difference will be large enough to be statistically significant but not so large as to have much social or practical utility. In the development of effective behavioral solutions to environmental problems described in this book, we will pay a good deal more attention to social than to statistical significance.

Admittedly, the treatment given factorial designs here is overly simplified and brief. The important point is that they can be used to answer more specific questions than those dealt with in two-group experiments. Of course, their use is more difficult and expensive than that of the simpler design. For this reason they are usually employed *after* gross cause/effect relationships have been documented in experimental-group/control-group studies. It may help to think of the relationship between the two types of design in terms of "whether" and "why" questions. The two-group true experiment tells us *whether* the course produces more efficient electricity use. The factorial experiment helps answer *why* (what aspect of) the course has that effect. The 2 × 2 design presented here is the simplest of the factorials. Many more complex possibilities exist and are often found in the psychological literature. They have been used in some behavior/environment studies and will no doubt be used even more frequently as more and more complex questions are asked.[1] The use of factorial designs in applied

---

[1] Interested readers should see the excellent example of a factorial design used to investigate the separate and interactive effects of personal, social, and physical environmental characteristics on perceptions of crowding by Stokols, Rall, Pinner, and Schopler (1973).

behavior-analytic studies of environmental problems is rare, with most investigators preferring the intrasubject designs discussed in the next sections.

Time-Series Withdrawal Designs

The defining characteristic of intrasubject designs is the repeated measurement of the dependent variable over a period of time during which the independent variable is sometimes present, sometimes not. As mentioned earlier, proponents of the intrasubject approach usually prefer the intensive study of one or a few subjects over relatively long periods, but the logic of these designs applies also to large numbers of subjects. Indeed, many of the experiments in environmentally relevant psychology have involved the use of intrasubject designs to study large groups (see, for example, Hayes & Cone, in press). In *time-series* investigations the subject or subjects serve as their own control, and experimental effects are concluded from comparisons of data collected during times when the independent variable is present and times when it is absent. In the classic true experiment, control is provided by a group of subjects who are not exposed to the independent variable at all.

In the time-series design most frequently used in applied behavior analysis, the *withdrawal* design, repeated measurements are taken on the subject or subjects prior to the introduction of a change in experimental conditions. The change is then introduced, and measurement continues until differences in the data are clearly established. The experimental conditions are then returned to those existing initially, and measurement continues. If the introduction of the change in experimental conditions produced the differences noted in the data, they should now return to their original form. This design is commonly referred to as an *ABA* design; A = the baseline phase, B = the experimental phase, and A = the (return to) baseline.

An example of data from such a study is provided in Figure 4–1. In this example, from a study by Everett, Hayward, and Meyers (1974), data were collected over a 16-day baseline period (A phase) to establish the number of persons typically riding a campus bus each day at The Pennsylvania State University. To increase ridership, tokens were given each person boarding the bus during an eight-day experimental period (B phase). The number of rides occurring each day continued to be recorded. Finally, to determine whether the increase in rides noted during the experimental phase was actually related to the provision of free tokens, the tokens were withdrawn during the final phase and conditions thereby returned to those prevailing during the initial baseline period.

In this example it would appear that the independent variable (tokens) is functionally, or causally, related to the dependent one (rides per day). After all, systematic change in the latter is related to the presence or absence of the former. To be even more convinced, the careful investigator might attempt to replicate the A to B change by reintroducing the free tokens in a fourth phase and noting whether rides increase once again. The resulting *ABAB* design would provide the

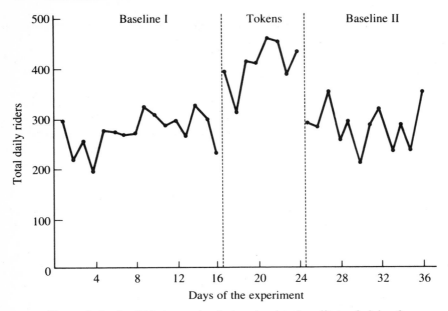

Figure 4–1. An *ABA* time-series design showing the effects of giving free tokens to bus riders. From "The Effects of a Token Reinforcement Procedure on Bus Ridership," by P. B. Everett, S. C. Hayward, and A. W. Meyers, *Journal of Applied Behavior Analysis,* 1974, *7*, 1–9. Copyright 1974 by the Society for the Experimental Analysis of Behavior, Inc. Reprinted by permission.

replicated effects more believable in science. Thus, *ABAB* designs are said to be more powerful than simple *ABA* ones for showing cause/effect relationships. Interested readers are referred to Hersen and Barlow (1976), Kratochwill (1978), and Leitenberg (1973) for examples of other types of *ABA* and *ABAB* designs.

Multiple-Baseline Designs

Another time-series design popular in applied behavior-analytic research is used when it is difficult to withdraw the independent variable and/or to return conditions as nearly as possible to those prevailing during the baseline period. As an example, consider our earlier question on the effects of instruction in appliance wattage ratings on the efficient use of electricity. Rather than using the classic true experiment, we might have chosen an intrasubject design. However, because of the nature of the independent variable (instruction), an *ABAB* design of the withdrawal variety would be difficult to use. It is hard to see how instruction once introduced in the *B* phase could subsequently be withdrawn.

When nonrecoverable variables such as this are being studied, *multiple-baseline* designs can be used. There are several variants of this design, but the one most appropriate to our example would involve first taking baseline data on

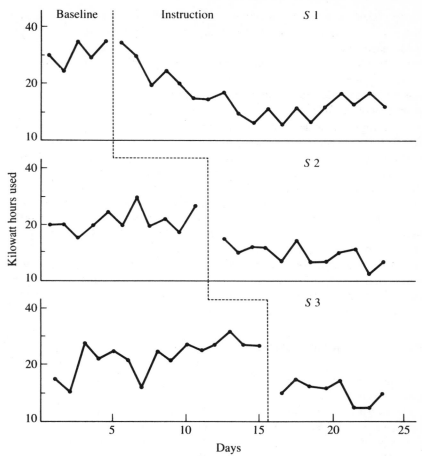

Figure 4–2. A multiple-baseline analysis of the effect of instruction in wattage ratings on daily level of electricity use.

the electricity usage of several different persons. Instruction in the wattage ratings of various appliances would then be given to one person while continuing to monitor the efficiency of that person's usage as well as that of the others. When the data on the first person have changed consistently, instruction would be introduced to another, and the data on all persons would continue to be monitored. When the second person's data have changed consistently, instruction would be introduced to the third, and so on. If each person's use of electricity remains essentially unchanged until instruction is given and then is altered systematically, there is a basis for concluding that instruction brought about the change.

Some fictitious data illustrating this example graphically are presented in Figure 4–2. The data for three different persons are portrayed in the figure, with the graphs stacked on top of one another. Note that the baseline for each person is either flat or showing a slight upward trend prior to the introduction of instruction. In each case, instruction is then associated with a consistent decrease in kilowatt hours used per day. Because the data remain relatively unaffected until the experimental phase is introduced and then change remarkably, a case can be made for concluding that a causal relationship exists between the independent and dependent variables.

As suggested earlier, the essence of believability in science, whether basic or applied, is repeatability. We noted that an *ABAB* design is more powerful than its *ABA* component alone because of the provision for repeating the baseline-to-experimental change (*A* to *B*) at least once. With multiple-baseline designs, of course, each additional subject provides an opportunity for an additional replication. In the example given in Figure 4–2, two replications are provided.

Multiple-baseline designs can be used in a variety of ways other than that illustrated here. Examples of their use in experimental studies of littering and electricity consumption are provided in Chapters 5 and 10, respectively. Moreover, *ABAB* and multiple-baseline designs can be combined in various ways to answer relatively complex questions while remaining in the intrasubject paradigm. The study of electricity use by Hayes and Cone (1977b) described in Chapter 10 is one example of such a combination.

MEASURING THE DEPENDENT VARIABLE

One very important aspect of behavior/environment research has not been touched on in this chapter due to space limitations. It involves the procedures used to measure the dependent variable. In the example given at the beginning of the chapter, we emphasized that before premises can be tested it is necessary to make some of their components measurable. How such operationalization occurs was not discussed further. The measurement of human behavior is, of course, an extremely complex undertaking; indeed, it is a science in its own right (see Cone & Hawkins, 1977; Wiggins, 1973). The measurement of environmental characteristics has been largely the province of the physical sciences. Thus, close, transdisciplinary working relationships among behavioral and physical scientists are obviously going to be necessary if we are to make serious efforts at the solution of environmental problems. Moreover, the training of effective problem solvers for the future will doubtless require extensive exposure to behavioral and physical sciences alike.

SUMMARY

This chapter has shown how environment/behavior scientists go about the business of studying relationships among variables. We noted that early in the life of most scientific undertakings a rather broad-brush, correlational/descriptive approach is taken in an effort to map out the important variables for further study. The establishment of correlations among things is often followed by controlled experimental studies that seek answers to cause/effect questions about the relationships among independent and dependent variables.

Two major experimental strategies were described: one in which differences between subjects are the basis for causal conclusions and one in which differences in the same subject or subjects during various phases of the experiment provide that basis. We noted that in applied behavior-analytic studies of environmental problems the latter design is generally favored. Indeed, most of the research illustrating the applied analysis of environmental problems in later chapters of this book relies heavily on intrasubject experimental approaches.

PART III

SOLVING PROBLEMS
OF ENVIRONMENTAL
AESTHETICS

Many of the problems that have been termed environmental issues—such as thermal pollution, noxious smells, litter, and noise—are chiefly aesthetic issues. Although all of these areas can be more than aesthetic concerns, they are considered problems even in their purely aesthetic form.

The earliest work in behavioral approaches to environmental problems emphasized the control of environmental aesthetics (with good reason, as we will discuss). Some of this earlier work paved the way for efforts in more difficult areas.

This part of the book summarizes work in two of the major aesthetic areas: litter control and noise control. Chapter 5 shows that a large and relatively well-developed set of techniques is now available for the control of litter. These techniques are effective and inexpensive, compared to traditional litter-control methods; unfortunately, though, the traditional methods are still far more popular. Chapter 6 describes the growing literature on noise control. We discuss noise in this part of the book because most studies to date have concentrated on the disruptive (rather than the health-related) effects of noise. The problem of noise control also provides a good example of the need to link behavioral technology and physical technology.

Chapter 5

ENVIRONMENTAL AESTHETICS: LITTER AND ENVIRONMENTAL DESIGN

LITTER

Americans generate about 145 million tons of trash every year (Kagan, 1977). Citizens of New York City alone produce 24,000 tons each *day* ("Treasure in the Trash Pile," 1978). Given such large amounts, it is not surprising that some of this trash ends up as litter in buildings, along roadways, and in parks and other areas frequented by the public. Nor is it surprising that the first serious efforts of behavior analysts to solve environmental problems began with the problem of litter. The choice was a reasonable one given the obvious magnitude of the problem, the relative ease of measuring litter, and the near-universal consensus that something should be done about it. According to the Keep America Beautiful campaign (Osborne & Powers, in press), the task of cleaning junk and trash from public settings cost taxpayers approximately $500 million in 1967. Clark, Burgess, and Hendee (1972) reported that the cost of cleaning up after campers in national forests reached $22 million in 1971. The cost has certainly increased since then. A national survey of highway litter (Research Triangle Institute, 1969) showed that trash accumulates to nearly 1 cubic yard per month on every mile of major highways. We all have our own data on the magnitude of the problem in those areas we visit frequently.

Solutions to the litter problem are discussed first in this section of the book because of their historical precedence in applied behavior analysis and because they are nicely illustrative of the principles of behavior and issues of measurement and research design dealt with in the previous two chapters. Various specific definitions of litter have been suggested, as the studies we review will attest. In a general sense, however, littering can be seen as one instance of the broader class of responses labeled pollution behaviors. Generating smog, contaminating water, and making noise would be other members of the same general behavior class (Cone, Parham, & Feirstein, 1972). Each of these behaviors can be conceptualized as operant in nature and thus controlled by stimulus changes subsequent to its occurrence. Viewed in this way, each can be subjected to experimental and applied analyses, with results having some possibility of generalization to other members of the class.

The litter problem can be thought of in terms of two major dimensions: inappropriately disposing of objects and cleaning or picking them up. More of the applied behavior-analytic literature has concentrated on the second of these dimensions than on the first. The basic rationale seems to be that it is easier to get people to pick up litter already on the ground than to keep them from throwing it there in the first place. Thus, preventive approaches to the problem have not been as plentiful as remedial ones. Traditionally, however, the reverse has been true. The majority of the more usual solutions involve large-scale education campaigns (for example, Keep America Beautiful), exhortations against littering, and threats of fines and/or imprisonment for doing so. The underwhelming success of these approaches is shown by the enormous monetary outlays for litter cleanup mentioned earlier.

In the sections that follow, the behavioral literature on solutions to littering is reviewed and categorized in terms of the general environmental context in which the problem was studied. Other reviews (for example, Cone & Hayes, 1977; Nietzel, Winett, MacDonald, & Davidson, 1977; Tuso & Geller, 1976) have used different organizational strategies, but the present approach seemed most in keeping with the problem-centered focus of the text in general.

Litter in Theaters and Football Stadiums

The earliest applied behavior-analytic study of litter dealt with trash left on the floor of movie theaters after Saturday children's matinees (Burgess, Clark, & Hendee, 1971). Using a series of withdrawal designs, Burgess and his colleagues examined the effects of two fairly conventional and one rather novel approach to the problem. Baseline amounts of litter were determined by collecting all the trash from the floor, weighing it, and comparing this weight with that of the trash appropriately disposed of in available containers. Only 11% to 24% of the total trash in the theater was found in the containers during the various baseline conditions. The rest was collected from the floor. The dependent variable in this study was thus "the percent of the total litter in the theater deposited in the trash cans" (p. 71).

The first procedure evaluated was the common suggestion of providing litter bags for holding trash for later disposal. Litter bags were given each child as he or she entered the theater, and each was told "This is for you to use while you are in the theater." The introduction of litter bags followed two Saturdays of baseline measurements and was associated with a slight increase in the percentage of litter deposited (from a mean of 19.5% to 31%) during the single Saturday it was tried. A return to baseline the next week resulted in a drop to 11%. In the next condition litter bags were again distributed, but an intermission announcement exhorted the audience to "Put your trash into the litter bags and put the bag into one of the trash cans in the lobby before leaving the theater." The single Saturday of this condition showed an increase in litter deposited to 57%, which dropped to 24% during the subsequent baseline period. The last procedure tried in this theater involved reintroducing the litter bags. Instead of the intermission exhortation, however, each patron was given a litter bag as he or she entered and told, "If you bring a bag of litter to the lobby before leaving the theater, you will receive one dime in exchange." The result of this approach was an increase to 94% in the percentage of litter disposed of properly. When this condition was subsequently withdrawn, this value dropped to 23%.

In a second theater Burgess and his colleagues evaluated two other common suggestions for solving the problem. Doubling the number of trash cans had no effect on litter, and neither did the showing of a Walt Disney cartoon entitled *Litterbugs*. However, when patrons entering the theater were given a litter bag and told "Each person returning a bag of litter will be given a free ticket to a special children's movie," the amount of litter appropriately disposed of again increased dramatically (to 95%). The authors concluded that alternatives to traditional approaches are needed and suggested that "littering might be reduced if immediate positive consequences contingent on anti-litter behavior could be scheduled" (p. 75). In a study similarly evaluating traditional and behavior-analytic approaches to litter with children, Lahart and Bailey (1974) came to comparable conclusions. Rewards were effective in getting children to pick up trash, while exhortation, lectures, and general educational approaches were not.

Zane (1974) evaluated similar procedures in a theater showing movies more oriented toward adult audiences. Using a dependent measure equivalent to that used by Burgess and his associates, Zane found that about 16.3% of the trash was appropriately deposited during baseline conditions. When three signs were posted instructing patrons to throw litter in the single trash can provided, 53.6% of the litter was disposed of appropriately. Similarly, the provision of one additional trash container was associated with the deposit of 56.4% of the litter. The offer of a free bag of popcorn (on a random basis to people putting trash in the can) was accompanied by a deposit rate of 60.9%. The baseline and instruction conditions of Zane's study produced disposal data remarkably similar to those of Burgess and his colleagues. The offer of a reward was probably not as effective as the positive consequences in the latter study because patrons were told only that "persons placing litter in the trash can in the outer hallway will have the chance to be rewarded." They were not told of the nature of the reward or exactly what chance they had of gaining it. All of the subjects in the other study could have earned the reward, and they were explicitly told that. The additional container may have been more effective in Zane's study because only one can was present previously. In the study by Burgess and his associates, though the containers were similarly doubled in number, there were multiple cans to begin with, and they may have been enough.

In another study aimed at theater litter, Geller (1973) found that flyers containing the cast of characters for a movie were less likely to be littered if they included an antilitter message asking people to "Please dispose of properly." Geller was more interested in evaluating the general usefulness of such prompts than in solving the trash problem in theaters, however. His research will be discussed more thoroughly in a subsequent section.

Baltes and Hayward (1976) extended the findings of Burgess and his colleagues to another setting, the football stadium at The Pennsylvania State University. Four different antilitter procedures were evaluated on two consecutive Saturdays in six sections of the stadium. Each of the procedures involved manipulating events antecedent to littering; that is, each involved altering stimuli thought to be discriminative for appropriate trash disposal. Thus, every third person entering a particular seating section was given a litter bag. In three of the four experimental sections, there was a message on each bag. Persons entering the fourth section received the bag but no message.

In the prompt-reward (PR) condition the message asked the person to "pitch in" and said the number on the bag might be a prize winner. The person was told to turn in the bag at the end of the game to see whether he or she had won. Note the similarity here to Zane's (1974) telling theater patrons that "persons placing litter in the trash can . . . will have the chance to be rewarded." As the people in the PR condition left the game, they passed a large sign bearing 20 randomly selected numbers. If their bag bore one of the 20 numbers, they were given $1 as they handed their bag to the experimenter.

In the positive-prompting (PP) condition every third person entering the section received a bag with a message asking him or her to "pitch in. . . , be a model for other people" and help "cut down cleaning costs." No reward was given for turning in the bag at the end of the game.

In the negative-prompting (NP) condition every third person entering the section received a bag with a message asking him or her to "pitch in" and not "be a litterbug." The message also warned that others might "disapprove of your littering" and that "litter can hurt."

In the litter bag-only (LO) condition every third patron was merely handed a bag with no message on it. Persons entering two randomly selected control sections received neither bags nor instructions.

The dependent variable consisted of the weight of the litter left on the benches and in the aisles after the game. This litter was collected in large sacks identified by section immediately after each of the two games.

The experimental design was a 2 × 5 factorial in which games (Saturday 1 versus Saturday 2) and experimental conditions (PR, PP, NP, LO, control) were compared. The most important finding was that, compared with control conditions, the PR, PP, NP, and LO procedures resulted in significantly less trash left on seats and in aisles. However, the four experimental procedures did not differ in effectiveness; that is, the offer of a reward in the PR condition was no more effective than merely giving patrons a litter bag without a message in the LO condition. Neither were those conditions more or less effective than the PP and NP procedures. Moreover, the same results occurred on both Saturdays. Overall, the four experimental procedures reduced littering by 45% when compared with the control conditions.

The importance of demonstrating effective antilitter procedures in football stadiums requires some discussion. After all, throwing one's trash on the ground in such settings seems very common and even to be expected. What is the value of showing various ways of reducing this activity? It can be argued that such studies have merit from both theoretical and practical points of view. Theoretically, as Baltes and Hayward noted, the production of changes in settings where social consequences actually favor littering has implications for settings in which it is inappropriate. Procedures found to be effective in stadiums and theaters can be refined in these more controlled settings before being tried in others such as parks and public campgrounds. Moreover, if something works where littering is generally seen as appropriate, it might be even more effective in a setting in which social sanctions are also working against littering.

From a practical perspective, cleaning up trash after movies and football games costs someone something. According to Baltes and Hayward, 24 workers spend six hours cleaning up after a typical Penn State football game. At $3 an hour, the cost of these efforts would be $432 per game, or $2160 for the usual five-game home schedule. Moreover, these costs do not reflect cleanup required on streets and walkways leading to the stadium. If the proper disposal of trash at games leads to reductions of litter in the area immediately surrounding the stadium, then the practical significance of studies such as Baltes and Hayward's is even greater. It should be noted that, although not exactly free, the cost of the litter bag-only procedure could be minimal. As Baltes and Hayward mentioned, local businesses might be convinced to donate litter bags with advertising on them. These businesses might even provide the labor needed to hand out the bags or to affix them to the backs of stadium seats before games.

Studies in theaters and football stadiums thus have their value, even though it may not be as immediately apparent as it seems in the research to be discussed in the next few sections.

Litter in Parks and Outdoor-Recreation Areas

Clark and his colleagues (1972) extended their earlier work with children to a campground covering more than 100 acres in the Wenatchee National Forest in the Cascade Mountains near Seattle. Again using an intrasubject design, they counted litter on the ground during two successive weekends in late summer. However, in a departure from previous studies, the authors deliberately planted items of litter on the ground in order to provide a constant level on both weekends. Four types of litter (crushed brown-paper bags, beverage cans, nondeposit bottles, and deposit bottles) were planted on the Thursday and Friday preceding each weekend. Marks on a map showed the location of each of the 160 pieces (40 of each type), so that it could be easily identified later.

Two observers, or counters, walked along a predetermined route on Thursday, Friday, Saturday, Sunday, and Monday of the baseline and intervention weekends. Each was responsible for counting a certain type of trash. On the

Saturday of the second weekend, seven families were asked to "help with the litter problem." Children of these families were told they could choose a prize from among several items (Smokey the Bear patch, Junior Forest Ranger badge, and so forth) if they agreed to help. They were then given 30-gallon plastic bags and told that the ranger would be back in the evening to pick up their bags and give them a reward.

The park rangers cooperated during the study by not picking up litter or encouraging others to do so. Interestingly, during the Thursday–Monday period of the baseline weekend, the number of planted items on the ground gradually decreased (from 160 to 56). Of the four types of trash, deposit bottles were most rapidly picked up during the baseline period, going from 40 to 3. When children were offered prizes for helping during the experimental phase, planted litter dropped from 160 pieces to 6. Thus, although people frequenting the campground seem to pick up trash without special efforts to get them to, they pick up even more when simple rewards are offered. Furthermore, as Clark and his associates observed, the rapid elimination of returnable bottles during the baseline period is evidence that nothing else is needed to encourage the collection of litter with a built-in value. The data on returnable bottles are directly supportive of legislative efforts to ban nonreturnable beverage containers. Requiring a deposit does seem to result in the bottles' being picked up quickly. Whether it would reduce their being thrown away in the first place cannot be determined from this study, of course. The returnable-bottle issue will surface again in Chapter 8, where the general topic of recycling is discussed in more depth.

The research just described is a useful extension of the efforts mentioned in the previous section. It shows the power of reinforcement procedures in dealing with litter in a natural setting and once again offers evidence of their cost effectiveness. Approximately 150–200 pounds of litter were collected by the 26 children participating, at a cost of $3 in rewards. It was estimated that an equivalent job by regular campground personnel would have taken between 16 and 20 hours at a cost of $50–$60. These results so impressed the U.S. Forest Service that the procedures have been extended to numerous other national-forest and campground areas (Burgess, Clark, & Hendee, 1974).

With the exception of the signs and extra trash container in Zane's (1974) study, the effective procedures described thus far have involved the active participation of research staff. Handing out litter bags, making announcements, and awarding dimes, dollars, and badges all take time and require the presence of some knowledgeable person. Such active, relatively labor-intensive strategies should be compared with the more passive, remotely administrable reinforcement procedures developed by Powers, Osborne, and Anderson (1973). These authors were interested in reducing ground litter in Green Canyon, an undeveloped U.S. Forest Service recreational area near Logan, Utah. The area was unsupervised, so there were no personnel available to administer antilitter programs.

The study followed an intrasubject withdrawal design in which bags of litter turned in per week and number of pieces of litter on the ground were the major dependent variables. Litter stations were constructed consisting of two 55-gallon oil drums, litter bags, cards, and a box for depositing the cards. A large sign asked people to fill a bag with litter, tie it, remove the card from it, and deposit the bag in one of the drums. The sign instructed the people to write their name, address, age, phone number, sex, and reason for coming to the canyon on the card and put it in the box.

The study was in effect for 15 weeks during the late summer and fall of one year and for six weeks during the subsequent spring. The overall design was *ABABABA,* with alternating baseline *(A)* and experimental conditions *(B).* After two weeks of baseline, the litter stations were modified to inform depositors that they could elect to receive 25¢ for their efforts or a chance at winning $20 in a drawing. The trash and cards were collected weekly, and letters were sent to the persons turning in cards. The letters contained 25¢ for those selecting this option or told them the number of chances entered in their name for the drawing. Drawings were held weekly, and a $20 check was mailed to the winner.

The experimental conditions were in effect for three weeks, followed by their withdrawal and a return to baseline for two weeks. Four bags of trash were turned in during the initial two-week baseline period, followed by 16, 24, and 19 during the first, second, and third weeks, respectively, of the initial experimental phase. Withdrawing the experimental procedures was accompanied by a drop to six and three bags per week during the two-week return to the baseline phase. Subsequent introductions and withdrawals of the experimental procedure were associated with respective increases and decreases in bags deposited. Overall, 187 bags (1658 pounds) of litter were deposited during the 21 weeks of the study. The majority of these (74%) were collected during the experimental conditions. An additional 219 pounds of loose litter were deposited in the drums. The two ground surveys similarly supported the efficiency of the remote-reinforcement procedure. An overall reduction of 41.5% was noted in litter on the ground between the first and second surveys.

A total of $208.50 was paid to participants in the study ($200 in ten lottery checks, $8.50 to those selecting an immediate 25¢). Most of the cards turned in (73%) selected a chance at the $20 drawing. Thus, 11¢ were paid for each pound of litter deposited during the study.

This research is a further example of the effective use of behavioral principles in solving the litter problem. The greatest significance of the study comes from showing the effectiveness of a relatively automatic procedure for reinforcing people for environmentally protective behavior. As will be noted later, more research needs to be addressed to developing similar procedures for use with other environmental problems.

The labor involved in implementing and maintaining such programs is only one aspect of their cost, however. When monetary payment is the reward, it can also elevate the cost of the procedure significantly. Baltes and Hayward (1976) reduced the overall cost of payments by a lottery drawing of 20 numbers worth $1 each. Similarly, Powers and his associates (1973) economized by offering the larger, more meaningful $20 reward to persons winning a lottery. Zane (1974) awarded a free bag of popcorn to an average of every tenth patron depositing a bag of litter on leaving the theater. None of these studies directly evaluated the effects of different payment schedules, however.

As part of an examination of litter reduction in the Woodland Park Zoo in Seattle, Kohlenberg and Phillips (1973) looked at this question. Using an intra-subject withdrawal design, they collected baseline data daily between 12 and 8 P.M. for two weeks. The principal dependent variable was the number of litter deposits each day in a 28-gallon garbage can located in the central portion of the zoo.

After the baseline phase a sign reading "At times persons depositing litter in this container will be rewarded" was installed near the garbage can. In addition, after a varying number of deposits the experimenter would approach a person who had just put something in the can, thank him or her, and present a coupon good for a Pepsi at the concession stand. The experimenter presented the coupons on a variable schedule such that the average number of deposits per reward was ten or seven during the first three days of the first experimental phase. The average number of deposits before a reward was then changed to 20 for the remaining 11 days of the phase.

Rewards were discontinued during the next two weeks, but the sign remained. Finally, rewards were reinstated for two weeks, with the average number of deposits per reward once again set at ten.

The total number of deposits varied systematically over the four phases of the study, with sums of 723, 4577, 2403, and 6023 for Baseline 1, Reinforcement 1, Baseline 2, and Reinforcement 2, respectively. Pictures were taken of the litter on the ground in the area near the can on most days of the last two phases of the study. Judges blind to the study rated these as containing significantly more litter under baseline than experimental conditions.

Thus, overall it would appear that reward procedures were once again effective in reducing litter by increasing appropriate disposal behaviors. In addition, preliminary evidence was provided to suggest a possible effect for reinforcer density. Except for the first three days of Reinforcement 1, in which Pepsi coupons were awarded after an average of seven or ten deposits (VP–7 or VP–10), the reward schedule was such that they were awarded after every 20th deposit on the average (VP–20). During Reinforcement 2 the coupons were presented after every tenth deposit on the average (VP–10) to obtain data allowing a comparison of the two reinforcement densities. That 4577 deposits (40.9 per hour) were made during the 14 days of Reinforcement 1, compared with 6023 deposits (53.8 per hour) during Reinforcement 2, is preliminary evidence that the reward schedule may have been important. At least, it appears that doubling the frequency of reinforcement was associated with a 32% increase in deposits.

However, the nature of the experimental design makes it impossible to say with any certainty that the difference in deposit rates was due to increased reinforcement density. One of the obvious problems is that the richer schedule followed the lean one, and increases in deposits may thus reflect merely the order in which the schedules were presented. Perhaps the first two weeks were necessary for people to catch on to the relationship between deposits and rewards, so that an increase would have occurred in Reinforcement 2 even if the same reinforcement schedule had been carried over from Reinforcement 1.

The issue of reinforcement schedule is a fascinating one that is just beginning to be explored in applied behavior-analytic work in the environmental area. It will come up again when transportation systems are discussed in Chapter 9. The results of extensive basic research on schedule effects are already available, however, and interested readers are referred to Ferster and Skinner (1957) for the classic treatment of this literature. Similarly, the suitability of intrasubject designs for answering comparative questions has been dealt with, and interested readers are referred to the paper by Kazdin (1973) and the book by Hersen and Barlow (1976) for a discussion of this issue.

The issue of reinforcement density is directly related to that of the cost effectiveness of various solutions to the litter problem. Although most of the studies described thus far have discussed this issue, none has directly compared the cost and effectiveness of experimental procedures with the litter-control tactics normally employed in a setting. Such a comparison was conducted in a study reported by Casey and Lloyd (1977).

These authors were interested in how effective reinforcement procedures would be when compared with the cleanup activities of maintenance personnel in a small, commercial amusement park in northern Iowa. They were also interested in whether children of different ages might be more or less affected by rewards for picking up litter. An *ABACAD* intrasubject withdrawal design was used in which percentage of litter removed from the grounds each day served as the dependent variable.

During the baseline *(A)* phases, litter was counted each morning before and after the maintenance people had cleaned the park. The difference in the two counts divided by the first yielded the percentage of litter actually removed from the grounds. During the *B* phase, children 12 years of age and under were awarded a free ticket for one of the amusement-park rides for every bag of litter turned in to the experimenters. During the *C* phase the procedures were extended to all ages, while during the *D* phase only those 13 and over were eligible.

Litter was divided into large items (cans, bottles, and large wrappers) and small, miscellaneous items, and separate counts were made for each. Data were also collected on the number of minutes the maintenance people spent cleaning up, the number of children and their ages, the number and size of bags filled, the number of tickets issued, and the cost of the rides for which they were used.

The results indicated that children consistently picked up more litter than the maintenance people. The mean percentage of litter removed during the *B, C,* and *D* phases, when children were involved, was 71.7% compared with 27% during baseline conditions, in which the maintenance people were responsible. During the *B* phase, when children 12 and under were targeted, 93% and 45% of the large and small litter, respectively, were removed. When all ages were included (*C* phase), 98% and 79% of the large and small litter, respectively, were removed. When only children 13 and over were involved (*D* phase), 94% and 80% of the large and small litter were removed. Thus, the younger children did not seem to remove the small litter as well.

In terms of cost effectiveness, the maintenance people spent about three hours each day picking up trash. At $1.90 per hour plus the cost of a litter sack (25¢), routine cleanup cost the park $5.95 per day. This figure compares favorably with total costs of $4.78, $6.35, and $7.90 for the *B, C,* and *D* phases, respectively. Casey and Lloyd report that the "cost-effectiveness index (cost for each percent of litter removed) was .22 for traditional maintenance and .09, .08, and .10" (p. 544) for the *B, C,* and *D* phases, respectively. Thus, routine maintenance procedures were approximately two-and-one-half times more expensive than the experimental procedures.

Interestingly, though the management of the amusement park was told of these results, they continue to use the routine maintenance procedures, reserving the others for occasional use as publicity and good-will gestures! More will be said about influencing decision makers to use proven solutions to environmental problems in Chapters 12 and 13. Suffice it here to say that this difficulty is not uncommon in applied behavior analysis generally.

Litter along Streets and Highways

Although most of the studies mentioned thus far have involved reinforcement procedures of one form or another, the problem of trash along streets and highways has been attacked somewhat differently. In the best-known studies in this area, Finnie (1973) examined a number of potentially influential factors, including the availability of trash receptacles, their attractiveness, and the initial cleanliness of the environment.

Finnie examined the first of these questions along three highways outside Richmond, Virginia. In an intrasubject withdrawal design trash cans were placed along the highways exactly .25 mile past a sign announcing their presence. Litter was counted in separate areas 1 mile and 5 miles past the can. Signs and cans were then removed and litter counted in the same two areas. Thus, the experimental condition was in effect prior to taking baseline data, resulting in a *BA* design. Finnie also included a condition in which the cans were present but the signs were not.

The presence of cans reduced litter by an average of 28.6%. Interestingly, this effect was comparable for areas 1 mile and 5 miles from the can (27.9% and 29.4%, respectively). Moreover, there was no statistical difference between the reduction occurring when signs were present (25.2%) and that occurring when they were not (32.0%). It seems the trash cans themselves were a sufficient cue for people to deposit their litter.

The availability of trash receptacles was also studied on sidewalks in downtown Richmond. A 6.8% reduction in litter occurred with the provision of one can every four blocks. When a can was placed on every block, 16.7% of the litter was removed.

In a third study Finnie evaluated the effect of the attractiveness of trash receptacles in St. Louis. A Clean City Squares can attractively painted with the names of corporate sponsors was compared with the usual 55-gallon oil drum. Although a somewhat greater reduction in litter on the sidewalks occurred when the Clean City Squares cans were present (14.7% versus 3.2%), neither type of can produced a practically useful reduction in overall litter. Finnie discussed some methodological problems with the study that may have resulted in an underestimation of the actual effects of the litter cans. Other studies showing that the design of the trash container can have an effect are reviewed by Geller (in press).

The question of whether initial environmental cleanliness is a factor was investigated together with several others in a more extensive study by Finnie in Philadelphia. Persons buying hot dogs wrapped in waxed paper from street vendors served as subjects, and the principal dependent variable was the statistical probability that a person would drop his or her wrapper on the ground. As might be expected, there was less littering on clean streets than on already littered ones. The presence of trash receptacles was also varied, and once again there was less littering when they were present. In addition, people under 19 years of age were found to be much more likely to litter than those who were older. Overall, Finnie reported 45.5% and 31.4% less litter in clean than in dirty environments, depending on whether receptacles were present or absent, respectively. Thus, as commonly suspected, litter begets litter, a finding also reported by Cone and his colleagues (1972) in a laboratory study of littering by young children, by Heberlein (1971) in a field study of handbill littering by college students, and by Geller, Witmer, and Tuso (1977) in a study of handbill littering in grocery stores.

To summarize, research described in this section shows that litter on sidewalks and along roadways can be reduced somewhat by keeping the areas clean to begin with and by providing appropriate trash receptacles. However, the effects of litter-prevention tactics such as these are not nearly as impressive as those of the litter-cleanup approaches mentioned earlier, a point to which we shall return in a later section (see Preliminary Conclusions and Unresolved Issues).

Litter on the Grounds around Buildings

Trash in the yards of apartment complexes and on the grounds around public buildings is an eyesore at best and a hazard to playing children at worst. Trash in apartment-complex yards was examined in a carefully conducted study by Chapman and Risley (1974) in a large, low-income, public-housing project in

Kansas City, Kansas. Two different reinforcement procedures were evaluated in an intrasubject withdrawal design in which the number of pieces of litter counted in yards served as the primary dependent variable.

The design employed a *BCACACDA* sequence of conditions in which verbal appeals to help pick up trash *(B)* were followed by payments of 10¢ per bag of litter turned in *(C)*, the withdrawal of payments *(A)*, and finally payment for producing a clean yard *(D)*. The authors noted that previous reinforcement studies of antilittering had made rewards contingent on volume of litter turned in rather than on producing some level of cleanliness in the area or areas of interest. They reasoned that payment contingent upon the absence of litter in assigned yards might lead to differences in litter counts.

Chapman and Risley's results were consistent with those of earlier studies in showing no noticeable effect for verbal appeals to help and yet quite sizable reductions when children were given 10¢ per bag of litter. When children were paid for turning in trash, the number of pieces of ground litter dropped 28.9% from its levels during the verbal-appeal and no-payment conditions. However, when children were paid for producing clean yards (about 10¢ per yard), an even greater reduction (68.4%) was noted. Although certain design limitations prevent strong conclusions concerning the separate and relative effects of payment for clean yards, the results at least point to this tactic as an alternative reinforcement strategy worth further study. Unfortunately, as Chapman and Risley noted, the effects seem to have been short-lived. Within 12 days of the discontinuation of the study, counts of ground litter showed it was once again approaching baseline levels. The authors estimated that a permanent antilitter program would require a half-time maintenance person to recruit and pay large numbers of children about $50 a week to keep the yards clean. For a 15-square-block, 390-unit housing project, they estimated the cost of such a program to be less than $1 a month per unit.

One of the advantages of the payment-for-clean-yards procedure used by Chapman and Risley was that the reinforcer was directly related to the environmental change desired. However, when rewards are offered for turning in trash, there is no assurance (1) that the trash actually comes from the area targeted for cleaning or (2) that enough is removed to produce satisfactory levels of cleanliness. Chapman and Risley found both of these problems with their payment-for-volume condition. Children were discovered to be bringing in trash from home or other areas to gain the reward. Also, frequently only the largest, most obvious items were turned in from actual target areas, leaving enough small trash—cigarette butts, gum wrappers, and so on—that the areas still had the appearance of being littered.

The trash-importation and small-items problems were tackled from a different angle by Hayes, Johnson, and Cone (1975). Their study was an attempt to clean up the litter on the grounds around buildings of a large, federal, youth-correctional facility, Kennedy Youth Center, in Morgantown, West Virginia. An intrasubject multiple-baseline design was employed, with number of pieces of litter on the ground as the dependent variable.

Four areas were marked off on a diagram of the buildings and grounds, and separate counts were made of the litter in each. Baseline counts were made for 17, 22, and 36 days, respectively, in Areas 1–3 and continuously throughout the study in Area 4. The inmates of the living unit bordering Area 1 were told by means of a flier that beginning on the 18th day the area around their cottage would be planted with undetectably marked items of litter. The inmates were told that they could voluntarily pick up trash in that area, place it in paper bags provided, write their names on the bags, and leave them in a designated trash can. They were also informed that the contents of the bags would be inspected each day and that persons having a marked item in their bags would receive a choice of 25¢ or a special privilege such as late bedtime or participation in a weekend "coffee house."

As a check on the effects of a verbal appeal similar to that used by Chapman and Risley (1974), the inmates of the first cottage were told that Area 2 was also their responsibility though it would not be planted with marked items. On the 23rd day a second flier told these inmates that the marked items had been extended to Area 2. The inmates in a second cottage were then introduced to the marked-item procedure 14 days later. They were told that Area 3 would contain marked items good for 25¢ and that Area 4 was also their responsibility even though it would contain no such items. Special privileges were not used as rewards with this group.

The baseline data for Areas 1–3 showed steadily increasing amounts of litter. With the introduction of the marked-item technique, the amount of ground litter dropped immediately and remained low. Litter counts in the three targeted areas dropped a mean of 71.3% from baseline, comparing favorably with Chapman and Risley's production of a 68.4% reduction with their payment-for-clean-yards condition.

The marked-item technique is an effective control over the sabotage possible with the trash-buying approaches discussed earlier because there is no advantage in importing litter to fill a bag and gain a reward. Moreover, since even very small pieces of litter might be marked, they tend to be picked up just as often as large items. Unfortunately, Hayes and his associates provided no formal follow-up data showing the permanence of the changes produced. It is very likely that ground litter once again accumulated when the marked-item procedures were discontinued. If so, it would be important to have data on the cost of maintaining the procedure on a continuing basis. Although these cost figures are not provided, Hayes et al. noted that one advantage of the marked-item technique is that program administrators "can control the upper limit of funding by controlling the number of items marked" (p. 386). Moreover, administrators can vary the density of the marked items to deal with areas having more of a litter problem than others.

Hayes and his colleagues also made suggestions for using the procedure on a large scale and for applying it to other types of litter such as junked cars. Large-scale uses might involve marking items with fluorescent paint and using a black light to detect them as Bacon and her associates have subsequently shown (Bacon, Blount, Pickering, & Drabman, 1978). Or items could be marked with an isotopic compound that would be sensed by a Geiger counter. Large bins could be automated such that sacks containing marked items would trigger a dispenser that would award money or raffle tickets automatically. Junked cars could be marked surreptitiously or their serial numbers recorded. Then large cash bonuses could be awarded persons turning in marked cars. Only some of the cars would actually have to be marked, making the procedure relatively inexpensive. Indeed, the cars would not even have to be marked physically, since they could be located and marked on aerial photographs that would be carefully hidden in a government vault somewhere.

Litter inside Buildings

A number of studies have involved attempts to solve litter problems occurring in buildings frequented by the public. The studies conducted in theaters would be examples of these but are not included because of their special status as places where throwing trash on the floor is a commonly accepted, socially sanctioned practice. The research described in this section was conducted in buildings where littering is generally considered inappropriate.

The most extensive work in this area is that of Geller (1973, 1975) and his associates (Geller, Witmer, & Orebaugh, 1976; Geller, Witmer, & Tuso, 1977; Geller, Wylie, & Farris, 1971). Geller's research is nicely summarized in Tuso and Geller (1976) and will be described here only briefly. In contrast to the cleanup emphasis of the bulk of the reinforcement studies discussed in the previous sections, Geller's focus, as was Finnie's (1973), has been on preventing inappropriate trash disposal in the first place. Generally, his approach has been to examine the effects of prompts (such as "Please do not litter") on subsequent littering by persons exposed to the prompts.

For example, in an early study (Geller, 1973) the use of already existing trash cans was prompted by written messages. In this study 34 college students entering a classroom were given free paper cups of lemonade. On half of the cups was written "Please dispose of properly." The dependent measure was to be the proportion of students in the message and no-message groups disposing of their cups properly. To Geller's surprise, however, all the students appropriately deposited their cups in the wastebasket. Nonetheless, the same general-prompt strategy did yield positive results in five other settings—a university snack bar, the lobby of a university classroom building, a grocery store, and two movie theaters. In a number of these settings, general prompts to "dispose of properly" were compared with specific prompts that also indicated where a trash receptacle could be found. As Tuso and Geller (1976) noted, "slightly more trash disposals occurred when the message included the location of the trash can" (p. 14).

In another study (Geller et al., 1977), two experiments examined the effects of specific prompts on the littering of handbills in a grocery store. Patrons entering the store received a handbill listing the week's specials. On some of those, a specific prompt was included: "Please don't litter. Dispose for recycling in the green trash can located in aisle one." On others no prompt was included at all. The first experiment showed that about 30% of the 1146 customers receiving the antilitter prompt did indeed use the suggested trash can. When the message was omitted from the handbills of an additional 1231 customers, only 9% disposed of them properly.

In the second experiment, handbills were deliberately strewn about the store in one condition (dirty) and not in another (clean) to examine whether littering is more likely in already trashy environments. As you may recall, Finnie (1973) found more littering of hot-dog wrappers on the streets of Philadelphia when they were already littered than when they were clean. In the littered-store condition Geller and his associates found that a somewhat higher percentage of customers littered than when the store was free of littered handbills (5.09% versus .9%). Overall littering in this experiment was too infrequent to draw firm conclusions from this difference, but the results are consistent with those of Finnie and of Cone and his colleagues (1972) and Heberlein (1971) mentioned earlier.

The last study (Byers & Cone, 1976) to be described in this section dealt with the problem of litter in a large cafeteria in the student union of West Virginia University. Though a number of employees were responsible for clearing tables of trash not voluntarily removed by users, the large volume of business during the noon hour typically resulted in many tables covered with trays and trash. Already crowded conditions became worse as people crowded around clean tables while avoiding trashy ones. In an intrasubject withdrawal design Byers and Cone examined the effects of (1) a small sign on each table saying "Please reshelve your tray" and (2) randomly awarding coupons good for free hamburgers to persons who did reshelve their trays.

The primary dependent variable was the percentage of persons reshelving trays during the 50-minute period from 12:00 to 12:50 P.M. each day. Trained observers counted the number of trays passing by the cashiers during this period and the number placed on tray carts or conveyor belts after their use. In an *ABAB* *(C + B)* design, baseline data showed that 52.6% of the trays were reshelved. When the signs urging reshelving were placed on the tables during the first experimental phase, the percentage increased to 64.1%. A drop in tray reshelving during the subsequent baseline period established the effect of the signs. When the signs were reintroduced, reshelving climbed to 67.9%.

During the last phase a coupon good for a free hamburger was awarded every 14th person, on the average, who reshelved a tray. The signs were also retained in this phase, and the combination of signs and coupons was associated with 73.3% of the trays being reshelved. Unfortunately, time constraints prohibited a clear isolation of the effect of hamburger coupons alone, but the table signs did appear to be effective.

The results of this small study are consistent with those of earlier investigations using prompt-only approaches and with those of studies using reinforcement procedures. It would appear that the latter were potentially more effective in this study in that a higher percentage of trays was reshelved when hamburgers were awarded on a random basis. Unfortunately, design limitations and too few data make conclusive statements about the relative superiority of the reinforcement procedures premature at this time.

Community-Wide Cleanup Campaigns

The research discussed up to now convincingly demonstrates the power of behavioral approaches to litter problems that are clearly defined and generally restricted to rather small areas. Litter is a community-wide problem, however, so the technology evaluated in these small-scale pilot investigations will eventually have to be tried out in much larger projects. Some work of this scope has already begun, sponsored by Keep America Beautiful, Inc. (KAB) and referred to as the Clean Community System (CCS).

Space limitations do not permit a complete description of the KAB program here, but interested readers can find a very thorough analysis and critique of its various aspects in an excellent article by Geller (in press). Briefly, the Clean Community System approach involves the following steps:

1. Recognition by community leaders of problems in solid-waste disposal.
2. Applying to KAB to become a CCS participant.
3. Purchasing materials from KAB and obtaining funds for the program.
4. Sending a team of community representatives to KAB for training.
5. Performing thorough solid-waste analyses to determine existing laws, education programs, litter-control technology, and ratings of the cleanliness of various locations throughout the community.
6. Obtaining baseline photographs of the cleanliness of various community locations.
7. Training community leaders from the business, government, and private sectors.
8. Organizing a Clean Community Committee and hiring a coordinator.
9. Establishing various subcommittees, such as commercial (to work with business and industry); communications (to publicize CCS efforts); community (to promote volunteer projects and so on); municipal (to upgrade laws, improve technology, and so on); and education (to influence efforts to teach effective waste-disposal practices in schools and other educational contexts).

This cursory listing of some of the steps involved in the program does not completely indicate its complexity, but the list should give some idea of the breadth of the CCS effort, and it demonstrates the potential for large-scale, community-wide applications of the behavioral technology discussed in the earlier sections of this chapter. More specific information about the CCS program can be obtained from Keep America Beautiful, Inc. (99 Park Ave., New York, N.Y. 10016).

Preliminary Conclusions and Unresolved Issues

The questions raised at the beginning of the chapter have been answered more or less definitively in the subsequent review of approaches to the problem of littering in various environmental contexts. It is clear that the problem is extensive and costly to deal with in traditional ways. It is also now clear that various solutions have been proved effective, at least on a limited basis.

Although we did not organize the present chapter in this way, it is possible to separate research on litter into those studies dealing primarily with events antecedent to the act of littering and those dealing with litter already on the ground (see Tuso & Geller, 1976). The antecedent, or preventive, approaches have examined the effects of initial environmental cleanliness, availability of trash receptacles, personal vocal appeals not to litter, an antilitter cartoon, and signs and written messages not to litter. These preventive approaches have not all been consistently effective, but enough evidence is available from different studies to suggest that more littering is likely in trashy than in clean environments, that the availability of receptacles reduces litter, that personal vocal appeals are not very effective in preventing litter (at least with children), but that signs and written messages are, at least over the relatively short periods investigated in studies to date. The last finding is of interest to companies packaging products in disposable containers. Messages to "dispose of properly" do seem to have some effect, at least when printed on handbills and paper cups. We are not aware of any study that has directly examined the effects of such messages printed on packaging more relevant to the litter problem, such as beer cans, candy wrappers, cigarette packages, and pop bottles.

The research using reinforcement procedures to deal with litter already on the ground has been more ingenious and more voluminous than that focusing on prevention. It is now possible to say that the technology exists for effecting rapid cleanup of areas by users who may not have even contributed to the litter in the first place. Moreover, the innovative approaches we have described seem no more expensive than traditional cleanup procedures, and in some cases (for example, Casey & Lloyd, 1977) have been shown to be less expensive while considerably more effective. Whether one uses the relatively labor-intensive trash-buying approaches of Baltes and Hayward (1976), Burgess and his colleagues (1971), Casey and Lloyd (1977), Chapman and Risley (1974), Clark and his associates (1972), Kohlenberg and Phillips (1973), and Zane (1974) or the more economical, remote-reinforcement procedure of Powers and his associates (1973), sizable reductions in ground litter seem to result.

These promising findings notwithstanding, however, a number of issues are still unresolved. Many different antecedent/preventive and reinforcement/ cleanup approaches have been evaluated and found to be more or less effective. Although the former are not overwhelmingly successful in preventing litter (reductions as high as 25% are unusual), they are somewhat effective, and certainly more economical than the latter. What would seem to be called for now is some definitive research on the most effective technique within each general strategy (that is, preventive versus cleanup) separately, and then an evaluation of the most effective combination of the two. For example, a combination of (1) specific antilitter prompts (such as "Please don't litter. Put the pop top in the can and place both in the Peli-can") and (2) automatically rewarding people for throwing bags of trash containing a marked item into an automated bin might be the most cost-effective overall strategy for handling litter. Of course, the best combination might vary from area to area, and even within an area, depending on the population frequenting it.

In future research a number of limitations of earlier studies will no doubt be addressed. For example, most research efforts to date have been short-term demonstration projects conducted in proscribed, relatively well-controlled settings. The more effective of these early tactics should now be examined over longer periods and in larger geographic areas. Entire national parks, whole downtown shopping areas, and extensive stretches of highways and public beaches should be studied. Moreover, the procedures used should be maintained long enough for temporal variations in their effects to be documented. The community-wide, comprehensive approach of Keep America Beautiful, Inc. is an example of the scope of projects needed now. Indeed, future research on the various components of the CCS, if it is responsive to some of Geller's (in press) excellent suggestions, could lead to a quantum leap in the technology of solid-waste management.

Although research sophistication continues to improve, partial solutions to the litter problem are already in use in some places. For example, the state of Oregon has banned the use of no-deposit beverage containers, in effect requiring all such containers to possess some built-in value. As Clark and his associates (1972) have demonstrated, this type of litter is more likely to be picked up than trash with no such value, thus indirectly supporting the logic of the Oregon law. Though it is difficult to see how a similar approach could be extended to all forms of litter, the fact that beverage containers account for between 17% and 38% of highway trash and about 12% of urban trash (Finnie, 1973) shows the importance of similar legislation in other states.

Incidentally, as Nietzel and his colleagues (1977) have noted, the common suggestion that container legislation would put thousands of workers out of jobs has not been supported by the evidence in Oregon. There the deposit law "resulted in the loss of 350 production jobs, and the creation of 140 truck driving and 575 warehouse and handling jobs" (p. 316), for an overall gain of 365 jobs.

Other partial solutions are in effect in places having laws making littering punishable by fines and/or imprisonment. Unfortunately, to our knowledge there have been no systematic evaluations of the effects of such laws. Their existence concurrent with a continuing litter problem suggests, however, that they are probably not very effective. Moreover, these solutions are costly. Think of the obvious (and hidden) expense involved in catching a litterer and bringing legal action against him or her. There is sure to be more cost involved in such an approach than in the reinforcement tactics discussed here.

In the research we have just surveyed, there has been an interesting omission of almost any reference to theoretical issues. Other than viewing littering as operant behavior and thus potentially understandable in terms of the laws and concepts applicable to operant behavior generally (see, for example, Burgess et al., 1971), little of a theoretical nature has been said about it. Wohlwill and Carson (1972) warned of the dangers inherent in taking too practical or problem-focused a view of environmental psychology, and we have discussed the problem of theoretical emaciation ourselves (Cone & Hayes, 1977).

A number of potentially interesting theoretical issues seem to underlie the research cited earlier. If littering is viewed as merely one member of the larger class of pollution behaviors, then lessons learned from the study of littering should have general applicability; that is, littering should be controlled by the same variables that bear on the corporate pollution of waterways and air. Further research will be necessary to determine the nature of such response classes.

A careful look at littering as a response suggests some interesting parallels with other forms of human behavior. If we view the act as ridding oneself of an aversive stimulus (trash), the ridding is probably negatively reinforced (by the removal of that aversive stimulus). The prevention of littering in the individual would thus seem to center around increasing the time between the appearance of the aversive object and its removal by the person; that is, trash would need to be retained long enough to get it to an appropriate receptacle for disposal. Viewed in this way, any behavioral-science literature dealing with the shaping of delay in escape from mildly aversive circumstances would seem to have potential relevance to the study of litter prevention. Thus, in terms of the theoretical notions embodied in Platt's (1973) concept of social traps (discussed in Chapter 1), it would be necessary to find ways of avoiding or overcoming the short-term negative consequences of holding onto trash in order to bring about the long-term positive consequence of a cleaner environment (see Table 1-1).

All this may seem a bit abstract and far afield of the more prosaic practical problems dealt with up to now in this chapter. To some extent it is. However, as mentioned in Chapter 2, we shall endeavor throughout this book to present applied behavior-analytic solutions to environmental problems as more than a bag of tricks having no conceptual underpinnings or common theoretical ties. On the contrary, we have tried to show how the various practical solutions to the litter problem are derived from the common principles described in Chapter 3. Future chapters will show this same relevance to principle.

DESIGNING ENVIRONMENTS TO MINIMIZE LITTER AND PERPETUATE THEIR OWN ATTRACTIVENESS

In Chapter 2 we noted that a great deal of research has examined reactions people have to their built environment. The way furniture is arranged can affect social interaction. The way buildings are designed can affect movement, social interaction, crime rates, and numerous other human activities. Research establishing these reactions has generally not been of direct value in solving environmental problems, so we have not reviewed it extensively. Environmental design is important in issues of aesthetics, however, from at least two slightly different perspectives.

A building, a chair, or an outdoor landscape can be designed in accordance with societally prevalent notions of what is aesthetically pleasing or satisfying. Data establishing these notions are derived largely from reactive research. Once environments are built, their maintenance in an aesthetically satisfying condition is dependent on certain behaviors of their users. Previous portions of this chapter have shown ways of effecting behavior change to improve or maintain the environment at levels consistent with prevalent judgments of what is aesthetically satisfying. In addition to these after-the-fact behavior-change efforts, however, it is possible to design environments initially in ways that will help them continue to meet those aesthetic criteria indefinitely. In other words, environments can be designed that are self-perpetuating, that promote and maintain environmentally protective behavior toward themselves.

In recognition of this possibility, students of design are often encouraged to consider carefully just how behavior will be affected by their efforts. To date, however, there is not much experimental evidence available to help guide design decisions (see Bell, Fisher, & Loomis, 1978, for an excellent summary). These decisions are typically quite complex, and completely adequate theoretical accounts of the effects of the built environment on behavior have not yet been developed. In their absence, several empirical strategies are available that might be useful in encouraging designing from a human behavioral standpoint; that is, guesses about features that will lead to greater aesthetic self-perpetuation can be assisted by gathering some data before finishing the design.

One way to do so would be to set up laboratory studies analogous to real-life environmental circumstances. The advantage of this approach, of course, is the simpler, better controlled conditions of a laboratory setting. Another approach to getting data before finishing the design would be to construct temporary, life-sized models of environmental spaces and observe behavior in them. Both approaches have been used and will be examined next.

Laboratory-Analogue Research on Design

Suppose you were designing a plaza and were concerned that it remain relatively litter free. You could place a number of attractive trash cans throughout the area and keep it clean (see, for example, Finnie, 1973), but you are reluctant to do so unless it is really necessary. Small amounts of trash, you believe, may detract less from the environmental appearance than even attractive trash cans, and besides, there will be plenty of janitorial help. The question, then, is this: will litter on the ground cause even more litter to be thrown down? If so, your new plaza may quickly become a dirty and unattractive environment. Conversely, if a bit of litter on the ground has little effect, you may wish to rely simply on normal janitorial care without the large number of potentially unsightly trash cans.

This kind of question can easily be asked in a laboratory environment, and, in fact, it has been. For example, Cone and Parham (1973) examined the effects of clean and dirty environments on littering in children (this study also looked at modeling influences, but this is irrelevant to our present purposes). Children engaged in several different kinds of play, each of which produced quite a bit of trash. The children were allowed to throw the trash on the floor or deposit it in a trash can. The room itself was either clean or littered when the children entered it. Cone and Parham found that the cleanliness of the room itself had a very strong effect. Simply put, littered environments produced more litter, while clean environments produced less.

Armed with this information, you would want to include trash receptacles in the overall plan for the plaza. However, because you are still bothered by the effects such containers are likely to have on the aesthetic integrity of the plaza, you are now confronted with the issue of container design, location, and number. Trash receptacles can be built into the environment so as to be relatively unobtrusive and thus have minimal effect on its overall aesthetic qualities. However, less obtrusive containers will probably need to be located carefully so people will see them and use them. And, because the containers blend in better with the overall design, it may be necessary to have more of them, even if carefully located. Each of these issues (design, location, number) could be framed as an experimental question and data gathered to answer it in laboratory-analogue research. An alternative would be to investigate these issues on a temporary basis in an environmental context similar to that being designed. Or the environment being designed might be built with a certain degree of impermanence, so that data on the best design could be obtained before it is finished. This possibility is discussed in the next section.

Temporary Environmental Structuring

Many design decisions can be based on data from preliminary, impermanent structuring. For example, it is often possible to construct movable walls, temporary barriers, experimental paths, and so on. Dwight D. Eisenhower, when president of Columbia University, was reported to have made a clever use of this principle. Frustrated with the development of dirt pathways across lawns on the campus, he decided that the grounds around any new buildings put in would not have permanent walkways installed or landscaping completed. Rather, he simply waited for students to form the pathways to and from the building and then paved these, landscaping around them.

Hayes and Cone (1977a) have provided another example of this strategy. The problem area in this study was a small university park composed of rock-aggregate pathways around grass islands. During certain hours, such as lunch-time, hundreds of students and faculty members traversed the area. Unfortunately, many of them walked on the lawns, so that the new park was crisscrossed with large, ugly, and destructive dirt paths. The park was built at a cost of several thousand dollars, so it was not possible to change its structure significantly, but the dirt pathways had made the area useless as a park. At the time of the study, the university was about to place some benches throughout the area in hopes that they would alleviate the situation and cause the area to be used as a park.

It should be noted that the designer had apparently failed to consider how the park should be laid out so as to avoid this problem. The layout of the park is shown in Figure 5–1. Most of the traffic entered at the bottom left-hand or top right-hand corner of the park and went diagonally across it. As you can see, this meant that pedestrians had to zigzag through the park in order not to walk on the grass. Most pedestrians naturally took a straight route. Distressingly, the benches that were about to be placed in the park were to be arranged according to another "good idea" some designer had, and not according to an experimentally proved plan. Permission was obtained from the school to delay the implementation of the proposed "solution" until some data could be collected.

Several interventions were tested. (See Figures 5–1 and 5–2 for maps of the layouts of these interventions.) Three interventions were tested that made it more or less difficult to walk through the park from corner to corner (labeled A and AR or E and ER in the figures). In the benches/university-placement condition (labeled BU in Figure 5–1), the 2-foot by 3-foot redwood benches were arranged in the manner the university designer had determined would solve the traffic problem. However, note that this placement actually made it *more* difficult to stay on the rock pathways while walking from corner to corner. In the benches condition (BC in Figure 5–1), an effort was made to place the benches so that pedestrians would have a hard time walking across the lawns. The chained-pathways condition (CP in Figure 5–1) was designed to make walking on the pathways very difficult. This condition was expected to make the problem worse and was used to test the generality of response difficulty as an idea guiding the development of various interventions.

A fourth condition was termed the chained-entrance condition (CE in Figure 5–2). The idea here was that if walkers entering the park from the lower left-hand corner were forced at least to start out on the pathways, they might then stay on them.

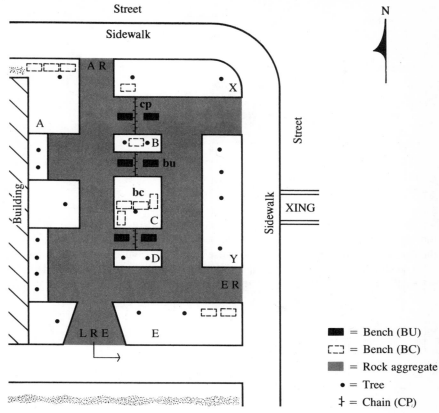

Figure 5–1. The layout of the park and the arrangement of the BU, CP, and BC conditions. From "Decelerating Environmentally Destructive Lawn-walking," by S. C. Hayes and J. D. Cone, *Environment and Behavior*, 1977, *9*, 511–534. Reprinted with the permission of Sage Publications, Inc.

Finally, there were two prompting conditions. One simply used the thematic prompt provided by placing park benches throughout the area (benches-only condition; BO in Figure 5–2). The idea here was that merely by identifying the area as a park, some more environmentally protective behavior might result. The benches were placed on the periphery of the park so as not to obstruct common walking patterns. The last condition was two signs (S in Figure 5–2) that were placed near the lower right-hand corner of the park. These signs said, "University Mini-Park—Please Don't Trample the Grass."

All the treatment conditions were tested in *ABA* designs during the high-traffic part of the day. Walkers entering the park from the lower left-hand corner and leaving from the upper right-hand corner were observed by raters from the roof of a nearby parking garage. The raters counted the number of targeted grass

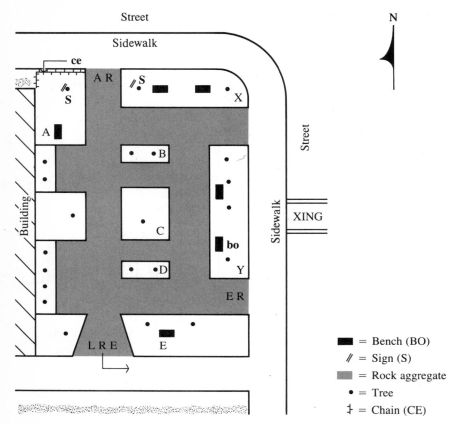

Figure 5–2. The arrangement of the CE, BO, and S conditions. From "Decelerating Environmentally Destructive Lawnwalking," by S. C. Hayes and J. D. Cone, *Environment and Behavior,* 1977, *9,* 511–534. Reprinted with the permission of Sage Publications, Inc.

islands walked on by the pedestrians (the targeted islands were those with letters on them in the figures). A total of about 1300 walkers was observed.

The results are shown in Figure 5–3. It presents the mean number of islands touched by walkers under the various conditions. This figure shows some surprising things. Note that the condition designed by the university (BU condition) actually made the problem worse! Simply placing benches around the area (BO condition) had no strong effect; a similar result was found with the chained-off-pathways condition (CP). Part of the reason the chained-pathways condition had little or no effect (recall that it was expected to make the situation worse) was that many walkers avoided the whole area when they saw those chains. They seemingly were shocked by their placement (several people stopped and stared at the chains and then turned and walked away from them). The successful condi-

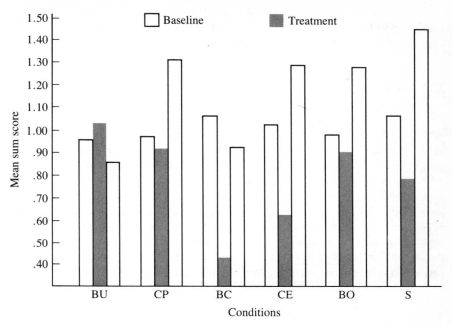

Figure 5–3. The effects of the six conditions on the average number of grass islands touched by a walker. From "Decelerating Environmentally Destructive Lawnwalking," by S. C. Hayes and J. D. Cone, *Environment and Behavior,* 1977, *9,* 511–534. Reprinted with the permission of Sage Publications, Inc.

tions were, in ascending order of effectiveness: signs, chained entrance, and benches in the pathways. These findings give future designers a place to begin.

The findings also enabled us to make some recommendations to the university about the placement of the benches that were about to be installed. We recommended that the corner islands be chained off, that the signs be placed in each corner, and that the benches be placed as they had been in the BC condition. Unfortunately, not all these recommendations were followed. The university staff in the designing and physical-plant offices read the report we prepared, but it *seemed* to them that certain other arrangements would be even better, and these arrangements were implemented. Essentially, some benches were placed as in the BO condition and a few as in the BC condition. Unfortunately, the overall protective effect was greatly reduced. The park is still there (several years now after our study of it), but it is gouged by large and ugly dirt paths.

Thus, these examples of the prior empirical evaluation of design options to perpetuate environmentally protective behavior are instructive. Though the examples illustrate reasonable ways of approaching the problem, they are based on a yet-to-be-verified assumption: that designers are influenced by available data showing what behavior will be like in their final design. It is probably likely that designers have not yet come to value such data and to alter their own plans accordingly. In retrospect, it is probably naive to think they would have, a point to which we shall return in the last chapter of the book.

SUMMARY

Two approaches to problems of environmental aesthetics have been presented in this chapter. In the first section, emphasis was placed on cleaning up environments that have been littered. In the second section, the focus shifted to designing environments that perpetuate their own inherent beauty and appeal.

We discussed various approaches to the removal of litter from the floors of movie theaters and football stadiums, the grounds of parks and outdoor recreation areas, the sides of roads and highways, the grounds around buildings, and the floors and tables of classrooms and university cafeterias. Most of the studies cited arranged positive consequences to follow the picking up of trash, even paying participants in some cases. A few of the studies relied on appeals (verbal prompts) to prevent people from littering in the first place.

Almost all of the research we cited produced positive effects. People can be induced to pick up trash from an already littered environment, and they can be discouraged from littering in the first place. Indeed, some procedures reduced litter by as much as 94% (Casey & Lloyd, 1977). In general, we noted that cleanup approaches have produced consistently greater results than preventive approaches.

Although most of the evidence for the effectiveness of behavioral solutions to the problems of litter has come from small-scale experimental or pilot projects, we discussed at least one very large-scale, community-wide approach. The Clean Community System of Keep America Beautiful is a very comprehensive strategy that involves many segments of the community in the overall analysis and improvement of its solid-waste management technology. A rigorous analysis of the effectiveness of this comprehensive approach will provide valuable information leading to improved behavioral solutions to litter and perhaps other environmental problems as well.

The second section of the chapter dealt with the design of environments that prevent aesthetic deterioration. Preliminary research was cited to show the potential of such an approach. It was noted that laboratory analogues of future environmental space can be developed and behavior monitored for its potential impact on aesthetics. Or, environments can be designed as temporary, pending an examination of their effects on behavior, which will affect their aesthetics. Examples of the latter approach were described as they were applied in the design of pathways across university campuses. Having examined the effects of the environment in its temporary form, appropriate adjustments could be made before finalizing the design and constructing the permanent space. Of course, it is important to remember the underlying assumption of such an experimental approach to environmental design—that designers will be affected by the data it produces. It seems reasonable to expect that a little prior evaluation will produce more cost-effective and longer-lasting benefits than the remedial approaches necessary after the environment is already there.

In this chapter, we have tried to show how each of the solutions has been derived from the principles of behavior described in Chapter 3. The importance of tying practice to theory was stressed repeatedly. More examples of the value of this tactic are described in the following chapter which deals with noise.

SUGGESTED PROJECTS

Litter Prevention

If you are a student, look around on the floors of halls and classrooms you frequent and determine whether there is a litter problem. You might also make similar observations about the grounds around the buildings of your school. When you have located areas that look as though they could benefit from cleaning up, decide how you might go about it.

Step 1: Define litter. First, it will be necessary for you to "objectify" some of your assumptions (see Chapter 4). In other words, you will need an operational definition of litter in order to measure it and determine whether it is as bad as you assume from casual observation. Consult Finnie (1973), Hayes and his colleagues (1975), or Geller (in press) for examples of definitions of litter. When you have written a definition, then decide the specific boundaries of the area (or areas) you are going to improve. You will need to do this in order to know exactly where to perform your litter counts.

Step 2: Try out your definition. Have a friend read the definition, and explain the boundaries of your area. Then both of you should walk around the area and count the litter. Make these counts independently. Now compare your counts. If you have a reasonably large area, it is helpful to divide it into several smaller ones and make separate counts in each. When you compare your data with another's in this fashion, you are performing an interobserver-agreement check. The purpose of such checks is to determine the accuracy of your measurement system and the adequacy of your definitions. If you are interested in more information about these issues, see Kazdin (1980, pp. 89–94).

Although there are a number of ways of calculating interobserver agreement, the most reasonable for the present purpose is to divide the smaller sum by the larger and multiply by 100; that is, if you counted 30 pieces of litter and your helper counted 34, your agreement index is $30/34 \times 100$, or 88.2%. Obviously, if you had both counted exactly the same number of pieces of litter, your agreement would have been 100%. Generally, values over 80% are indicative of sufficient accuracy in your measurement system to warrant its continued use. Two observers rarely agree 100% of the time, so do not be concerned about falling short of this value.

Step 3: Select a design. Prior to collecting baseline data, you will have selected an appropriate experimental design. We suggest an intrasubject withdrawal design of the *ABAB* variety for this project, but you may prefer another one depending on the procedure you want to evaluate, resources available, and so forth.

Step 4: Collect baseline data. When you reach a satisfactory level of agreement with your partner, begin collecting baseline data. Decide whether you will make your counts daily, every other day, weekly, or on some other schedule. As you collect these data, plot them on a graph so you can watch the trends in litter over time. If you have selected a setting in which the trash is cleaned up regularly, you should notice a fairly constant or slightly increasing level of litter from day to day (or week to week and so on). When your graph is fairly level (showing no definable trend) or when it is consistently moving upward, you should introduce your litter-reduction procedure. Note that a downward trend in the graph would suggest the problem is taking care of itself and needs no help from you.

Step 5: Intervene. You may have your own ideas about the procedure to use to reduce littering, but remember that this project has to do with *preventing* it. The next project deals with cleaning up the area if your preventive strategy fails. We would suggest you try one of the interventions mentioned in the earlier portions of this chapter, such as signs asking people not to litter, signs directing them to the location of the appropriate receptacle, increased numbers of receptacles, and personal appeals to persons using the area. Or you might want to have confederates (stooges) model appropriate trash disposal by exaggeratedly depositing some trash in a receptacle when passers-by are watching.

Whatever procedure you use, continue it long enough to determine its effects, if any. In other words, the litter counts you continue to make with the same frequency as during your baseline period should show some consistent trend away from those of the baseline counts.

Step 6: Withdraw your experimental variable. When such a trend is evident, discontinue (withdraw) your procedure and keep collecting your data. If your procedure was having an effect, you should begin to see the data return toward their baseline level.

Step 7: Reinstate your experimental variable. When baseline frequency has been reached again, reintroduce your procedure. You should see a trend away from baseline, just as with your first introduction of the strategy. Continue this last phase until a clear trend appears.

Step 8: Analyze data and plan follow-up. When the above steps have been followed, you will have completed a four-phase *ABAB* intrasubject withdrawal design. You can now label the phases on your graph, using dashed vertical lines between them. Observation of systematic changes in your graph concurrent with introductions and withdrawals of your experimental procedure should show whether you successfully altered littering in the area of concern.

Finally, you may want to examine the permanence of any changes apparently produced. To do this, you might simply leave your experimental procedure in effect for an indefinite period and return occasionally to count litter in the area. You might plot these counts as follow-up data on your graph, thus providing a visual representation of the maintenance of any effects over time.

Remember, the most important part of your project is the collection of data accurate enough to permit an evaluation of your experimental procedure. After you start the study proper, you should continue to check interobserver agreement periodically to make sure your counts are still accurate.

Litter Cleanup

The second project focuses on getting people to pick up litter already on the ground in the area or areas of interest. Familiarize yourself with the suggestions given for conducting the above prevention project. The cleanup study will follow the same procedures except that the intervention will require some clever way of getting litter picked up.

After deciding on the area, the research design, the definition of litter, and the data-collection procedures, check interobserver agreement and start obtaining baseline counts of litter. When you are satisfied with the baseline data, try one of the reinforcement procedures discussed in this chapter or something entirely innovative. Keep collecting data. If your procedure works, you should begin to count less and less litter in the area. When a difference from baseline is established, withdraw your procedure and see whether the litter counts once again approach baseline levels. When they do, reintroduce your procedure and continue your counts.

The design of the second project is identical to that of the first. As with that project, you may want to continue to make counts periodically in order to examine any long-term effects. In addition, you will want to make occasional interobserver-agreement checks to document the continuing accuracy of your measurement system.

Empirical Evaluation of Environmental Barriers

Dirt pathways are a real problem to many institutions. Many colleges and universities find them particularly distasteful. This project should be something you could test in your own school. Here is what to do.

Step 1: Select target areas. Find two or three areas where a number of people cut across the lawn and where you can observe the areas without being seen.

Step 2: Get materials. Find some lengths of 2-inch by 2-inch lumber and chain. The chains will need to be at least 5 to 6 feet long.

Step 3: Record baseline data. Decide on some times during the day when you can observe the lawn areas. Get a friend to help you observe. Count how many (and what percentage) of the passing pedestrians step on the lawns. Record these figures for a day or two, breaking your observations into several time periods. Keep the data separate for each area.

Step 4: Calculate interobserver agreement. To get some idea of the accuracy of your counts, you and the second observer will need to record your data independently of each other. After doing so, compare the two counts for the different time periods separately. A good way to do this was described in Step 2 of the litter-prevention project.

Step 5: Intervene. Construct chain barriers around the grass areas. Randomly vary the height of the chain from the ground (see Hayes & Cone, 1977a) between the different lawn areas. For one area have a low chain (say, 18 inches); for others have it higher (24 inches), higher (30 inches), higher (36 inches), higher (40 inches), and higher still (48 inches). If you do not have enough areas to look at all of these heights, select some high, medium, and low heights. Record the same information as in Step 3 for several days. Also keep track of how many walkers step over or duck under the chain barriers.

Step 6: Withdraw the chains. When the results seem clear, take out all the chains and continue to record the data. You have now completed an *ABA* design. Your data should be of considerable interest to designers and physical-plant personnel. Many of the chain barriers you see around town will be very low; few are high. Yet Hayes and Cone (1977a) noted that people would step over low chain barriers. Which chain height was most effective in your study? Why?

Step 7: Disseminate your findings. Simply presenting your data to the appropriate officials may not result in much action on their part. If you are serious about wanting to improve the looks of your campus, you may have to bring public pressure to bear on these officials. This can be done in a variety of ways. One of the more effective is simply to make the results of your study widely known. Have an interview with a reporter from the campus newspaper, or write a story yourself and send it to the paper. If you find differences between your most effective chain heights and those commonly in use around campus, these differences should be highlighted in the article. Better yet, try to include side-by-side photographs showing the two chain heights.

Chapter 6

NOISE AND
ITS CONTROL

Joshua said unto the people, Shout; for Jehovah hath given you the city. . . . So the people shouted, and the priests blew the trumpets: and it came to pass, when the people heard the sound of the trumpet, that the people shouted with a great shout, and the wall fell down flat . . . [Joshua 6:16–20].

The destructive effects of noise have been known to us for millenia, as the above quotation may indicate. Of all the current environmental problems, perhaps the most pervasive is noise. All you have to do is to attend to the environment to realize how much we are bombarded with auditory stimulation. As this chapter is being written (in a "quiet" library), there is the sound of clattering typewriters, ringing telephones, stomping feet, loud talk and laughter, and a periodic buzzer signaling the library stack worker that can only be described as incredibly loud. Try a brief experiment: stop right now and listen carefully to all the sounds you can hear. Chances are good that there are many sounds where you are—perhaps even many unpleasant or loud ones. As we go through our day-to-day lives, we are exposed to noise levels—from cars, trucks, trains, fans, motors, horns, other people, and so on—far above those for which we have been evolutionarily prepared.

Applied psychological research in noise control has been slow. It has been hindered by several problems, not the least of which is the very definition of noise itself. In earlier chapters we have pointed out that "reactive" environmental research can be of real value in discovering the dimensions of certain environmental problems. The problem of noise shows just how reactive research can be of assistance. What, after all, is noise? Think about it for a minute. You might be tempted to say "Well, noise means loud sounds." Clearly, the loudness of sound is one important dimension of noise. But loudness itself is certainly not the only thing we mean by noise. The roar of the waves at the beach may be loud but relaxing; the sound of fingernails on a blackboard may be quiet but positively unbearable. Reactive research can help specify the critical nature and impact of the phenomenon of noise.

This chapter describes the nature of sound and its measurement; delineates dimensions of sound that produce undesirable effects and documents those effects; and, finally, examines the small but growing body of literature on behavioral noise control.

SOUND AND ITS MEASUREMENT

First, let us review briefly what sound consists of. There are at least four main dimensions of sound—and each may be important in the definition and impact of noise.

Frequency

All sound is created by vibration. The back-and-forth movement creates alternating states (a "wave") of positive and negative pressure as the transfer medium (usually air) is alternately compressed and rarefied (by "positive and negative pressure" we mean above and below atmospheric pressure, respectively). The rate at which these pressure states alternate is the *frequency* of sound (see Figure 6–1). The standard international unit used to describe the frequency of sound is the *hertz (Hz),* which refers to the number of complete cycles occurring each second. For example, suppose you strike a cymbal that produces 1000 complete cycles of first a positive and then a negative pressure change each second. This sound would have a frequency of 1000 Hz.

In general, we perceive the frequency of sound as *pitch.* A low (bass) tone has a lower frequency (that is, a lower hertz value) than a high-pitched tone. The human ear can typically perceive sounds between 20 Hz and about 20,000 Hz. Vibrations below 20 Hz are termed *infrasound*—they may be felt as vibration if sufficiently intense, but they will not be heard. Similarly, above 20,000 Hz is *ultrasound,* which is inaudible to humans but may nevertheless be felt in other ways (for example, as heat).

Amplitude (Intensity)

Because sound involves alternating positive and negative deviations from the baseline pressure impinging on the ear, another characteristic of sound is the degree of deviation. This is termed the *amplitude* or *intensity* of sound and is largely perceived as *loudness.* Sounds in which the degree of deviation is small

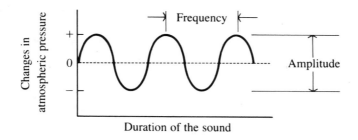

Figure 6–1. A schematic description of the characteristics of sound.

are softer than those in which the alternating pressure changes are very large. One way you can picture this is to think of sound waves as you would waves in the ocean. A very small wave (say, 1 foot high) has less energy behind it and will not strike you with the force of a large wave (say, 7 feet high). Similarly, a large pressure wave will strike your eardrum with far more force (and will be perceived as louder) than a small one.

The major unit used to measure the amplitude of sound is the *decibel (dB)*, named after Alexander Graham Bell. This unit is a bit confusing at first, but it is critical to persons interested in noise pollution. First, the most common type of decibel (*SPL,* for sound-pressure level) starts with the physical pressure of the sound (the "height" of the wave) and divides it by the pressure level of the softest 1000-Hz tone humans can hear under ideal circumstances. Thus, a given sound may have a pressure level that is, say, ten times larger than the softest sound we can hear. This ratio (measured sound to softest sound) is then converted into a logarithm. This sounds confusing, but it need not be. One reason decibels are logarithmic is that the range of stimulus intensities that can be dealt with by the human ear is incredible. The sound-pressure level of the loudest sound we can hear is about a *thousand million* (1,000,000,000,000) times greater than the pressure level of the softest sound we can hear! Such large numbers would be cumbersome to deal with. By changing these ratios to logarithms, more reasonable numbers are produced. The loudest sound we can stand, for example, is about 180 dB.

Because of the nature of the decibel, it is important to remember that changes in decibel values represent multiples of physical sound intensities. For every 6-dB increase in sound, the physical sound pressure doubles; for every 20-dB increase, the sound pressure increases tenfold. This means that at high decibel levels, very small changes in decibel values represent enormous changes in sound-pressure levels. For example, if you have a 134-dB sound and double it (to 140 dB), the actual change in sound-pressure level is huge (about a million times greater than the increase that occurs when you double a 0-dB sound to 6 dB). A better intuitive understanding of the decibel system can be had by examining Table 6–1.

Decibels are typically measured with a sound-level meter. An interesting finding by psychophysicists has been built into many of these meters: there is a psychological interaction between sound frequency and amplitude. Simply put, low tones with a given sound-pressure level *sound quieter* than high-pitched tones of the same objective intensity. Therefore, several popular adjustment curves have been developed to yield decibel values that are psychologically more equivalent across various frequencies.

Complexity

Tones can be more or less complex. Most sounds we hear are in fact mixtures of several distinct frequencies.

Table 6–1. The Decibel Level of Various Sounds (on the Average)

Source	dB[a]	Comments
	0	
Normal breathing	10	Lowest audible level
Faint whisper	20	
Room in a quiet house at midnight	30	
Easily audible whisper	40	
Average quiet house	45	
Average office (few machines)	50	
Window air conditioner	55	
Conversational speech	60	
Busy restaurant	65	Level of possible annoyance
Loud speech	70	
Alarm clock	75	
Inside an auto on a freeway	80	
Loud orchestra music in a large room	85	Ear damage possible (if sustained)
Food blender	90	
Power lawn mower	95	
Noisy construction site	100	
Motorcycle	105	
Air hammer	110	
Diesel truck accelerating	115	
Loud rock band	120	
Hydraulic press	130	
Rifle	140	Usual threshold of pain
A jet plane, up close	150	
Cap pistol	160	
Wind tunnel	170	Eardrums can burst
	180	
Rocket engine, nearby	190	
	194	Theoretical maximum

[a]Technically, there are different types of decibels. The values given here are in SPL decibels.

Duration and Spacing

The last important aspect of sound is its occurrence in time: the continuous length of the sound, the spaces between sounds (their length and regularity), and the total duration of the sounds across a large unit of time (that is, the sum of their individual lengths).

THE DEFINITION OF NOISE

Well, you may ask, all this information about sound is fine, but what about *noise?* Surely the two concepts are different.

The definition of noise can be exceedingly complicated, but a working definition is this: noise is sound that produces undesirable physical or psychological effects. The effects, for sound to be called noise, must be due to the sound itself, not to its informational value (see Azrin, 1958). For example, obscene words may disturb people not because of the sound itself, but because of the meaning of the words. This is the definition of noise we will use. However, there are a number of simpler definitions that are equally workable in most instances. For example, noise has been defined as sound that is unwanted (Berrien, 1946; Lipscomb, 1974; Rodda, 1967), destructive (Baron, 1970), or obnoxious (Bergland, 1970).

The preceding discussion about the important dimensions of sound (frequency, amplitude, complexity, and duration and spacing) paves the way for a more sophisticated question about the definition of noise: what are the important dimensions of sound that lead to damaging psychological or physical effects? You can immediately see that this is a question calling for reactive research.

The nature of unwanted sound can be classified according to our four dimensions of sound, as the following brief discussion shows.

Amplitude

The most important dimension that turns sound into noise is its amplitude, or loudness. The increased industrialization and mechanization of modern society have raised the "normal" levels of sound markedly over the years—well beyond any level for which we are likely to have been evolutionarily prepared. It has been claimed that the average noise level in our cities jumped 30 dB (about 1 dB per year) over the middle part of this century (Knudson, 1955). Although that estimate may be very high, remember that even an increase of only one-fifth that size (that is, 6 dB) would mean a *doubling* of sound pressure. Clearly, we live in a louder world than did our forefathers.

Frequency

We have already noted that the psychological impact of noise in higher frequencies is greater than that in lower frequencies, given the same sound intensity. The decibel level itself is commonly corrected to reflect this fact.

Complexity

Certain discordant mixtures of sounds are more noticeable and aversive than relatively pure tones. Examples include the sounds produced by fingernails on a blackboard, knives on a plate, and the sounds in some police sirens (a practical application of the principle). The very definition of the word *noise* is often tied to the concept of the mixture (that is, excessive complexity) of sound (see, for example, Burns, 1969). However, pure tones are more likely to be physiologically damaging (Bergland, 1970).

Duration and Spacing

In general, sounds that are constant or of long duration produce greater physiological effects and lesser psychological effects. If the total duration is kept constant, as more frequent rest spaces are added the physiological effects diminish while the psychological effects increase. Psychological effects are greatest when noise is intermittent, aperiodic (unpredictable), and uncontrollable (Glass & Singer, 1972).

THE EFFECTS OF NOISE

The effects of noise can be broken down into two main areas: behavioral (social and psychological) effects and physical effects. A great deal of research evidence has accumulated over the years. Even in a review of the effects of noise published in 1970, Kryter was able to cite nearly 1000 references on the subject.

Social and Psychological Effects

The effects of loud noise on the social and psychological functioning of individuals and groups have been the subject of some reactive research. Loud noises may disrupt effective social intercourse. For example, they may mask conversation by lowering the "signal-to-noise" ratio (Kryter, 1970), which is what happens when a plane passes overhead during a conversation. A sound of more than 80 dB may disrupt normal conversation (Lipscomb, 1974). Further, exposure to very loud noises (such as that made by a power lawn mower) may produce a temporary hearing loss that can have much the same effect (Shearer, 1968). The types of social activities commonly disrupted by noise are numerous—for example, eating, talking, watching television, and working (Bragdon, 1971).

The psychological effects of very loud noise are a somewhat less prominent concern in the noise-control literature, which has greatly emphasized the effects on hearing itself. However, labor officials (for example, Wood, 1973) and others have repeatedly called for more emphasis on reactive psychological measures. Part of the problem seems to be that most noise-control programs are in the hands of engineers and audiologists, not behavioral scientists. Thus, the many psychological studies that have documented some of the behavioral effects of noise may not be well-known. Obviously, any noise can influence the performance of auditory tasks, if it is loud enough and of the right frequency and duration, simply by masking the perception of essential auditory signals (Kryter, 1970).

However, several studies have shown that noise can influence nonauditory tasks as well. The available evidence indicates that loud noise is particularly likely to produce decrements in the performance of nonauditory tasks if the tasks are complex (Boggs & Simon, 1968); if the noise is sufficiently loud—about 90 dB or more (see, for example, Broadbent, 1957); or if it is aperiodic, unsignaled, or uncontrollable (Glass & Singer, 1972). High frequencies, above about 2000 Hz, are most disruptive (Kerbec, 1972). Not surprisingly, subjects who are described by various personality measures as "anxious" or "somatically responsive" are more sensitive to the effects of noise (Bergamasco, Benna, Furlan, & Gilli, 1976; Kryter, 1970).

Physiological Effects

The effect of noise is felt temporarily by a number of bodily systems other than the ear, such as the cardiovascular system. With some exceptions (see, for example, Brewer & Briess, 1960), surprisingly there is little evidence that noise itself can damage these systems to a clinically significant degree (Kryter, 1970), especially because humans adapt so rapidly to stimulation. The damaging effects of noise on the ear, however, are indisputable. These effects are manifested in both temporary hearing defects and, under certain conditions, permanent hearing loss. Hearing defects are more likely as (1) noise increases in frequency— generally, the higher, the more damaging (W. D. Ward, 1963); (2) the total duration of noise increases (Beales, 1965; Burns & Littler, 1960); (3) noise is presented more continuously (W. D. Ward, 1976), with few rest periods; (4) noise consists of relatively more pure tones (Kryter, 1970); and (5) decibel levels increase above 80 dB (Kryter, 1970).

Finally, in addition to its effects upon hearing, noise may interfere significantly with sleep (see, for example, Bergamasco, Benna, & Gilli, 1976). Whether this interference is a health hazard or a mere annoyance is unclear; it is probably primarily an annoyance except, perhaps, to hospital patients and others in poor condition (Kryter, 1970).

In summary, research on the effects of noise has documented both the major areas in which its effects are felt and the dimensions that are most likely to produce undesirable effects. The effects of noise can be broken down into two relatively clear-cut categories: behavioral (social/psychological) and physiological. Interestingly, the dimensions of noise that produce effects are different, even opposite at times, in the two areas. For example, though intermittent sounds are more behaviorally disruptive, continuous sounds are more physiologically disruptive.

What experimental literature there is on psychological efforts at noise control has been aimed at the behavioral effects of noise. However, the possible contribution of behavioral programs in the hearing-loss area is great indeed, as we will show. Let us turn now to these topics as we examine the control of noise.

THE CONTROL OF NOISE

Although increased legislation has produced more physical technology on noise control, the problem has received little attention from social scientists. The reasons seem largely due to the lack of a permanent product, the rapidity with which we adapt to noise, and a more general lack of awareness of noise-control problems. However, when noise produces an immediate disruptive effect on behavior, these problems are not easily bypassed. Not surprisingly, then, the behavioral noise-control literature is oriented almost exclusively toward control of the disruptive behavioral effects of noise.

Noise Control: Behavioral Effects

Several behavioral investigations of noise control have been reported. All have been done in educational settings, and all have looked at a single dimension of noise: peaks in decibel level. The control of noise in classrooms is a logical place for behavioral noise-control efforts to have originated. For one thing, there is evidence that noise can negatively influence student performance (see, for example, Baker & Madell, 1965). Further, students and especially teachers frequently complain about noise in the classroom.

Schmidt and Ulrich (1969) reported the first behavioral study in this area. In a series of two experiments, they examined the effects of group contingencies on noise levels in a fourth-grade classroom. Group contingencies consist of an arrangement whereby (1) the behavior of an entire group is consequated and/or (2) the consequences that follow an individual's behavior apply to the entire group (see Litow & Pumroy, 1975, for a review of classroom applications of group contingencies). The contingencies used in the Schmidt and Ulrich study were group contingencies in both senses of the word.

The classroom had been "excessively noisy" during a morning "free study" period. Data were collected each day during this time by periodically reading a sound-level meter (for example, once every 60 seconds). To make sure the readings were correct, a second person also read the meter every so often, and the two readings were compared. There was a high degree of agreement, as you might expect. The sound level in the classroom measured about 36 dB when empty, but during the free study period the average sound level was about 52 dB (more than ten times as loud). The experimenters decided to aim for a reduction to about 42 dB—a level the teacher felt was appropriate.

What they did was very creative. A timer was set for ten minutes. If the class went the entire ten minutes without any noise above 42 dB, they received (1) two extra minutes of gym period and (2) an immediate two-minute break from the study period. A buzzer indicated the end of the ten minutes. If, however, the class became noisy, a whistle was blown and the ten-minute clock was reset. In other words, the entire class was on a ten-minute, fixed-interval schedule in

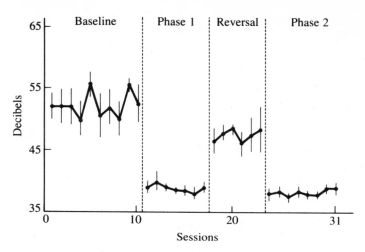

Figure 6–2. The effects of Schmidt and Ulrich's sound-level-control proce-
dure on classroom noise. Each point represents the average sound-level
reading for one session. From "Effects of Group Contingent Events upon
Classroom Noise," by G. W. Schmidt and R. E. Ulrich, *Journal of Applied
Behavior Analysis,* 1969, 2, 171–179. Copyright 1969 by the Society for the
Experimental Analysis of Behavior, Inc. Reprinted by permission.

which any classroom behavior other than excessive collective noise would be
consequated (this procedure is often termed *DRO,* which stands for differential
reinforcement of other behavior). Note that the consequences applied evenly to
the entire class.

The effects of the procedure are shown in Figure 6–2. There was an
immediate and stable reduction in noise to about 39 dB, a level near that produced by the empty room. However, to make sure this effect was due to the
group contingency and not to some other, uncontrolled variable, the procedure
was terminated (the class was simply told that the previous conditions were no
longer in effect). The noise levels immediately increased again. Finally, when
the group contingency was reinstated, the noise levels dropped once more, thus
proving conclusively that the program was responsible for the improvement.

Schmidt and Ulrich noted that this rather simple procedure seemed to have
effects on other behaviors as well; that is, students seemed generally more well
behaved. Indeed, reduction of noise at these decibel levels is important only if it
leads to a more positive and productive environment, since there are no risks of
hearing damage at 52 dB. It is possible that such a program would improve the
atmosphere in a class. For example, the teacher might now be less critical of
students (less of "Sit down!" or "Be quiet!"); students might sit down and study
more; most desirably, students might learn more if it is quieter. To examine some
of these possible benefits, Schmidt and Ulrich replicated their study and collected
data on behaviors other than noise.

This time they selected a noisy second-grade classroom during a one-hour reading period. Decibel readings were taken as before, and, in addition, the number of students out of their seats and the number of teacher reprimands (such as "Be quiet!") were recorded (once again, with good inter-observer agreement). The data showed that the class was indeed noisy (above 50 dB) and that in each class there were some 175 instances of being out of one's seat and about 15 to 20 teacher reprimands.

After this initial baseline phase a program quite similar to the previous one was begun. However, in this instance the timer was set for only five minutes. Each time five minutes went by at below 42 dB, two extra minutes of gym time were earned for the entire class. Noise above 42 dB resulted in a resetting of the clock (signaled by a tone). Note that the potentially disruptive consequence used in the previous experiment (getting an immediate two-minute break in the free study period) was not used in this experiment.

The effects of the group contingency on decibel levels paralleled those found with the fourth-grade students. The noise level of the class stayed below 40 dB. In addition, as the class became quieter, it received fewer reprimands from the teacher (down to about five per class). However, the procedure had very little effect on the number of children out of their seats. Accordingly, an additional procedure was tried. In this phase, all of the gym period was earned by quiet. Now each five minutes of quiet earned three minutes of gym for the class. If individual students made the noise level go above 42 dB (for example, by yelling), these students lost five minutes of gym time. Finally, students out of their seats when a timer went off (about every five minutes) also lost five minutes of gym time. This procedure, then, is a mixture of individual and group contingencies for both making noise and being out of one's seat.

The results showed a continuation of the noise reduction, with further decreases in teacher reprimands to a very low level (one or two per class period). In addition, the number of students out of their seats dropped dramatically (about ten to 15 instances per class).

The procedure was then terminated. A slight worsening of the behaviors resulted. Amazingly, a follow-up during the next school year showed that the class remained quiet and in their seats, and teacher reprimands stayed low (however, the teacher was different).

All in all, these data support the view that it is possible to use naturally occurring consequences (for example, gym time) to keep classrooms quiet. However, the procedure had little effect on out-of-seat instances until those were specifically treated. Further, no data were taken on the actual academic performance of the children. Presumably the reason we want classrooms relatively quiet is so the children will learn better. This study was done quite a few years ago, before some of these critical questions were common (see, for example, Winett & Winkler, 1972). Unfortunately, as it stands this study has shown only that you can get a classroom to be quiet, not that this is helpful in achieving the goals of the school. You may recall that a similar issue was raised in Chapter 2. Simply put, we should never assume that behaviors are environmentally relevant. Rather, we must demonstrate it. Nevertheless, the Schmidt and Ulrich study is a good beginning. One serious practical problem that would limit its applicability is its reliance upon observers to read the sound-level meter and keep track of the consequences. Clearly, no school could afford to pay people to do this permanently.

This problem has been addressed in two very clever studies that automated the entire procedure. Wilson and Hopkins (1973) reported the first such study, on the effects of an automatic, music-based contingency system in four junior high home-economics classes. The classes involved the completion of individual sewing assignments. Naturally, the classes were quite noisy with about 20 sewing machines running, but the additional contribution of student noise had created a serious problem in the opinion of the teacher.

The experimenter set up an automatic system that relied on a voice-operated relay, set to switch whenever noise levels exceeded 76 dB (in the case of one of the classes) or 70 dB (in the other three classes). The teacher allowed the students to listen to music on their favorite radio station during class. Under some conditions, noise above the set levels (70 or 76 dB) turned off the radio for at least 20 seconds. When the noise level dropped below the set threshold for 20 seconds, the radio came on once more. The number of noise instances was automatically recorded. This, then, is an entirely automatic system in which noise turns off music and quiet turns it on.

There were three different conditions in this investigation: baseline, radio turned on contingent upon quiet (as just described), and radio turned on contingent upon noise. This last condition was inserted simply to see whether it really was the radio producing the effects. In it the radio stayed on only if the class stayed *above* the decibel limit. Dropping below the limit turned off the radio for 20 seconds.

The results for the four classes are shown in Figure 6–3. In Groups B, C, and D, the radio-turned-on-for-quiet contingency was successively introduced after a baseline period, and, as you can see, led to rapid and stable reductions in the percentage of time the class was noisy (above threshold) compared to their normal level. In Group A a different design was used. In the first three phases the radio for quiet was tried, withdrawn, and tried again. The results showed corresponding changes. Just to make sure it was the radio producing the effects, Wilson and Hopkins then reversed the contingency (the radio was turned on when the class was noisy). Once the class figured this out, they stayed noisy almost constantly. Finally, when the radio-for-quiet condition was reinstated, the class became quiet once again.

This procedure is a very creative attempt to use immediate, inexpensive consequences to control classroom noise. As can be seen, the procedure did that very well. Note that this strategy, unlike Schmidt and Ulrich's, took no teacher time and, once set up, functioned automatically. The devices involved are not very expensive and could be permanently implemented in a particularly noisy class.

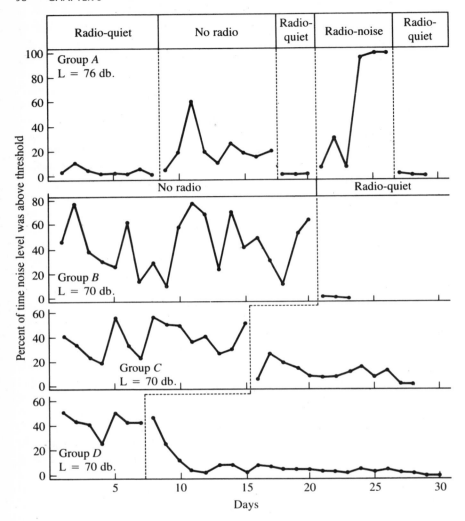

Figure 6–3. The percentage of time that the intensity of noise exceeded the teacher-determined threshold for all four classes. From "The Effects of Contingent Music on the Intensity of Noise in Junior High Home Economics Classes," by C. W. Wilson and B. L. Hopkins, *Journal of Applied Behavior Analysis,* 1973, *6,* 269–275. Copyright 1973 by the Society for the Experimental Analysis of Behavior, Inc. Reprinted by permission.

Although the experimenters did not collect systematic data on student productivity, the teacher did report that the students were more productive when it was quiet. The noise data are more impressive when one realizes that, while it was quiet, the radio was turned on (contributing some 52 dB to the sound levels).

Thus, the students had to remain extra quiet in the radio-for-quiet condition because the ambient noise level had been raised.

The effects of contingent music would not be of much assistance when background noise levels need to be kept very low (as in the Schmidt and Ulrich study). It is still possible, however, to automate these consequences using a different sensory mode. This was attempted by Strang and George (1975). The system was very similar to that used by Wilson and Hopkins, but instead of music, continued quiet lit up lights on a clown figure. There were 13 lights, forming buttons, a smile, eyes, and a nose. For every 20 seconds of quiet below a set threshold, a light was turned on—first the buttons, then the face lights. If excessive noise occurred, the clown gasped and all the lights went out.

The system was tested in first-grade and third-grade rural classrooms. After establishing a baseline, the lights-for-quiet contingency was begun. In both classrooms, but especially in the first-grade class, this contingency produced an immediate and stable reduction in noise below the decibel threshold set by the teacher (unfortunately, the article fails to mention the decibel level used). Thus, apparently very simple forms of sensory stimulation (music, lights on a figure) can serve as reinforcers for quiet behavior in children.

Unfortunately, the authors failed to measure schoolwork, so we do not know whether the intervention did more than produce quiet. However, the authors were sensitive to the issue and included a discussion of the ethical implications of their work.

Our last study of noise itself in the classroom is an infrequently cited experiment by Grobe, Pettibone, and Martin (1973). This study, unlike those just described, manipulated antecedent stimulus events rather than consequent events. In the experiment the instructor of a large college psychology class lectured at three different speeds: slow, medium, and fast. At the same time noise levels were recorded in the classroom. The data showed a U-shaped function; that is, classroom noise was high when the lectures were either fast or slow, and noise was low when the lectures were given at a moderate pace.

Unfortunately, this study used somewhat confusing measurement procedures (as in the Strang and George study, decibel levels are not given), and teacher-generated noise was included as part of the classroom noise. Student learning was also not measured. However, the examination of antecedent events is a very fine idea. Perhaps students attend less to the lectures when they are given either very slowly ("boring") or very rapidly ("impossible to follow") and begin to talk to neighbors and generate additional noise. If so, noise may be controllable by arranging for interesting situations that demand quiet, without using any explicit consequation of noise as such.

Noise in the classroom has also been addressed indirectly by many studies on "disruptive behavior" in the classroom. These studies have concentrated specifically on "inappropriate verbalization" (for example, McLaughlin & Malaby, 1972) as well as on more general descriptions of disruptive behavior in which talking out of turn in class may be only one of a number of behaviors recorded (for example, Ayllon, Garber, & Pisor, 1975; Drabman, Spitalnik, & Spitalnik, 1974; Ellery, Blampied, & Black, 1975; Grandy, Madsen, & Mersseman, 1973; Harris & Sherman, 1973; Medland & Stachnik, 1972). These, however, are not reviewed here, since the definitions used were not related to characteristics of sound as such (for example, decibel level, frequency) but to a specific type of meaningful sound (for example, talking out of turn). As we have used the term, these studies are not, therefore, concerned with noise itself. The reader particularly interested in the control of classroom noise may nevertheless wish to examine this literature.

In probably the most elaborate behavioral noise-control study to date, Meyers, Artz, and Craighead (1976) examined noise levels in a college dormitory. About one-third of the students in the dorm were not able to study there because of the noise, and two-thirds reported occasional difficulties in sleeping in the dorm because of noise.

Four dormitory floors were selected for study. A voice-operated relay (set between 82 and 84 dB) monitored the noise levels in the main hallway on each floor. Because almost all high-intensity noises seemed to be of short duration (yells, laughter, running), the equipment was set to record the number of loud noises, not their duration. The treatment package consisted of several elements:

1. *An instructional/modeling component.* A meeting was held, and the residents were instructed that excessive noise is a learned behavior. In a series of scenes, the experimenters also modeled the behaviors appropriate for giving and reacting to negative feedback for quiet.
2. *Feedback.* A doorbell rang each time a noise transgression occurred. Scoreboards kept track of the daily noise transgressions. They also indicated the target number of noise transgressions for each day that week. Staying below this target earned points for the residents on that floor.
3. *Reinforcers.* Two types were used in this study: money and academic grades. The monetary contingency consisted of a system through which the students together could earn as much as $100, based on the number of points earned by the floor, during the course of the treatment condition. In the grade-contingency condition, students signed up for a course in which their grade was tied, in part, to reductions in noise transgressions as a group.

Two floors were used to evaluate the instructions, feedback, and contingency package. The package was implemented in a multiple-baseline design with changing criteria and withdrawal conditions. The changing criteria consisted of the gradual reduction of the number of daily noise transgressions beyond which no points toward the monetary payoff would be earned. The package produced a clear reduction in noise transgressions, from 345 per day during baseline (summed across floors) to 148 per day during treatment.

For the third floor the treatment package was similar, but a group academic-grade contingency in a special psychology "class" was used instead of money. This package was evaluated in an *ABA* design with changing criteria. Once again, instances of excessive noise were dramatically reduced, from about

950 instances per day during baseline to about 150 instances per day during treatment.

On the last floor the treatment package was identical to that of the other floors except that rewards were omitted. This condition was also evaluated in an *ABA* design with changing criteria. Although the results for this floor were less dramatic, the package produced a clear reduction in noise transgressions, from an average of 1253 per day during baseline to 709 per day during treatment. Return to baseline led to an increase to 1123 per day. Changes in criteria led to corresponding changes in the number of noise transgressions even though the reductions were not associated with experimentally delivered reinforcers other than the points themselves.

Taken as a whole, the existing behavioral noise-control research, though limited and preliminary, has shown conclusively that excessive noise levels can be rapidly and inexpensively controlled. Unfortunately, to date the behavioral noise-control studies have concentrated on decibel levels, to the exclusion of other dimensions of noise. This neglect may be due to the salience of sound intensity as a critical aspect of noise, to an ignorance of the other disruptive dimensions of sound, or to the more expensive and complicated instrumentation needed to measure and control sound frequency, duration, complexity, spacing, and so on. In addition, the available literature has drawn from a short list of settings. The interest in classroom noise has perhaps diverted attention from other settings in which the behavioral effects of noise are undesirable.

Noise Control: Hospital Noise

One prime unexamined area, which sits on the boundary between socially or psychologically relevant noise and health-related noise, is noise in and around hospitals. A considerable amount of literature suggests that hospital noise, at the least, is annoying to patients and handicaps their ability to rest normally and, at the most, may actually be dangerous to their health (see, for example, the studies listed in Floyd, 1973, under "Hospital Noise"). Patients complain most about noises created directly by the staff and other patients (Whitfield, 1975), and these would seem to be precisely the kinds of noises that could readily be controlled through, say, simple feedback or consequation systems. To date, no such programs have been reported. Instead, hospital noise-control programs have relied upon either physical technology (such as quieter heating and cooling systems) or commonsense but untested recommendations. Whitfield (1975), for example, suggested that nurses should be sure to wear shoes that do not squeak.

Noise Control: Health-Related Noise

Although this chapter appears in the section on environmental aesthetics, we do not, of course, mean to imply that noise cannot have negative effects on health, especially hearing. But virtually no studies have approached the direct control of health-related noise (intense, long-duration, constant, pure, or high-frequency sound) from a psychological point of view. A major theme of this book is that a psychological approach to environmental problems, though not a complete solution, presents an exciting and productive new way to better our environment. Put another way, there is a growing need to complement physical technology with behavioral technology.

The extent to which physical technology dominates current noise-control efforts, especially as noise influences health, can hardly be overstated. The very field of noise control is often all but defined as an engineering enterprise. Indeed, Thurmann and Miller (1976) have listed 16 journals concerned with noise and its control, but *none* of them is concerned with the development of behavioral technology. The noise literature is now so extensive that entire bibliographies are published yearly on the subject (see, for example, Floyd, 1973). Of the thousands of studies listed there, very few involve an experimentally derived behavioral technology. Instead, these articles are either calls to arms or describe reactive research or research on physical technology.

How might a psychological approach influence health-related noise? In the absence of solid data, we can only point out some of the potentially useful ways a behavioral technology could contribute. You can conceive of noise as consisting of three phases: (1) the sound has reached the organism, (2) by traveling a distance through a medium, such as air or water, (3) from the original source. Noise-control efforts can be usefully applied to each of these areas.

The organism. One of the main ways in which health-related noise is currently controlled—in factories or at airports, for example—is through the use of ear-protective devices that reduce the impact of noise on the organism. These devices include both earmuff-type and earplug-type protectors, some of which actually are able to filter out only high-frequency sound. Nevertheless, these devices are cheap and effective (Rice & Coles, 1966; Scott, Thomas, & Royster, 1973). Parenthetically, it is interesting to note that some of the best ear-protective devices (better than earplugs or earmuffs) are always with us, although hardly convenient: our fingers, palms, and tragi—the little flaps in front of our ear canals (H. H. Holland, 1967).

The problem with ear-protective devices is that very often they are not used. As has been pointed out somewhat ruefully, "It is perhaps ironical that the accumulation of permanent noise-induced hearing loss could be brought to an end overnight were it possible to ensure that earplugs or earmuffs were worn wherever necessary" (Shaw, 1975, p. 58). Of course, getting people to use available environmentally protective technology is a problem in a number of different areas, as will be mentioned in the chapters in this book dealing with population control, mass transit, conservation of water, and energy production. Increasing the use of available technology is one of the greatest challenges facing behavior analysts in the environmental area. For example, in Chapter 11 we note that inexpensive, easily installed devices can save up to 40% of the water normally used inside houses.

In the early 1960s only 22% of the factories with dangerous noise levels had reasonably successful programs to ensure the use of ear-protective devices (Maas, 1961). The increase in noise-control legislation seen in the 1970s and regulation by the federal Occupational Safety and Health Administration altered this situation for the better by requiring hearing conservation programs. Nevertheless, it remains widely recognized as a significant management problem (Harmon, 1974; Melnick, 1969). With a very few exceptions (for example, Esler, 1978), only anecdotal reports of programs intended to increase the use of ear-protective devices have been reported to date (see, for example, Grzona, 1961).

The behavioral principles underlying the problem seem understandable enough. As was mentioned in Chapter 3, the effect of a stimulus event on behavior is related in part to the immediacy and certainty of that event's following the behavior in question. Wearing or not wearing ear protection has both long-term and short-term effects, as shown in Table 6–2. Recall that the general schema for representing the short-term and long-term effects of environmentally relevant behavior was described in Chapter 1.

Like many pollution-related behaviors, the weight of the short-term consequences favors *not* wearing the protectors. Only in the long term will most of the benefits of wearing ear protection be felt, another example of a behavioral trap. Just as with other such traps, the task becomes largely one of (1) increasing the salience of long-term effects, (2) decreasing the short-term negative aspects of wearing the protectors, and (3) providing short-term rewards for wearing the devices. Long-term effects are usually made more salient through demonstration films, educational programs, repeated hearing examinations, and the like. The short-term aversiveness can be reduced by using the most comfortable and convenient devices available; for example, earmuffs are typically strongly preferred over earplugs by employees (Maas, 1961). They are also more effective (Melnick, 1969), although more expensive. Finally, other short-term reinforcers can be increased for compliance. Thus, use of protective devices might be monitored (another advantage of earmuffs over earplugs), and effective consequences, such as social praise, promotional advantage, public or individual feedback, monetary rewards, and so on might be provided. Perhaps behavior analysts in industrial settings will soon begin to evaluate these and similar suggestions.

Route through a medium. The pathway along which noise travels to the ear determines how much sound energy will be left to strike the eardrum. The greater the distance sound travels, obviously, the less the sound intensity that will strike the ear. This is so because the energy is being spread over a greater and greater area as the distance increases. Further, if sound can be made to travel around or through barriers, much of its energy will be reflected away or lost in the form of heat.

Many of the current laws and regulations (such as tax breaks for thermally insulating homes or buildings—an intervention with the possible side effect of

Table 6–2. The Matrix of Long-Term and Short-Term Consequences of Wearing or Not Wearing Ear-Protective Devices

Antecedents (S^Ds)	Behavior (R)	Short-Term Consequences (S^R short)	Long-Term Consequences (S^R long)
Noise Entering work Other	Do not wear ear-protective devices.	You get used to the noise. Easier to communicate with others. Don't have to worry about keeping track of and remembering to wear muffs.	Possibility of hearing loss. The hearing loss is usually difficult to notice until it is very advanced. The hearing loss will not hinder functioning in the noisy environment itself until very advanced. Will only be noticeable in quiet environment.
		$^+$ short	S^{R-} long
Noise Entering work Other	Wear ear-protective devices.	May be difficult to communicate with others. Uncomfortable, bulky, awkward, they get lost, look foolish, are inconvenient.	No hearing loss.
		S^{R-} short	S^{R+} long

noise reduction) can be thought of as efforts to control behavior in this area (Bragdon, 1971).

The source. Finally, noise can be controlled at the source. This involves influences on the development and production of needed physical technology, of course, but once again also involves its purchase and use, by contractors, organizations, or individual consumers. Advertising agencies have long known that it is most effective to point out how quiet a particular car or appliance is. Bragdon (1971) collected an interesting and at times humorous list of such claims. For example, Chevrolet Vegas were said to "hum along with a degree of quietness that is all too unusual for little cars." Yet, according to Bragdon, a Vega was almost twice as loud as a Ford Pinto! Similarly, the Dodge Challenger and the Plymouth Satellite were both promoted as having a "torsion-quiet ride" (whatever *that* is). Yet the Dodge was twice as noisy as the Plymouth. Bragdon's figures show that cars supposed to be quiet ranged in loudness from decibel values of 66 or 67 to 83 or more. From the lowest to the highest, the noise levels increased 16 times—all in so-called quiet cars.

These problems arise because claims of quietness are not necessarily accurate or informative. Since there are no standards regulating the use of these general claims (for example, what is a "quiet ride"?), consumers are unable to know when they are actually buying the best available sound-control technology.

One way this situation might change would be the compilation of simple sound ratings or standards, just as has been done in the energy area (R values for insulating material, for example). In this way, consumers could see the true relationship between their purchase decision and the actual consequence (degree of quiet). It may even be possible to express the sound-rating value in a way that increases the salience of the long-term effects of this decision. For example, in addition to decibel or other ratings, the likelihood of long-term hearing damage from the appliance under set conditions could be estimated and reported.

The area of noise control is an exciting frontier for environmental research generally and the development of behavioral technology in particular. The need is there; the measurement systems are available; and several obvious and important programs are just waiting to be developed. With the tremendous increase in behavioral/environmental research over the past decade, it hopefully will not be long before a psychological approach is more widely used to control the din.

SUMMARY

Sound has several important dimensions: frequency, amplitude, complexity, and duration and spacing. Noise is sound that produces undesirable physical or psychological effects, and it is influenced by each of the four main dimensions of sound. In general, psychologically damaging noise is loud, discordant, high pitched, intermittent, unpredictable, and uncontrollable. Physically damaging noise is loud, high pitched, pure toned, and constant.

Psychological approaches to noise control have emphasized the control of psychologically disruptive sound, typically in classrooms. Research has shown that noise can be controlled by feedback, sensory reinforcement, and token systems backed up by a variety of reinforcers.

Few studies have approached physically destructive noise from a behavioral viewpoint. However, one particularly promising area is the use of behavioral methods to increase the use of physical technology in the area, such as earmuffs.

SUGGESTED PROJECT

1. Start by selecting a particularly noisy environment, such as a dormitory.
2. Decide upon the target type of noise, and select a measurement system. First survey the residents of the dormitory (you might want to make up a question-

naire). Find out what kind of noise disrupts what kinds of activities and when. (Notice that this is a good use of reactive research.) The survey might lead to the selection of the overall level of noise or particular types of noise (such as yelling) at particular times. If the problem is the overall level of noise and you cannot locate a decibel meter, try the following procedure. Select several noise makers that produce distinctive sounds of consistent loudness each time they are used (a car horn, air horn, cap pistol, and so on) and that range from making a loud to making a soft noise. Have someone periodically set off these noises outside the dorm while another person in the dorm records which of the noises were audible. In this way the current level of noise can be estimated. If the target noise is periodic, you may wish to rely on subjective loudness ratings by observers (check their reliability) or simple frequency counts of the number of yells, shouts, or whatever.

3. Collect these data for a few days or a week. You should now have an idea of how noisy it is in your chosen setting. Now choose a method you think will reduce the noise level or number of undesirable sounds. Some ideas:
   a. *Prompts.* Put up several signs asking for quiet. Try a catchy phrase.
   b. *Direct social feedback.* Try systematically approaching persons who have created excessive noise and asking them not to do it again. If they are bigger than you, this might be a bit risky, so be tactful!
   c. *Decibel feedback.* Simply post your decibel levels (or frequency counts and so on) for all to see.
   d. *Information.* Post information about noise and its effects.
   e. *Your own idea.* Be creative. What do you think might work?

4. Implement your chosen method. Now continue to measure the noise in the setting for at least a few days. Did the noise go down? If it did, you might take away your intervention to see whether the noise will then return to its previous level. If nothing happened, think through the problem some more, and go back to Step 3.

PART IV

SOLVING HEALTH-RELATED AND RESOURCE-RELATED ENVIRONMENTAL PROBLEMS

When people are asked about "environmental problems," they probably think of the serious, life-threatening difficulties we face in our biosphere. These are the kinds of problems addressed in this section. The next five chapters describe the work of behavioral scientists in population control, recycling, transportation, residential energy consumption, and residential water consumption. Although the advances made in each area may presently be somewhat limited, taken together these chapters should show dramatically the potential contribution that behavioral scientists can make to the solution of environmental problems.

In Chapter 7 we describe the worldwide efforts being made to control population. Some of these programs represent the most ambitious attempts to use behavioral technology ever undertaken, encompassing as they do entire states or even countries. Chapter 8 documents some of the resource problems caused by inadequate recycling and shows how recycling can be increased. Chapter 9 deals with the effect of behavioral technology on transportation patterns and corresponding fuel use. In these days of gasoline shortages and price increases, this information seems particularly timely. Chapter 10 shows that we now have several simple and inexpensive methods for conserving residential energy and that implementing them throughout the United States could substantially reduce the amount of energy we consume. Chapter 11 deals with the impact that behavioral scientists might have on water conservation, an area of growing concern in which there has as yet been no extensive behavioral research.

Chapter 7

POPULATION CONTROL

> Then there is the story of the family-planning worker showing the village men about condoms. Discreetly he took a bamboo pole and put a condom over one end to show the men how it was to be done. All nodded understanding. On his next visit he found each hut magically protected against pregnancy by a bamboo pole stuck in the ground outside the door—each with a condom fitted over the end [Pohlman, 1971, p. 119].

The population "bomb" has been accompanied by an equally impressive explosion of public concern over our growing numbers. This concern is seen most prominently in the media—books, news stories, and documentaries on the subject abound. Less obvious, perhaps, are the thousands of actual family-planning programs, groups, and clinics that seek to educate the public (as in the above humorous example) and to increase the availability and use of contraceptives.

It should come as no surprise to readers of this book that the history of efforts in population control shows much the same pattern we have seen with other environmental problems: recognition of the problem; efforts in physical technological solutions to the problem; partial realization of the behavioral nature of the problem; studies conducted in the areas of attitudes, information, knowledge, and the like; efforts to educate the public; and, finally, the beginnings of a broad-based behavioral technology. In population control this sequence has unfolded quite rapidly, perhaps because, of all the environmental problems discussed in this book, population control is the most obviously behavioral and efforts in this area have produced the most impressive results. A distinct and salient set of human actions leads both to the conception of children and to the prevention of conception. Physical technology, while still developing, has long been basically adequate to the task of preventing unwanted children—the problem has been in getting people to use it. Unfortunately, we are far from having an effective approach to population control as a behavioral problem. Despite our best efforts in the area of family planning, people continue to have more children than they want and to want more than the earth can comfortably support.

The population problem itself has several distinct facets. It is simple-minded merely to say that there are too many people. The problem has at least two primary dimensions:

1. Population as a social problem. The raw numbers of new persons in a given area may be important, but equally important is the distribution of these persons in time and among different social groups. For example, children born to poor parents, or children born too closely together in time, may present problems to families quite apart from any environmental damage caused by excessive numbers of persons in the overall society. Thus, family planning clearly would have value even if we were not a society of ever-increasing numbers. There are data, for example, supporting the view that large families are less happy, even when proper controls have been established for differences in socioeconomic status (see, for example, Moore & Holtzman, 1965; Silvermann & Silvermann, 1971). The children in large families are also less likely to be outgoing, self-confident, and self-reliant and are less likely to do well in school (Clausen, 1966; Douvan & Adelson, 1966). However, the social or psychological effects of population are matters that go beyond the scope of this book. Rather than examine the behavioral effects *of* the problem, we will examine the effects of behavioral intervention *on* the problem.

2. *Population as an environmental problem.* Ehrlich (1968) and others have been arguing for some time that every increase in the earth's population produces a real, if imperceptible, worsening of the environmental problems we face. According to this view, more people, given the current system, mean more goods consumed, more energy and other resources used, and ultimately more pollution produced.

There are counterarguments, however, that center on the phrase "given the current system" in the above statement. The system, some would say, *is* the problem. Pollution and resource depletion, these persons would point out (for example, Commoner, 1972), are rising at a rate in the industrialized world that far outstrips any increases in population. Much of the current environmental pollution clearly is not due to population growth.

For the purposes of this chapter, we will examine the results of efforts to control the overall rate of population growth. To do so need not imply that population is the only variable producing environmental damage. Indeed, the main point of this book is that it is human *behavior,* in many areas, that is largely responsible for our environmental problems. The number of behaving organisms is but one component of this formulation.

THE ETHICS OF POPULATION CONTROL

At the outset it is important to point out that population control is a complex matter that generates strong reactions from otherwise reasonable people. Population control unavoidably raises ethical, moral, and political concerns that are often emotionally laden. For example, the use of contraceptives is still officially considered sinful by the Roman Catholic Church. In the United States the question of abortion has produced widespread controversy over the past several years. Similarly, some Third World countries and some ethnic groups think of population control as another name for genocide (see Figure 7–1).

FORCED Steriliza-tion is a nice name for genocide.

Figure 7–1. Many people view sterilization as a type of genocide. This view is not entirely uninformed, as there have indeed been many instances of sterilization abuse, especially in Third World countries. Drawing by Peg Averill of the Liberation News Service. From Fact Sheet #1 by CESA, the Committee to End Sterilization Abuse.

In this type of atmosphere, it is probably difficult to avoid offending certain readers. However, our focus in this book is on the alleviation of environmental problems. From that perspective it seems clear that population control or reduction is likely to be a "good," whatever one's ethical, moral, or political judgments of it may be. Accordingly, though recognizing these other issues, we will treat population control as if it were a desirable goal. You may wish to keep some of the ethical issues in mind as we describe the procedures that have been used in population control.

VIEWS ON POPULATION CONTROL

On one level it is very easy to describe the variables influencing population: the number of persons on the earth is a function of birth rate and death rate. Accordingly, in order to control population, only two options are available —decrease the birth rate or increase the death rate.

A number of views on population approach the question at just such a global level. Population matters are traditionally the concern of demographers, sociologists, and economists. We know, for example, that there is a strong inverse relationship between the socioeconomic level of a society and its fertility rate (Adelman & Morris, 1966). However, showing such a relationship at a global level is not particularly helpful in developing effective population-control programs. Global forces such as urbanization, industrialization, education, economic development, and the like are strongly predictive of fertility rates only at a large-group level. Further, identifying these forces alone can lead to few new fertility-change strategies because most major societies are seemingly already working as best they can toward modernization.

The hallmark of a psychological approach to population is the emphasis on the individual or the individual within a small group (Fawcett, 1970, 1973). M. Brewster Smith (1973) has described it this way: "Since it is individual men and women, not cohorts or social strata, who have babies, these social facts should have their psychological counterparts, and a sound psychological perspective on fertility should be an essential component in developing social strategies to bring the growth of population under control" (p. 4).

Unfortunately, as Smith himself recognized, the social and behavioral sciences have only begun to contribute to the solution of population problems. As we have argued throughout this book, the reason is clear enough: social scientists have generally been content merely to assess and interpret the current situation (reactive research) rather than intervene. Such efforts have not been particularly successful, even on their own terms (for example, see Westoff, Potter, & Sagi, 1963; Westoff, Potter, Sagi, & Mishler, 1961) or in terms of fertility control.

Considerable research has been conducted on such topics as the perceived value of children (Hoffman & Hoffman, 1973); the effect of religion on sterilization (for example, Presser, 1970); the psychological impact of population density on human behavior (for example, Stokols, 1978); and other psychological precursors or consequences of population behavior. This research may yet prove to have considerable value in actual efforts in population control. Reactive research can be especially important in pointing to the (potentially changeable) motives for and against a particular course of action. But unless actual action is taken to change these motives and the behaviors associated with them, little benefit should be expected from such research. It is one thing to know that contraceptive use relates to measures of "internal control" (MacDonald, 1970), "modernity" (Fawcett & Bornstein, 1973), or "planning ahead" (Keller, Sims, Henry, & Crawford, 1970). It is quite another thing to use this information to control fertility.

The possible sources of influences over fertility can be classified in several ways. A schema for considering these variables is presented in Table 7–1 (compare Davis & Blake, 1956; Hardin, 1968; Lipe, 1971; Zifferblatt & Hendricks, 1974). By considering these factors, the nature and source of several areas of difficulty in fertility control can be assessed. The following summary is not intended to be comprehensive, but it should suggest the range of possible psychological influences on fertility.

Intercourse Variables

Sexual intercourse surely most often occurs for reasons other than the production of children. Unfortunately (for population control), these reasons (for example, sexual satisfaction, development of relationships) are very immediate and often very intense. Sexual intercourse could be limited in several ways, such as decreasing the availability of appropriate partners or settings, keeping children ignorant of the nature of sexual activity, increasing moral or ethical proscriptions on heterosexual intercourse, or encouraging alternative sexual behavior (for example, masturbation or homosexuality). For obvious reasons, none of these steps is likely either to be tried or to work. In our current social environment heterosexual intercourse is likely to occur even more often and at an even younger initial age.

Contraceptive Variables

The next step in the chain of fertility behavior is the use or nonuse of contraceptives or sterilization to avoid conception. The variables involved here can be broken down into short-term and long-term factors. Most of the long-term factors involve the benefits and costs of having children, while the short-term factors typically have more to do with the specific contraceptive. We will consider each briefly.

Short-term factors. In order to be used, a method must be known and available. Contraceptives are more likely to be an effective means of population

Table 7-1. A Schema for Analyzing Sources of Control over Fertility-Related Behavior and Some Examples of These Sources

| | Steps in the Chain of Fertility Behaviors | | | | | |
| | Intercourse Variables | | Conception Variables | | Gestation Variables | |
Types of Available Psychological Controls	Engaging in Heterosexual Intercourse	Not Engaging in Heterosexual Intercourse	Using Contraceptives	Not Using Contraceptives	Having an Abortion	Not Having an Abortion
The availability and salience of stimuli prompting the behavior	Willing partner	Parental surveillance	Having a contraceptive in a prominent place	Seeing a copy of Pope Paul's encyclical on birth control	Ads for clinics	Antiabortion "Right to Life" demonstration
The relative valence of the consequence of the behavior	Is sex enjoyable?	It is good to remain "moral"?	Will it disrupt the sexual interaction?	Is it enjoyable to be "spontaneous"?	Is it murder to have an abortion?	Do I want a kid?
The magnitude of the consequence for the behavior	How enjoyable is sex for the person?	How important is it to remain a virgin?	How disruptive will it be?	How enjoyable is it to be "spontaneous"?	Will I go to hell if I have an abortion?	Will I lose my job if I have a kid?
The certainty that the consequence will follow	How likely is it that pregnancy will follow?	Will I really feel less frustrated tomorrow?	Perhaps he will not mind my taking a quick trip to the bathroom.	Maybe I will worry too much to make it fun.	Can I make up for this sin later?	Maybe I will spontaneously abort.
The immediacy of the consequence	I'll just go a little further into this.	I can't stop now.	Maybe I'll do it in a minute.	Will I be around nine months from now?	Will it hurt now or later?	I can always decide tomorrow.

control if they need not be deliberately used each time intercourse occurs, both because of stimulus-control factors (people forget) and because of the immediately disruptive effect special contraceptive measures may have upon spontaneous sexual activity. Thus, most family-planning programs throughout the world have concentrated on the use of the intrauterine device (IUD) or sterilization (tubal ligation or vasectomy). Use of oral contraceptives is also high, while the condom, vaginal foam, and the rhythm method are used far less consistently or prevalently (see Nortman, 1971). Other factors that may commonly affect the immediate value of various contraceptives are (1) reduction in genital stimulation (for example, by the condom), (2) cost, (3) fear of loss of sexual functioning (for example, from sterilization), and (4) the social embarrassment involved in their purchase or use (W. A. Fisher, Fisher, & Byrne, 1977).

Long-term factors. Having children produces many positive and negative changes in the parents' lives over the long term. One important source of benefit is social. Society often expects couples to have children, and this pressure comes in many forms, including:

a. Religion. In most religions, "barrenness" is a curse, while children are considered a heavenly blessing (Pohlman, 1969). There are also differences between religions. Catholics, for example, as a group say that they want to have considerably more children than do Protestants (Rainwater, 1965).

b. Nationality. Similarly, some nationalities or racial groups may view it essential that members reproduce at a high rate (see, for example, Dow, 1967).

c. Consolidation of the family. Having children is thought by some parents to demonstrate stability in the marriage (Rainwater, 1960) and to tie the marital partners together (for example, see Lopata, 1971).

d. Pleasure from children. Children are thought to be cute and stimulating. One has only to watch adults play with small children to be convinced that "fun" can be a major source of benefit from children. Researchers (for example, Komarovsky, 1950) have documented that this benefit is an objective of parents.

e. Monetary value and old-age security. In many societies one's children are a kind of combined labor pool and living Social Security system. In agrarian societies, for example, subsistence farmers may be unable to hire farm hands for seasonal work, and although children may cost some money to rear, they may also be the only feasible way to survive economically. Further, the cost of many children must be weighed against their value in the parents' old age. Subsistence-based economies cannot afford to support older persons at a societal level, so parents must turn to their children for help. In some agrarian societies only sons are of value in this respect because daughters go to live in their husbands' villages. Thus, the goal is to have many sons (Poffenberger, 1968).

Urbanization has a dramatic influence on this variable. In the United States, as in many other industrialized countries, there is virtually no evidence that economic gain is a factor, in parents' views, favoring having children (Hoffman & Hoffman, 1973). The commonly held conservative belief that welfare is an incentive for poor people to have more illegitimate children also appears mistaken (Cutright, 1970).

Gestation Variables

The last fertility behavior is gestation. Once not even a topic of polite conversation, abortion in the United States is now legal due to actions taken by the Supreme Court. The immediate effects of the liberalization of abortion have been positive in terms of maternal health, reductions in birth rate, and decreased illegitimacy (see, for example, Pakter & Nelson, 1971). This experience in the United States has not been atypical. The evidence indicates that abortion is a significant factor in the dramatic decline of birth rates in Japan (Davis, 1963) and Eastern Europe (Tietze, 1964). In many parts of the world, abortions are very common, at times exceeding the number of live births (Klinger, 1966, 1971).

There are, of course, profound psychological (David, 1973) and ethical implications surrounding the issue of abortion. Religious and other beliefs (see Knutson, 1973) undoubtedly bear a relation to the use of abortion by various groups. However, little currently can (or, many would say, should) be done to liberalize the use of abortion beyond the removal of legal and economic restraints. Abortion is still illegal in parts of the world, and legal measures in these areas may have an effect on population growth.

In summary, fertility is an enormously complex area in which many factors must be analyzed. Unfortunately, only a subset (conception variables) currently seems particularly amenable to the development of behavioral technology. The goal of most behavioral programs has therefore been to increase the use of contraceptives and sterilization.

The importance of work in contraception is underlined by research showing that most young, sexually active, unmarried American females rarely use any contraceptives at all, particularly when just starting to have intercourse (Eastman, 1972; Zelnick & Kantner, 1974). This distressing finding would undoubtedly be even more distressing in developing countries.

There have long been programs designed to increase the use of contraceptives. In part because of the complexity of the issue and the religious and ethical questions it raises, research in population control is very difficult, as we shall see next.

RESEARCH ISSUES

Although it is probably unnecessary to go into the methodological details of population research, you should have a sense of some of the general problems involved. Many of the programs we will describe have been carried out in relatively primitive countries or in countries with limited administrative capabilities. This can create real difficulties. For example, suppose you wish to give payments to small families, so long as the number of children stays low. In the United States this might be fine; in India it may well be impossible because of skimpy birth records. Even if you checked the homes, the parents might claim that the children are not theirs in order to receive the payments (the "these-three-are-the-children-of-my-dead-uncle" phenomenon). Research problems occur in the following major areas: dependent variable, independent variable, and design.

Dependent Variables

You might think that dependent variables in population control would be no problem. After all, it is impossible to be just a little bit pregnant or to sort of have children. But despite the concrete, all-or-none nature of the dependent measures often used, there are serious difficulties. For example, as just indicated, it is often difficult to get good records of actual birth and death rates without special efforts (see, for example, Cernada & Chow, 1969). This problem may be especially acute when one wishes to assess the effects of a program on a particular subset of the population. In a common type of study, researchers are interested in the effect of a program on its "accepters"—that is, on those who have agreed to participate in the program. In a country with limited, inaccurate, or unreliable record keeping, how could the researchers determine the effect? There are several strategies used. One is to ask for self-reports from persons about birth-control knowledge, attitudes, and practice—the so-called KAP studies. More than 400 KAP studies have been reported in the literature, and it is probably the most popular research tool in the area of population control. Unfortunately, we seldom know what relationship, if any, exists between these verbal statements and actual population behaviors. Thus, the reliability and validity of KAP studies are almost always suspect.

Another strategy is to conduct periodic pregnancy checks, in which a family worker sees the accepter and certifies that she is, in fact, not pregnant. This, too, is often a problem because the checks are of unknown reliability and because there have been concerns about fraudulent checks. For example, a family worker might be paid to report a lack of pregnancy.

Independent Variables

Experimental population research is still young, and, perhaps understandably, the interventions used have often had an everything-but-the-kitchen-sink quality about them. Family-planning programs are usually complex packages of procedures, some of which may work and some of which may be useless or even harmful. If programs work, we want to know why. Even if a correct design and correct dependent measures are used, many programs are not able to specify or monitor the actual independent variables. If, for example, you think that you are paying the equivalent of $4 to persons agreeing to have a vasectomy, it would be disturbing to find that this money is actually being skimmed off by local administrators (Pohlman, 1971). Yet this sort of thing apparently occurs regularly. Similarly, if a woman is paid to have an IUD inserted and then turns around and uses some portion of that money to have a local midwife remove it (perhaps so she can have another inserted and again be paid), the effectiveness of IUDs in preventing pregnancy can hardly be determined.

Design Problems

Even if good measures are available, it is often very difficult to demonstrate the effect of family-planning programs. Imagine that you have set up a family-planning clinic. You advertise the clinic when it first opens, and you quickly develop a clientele. The question is whether your clinic prevents births. If the program is not designed to influence an entire area (a state or country, for example), then you must measure its effect upon the accepters. Even if you have an adequate measure of births, how can you assess the impact? If the accepters have fewer births compared to nonaccepters, the reason could be that the accepters had previously decided not to have more children; this decision may have brought them to the clinic *and* lowered their likelihood of having children. The clinic itself may not have had a significant impact.

Because of these design questions, some research has encompassed entire areas. In this areal strategy, programs are implemented in some areas and not others, or are implemented in an area and then withdrawn, and changes in birth rate are noted. Difficulties inevitably arise because these program decisions are often highly political and occur in the face of purely scientific concerns. For example, public pressure may cause a clinic to change its program before it can be adequately evaluated. We will see some real-life instances of this problem later.

Thus, as you read the information that follows, keep in mind that despite researchers' best efforts, the dependent measures used are often of questionable reliability, family-planning packages are often poorly specified and monitored, and the designs are often weak (see Cuca & Pierce, 1977).

FAMILY-PLANNING PROGRAMS

Family-planning programs can be very roughly divided into three categories: informational, service, and incentive programs. Informational programs are designed to increase the knowledge about, or change attitudes toward, contraceptives. These programs may or may not be associated with a particular service or clinic. What we are terming service programs are programs that attempt to increase the availability and use of contraceptives by directly offering contraceptive services, such as by opening a clinic. Incentive programs are those that explicitly attempt to motivate clients (directly or indirectly) to accept and use contraceptives. Incentive programs are typically part of service-delivery programs.

Informational Campaigns

Informational campaigns have three principal goals. These are to make people aware of the need for family planning, know about the birth-control methods that are available, and seek out and accept the use of family-planning procedures. These three goals have been termed *awareness, knowledge,* and *acceptance* (or practice), respectively.

Informational campaigns have been found to be somewhat effective in all three areas. The most successful area is awareness. The media are clearly partially responsible for our general awareness of family planning (see, for example, Dubey & Choldin, 1967). However, awareness is not always a problem to begin with. Surprisingly, most people in developing countries (and, of course, in industrialized countries) *are* aware of the need for family planning (see, for example, Cernada & Lu, 1972).

Knowledge of specific techniques and available services has been shown to be influenced by a number of informational campaigns. For example, a media campaign in Taiwan increased familiarity with the IUD from 2% to 47% (among women aged 20–39) over a ten-month program; knowledge about contraceptive approaches not mentioned in the campaign increased only very slightly (Freedman & Takeshita, 1969). This finding has been confirmed in several studies (for example, Balakrishnan & Matthai, 1967; Cernada & Lu, 1972).

A stronger test, of course, is program acceptance. Here, too, informational campaigns are of some proven value. A large, "Madison Avenue" approach in the United States (Udry, 1974) yielded a significant increase in new patients at family-planning clinics when target cities were saturated with family-planning ads. Similar results were obtained in Taiwan (Cernada & Lu, 1972), Honduras (Stycos & Marden, 1970), Kenya (Black & Harvey, 1976), and other countries. There is some evidence that these campaigns are effective because people learn new things (about birth control, for example, or where to get contraceptives), not because they motivate people to change their ways (see Balakrishnan & Matthai, 1967). Persons already having the information may not be influenced by media appeals. This observation probably explains why informational campaigns are of some usefulness in population control but not in other areas (such as energy conservation—see Chapter 10) in which information may be more widely available.

There are several general guidelines for the design of informational campaigns. First, multimedia approaches, especially if combined with personal contacts (such as with village leaders), seem more effective than using only one type of medium (Freedman & Takeshita, 1969). Second, successful messages are catchy (Schramm, 1971), specific (Cernada & Lu, 1972), and carefully designed to avoid negative reactions (Udry, 1974). However, combining these three specifications can be tricky. For example, Udry found that the media objected to advertising campaigns that did such things as having a stork say "The love bird gets you when you don't watch out. And when I bring the baby it's too late to shout!" Consequently, these ads had difficulty getting air time.

Third, radio campaigns are effective in areas with low literacy rates (Cernada & Lu, 1972), while direct mailings are especially useful when smaller, specific populations need to be reached (Cernada, 1970). Mailings were shown in at least one study to be about as effective as door-to-door visits (Stycos & Mundigo, 1974).

Throughout this book we show that instructions are only a limited solution for environmental problems. Although informational campaigns are of some value, population control is not an exception. The purpose of information is to specify the desired behavior. If this is new information, it may get the behavior going, but the long-term success of a program is largely a function of other variables (Stycos & Back, 1964). To these we now turn.

Service Programs

The effectiveness of service programs depends upon their rate of acceptance (that is, how many people join them) and the continuation of contraception by the accepters. These are different problems and will be treated separately.

The rate of acceptance. Several methods, other than mass communication and incentives, are of use in increasing acceptance. First, professional field workers seem beneficial (Freedman & Takeshita, 1969). Traveling door to door and to group meetings, these workers explain the service and recruit accepters. However, little is known about the psychological principles involved in their work. These workers are often left to their own devices and are little trained. Some service programs have attempted to upgrade their training by using programmed instruction (Mullins & Perkin, 1969).

A major problem with field workers is cost, since they are typically salaried workers. Consequently, other, less expensive promotional systems have been attempted. In one particularly clever study (Fawcett & Somboonsuk, 1969), accepters were given cards to give to their friends. These cards promised "preferential treatment" for persons bringing them in. The cards were even stamped with an expiration date (two months hence) in order to give them added value and believability. This procedure produced an increase of about 30% in the number of new accepters at virtually no cost.

Another extraordinarily sensible approach has been to concentrate on an identifiable and psychologically reachable population: postpartum mothers (Zatuchni, 1971). These programs have grown considerably and are now part of the postpartum routine in many hospitals. They have resulted in impressive increases in the use of contraceptives (Jaffe, 1971). Further, postpartum accepters are younger than accepters in other programs, and this factor may lead to an even greater overall reduction in birth rates.

A last major variable in the rate of acceptance of service programs is the type of service offered. Most foreign programs have concentrated on the IUD or sterilization (vasectomies or tubal ligations); in the United States the pill has also been widely promoted. Sterilization, although obviously effective, is not fully accepted. These operations are inexpensive, safe, and easily done. An experienced surgeon can perform a vasectomy in the office (hospitalization is not required) in a matter of minutes. Sexual performance or satisfaction is not affected by the operation itself.

Still, there are difficulties. Concerns over vasectomies, for example, often center on the issue of the implications for a man's "manhood." Sterilization is widely practiced (if not fully accepted) in many countries, such as India and the United States (Presser, 1970). At any rate, there are regional and social differences in the degree of acceptance given to a particular contraceptive approach.

Continuation of contraception. The variables that influence the continuation of contraception can be divided into the characteristics of the accepters, the characteristics of the method of contraception, and the consequences of continued use. Accepters' characteristics, though potentially important, have been studied almost entirely in correlational research. For example, it is known that continuation is better among accepters who live in rural areas and who are using contraceptives in order to stop having children rather than simply to space them out (see, for example, Freedman & Takeshita, 1969). It remains to be seen how this kind of information will directly aid the development of successful family-planning programs.

The characteristics of the method of contraception itself offer more helpful information. A number of studies have shown that IUD continuation is generally higher than that for oral contraceptives. These data have supported the current emphasis on the IUD and on sterilization (a procedure with obviously high continuation rates, since it is often difficult or impossible to reverse).

Finally, the consequences of a particular method of contraception are important. For example, some of the failure to continue using the IUD can be accounted for by bodily rejection of the device or by pregnancy itself. Further research in contraception methods may produce techniques that minimize these kinds of consequences.

Incentive Programs

One of the truly major problems in population-control efforts is that not only do people have more children than they want to have, but they want to have more children than they should if our rate of population growth is to become manageable (Pohlman, 1971). Virtually all studies on family-size preferences have found that people desire between two and four children (George, 1973), far too many for population stability.

To the extent that this finding is valid, population control can be said to constitute a motivational problem with two basic dimensions: getting people to have only the children they want (and motivating them to do what needs to be done to accomplish their goal) and getting people to want to have fewer children. Even if there existed the perfect contraceptive (everyone knew of it and how to get it, and it was cheap, completely effective, and had no side effects), incentive programs would still be needed so that people would want fewer children. Thus, incentive programs are probably one of the most critical areas of population research.

Box 7–1.   Reduce Your Family Size, or Else!

One of the most successful and comprehensive population-control programs is that in Singapore. It includes many specific measures that cover the entire population of about 2.3 million.

1. Hospital fees.   Hospital costs for having a child go up as a person has more children. Although the fees are low for the first two children, they are quite high after the fourth child.

2. Income tax.   In many countries, families receive a tax break if they have children. For example, in the United States the more dependents you have, the more tax deductions you are allowed. In Singapore the tax law is reversed. Large families are not allowed tax breaks for additional children.

3. Education.   Not all eligible children can get an advanced education in Singapore. Children from large families are given low priorities for admission to school.

4. State housing.   Families with four or more children are given low priorities for admission to state housing projects. Having too many children after you move into a project can cause you to be evicted.

5. Maternity leave.   Women do receive paid maternity leaves in Singapore. Consistent with the overall policy, however, maternity leaves are allowed for only the first two children.

This collection of incentives (or, one might say, disincentives) has apparently reduced the birth rate over 50% since the late 1950s, from 44 births per thousand to about 21 births per thousand (Fook-Kee & Swee-Hock, 1975; Swee-Hock, 1975). Do you see any ethical issues involved in this program?

The explicit use of incentives has been widely discussed (see, for example, Pohlman, 1971; Ridker, 1971; Sirageldin & Hopkins, 1972), but until rather recently, well-controlled experimental projects were few. Most of the rigorous studies that have been done involve limited contraceptive programs rather than broad efforts to reduce the rate of population growth. Nevertheless, some of the latter type of programs are huge and potentially quite important, despite the lack of experimental rigor.

Incentives for what behavior? Pohlman (1971) has delineated several possible targets for incentives: postponing the first child; having an IUD inserted; getting sterilized; postponing marriage; paying women for remaining nonpregnant; paying for keeping families small. By far the most studied behavior, for a number of reasons, is accepting sterilization (usually vasectomies). As mentioned earlier, vasectomies are simple, relatively cheap, and highly effective. Complications are relatively uncommon, and once the operation is performed, no further effort need be spent in monitoring compliance. These characteristics make vasectomies a practical technique for population control, particularly in underdeveloped countries. (See Pohlman, 1971, for a discussion of the relative usefulness of other behaviors.)

Which incentives, when, and how much? Once a program is committed to a target behavior, such as accepting a vasectomy, how much of what will be given when for the behavior must still be determined. An obvious answer is cash, as much as can be afforded, and paid immediately following the vasectomy. Most programs have followed this strategy. After all, cash is something that anybody can use. There are problems here, however. First, cash payments may come under fire because of the image they present of buying off people (for example, see Enke, 1961). People do not want to feel that they have "sold" their future children. Second, recall that there are data indicating that part of the motivation for having children (at least in agrarian societies) is as a type of old-age security. If you receive a cash payment for a vasectomy, this security may not be forthcoming. Therefore, a better (meaning socially better—not necessarily more effective) incentive might be something like educational benefits for accepters' children, so they can support their parents better later on (see, for example, Finnigan & Sun, 1972; Wang & Chen, 1973); savings accounts or bonds that can be used after child-bearing age (Ridker, 1969; Ridker & Muscat, 1973); or pension payments. A number of additional incentives have been suggested (Pohlman, 1971) or used, such as health care, clothing (see Rogers, 1971), government favors, or food (Perkin, 1970). Nevertheless, most of the actual programs (for example, Repetto, 1968; Thakor & Patel, 1972) have used immediate monetary incentives.

Incentives for whom? A number of persons are involved in the sequence of events leading to program acceptance: the accepter, the person who found the accepter and explained how to participate, the physician or paramedical worker who implements the program. All of these persons may respond well to incentive procedures.

Most current programs pay the program accepter. To avoid public criticism of the program, sometimes this payment is said to be "mere compensation"—for transportation costs (for example, see Treadway, Gillespie, & Loghmani, 1976), for time off work (Repetto, 1968), or other such losses of income. Regardless, there are data to show that the accepters themselves are frequently motivated by the money or other incentive offered and do not see it as "mere compensation" (Srinivasan & Kachirayan, 1968).

A number of programs also offer substantial incentives to program staff members and to canvassers to find the accepters. With some exceptions (such as Porapakkham, Donaldson, & Svetsreni, 1975), these incentives are usually quite effective (see, for example, Chang, Cernada, & Sun, 1972). There is concern, however, over the ethical issues involved in paying people to find accepters (Veatch, 1977). Basically, the concern is that undue social pressure will be brought to bear or that misinformation may be used to gain acceptance of the program. Indeed, there are data showing that fewer complaints come from persons accepting vasectomies due to information provided by village officials or health staff as compared to paid canvassers (Srinivasan & Kachirayan, 1968).

These kinds of problems caused India to terminate payments to canvassers working with the country's vasectomy program. Unfortunately, this decision caused the effectiveness of the program to begin to deteriorate (Repetto, 1968), and the incentives were later reinstated. A side benefit was gained by these program changes, however. As was noted earlier, political decisions (such as this one) often interfere with the scientific evaluation of population programs. In this case the opposite occurred. Since data had been collected throughout, the removal and subsequent reinstitution of canvasser incentives constituted a single-subject design similar to the *ABA* designs cited so often in the previous chapters. In this case program acceptance was high when the incentives were used, low when they were not, and high again when they were reinstituted, thus showing their importance to the success of the program.

Some calls have been made for group-incentive programs. Group incentives have been shown to be effective in many environmental areas (see Chapters 6, 8, and 10). In such an arrangement, payments would not go to the accepter directly but to his or her town, village, or family. For example, one village was offered a well for cooperation with a family-planning program. Of the eligible couples, 100% adopted family planning, primarily vasectomies (Kulkarni, 1969). Other, similar programs have not produced such dramatic successes, however (Pohlman, 1971).

Research is badly needed on the relative value of these various types, frequencies, qualities, and recipients of incentives. As it is, we can say that experimental incentives have been shown to be an effective aid in the establishment of population-control programs. More detailed studies have often been attempted, but few have succeeded due to the combined effects of political decisions influencing the program, lack of proper measures, and other such difficulties (for example, see J. F. Phillips, Silayan-Go, & Pal-Montano, 1975).

Individualizing Family-Planning Efforts

One alternative to the broad strategies that have been used is to individual-ize these programs. As Zifferblatt and Hendricks (1974) have pointed out, the single behavior of using or not using a contraceptive occurs in a cultural/familial context. By analyzing the needs of a particular family, it may be possible to design a program that is more sensitive to this context. For example, a family living in a one-room house may rely more upon opportunities for intercourse that present themselves spontaneously than would families living in multiple-room houses. Accordingly, this family may be least likely to use regularly any con-traceptives that require prior planning (for example, vaginal foam).

The suggestion is quite sound theoretically, and though it might be quite useful to individualize such programs, there are no data on the practicality or success of this approach. Unfortunately, the kind of training that would be required for family-planning workers to understand behavioral principles may be beyond the reach of many societies. Still, pilot programs might be set up using this approach as ways of developing cookbook-style manuals for the individuali-zation of family-planning programs.

Some Examples of Large Family-Planning Programs

Although the number of well-controlled studies on incentives in family planning is small, these programs constitute perhaps the single largest use of behavioral technology to influence an environmental problem. Some of the pro-grams are massive, incorporating entire cities, states, or even countries. It may be helpful to describe some of these programs in more detail to show you how they are run.

The vasectomy camps.   India has experimented with the camp approach to population control. In these efforts massive camps (or at times a number of smaller camps) are established with the goal of performing as many sterilization operations (both vasectomies and tubal ligations) as possible in as short a time as possible. For example, in the Ernakulam district of Kerala State in India, three separate one-month to two-month camps were held in 1970, 1971, and 1972. Nearly 95,000 sterilizations were performed at the camps. Of this number, about 50,000 were on people from the district, which had about 300,000 eligible couples. Thus, in only three years an incredible one out of six eligible couples was sterilized. Similar programs have been conducted covering the entire state of Gujarat in India (nearly 27 million people).

The camps are accompanied by extremely intensive publicity campaigns before they begin, including door-to-door canvassing by paid "motivators." Accepters are given incentives in the form of cash and gifts; there is even a lottery from a large sum of money. The motivators are given lesser, but still substantial, cash payments. The net effect of these procedures is a circus atmosphere surrounding the camps. They become events, drawing thousands of persons to them to partake of the excitement (Krishnakumar, 1972, 1974; Thakor & Patel, 1972).

The camp approach concentrates efforts into a shorter period of time in a particular area. The success of such an approach is understandable when we consider behavioral principles. First, most of the residents of the area will be exposed to canvassers or friends who will inform the residents of the existence and nature of the camp (an S^D and a powerful one, given our tendency to do what others do). By using incentives of various sorts, the strength of the short-term consequences of sterilization may be increased to the point that other, competing short-term and long-term consequences (such as desire to have more children, fear of the operation) are overcome. The circus atmosphere may increase the short-term effects even more as social pressure is brought to bear to get in on the act.

An educational-bond program. This program encompasses several rural townships in Taiwan. Participants are given an annual cash reward for limiting family size. The size of the payments increases over the years if the family stays small. By the time the families are in a position to redeem the bonds when the children reach high school age, they could have as much as $400 in the account for each child's education (if they have had no more than two children). The promotional materials stress that achieving old-age security is dependent upon having successful children and that success can be ensured by having the money to pay for high school and college tuition (Finnigan & Sun, 1972). Complete results of the study are not yet in, but you should note that this approach relies far more upon long-term reinforcers than upon short-term ones. The likelihood of its success seems less, due to this orientation. Indeed, early results of the study are somewhat discouraging (Sun, 1976).

The undeniably behavioral nature of population control has produced efforts in this area that outstrip in scope and impact those discussed elsewhere in this book. Nevertheless, these efforts are still preliminary. Population control, after all, is an area in which research is difficult. It is beset with religious and ethical concerns. It is often a matter of some political debate. Most of the programs described in this chapter were not developed by behavioral scientists but were practical responses to local problems by the officials involved. Still, one has to be impressed by the boldness of these efforts and by their apparent success despite the obstacles. The thesis of this book is that viewing environmental problems as largely behavioral will yield significant benefits. Population control is one area in which there are data on programs of such a nature and scope as to bolster that claim.

SUMMARY

The behavioral chain that leads to the production of children contains three elements: intercourse, conception, and gestation. Only conception variables seem particularly amenable to intervention. Many family-planning programs have been established that attempt to inform, provide services, and motivate people to accept these services. Information is of some help in initiating cooperation, but not in maintaining it. Cooperation over the long term is more heavily influenced by accepter characteristics, the type of contraception, and incentive schemes. Individualization of programs may bring benefits, but most of the programs to date have been more rigid. Several broad-scale programs have been used, such as the Gujarat camps.

SUGGESTED PROJECT

The purpose of this project is to examine the relationship between the accurate knowledge of contraceptives and their use.

1. First, devise an anonymous questionnaire consisting of multiple-choice questions about the nature of various methods of contraception and their use, effectiveness, and availability (for example, where they can be purchased and for how much).
2. Have a second section of the questionnaire ask the subjects about the likelihood (or perceived likelihood) of their use of each of these methods of contraception. Here is a sample question:
   If you wished to engage in heterosexual intercourse and had not otherwise used a birth-control device, how likely is it that you would use (or encourage your partner to use) a condom?

0	1	2	3	4	5	6	7
Not at all likely			Somewhat likely			Extremely likely	

3. Give the questionnaire to a number of persons (keep them totally anonymous).
4. Total the score (number correct) on the knowledge section, and total the score on the likelihood-of-use section.
5. Plot the pairs of scores (for knowledge and likelihood of use) on a graph:

6. If the two measures are correlated, you should see a tendency for the points to collect in a linelike fashion, like this:

7. Look up the formula (or get a good calculator), and determine the exact correlation.

8. If you wish to, you might pass out contraceptive information to the subjects and then have them fill out the questionnaire again. Repeat Steps 4, 5, 6, and 7. See whether the correlation then changes.

Chapter 8

RECYCLING

We are not consumers; we are users [Small, 1971].

Perhaps one reason we are careless about the way in which we generate and dispose of used material is that we have thought of the earth as the source of materials we can consume. If you think about it, you will see that the earth is a relatively closed system. Any material you use will still be in the system somewhere when you are finished with it. It may be in a dump, your backyard, an incinerator, or a collection point. Therefore, we reuse goods all the time in some sense; the question is how well. We can put our used materials in a place where their practical future use is limited and their effect upon the environment is detrimental. Or we can put them where they can most easily and efficiently be used again.

Although many people use the term in a narrower sense (Geller, in press), in this chapter we will use the term *recycling* to refer to any attempt to reuse, reclaim, convert, remanufacture, or recover the resources in used goods and material. Such a definition covers many different strategies designed to reduce resource consumption, pollution, or the generation of waste. As an example, consider a few instances of what could be done with a used glass bottle. It can be returned to be refilled (reuse); it can be crushed into cullet and melted down to make more glass (remanufacture); it can be crushed and used as a base for a road (conversion or reclamation); or it can be cut and made into a drinking glass (conversion or reclamation).

In this chapter we will consider all of these types of approaches. We will examine the problem of waste and the factors that restrict the recycling of goods. Methods to reduce waste or to recover the resources in waste will also be described, including those projects using physical technology, behavioral technology, or both.

THE PROBLEM OF WASTE: WHY RECYCLE?

The number of materials we now know how to recycle efficiently is very large. It includes oil, glass, metals of nearly every variety, paper, plastics of certain types, sewage, and vegetable material. When the term *recycling* is used broadly, as it is in this chapter, virtually every form of goods we consume can be said to be effectively recyclable.

Recycling can have an enormous effect upon our resources, upon pollution, and upon the management of waste. As a general example, consider the case of paper recycling. It is the most salient form of recycling to most consumers (with the possible exception of glass bottles and aluminum cans), and it is the most studied by far from a psychological point of view. Although the specific costs and benefits of paper recycling may not fit every form of recycling, it does seem to be a representative case.

The paper industry derives its raw material from two main sources: wood and wastepaper (years ago a third source was also widely used: cotton fiber, largely from rags). Over the years paper production has increased enormously, from about 29 million tons in 1950 to 54 million tons in 1970 to a projected 91 million tons in 1985 (Franklin, Hunt, & Sharp, 1973). However, as the demand for paper *grows,* the percentage amount of production based upon wastepaper is *decreasing.* In 1970, less than 25% of the production of paper was from recycled sources, while during World War II the recycling rate was above 36% as a national effort was marshaled to reduce waste to aid the war effort (Franklin et al., 1973). Currently, only about 15% of the paper produced is recycled (*Fourth Report to Congress,* 1977).

What these figures mean, of course, is that many millions of tons of wood will be consumed that otherwise would not have been used. Fortunately, at present our forests are still growing faster than we cut them. However, consumption of wood is not the only concern. Making paper from virgin wood versus recycled sources has complex energy, resource, pollution, and waste effects. The complexity of this environmental impact is worth a closer examination because it demonstrates the interrelationships that we must consider. The effects of recycling paper lie in the following areas (from Turner, Grace, & Pearce, 1977).

Water Consumption

Huge quantities of water are used to process paper. In making low-grade paper, recycling saves about 60% of the water used to make paper from virgin fiber. Recycling also saves water when high-grade paper is made, but the savings are less (about 15%). As will be discussed in Chapter 11, the consumption of water is an important issue in its own right, and reduction in water consumption is a significant environmental issue.

Energy Consumption

Energy consumption is one of the most important environmental concerns in the world today, as we will discuss in Chapter 10. The harvesting and trans-

porting of the raw materials used in making paper and the manufacturing processes involved consume large amounts of energy. In order to make 1000 tons of
high-grade paper from virgin fiber, for example, you need to consume some 23
billion BTUs (British thermal units). Making paper from recycled sources saves
up to 70% of this energy.

Air Pollution

In addition to consuming energy, of course, all of this activity generates air
pollution from the trucks, power plants, paper plants, and other machinery involved. Recycling reduces the resultant air pollution by 60% to 73%.

Solid Wastes from the Manufacturing Process

The effects here depend upon the type of paper being made. Because of the
higher grade of fiber and higher degree of "brightness" required for high-grade
paper, less recycled material can be easily used. Compared to virgin paper, the
amount of solid waste generated by recycling is much less (about 39% less) when
low-grade paper is being manufactured but is much more (over twice as much)
when high-grade paper is made.

Water Pollution

The amount of water pollution also depends upon the type of paper being
made. In the case of low-grade paper, recycled materials generate less water
pollution. However, for high-grade paper the situation is reversed. The ink-
removal process used in making high-grade paper from wastepaper is extremely
polluting, generating several times as much water pollution as making the same
paper from virgin fiber. It is a mistake to think of recycling in all its forms as
cost-free.

Waste Management

Because recycled paper is taken from the waste-disposal stream, it has the
added benefit of reducing the amount and cost of waste disposal, already one of
the largest items in the average municipal budget. Since the average American
generates an estimated *ton* of solid waste each year (Zikmund & Stanton, 1972),
any savings in this area are important indeed in reducing the environmental
destruction from landfill, ocean dumping, and the like and in reducing the cost of
waste disposal to the taxpayers.

In the current state of physical waste-disposal technology, anything that
increases the production of solid waste has a number of environmental effects.
Solid-waste disposal in "sanitary" landfills, for example, may result in ground-

water contamination from "leachate" (Shuster, 1976) and in dangerous (albeit potentially beneficial and recoverable) production of methane gas (Collins, 1976; Pacey, 1976). Open dumps, still quite popular as a method of waste disposal (Subcommittee on Transportation and Commerce, 1976), may also contaminate ground water and present the additional hazards of air pollution, direct poisoning, an increase in rodents, the spread of disease, and contamination of the food chain (Subcommittee on Transportation and Commerce, 1976). Another popular method of waste disposal, incineration, is extremely polluting if the best available technology is not used.

Miscellaneous Effects

A number of other effects can be pointed out. Recycling may lead to less litter, for example. Logging practices have many environmental drawbacks of their own, such as land erosion, aesthetic damage, and water pollution. Therefore, recycling may reduce this damage. However, since much of the wood for paper manufacture comes as a by-product of logging for lumber (for example, the short pieces of wood are used that are not suitable for making lumber but are left over from the logging), increased use of recycled sources may lead to more aesthetic deterioration of areas that have been logged because more material would be left behind. Conversely, the left-behind material might reduce land erosion and would be good for the forest soil.

You can certainly see that there are many issues to keep track of in determining the degree of costs and benefits from recycling paper. Overall, however, it seems clear that recycling paper is a desirable environmental goal and could easily be made even more beneficial (for example, by eliminating needless brightness standards for paper products). As with other materials that can be recycled (we are using paper only as a specific example of a more general phenomenon), the benefits of paper recycling can be organized into three major areas: decreased consumption of resources, decreased environmental pollution, and decreased problems of waste management. In the current system it is possible to make some of these problems worse with recycling (for example, by removing ink from paper), a fact that should underline the importance of *demonstrating* the environmental relevance of given programs. The term *recycling* should not be taken to denote a process that is, a priori, always and everywhere environmentally desirable.

THE FACTORS INHIBITING RECYCLING

If recycling is generally desirable, it seems surprising at first that more material is not recycled. What prevents us as a society from doing the apparently sensible thing? This section examines the limits upon recycling, which occur in several categories. (See Bidwell, 1977, for a parallel discussion of this issue.)

Cost of the Recycled Product

In some cases it may actually cost more to recycle goods than to make them from scratch. This depressing economic fact of life stems from several sources. First, sometimes the development of needed physical technology for the processing of materials to be recycled is less advanced than that in the raw-material area. In part, this is due to the greater experience with virgin materials in manufacturing—an example of the vicious circle of the status quo. The development of physical technology of relevance to recycling sometimes lowers costs and increases the availability and practicality of recycled materials. For example, when better processes of making steel were developed, they worked against the use of scrap steel because fewer impurities could be allowed in a furnace charge than with the older, open-hearth furnaces. Then, around 1960, a shredder was developed that could chop automobiles, a major source of ferrous scrap, into little pieces, so that more of the impurities (plastic, rubber, and so on) could be removed. As a result, the use of scrap is once again on the rise in the steel industry (Bower, 1977).

A second problem is that the collection of recycled goods is often difficult or expensive. There are two basic ways in which most recyclable goods can be collected and placed back into the stream of available resources: materials can be segregated by the user (at the point of consumption or at a collection center), or they can be collected in aggregate form and subsequently separated into usable units by a machine. In other words, the collection and separation of recyclable goods involve either primarily behavioral or primarily physical technology. We will have much more to say on this later, but the point is raised here because both types of technology are often inefficient, poorly developed, or expensive.

A third and most important factor in the price of recycled goods is the complex economic and political realities that actually tend to subsidize environmentally undesirable manufacturing processes (Subcommittee on Transportation and Commerce, 1976). The way in which this can occur is instructive, so we will examine it in some detail.

Consider this fact: it costs an estimated $30 per ton to collect and dispose of solid waste in large cities in the United States (*Fourth Report to Congress,* 1977). At that rate the yearly cost to American taxpayers for the collection and disposal of wastepaper alone is well over $1 billion! Note that most of this money is not paid by paper manufacturers or even paper users, but by the general taxpayer. Put more generally, the true "environmental cost" of products is frequently, indeed typically, passed on from business to taxpayers. Of course, this means that a firm that decides to manufacture products from recycled material is often at a disadvantage because part of the environmental cost must then be borne by the firm. If a recycling firm, for example, collects the needed waste, it is paying part of the environmental cost (that is, disposal) of that product that would normally be paid by government. The fundamentally regressive nature of this system has often been noted, and solutions have been proposed, from putting a tax on virgin materials (Page, 1977) to putting a pollution tax on products that reflects the expense they will create for the society and the environment (Bingham, 1977; *Fourth Report to Congress,* 1977; F. L. Smith, 1977) to giving tax breaks or other incentives to recycling firms (Bidwell, 1977).

Box 8–1. Cars in Sweden: Doing Away with the No-Deposit/No-Return Mentality

A number of steps have been taken around the world to shift the economic burden of waste disposal away from the general taxpayer and place it upon the manufacturer or user of the particular products. For example, in Sweden all cars have a hefty disposal tax levied upon them. But rather than simply using this money to pay for government disposal efforts, Sweden has done something far more clever. Each year all car owners pay a car tax, whether or not the car is running. Thus, there is a cost to merely owning a car. In order to stop paying this tax, the owner must deregister the car—that is, take it off the roll of cars in the country. But the owner cannot deregister the car until an authorized scrap yard issues a certificate showing that the car has been received for scrapping. In a particularly creative use of incentives, the law provides that car owners who deregister their cars will receive a substantial cash payment. This payment is funded by the disposal tax levied when a car is purchased. Thus, the car buyer, not the general public, pays for what amounts to a return-deposit system on cars (from Bidwell, 1977). Imagine how different some of our blighted areas would look under this system. The front yards of some rural people in Appalachia would become veritable gold mines.

There are a host of other ways in which the apparent cost of recycled goods relative to virgin goods is increased. Tax breaks often openly favor virgin materials. These breaks include depletion allowances, capital-gains treatment, and foreign-tax allowances (Subcommittee on Transportation and Commerce, 1976). Together, they may make it cheaper to risk a loss on, say, a large tract of timber than to buy recycled paper. The wide fluctuations in price, which have been the bugaboo of secondary-materials firms, may make the small recycling firms charge more to build a reserve against lean times (several of the chapters in Pearce & Walter, 1977, contain excellent discussions of this issue). Allowing firms to own companies that are involved in each step of the production of a product, from raw materials to transportation to final manufacture, may also encourage these firms to use virgin materials. Given a close economic decision, it may be better to "buy from oneself" (make a profit each step of the way) than to buy secondary materials. Unfortunately, few firms have integrated recycling companies into their vertical structure because of the economic and tax realities.

Quality of the Recycled Product

Although most recycled products are functionally equivalent to the same product made from virgin material, there are many regulations and standards that are prejudicial to recycled material. For example, there are standards for the brightness of paper stock, even for such uses as paper towels. Although paper towels are just as good if they are brown or tan rather than white, brightness standards may prevent the use of much recycled furnish in the production of paper (Bower, 1977). Similarly, the use of recycled glass may result in a product that is not quite as clear as virgin glass. For some uses this lack of clarity may be functionally detrimental, but in most cases it is solely an aesthetic issue. France has dealt with this problem in an interesting manner. For example, the country prohibits advertising that points out the absence of recovered materials in products (such as "made of virgin cotton"). Also prohibited are standards that discriminate against recycled material, such as the Woolmark standards that prohibit the use of recycled wool (Bidwell, 1977).

Wastefulness in Manufacturing or Packaging

It is one thing to buy a bottled soft drink on which a deposit is paid, thus increasing the likelihood of return; it is another to take a nonreturnable bottle to a glass-recycling center with no or very little monetary payoff. Wastefulness can be influenced at the source (before goods enter the waste stream) by (1) increasing the use of returnable goods or easily reusable goods, (2) decreasing the resource intensiveness of goods (for example, encouraging the manufacture of smaller automobiles), (3) increasing the durability of goods, and (4) decreasing the overall consumption of goods (Subcommittee on Transportation and Commerce, 1976). Each of these measures would reduce the stream of waste before it needs to be recycled in more difficult ways. It has been estimated that the United States could save 1174 trillion BTUs each year by simply eliminating unnecessary packaging and using only returnable beverage containers. This value reflects the equivalent of 555,000 barrels of oil per day (Subcommittee on Transportation and Commerce, 1976).

METHODS OF WASTE REDUCTION AND RESOURCE RECOVERY

Efforts to increase recycling fall into at least two major categories, with further subdivisions in each. One category is that of waste reduction, which means reducing waste at the source, before it enters the stream of solid waste. The second major category consists of the recovery of resources from postconsumer waste.

Waste Reduction

Waste-reduction methods are designed to decrease the amount of solid waste that is produced in the first place. Several states have already passed beverage-container legislation, and a few have enacted packaging laws. Further, several behavioral-research projects have identified ways to increase consumers' selection of low-waste products.

Oregon's bottle law. Probably the most famous effort at waste reduction to date is Oregon's bottle bill. Passed in 1971 and since imitated in several states (for example, Vermont, Maine, Michigan, South Dakota) as well as in all federal agencies, this law requires beverage containers to have a minimum refund value (5¢ for most bottles) and outlaws pop-top cans (McEwen, 1977). A number of papers (for example, Claussen, 1973; Gudger & Bailes, 1973; Waggoner, 1974, 1976) have evaluated the impact of the bill on litter, price, energy consumption, and other dimensions. (See Geller, in press, for a summary.)

The results of these studies seem to show, first, a significant reduction in beverage-container litter. It has long been known that returnable bottles are not improperly disposed of as often as nonreturnables. Moreover, as children have long shown with their bottle hunts, returnable bottles are rapidly picked up from indigenous litter (see, for example, Clark, Burgess, & Hendee, 1972; Finnie, 1973). The estimated effects of the bottle bills range as high as a 65% reduction in beverage-container litter (*Fourth Report to Congress,* 1977; J. H. Skinner, 1977a). Second, bottles are reused many times (Loube, 1976). In other words, the containers are not only returned but are returned in a condition that permits their refill, up to as many as 19 times by design (Hunt & Franklin, 1974), with reported average refills as high as 27 (*Fourth Report to Congress,* 1977). Finally, since containers are being returned and refilled, bottlers have been buying significantly fewer containers. This reduction in container purchases has an important effect on the amount of energy consumed—about 60% less than one-way containers (Hunt & Franklin, 1974; Hunt, Welch, Cross, & Woodall, 1974)—and the amount of solid waste generated (Waggoner, 1974, 1976).

There have been negative effects produced by the law (J. H. Skinner, 1977a), but most of these seem temporary and somewhat inconsistent with national trends. For example, the price of beverages increased in the year following the implementation of these laws (from 20¢ to 60¢ per case of beverage, according to Loube, 1976). Presumably, this rise in price is due to the increased handling and storage problems associated with returnables (Loube, 1976). However, given the controversial nature of the laws, bottlers may have overestimated and overreacted to the possible impact of the laws. A recent survey in the Washington, D.C., area, for example (Peterson, 1976), showed that consumers could *save* an average of 26¢ per six-pack by purchasing beverages in returnable containers. Further, when the true environmental costs of various container options are considered comprehensively (including, for example, the hidden cost of disposal), there can be little doubt that returnable bottles are "definitely cheaper for consumers" (Peterson, 1976) and definitely less destructive to the environment (Hunt & Franklin, 1974; Hunt et al., 1974). Nevertheless, bottle-bill legislation has been the subject of vehement industry (for example, King, 1977) and labor (for example, McGlotten, 1977) opposition. The implementation of bottle-bill legislation will clearly be slow and subject to setbacks (*Fourth Report to Congress,* 1977; Ruvin, 1977), despite the large benefits to be gained, especially if implemented nationally (*Fourth Report to Congress,* 1977).

The Minnesota packaging law. A related legal development is the 1973 Minnesota packaging law, which gives the state the right to review the nature of product packaging and to act to reduce the number of overpackaged products by prohibiting their sale. Challenged by a group of packaging manufacturers and others as vague, burdensome, and unconstitutional, the law has been tied up in court from the outset. However, a 1976 lower court decision upheld the law (*Fourth Report to Congress,* 1977). It is currently being appealed. The literature on the law (for example, Wendt, 1975) is still sparse, but it may provide a model for the control of solid-waste generation in this important area.

Increasing the voluntary purchase of returnable containers. It would seem, in light of the economic facts (Peterson, 1976), that consumers would highly prefer returnable containers. These containers are not always widely available, however, particularly with some products (such as beer; see Peterson, 1976). Also, there once again seems to be a short-term versus long-term contingency problem here (see Chapter 1). Consumers who purchase beverages in returnable containers pay a deposit on these containers. This has the effect of making the returnables more expensive in the short term, until the bottles are brought back and the deposit refunded—a fact that industry has used to fight bottle bills (Ruvin, 1977). Further, the bottles have to be saved and carried back to the store. In this day of throwaway lighters, throwaway shavers, throwaway pens, and so on, consumers may not be happy with this small increase in work on their part. Unfortunately, little has been done to measure consumer reaction in this area systematically (Geller, in press).

Although some states have begun to deal with the generation of solid waste at the source through legislation, an immediate reduction in waste might be produced by increasing the voluntary purchase of returnable containers, underpackaged goods, and easily reusable products (such as products in jars that can be reused for storing other things or as drinking glasses). Several studies have attempted to do just that (see Geller, in press, for a good parallel review of this material).

Geller and his students have conducted a series of pioneering projects in this area. In one of the first behavioral studies addressed to environmental issues, Geller, Wylie, and Farris (1971) studied the effects of prompting on the purchase of returnable bottles in three markets. Observers posted at the check-out counters recorded the percentage of consumers who purchased more returnable than non-returnable bottles (given that both were available in the store for that product). After this initial baseline period, consumers entering the store were handed a flier that said such things as *"Buy returnable soft-drink bottles. Save money.* Considering deposits, returnable bottles are 10% cheaper per carton. *Fight pollution. . . ."* If consumers in fact did buy the majority of their drinks in returnables, the observer said to them as they checked out, "Thank you for your help in fighting pollution by buying your drinks in returnable bottles." The intervention was used for one hour each day for a week, and then follow-up data were collected periodically over the next six weeks.

The procedure was shown to have an effect in a small convenience store but not in the two large supermarkets. In the convenience store there was a 32% increase in returnable-bottle customers during the intervention period compared to the preceding baseline period. During follow-up the returnable-bottle customers decreased once again.

There are several possible reasons that the large stores did not show the same effect. First, the measure used (a dichotomous categorization of consumers into returnable-bottle or nonreturnable-bottle types) is probably more easily influenced when only a few bottles are being purchased, as would likely be the case in a convenience store. A more sensitive measure might have been used, such as the average percentage of returnable bottles out of the total number of bottles purchased. Second, in a large store, consumers may have plenty of time to forget the prompt (in the process of doing considerable shopping) as compared to the quick in-and-out of a convenience store (Geller et al., 1971). Finally, since the large stores had sales on soft drinks and the small one did not, it is possible that the effects of sales were too strong and that prompting will only have an effect on buying returnables given the economic equivalence of the alternatives, an explanation now favored by Geller himself (Geller, in press).

Unfortunately, a program such as that just described would also create a good deal of litter in the store. To Geller's credit, this observation led him to conduct a series of litter-control studies in grocery-store settings (previously reviewed in Chapter 5). It is conceivable that a prompting program could be set up using signs and comments from the check-out clerk (rather than fliers) to minimize any undesirable side effects in the form of litter.

Geller, Farris, and Post (1973) conducted a follow-up study at the same convenience (7-Eleven) store used in the first study. Over a month-long period six different conditions were tried out (for two hours each) in a semirandom order (in what is technically known as a Latin-square design). The six conditions were a baseline condition, a prompting procedure similar to that used in the first study, and four variations of a prompting-plus-feedback condition. In the last four conditions, consumers entering the store were given a flier asking them to buy drinks in returnable bottles. In addition, a large "pollution chart" was placed near the exit from the store, and a student recorded whether a given consumer was a returnable-bottle consumer or a nonreturnable-bottle consumer (that is, whether the majority of the bottles purchased by the consumer were returnable or not). In the four conditions the number and sex of the persons handing out the fliers and posting the results on the pollution chart were varied. The results showed that all five prompting or prompting-plus-feedback conditions had significant effects on the percentage of returnable-bottle customers, but no difference was shown among the five conditions. On the average a 22% increase in returnable-bottle consumers was recorded in the treatment conditions as compared to baseline.

In some ways it is surprising that the baseline behavior differed, since customer interviews showed that most of the 7-Eleven customers shopped there often. Many customers in the baseline phases had presumably experienced one or more of the treatment conditions. Geller and his colleagues saw this as an indication that prompts have only temporary effects, a finding in line with much of the literature in the area, as you already know from preceding chapters.

These results point to the possibility of a significant effect on consumer purchasing patterns through prompting. However, we would need to examine more closely the influence of these prompts under conditions that more nearly approximate the actual form such a program might take. Clearly, it is not practical to have an employee do nothing but pass out fliers. It may be, however, that large signs would influence the purchase of returnables in much the same manner. If so, a very inexpensive program could have a significant effect on purchasing patterns. Such a program is outlined in the projects section at the end of this chapter.

The Red Owl program.   Another approach to the reduction of solid waste was attempted by the Red Owl food stores, a Midwestern chain of 130 supermarkets. In this program, customers were paid small rebates for the use of used packaging materials. For example, a customer could bring in an egg carton, fill it with eggs, and receive a 3¢ refund. Other products on which refunds were paid included grocery bags and refillable milk containers. In a particularly creative twist, the consumers were given their refunds in cash after the clerk rang up the purchases instead of simply deducting the refund from the tape total.

The Red Owl program was evaluated in an eight-week market test (Greene, 1977) in about 10% of its stores. The program received a good deal of free publicity due to media interest and was accompanied by a large-scale advertising effort to acquaint consumers with the program. The results seemed to show that there was only a small increase in overall sales but that most consumers and store managers liked the program. The biggest appeal to the consumer was the economic aspect of the program. Several factors seemed to influence the success of the program in individual stores, ranging from in-store prompts to the enthusiasm shown by store employees toward the program.

Other avenues.   There are several other avenues available for waste reduction for which little or no new physical technology is needed (*Fourth Report to*

Congress, 1977). First, waste reduction can be achieved by developing and using products that require less material. A good example is the promotion and purchase of smaller cars. Over the past several years the average weight of automobiles sold in the United States has dropped significantly and will drop even further as a result of gas-mileage legislation passed by Congress (*Fourth Report to Congress,* 1977). Waste reduction can also result from developing and using products that have a longer lifetime and are more readily and cheaply repairable. One good example is the automobile tire. As the lifetime of tires increases to 40,000 miles and eventually as high as 100,000 miles, corresponding savings would be experienced in solid-waste generation (Westerman, 1977). Legislation or programs that influence voluntary consumer decisions in this area could result in important environmental gains. Finally, another area of waste reduction is the substitution of reusable products for disposable ones. Bottles are only one example. Another hopeful sign of what could be done is the greatly increased demand for reusable home-canning jars (Sadd, 1977).

Waste reduction: What can be done?   The current state of behavioral technology in the waste-reduction area is clearly poor. With the exception of legislative avenues, about which we know little from a scientific point of view, psychologists and other behavioral scientists can point to few successes resulting from the systematic modification of human behavior as it influences the generation of waste. (The successful litter studies reviewed in Chapter 5 did not influence waste generation—only the location of waste.)

There are areas that might be usefully explored, however. To date, behaviorally oriented efforts have emphasized antecedent controls, such as the fliers used by Geller and his colleagues (1971, 1973). Although this is a very promising area, stronger effects could be expected from manipulation of the consequences of reducing waste. Actually, natural economic forces may be acting toward that end. The energy crisis has led to the purchase of smaller cars, beverages in returnable bottles are cheaper, and so on. The problem in many of these areas is that the current system cannot be easily changed by legislation due to the disruptive effect on industry and labor (see, for example, King, 1977; Sadd, 1977; Taylor, 1977) and the resulting power wielded against such changes (Ruvin, 1977). Even more important, perhaps, the economic benefit of waste reduction is diffuse, uncertain, or felt only in the long term. To take a simple example, beverages in returnable bottles cost more at the point of purchase than do nonreturnables. Never mind that the total cost, after deposit refund, is less. The most important psychological fact is that the immediate, certain cost of returnables argues against their purchase. Instead of requiring deposits on *all* containers (desirable but politically difficult), another program might put a tax on nonreturnables such that, *counting* the deposit, the costs of returnables and nonreturnables would be equivalent (in effect, the returnables would then obviously be cheaper). Since industry and labor would probably oppose this tax, one solution would be to use this tax in ways of benefit to consumers, industry, and labor, such as supporting industry recycling efforts. A psychological approach may yet add to the development of such incentive systems (*Fourth Report to Congress,* 1977) despite the current lack of use of psychological knowledge in the area (Geller, in press).

An alternative to waste reduction is to recover the large amount of waste we produce. Several innovative approaches have been developed, and to these we now turn.

Resource Recovery

The term *resource recovery* refers to the salvage of materials from the postconsumer solid-waste stream and the channeling of those materials into useful areas. There are two basic strategies available for resource-recovery efforts: source separation and centralized treatment of mixed waste, or what has been referred to as low-technology and high-technology solutions, respectively (Geller, in press). Another way to characterize the two approaches is that source separation uses primarily behavioral technology, while mixed-waste resource recovery relies primarily on physical technology.

The treatment of mixed waste. Resource recovery from mixed waste is just now beginning to become a technical possibility. Through a variety of innovative programs, several hopeful avenues seem to be open. However, as the government has pointed out (*Fourth Report to Congress,* 1977), these efforts at best will be handling only 10% of the nation's solid-waste stream by 1985. If current difficulties continue, they may handle far less.

There are two basic efforts being advanced in mixed-waste processing: the recovery of energy and the recovery of raw materials such as glass and metal. The energy content of solid waste is enormous. In 1971 some 125 million tons of solid waste were discarded with no attempt to recover the energy it contained. By 1980 this figure will be 175 million tons; by 1990 it will be 225 million tons. Each ton has about 9 million BTUs of energy. Together, the solid waste we generate each year has a heat value of 1575 trillion BTUs (based on 1980 values), a value that represents about 258 million barrels of oil a year (Government Accounting Office, 1979; Levy, 1974; Lowe, 1974).

In addition to the energy content, much of our solid waste is recoverable material. Several systems have been developed to separate glass and metal (the major forms of inorganic waste) and other materials automatically from mixed-waste sources. In a typical system this involves shredding the waste into small pieces, which may be sorted for size and weight, the use of electromagnets to acquire the ferrous metal, and the use of flotation tanks or other devices to separate the glass, aluminum, and other waste materials (see, for example, *Fourth Report to Congress,* 1977; Levy, 1975; Sussman, 1975). However, all of these systems are either not yet fully developed or are developed but not widely implemented. As an EPA report to Congress has stated:

Virtually all of the wastepaper, aluminum cans, and glass containers currently recovered from postconsumer wastes are separated at the source and routed via community collection centers or scrap dealers to industrial processors. Numerous communities are now separating ferrous metal from mixed waste by magnetic separation, but the quantities processed have thus far amounted to a very small percentage of the ferrous metal available in the U.S. mixed waste stream [*Fourth Report to Congress,* 1977, p. 51].

The energy in solid waste can be acquired by several techniques. First, it can be burned to produce steam. With the availability of modern pollution controls, the burning of solid waste has become environmentally practical. The heat produced by burning the processed solid waste directly can be used to produce steam for a "steam-district" distribution system to heat buildings. This is an advantage because lower-temperature, lower-pressure steam can be used in such systems. Higher-temperature steam can also be produced, however, and can be used in factories or electricity generators to drive turbines or other machines (Levy, 1974; Lingle & Holloway, 1977).

Second, the solid waste can be reprocessed into a conventional fuel. A number of techniques have been developed to acquire gaseous or liquid fuel from solid waste. For example, demonstration plants in Baltimore and San Diego County are using the process of pyrolysis (the thermally produced decomposition of organic material in an oxygen-free atmosphere) to process waste. The plant in San Diego County yields a product similar to fuel oil that can be burned in electricity generators that have had minor modifications made on them (Levy, 1975). Another promising approach is to recover methane from the anaerobic degeneration of solid waste, either in landfills or in specially designed facilities (Collins, 1976; *Fourth Report to Congress,* 1977; Lowe, 1974).

The main disadvantages of mixed-waste processing are threefold. First, as has already been mentioned, current technology does not yet have all the answers to the automatic separation of valuable materials from mixed waste. Second, although some forms of energy generation from solid waste have been well tested in Europe and Japan (such as water-wall incinerators), few economically feasible efforts have been proved in the United States. Simply put, mixed-waste processing is currently expensive and unreliable, probably because U.S. efforts have emphasized huge plants, processing 2000 to 8000 tons of solid waste per day, and have used more exotic technology. Some of this technology has been used to produce "superheated" steam, such as that needed for electricity generation, rather than the lower-temperature, lower-pressure steam useful for direct production of heat. Of the current EPA-supported projects for processing mixed waste, virtually all of them are well over their original budgets (*Fourth Report to Congress,* 1977). For example, the Baltimore pyrolysis project has had cost overruns of more than $11 million, and it now appears that the plant will never be fully operational. In fact, the major contractor, Monsanto, at first recommended that it be shut down, this *after* the expenditure of $27 million (*Fourth Report to*

Congress, 1977). The project is currently operating at a greatly reduced load despite the very high cost per ton this incurs. Another example of the high-cost, high-technology approach to mixed-waste processing is a gigantic facility in St. Louis whose planned cost (a figure very likely to increase if and when the project begins) is more than $70 million (McEwen, 1977)! The third problem is that many of these plants are polluting, less energy efficient than waste reduction at the source, subject to marketplace fluctuations, and hurt by successful source-separation efforts (Geller, in press). For example, if wastepaper recycling increases greatly, the heat value of municipal waste will drop, perhaps by as much as 10% (Lowe, 1974; J. H. Skinner, 1977b). This drop may seem small, but it may be enough to affect significantly the economic practicality of energy-from-waste efforts.

Source separation. Mixed-waste processing may someday be feasible and widely practiced, but there is another alternative:

> Although efforts to devise and build automatic machines capable of extracting usable products, one by one, from mixed waste collections should continue to be encouraged, the same objective could be accomplished by research into methods of motivating the producer and discarder of wastes . . . to deposit them, in a clean condition, into a number of separate containers reserved for tin cans, aluminum cans, paper and cardboard, glass, garbage and garden debris, non-ferrous metals, plastics, and non-burnable, nondisposable items such as ashes [Melvin First, as quoted by Small, 1971, p. 107].

In source-separation systems it is the user who divides the waste into recyclable and nonrecyclable categories. The number of categories into which waste is divided depends on how comprehensive the program is, but a practical program may separate waste into at least four categories: metal, glass, paper, and mixed waste. Dividing trash into these categories would take a household only a few minutes per week and would cost very little.

After the waste is divided into categories, one of three things can happen: (1) the user can deliver the waste to a central recycling area. This is perhaps the type of program most people think of when they think of recycling. Unfortunately, these programs are almost always small, if well-meaning, efforts by local ecology groups and the like. It is certainly fair to say that their impact to date has been slight. Further, a logical extension of data reported later in this chapter would make the likelihood of success seem dim. It has been shown that apartment dwellers often will not deliver newspaper to a central location in an apartment complex. So why would people drive to even more remote locations to deliver glass, metal, and paper? (2) The recyclable and nonrecyclable waste can be picked up separately. In such a program separate systems are set up for the collection of mixed waste and recyclable material. This procedure has some advantages. For example, small trucks or even handcarts arranged into a local network can readily collect the recyclables (see Duncan, 1976) and leave the messy business of mixed-waste collection to the regular trash collectors. But there are also possible disadvantages to such a dual-collection system. First, it may waste energy, since two vehicles are involved rather than one. Second, since householders may have to remember two different days to put their trash out, the likelihood of compliance with the program may drop. Successful programs of this type have been established, however, and will be described shortly. (3) All trash can be picked up at the same time and placed into vehicles designed for segregated collections. This tactic has the advantages of lower transportation costs and higher probable compliance. It has the disadvantage of requiring at least cooperation from government (Duncan, 1976).

A number of community-wide programs have been attempted (see Geller, in press, for a review). For example, an EPA-sponsored source-separation effort is underway in Somerville and Marblehead, Massachusetts (Resource Planning Associates, 1976). In this project the city collects trash, which the residential user has divided into recyclable categories. The categories to date are clear (not colored) glass, flat paper, cans, and mixed waste. The program has been heavily promoted by a coordinated educational effort. Significantly, compliance with the program has been mandatory, and there are provisions for fining violators. To ensure a stable and fair market for the collected goods, a long-term contract was signed with a local recycling firm that guaranteed a floor price for the materials. In addition, scavenger-prohibition laws were passed so that the recyclable goods placed at curbside could be collected only by authorized persons.

This program is still too new to have produced much, but early data suggest a high degree of compliance (increasing as time goes on) and a large decrease in the amount of mixed waste deposited in landfills. Unfortunately, the design of the project is such that a clear experimental demonstration of its value is unlikely. In this the Somerville/Marblehead program is not unlike most other community programs. Indeed, the great majority of the literature in the area is promotional in nature. Further, in marked contrast to the results found through experimentation in the area of litter control and energy consumption (Chapters 5 and 10, respectively), most of these programs have heavily emphasized education of the public (Hansen, 1975). Unfortunately, since most of the community-wide source-separation efforts have set up programs without experimentally evaluating the elements needed for success, it is not at all clear which components of the existing programs are needed or beneficial.

A very exciting approach to resource recovery is the ORE (so called because of its development in Portland, Oregon) recycling plan (Duncan, 1976). Under this system individual households and businesses contract with a private firm (Cloudburst Recycling, Inc.) for trash collection. The fee (about $5 per month) is lower than that of competing trash-collection services in part because of the recovery of materials. Consumers must sort their trash into six categories: glass, steel cans, aluminum cans, paper, kitchen scraps, and mixed waste (see Figure 8–1). There are plans also to pick up refundable beverage containers (crediting some of the refund to the customer's account). Small trucks or electric carts collect the waste in weekly neighborhood runs. The loads are then taken to local centers. The plan is to connect these centers into city-wide and ultimately regional networks. In fact, Seattle has recently contracted for an 18-month test

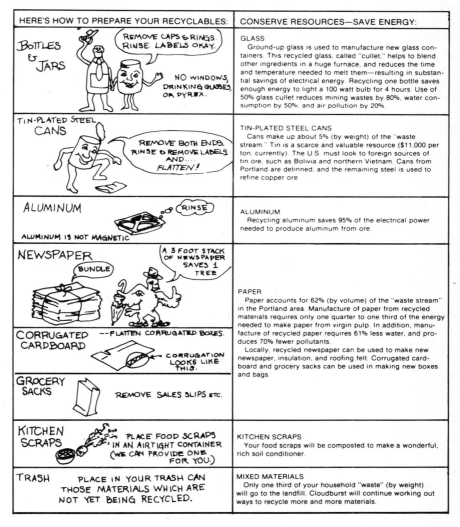

HERE'S HOW TO PREPARE YOUR RECYCLABLES:	CONSERVE RESOURCES—SAVE ENERGY:
BOTTLES & JARS — REMOVE CAPS & RINGS. RINSE. LABELS OKAY. NO WINDOWS, DRINKING GLASSES, OR PYREX.	**GLASS** Ground-up glass is used to manufacture new glass containers. This recycled glass, called "cullet," helps to blend other ingredients in a huge furnace, and reduces the time and temperature needed to melt them—resulting in substantial savings of electrical energy. Recycling one bottle saves enough energy to light a 100 watt bulb for 4 hours. Use of 50% glass cullet reduces mining wastes by 80%, water consumption by 50%, and air pollution by 20%.
TIN-PLATED STEEL CANS — REMOVE BOTH ENDS. RINSE & REMOVE LABELS AND.... FLATTEN!	**TIN-PLATED STEEL CANS** Cans make up about 5% (by weight) of the "waste stream." Tin is a scarce and valuable resource ($11,000 per ton, currently). The U.S. must look to foreign sources of tin ore, such as Bolivia and northern Vietnam. Cans from Portland are detinned, and the remaining steel is used to refine copper ore.
ALUMINUM — RINSE. ALUMINUM IS NOT MAGNETIC.	**ALUMINUM** Recycling aluminum saves 95% of the electrical power needed to produce aluminum from ore.
NEWSPAPER BUNDLE — A 3 FOOT STACK OF NEWSPAPER SAVES 1 TREE. CORRUGATED CARDBOARD — FLATTEN CORRUGATED BOXES. CORRUGATION LOOKS LIKE THIS. GROCERY SACKS — REMOVE SALES SLIPS ETC.	**PAPER** Paper accounts for 62% (by volume) of the "waste stream" in the Portland area. Manufacture of paper from recycled materials requires only one quarter to one third of the energy needed to make paper from virgin pulp. In addition, manufacture of recycled paper requires 61% less water, and produces 70% fewer pollutants. Locally, recycled newspaper can be used to make new newspaper, insulation, and roofing felt. Corrugated cardboard and grocery sacks can be used in making new boxes and bags.
KITCHEN SCRAPS — PLACE FOOD SCRAPS IN AN AIRTIGHT CONTAINER (WE CAN PROVIDE ONE FOR YOU.)	**KITCHEN SCRAPS** Your food scraps will be composted to make a wonderful, rich soil conditioner.
TRASH — PLACE IN YOUR TRASH CAN THOSE MATERIALS WHICH ARE NOT YET BEING RECYCLED.	**MIXED MATERIALS** Only one third of your household "waste" (by weight) will go to the landfill. Cloudburst will continue working out ways to recycle more and more materials.

281-8075   cloudburst   281-8075

Figure 8-1. A copy of a flier sent to homes participating in Cloudburst's ORE program. Used by permission of the Cloudburst Recycling Corporation.

operation of the plan for about 14,000 homes (Duncan, 1978). Note that this system is voluntary, profit making, decentralized, and energy efficient. Many cities would resist such a plan, since trash collection in some areas is a government monopoly.

Another approach to the problem of source separation is to look at smaller, experimental programs in which a number of variables can be examined systematically. Several studies have followed this approach in the area of wastepaper recycling. These efforts seem less oriented toward paper recycling as such than toward a sounder understanding of methods for setting up recycling systems in general.

Geller, Chaffee, and Ingram (1975) published the first such study. Interestingly, they examined the functioning of an ongoing paper-recycling campaign. For several months a campus ecological group had been collecting wastepaper from college dormitories and selling it to a wastepaper firm (for a pathetically low $5 per ton). Each dorm had a small storage room that had been designated as the paper-recycling area, and large posters were placed throughout the dorm indicating the location of the storage room and encouraging participation in the program. Note that this approach is exactly the kind of public-education approach so often touted in the informational literature on recycling.

Geller and his colleagues decided to see whether this approach was maximally effective. Six dormitories were divided into three pairs. The students in each pair received two weeks of each of three conditions: baseline, contest, and raffle (the order of the conditions was varied to control for time and sequence). The baseline condition consisted of the current system, with the exception that data recorders were in the storage rooms to weigh the paper brought in. In the contest condition each pair of dorms was divided and the two dorms pitted against each other in a contest. The dorm that delivered the most paper each week would receive a $15 prize. In the third (raffle) condition, students received a ticket to a raffle for each sheet of paper or cardboard brought in. Prizes were donated by local merchants, and drawings were held once each week.

The results showed that the contest and raffle conditions were superior to the baseline (educational) approach. During the baseline phase only about 845 pounds of paper were delivered every two weeks. In the contest phase the figure was more than 1400 pounds, and in the raffle condition more than 1500 pounds of paper were recovered.

One possible criticism of this study is that the educational program did not work because contact with the program was limited (through posters placed in the dormitory halls). It may be that the students would have contributed more if they had all known that such a program was taking place. Witmer and Geller (1976) controlled for this possible variable by replicating the earlier study, but this time with fliers distributed to each dormitory room. In the prompt-only condition a flier was distributed once each week to every room. This may have been a fairer test of the educational approach to increasing recycling, since some degree of contact with the program and its importance was ensured for each resident. The raffle and contest conditions were each also promoted with a flier and were similar to the corresponding conditions used in the 1975 study by Geller and his associates except that raffle tickets were given for each pound of paper delivered rather than for each piece. As Geller (in press) noted later, the piece contingency "resulted in some residents undermining the system by stacking their paper outside of the door to the collection room and then repeatedly delivering individual sheets of paper to the data recorder, receiving a raffle ticket for each delivery." The pound contingency avoided this problem. As we saw in our discussion of litter (Chapter 5), people will subvert programs if the contingencies are not properly designed.

The Witmer and Geller study used an *ABA* design in which the students in three pairs of dormitories (not the same ones used in the earlier research) received three weeks of the prompting, raffle, or contest conditions, preceded and followed by baseline phases of two and three weeks, respectively.

The results closely paralleled those of the earlier study. Prompting alone did not result in large increases in the number of pounds of paper collected. About 50 pounds of paper were recovered per week during the prompting phase, only slightly more than during the baseline phase. The raffle and contest conditions, however, led to large weekly increases, up to about 550 pounds in the contest phase and 820 pounds in the raffle phase. Note that even with frequent and individualized prompting, little effect was obtained with prompting alone. This finding has grave implications for public programs that rely upon educational programs to ensure compliance with recycling efforts.

Ingram and Geller (1975) conducted a third study replicating the others and again examining the possible effects of an antecedent-based (education) program, as opposed to reinforcer-based efforts. This study used a prompting condition and a raffle condition very similar to that used by Witmer and Geller. In addition, a condition was included in which the experimenters personally delivered the fliers to the dormitory students and personally invited the students' participation. The students living in four dormitories were used as subjects. The results were very similar to those of the earlier studies. Prompting had only a small effect, and there was little difference between the two types of prompting. The raffle condition had the greatest effect.

Couch, Garber, and Karpus (1978) examined a similar raffle-based program in two college dormitories. In this study the amount of paper needed to earn a raffle ticket increased as the study went on. The number of pounds of paper collected remained fairly high, indicating that project organizers might use this device to influence the cost effectiveness of their programs.

Together, these results seem to support the view that antecedent-based programs, in the absence of significant consequences for participation, have little effect on recycling. Consequence-based programs, however, have generated larger increases in recycling, at least over short periods.

Recycling might also be increased by reducing the effort required to recycle. It has already been demonstrated repeatedly throughout this book that the cost of a response strongly determines its strength. Recycling, if it is to be successful, must be an easy thing to do. This is one rationale for curbside pickups of recycled material.

Reid, Luyben, Rawers, and Bailey (1976) examined this issue experimentally in several apartment complexes. A paper-recycling program had been in force for several months in each of four target complexes. The program, sponsored by a local environmental group, included educational campaigns and the placement of a newspaper-deposit box in one of the laundry rooms in each complex. Unfortunately, participation was low.

The intervention, evaluated in a multiple-baseline design across the individual apartment complexes, consisted of a personal prompt (a door-to-door program explanation) and the placement of additional newspaper-recycling containers in the parking lots near the garbage dumpsters. In this way the residents could recycle their newspapers more easily because the containers were closer to their apartments.

This intervention led to an increase of from 50% to 100% in pounds of paper collected. Since it is unlikely that the prompt condition alone would be so effective—given the literature discussed earlier—it seems that mere proximity to the recycling container has significant effects on recycling behavior. It should be noted that Geller observed a similar phenomenon in his dormitory studies. He found that students who lived near the recycling rooms in the dormitories recycled paper significantly more often than those residents with distant rooms (Geller, in press).

In a larger and more complex follow-up study, Luyben and Bailey examined the relative contribution of container proximity plus prompts versus reinforcement plus prompts. Four mobile-home parks were used. During the baseline period one recycling container was placed near the entrance to each of the parks. In two of the parks, a proximity-plus-prompt condition was implemented in multiple-baseline fashion. As with the study by Reid and his colleagues, several additional recycling containers were distributed throughout the area, and fliers announcing the change were given to each household. In the reinforcement-plus-prompt program, park children were given toys for bringing in pounds of newspaper. This condition was tested in the two remaining parks, also in a multiple-baseline fashion. The data supported the usefulness of both approaches. Collections increased 150% over baseline in the proximity condition and about 250% over baseline in the reinforcement condition.

A problem with the reinforcement approach used in this study, however, is that the toys delivered were actually worth more than the paper collected. Although this may be acceptable in a demonstration program, it is clearly impractical in a full-scale effort. A further difficulty is that it would be easy for children to raid the residents' front porches to collect wastepaper, a problem similar to that discussed in Chapter 5.

Hamad, Cooper, and Semb (1977) and Hamad, Bettinger, Cooper, and Semb (1978) have examined the use of elementary schools as agents for wide-scale recycling operations. Their idea was that children could be induced to bring wastepaper to school and deposit the paper in a central location. This system would take advantage of the fact that schools are one of the few places where substantial numbers of people gather regularly. A successful school-based program could conceivably reach a large portion of society without any additional transportation costs.

In the 1977 study the classrooms involved were pitted against one another in a contest. Within each level (Grades 1–2, 3–4, 5–6), the classroom bringing in the most paper was awarded certificates (redeemable for hamburgers) for each student who brought in any paper. In a *BABA* design (treatment, baseline, treatment, baseline), it was shown that the group contest had a substantial impact on the amount of paper collected. The average amount of paper collected each week during the contest was about 3000 pounds in the first treatment phase and about 1500 pounds in the second. During the baseline period, children were encouraged to bring in paper, but no prizes were offered. The average weekly collection was 100 to 200 pounds during the two baseline phases. Although the somewhat similar 1978 study was less successful, the idea of using school systems to support recycling may be a good one.

Other areas.   Virtually all of the work on source separation from an experimental point of view has used wastepaper as the targeted material. However, a number of other recoverable materials might be examined. Along with the usual programs for the recovery of glass and metal, researchers might well consider such problems as abandoned cars (Dehn, 1974) and scrap tires (see Stone, Buchanan, & Steimle, 1974, for a particularly creative use of scrap tires). Many communities have the facilities for the collection and proper use of abandoned cars and other large pieces of waste material, but often it is required that their presence be reported to the authorities for collection. Hayes, Johnson, and Cone (1975) suggested that the marked-item procedure developed for litter control may be of use. It would be possible to mark a number of abandoned cars and pay a large sum of money to those reporting their existence. Since the reporting individuals would have no way of knowing that cars had been marked, such a program should produce a large increase in requests for disposal at a low overall cost. Tax incentives, such as those used in Sweden (see Box 8–1), may also be helpful.

The physical-technology approach to waste reduction and waste recovery is clearly only part of the solution to our resource-use problems. If we are to make a significant dent in the consumption of resources, it will be through the increase of environmentally protective behaviors, such as source separation of recyclable goods, and the decrease of destructive behaviors, such as purchase of wastefully packaged materials. Despite the apparent truth of this statement, it must be admitted that our knowledge about needed behavioral technology in the area is slim. This chapter is less a description of what has been done than a vision of what could be done if a behavioral solution to resource consumption were attempted.

SUMMARY

The reduction and recovery of waste is important for a number of environmental reasons, including water conservation, energy conservation, air pollution, and water pollution. At the present time recycled goods are often less competitive than virgin goods due to policies that artificially inflate the price or restrict the production of recycled goods. Waste reduction is preferable to the more difficult resource-recovery strategies but has not been well developed. Resource-recovery systems are further along and hold out some real hope for progress.

Research in the area has shown that several antecedent conditions (for example, prompts or proximity of recycling containers) can influence recycling. Systems that do not require a great deal of effort on the part of the consumer are much more likely to be successful. Governmental bodies have also had success in setting up incentive-oriented programs (for example, Oregon's bottle law). A careful use of behavioral technology could contribute in significant ways to the management of waste.

SUGGESTED PROJECT

This project will require the cooperation of a local grocery store.

1. Have one or two raters count the number of returnable and nonreturnable bottles purchased during specified times of the week.
2. Collect these data for several days, and then graph the percentage of returnable bottles purchased (if the grocery keeps a careful inventory, it could be used to supplement your ratings, since you will probably be there only several hours out of the week).
3. Select an intervention strategy. Two ideas: (a) Place a large sign in the beverage area that promotes the economic and environmental advantages of returnable bottles. (b) Give people purchasing a sufficient number and percentage of returnable bottles tickets to a raffle. Get a local merchant (perhaps the store itself) to donate the prize. Give out the tickets on a VP schedule (see Chapter 3).
4. Implement the strategy, and continue to record your data.
5. When the effects (if any) of the program are clear, stop the program, but continue to collect your data. If there are no effects, rethink the problem and try another strategy.

Chapter 9

TRANSPORTATION

Moving people and products from one place to another quickly and efficiently has become an extremely important characteristic of industrialized societies. Indeed, since productivity is greatly affected by the access of people to materials and goods, our whole standard of living is closely related to the effectiveness of our transportation system. However, the development of transportation systems brings with it serious environmental consequences as well, and scientists have recently begun looking at these more closely.

With the realization that transportation behavior can have serious environmental effects, researchers have also begun examining ways people move themselves and their possessions from one place to another. In this chapter we will take a look at some of the things that have been done to alter transportation behavior. We will see whether and how people can be induced to drive their automobiles less, how they can be coaxed into using public-transportation systems more, and how they can be encouraged to form car pools and van pools. We will also discuss the role that large corporations and governments can play in changing transportation habits.

Throughout the chapter some of the deficiencies in present research and some of the gaps in our knowledge will be mentioned. We will also discuss numerous issues related to research in this area, such as the need to study transportation providers as well as users, the need to look at patterns as well as levels of use, the value of simulation studies, and the cost effectiveness of experimental approaches evaluated thus far. Finally, this chapter will show the relevance of lessons learned from behavioral approaches to other environmental problems discussed elsewhere in this book.

THE ENERGY USED IN TRANSPORTATION

According to the Federal Energy Administration (1974), the energy used for transportation increased 100% between 1950 and 1974. Simultaneously, the relative availability of dependable sources of energy has decreased, with the result that the United States is increasingly dependent on foreign sources for the oil necessary to support its vast network of public and private transportation. The dramatic increases in the price of foreign oil are well-known, and the effects of those increases on our national balance of payments have become alarmingly clear. The result of this fiscal situation is a spiral of ever-increasing energy costs that some say threatens national bankruptcy.

The use of large quantities of fossil fuels to move people and products from place to place is the most obvious environmental effect of transportation, but it is not the only one. The building of more and more highways and parking lots also affects the environment, as does the use of valuable resources in the production of cars, buses, planes, and other vehicles. In addition, we are all only too familiar with the by-products of our transportation practices in the form of air and noise pollution.

The average U.S. family spends 18% of its income on transportation ("Gauging Prices—and Spending," 1978). In the United States as a whole, all forms of transportation account for 30% to 40% of our fuel use (Everett, 1977). Of that, approximately 25% to 30% is consumed by private automobiles (Stanford Research Institute, 1972), while the movement of persons generally accounts for about 43% of the fuel used in all transportation activities (Stuntz & Hirst, 1976).

With such a large portion of our energy-related resources at stake, it is clearly important to transport people in efficient ways. The increased use of mass-transit systems seems critical in view of Commoner's (1972) finding that such systems are from 300% to 600% more efficient than private automobiles in terms of passenger miles traveled per unit of energy expended. It is to the mass-transit studies that we turn first in this chapter.

ALTERING THE USE OF MASS-TRANSIT SYSTEMS

Various experimental approaches have been taken to increase the use of public-bus systems. These can generally be categorized as informal efforts by transit authorities, on the one hand, and more formal behavioral studies, on the other.

Informal Studies

If you were given the responsibility of attracting more users to a public-bus system, what approach do you think you would take? You might assume that a lot of people do not use buses because they are unfamiliar with them. They are not sure when they travel, where their routes are, whether they are comfortable, and so on. If people could just be encouraged to try the bus once or twice, they might continue to use it and leave their cars at home.

On the basis of similar reasoning, numerous communities have tried innovative procedures to attract more users to their systems. One of the simplest ways of doing this is to offer free rides in certain clearly defined areas of town.

Other approaches have involved lowering the fares for certain periods. The offering of free bus rides has been a particularly popular approach in congested downtown areas. The intent of such area-specific free transit is to reduce the number of private automobiles by increasing the attractiveness of alternative systems. In Dallas, for example, a "Freebus" gives free rides to users "as long as the origin and destination of their trip falls within a prescribed downtown metropolitan area" (Everett, 1977, p. 10).

A somewhat different approach involves varying the route (area) for free transit. In Pittsburgh, for example, the "Wild Card Bus" program involved different buses giving free rides on a daily varying basis such that riders could not predict whether their bus would be a free one. Each designated bus had a fare box decorated as a joker card, which signified free rides to all passengers boarding that day.

Sometimes entire communities, not just limited geographic areas, have been involved. An example of a system-wide reduced-fare strategy is the "Big Buck Pass" approach, also attempted in Pittsburgh. In this scheme unlimited weekend travel on the city's buses was permitted families who had purchased a pass for $1. As reported in *Passenger Transport* (1975), this program generated tremendous increases in the use of the bus system during the period of its implementation. On several different weekends as many as 350,000 riders were counted on the buses.

Other informal approaches to increasing bus riding have involved making buses more attractive by increasing their speed. This is generally accomplished by reserving one lane of a freeway expressly for bus use ("Diamonds Are Forever," 1976; Rose & Hinds, 1976). When this procedure is used, riders are presumably positively reinforced by getting to their destination sooner and negatively reinforced by avoiding the even greater congestion now encountered by automobile users restricted to fewer lanes.

In one effort to evaluate priority bus lanes, Rose and Hinds found bus-travel time improved by as much as 15–20 minutes. This was largely the result of reserving one lane of a 5.5-mile stretch of a highway south of Miami to buses and automobiles carrying two or more passengers. Single-occupant automobile-travel time increased by about 15 minutes because of the slight increase in congestion due to being restricted to fewer lanes. Bus ridership increased during the experiment, and surveys showed that 77% of the new bus travelers had used automobiles for the same trips prior to the experiment. The study seems therefore to have produced a significant shifting in mode of travel, with the majority (77%) reporting that convenience was their primary reason for switching.

Formal Studies

More formal approaches to the problem of increasing bus use have been taken at The Pennsylvania State University by Everett and his colleagues. The first study (Everett, 1973) looked at the effects of paying people to ride the bus.

After a 20-day baseline period, each person boarding the bus during a three-day experimental phase received 25¢ (after paying their usual 10¢ fare). By the third day of this procedure, ridership had shown a 149% increase over the mean of the baseline phase (to 260 persons per day). When the payments were discontinued in a seven-day return-to-baseline phase, ridership dropped to a mean of 205 persons per day. To be sure that the 25¢ payment was responsible for the apparent increase, Everett reinstated it together with a newspaper announcement of the payments. This newspaper-and-payment phase lasted only one day, but during it ridership jumped to 370 persons, a 180% increase over the previous baseline phase. After the payments were again discontinued, ridership dropped quickly to a mean of about 250 persons per day during the final phase of the study. Thus, relatively clear-cut evidence was provided that students will ride buses more frequently if they are paid to do so.

Of course, the expense of such a procedure makes it impractical as a long-term solution. For this reason a less expensive token system was evaluated in a second study by Everett, Hayward, and Meyers (1974) on the same campus bus line. After a 16-day baseline period, every person boarding the bus was given a token redeemable for goods and services made available by local merchants. The actual reimbursement value of the tokens ranged from 5¢ to 10¢ each. During the eight days of this token-reward phase, ridership jumped to a daily mean of 420, 50% higher than the previous baseline level. When the token procedure was withdrawn, mean daily ridership returned to the baseline level. A control bus, in which riders were counted but not rewarded, showed no systematic changes in ridership levels throughout the three phases of the study.

These two investigations have shown the relative ease with which large increases in the use of public-bus systems can be produced by offering rewards to riders. The substitution of tokens for quarters in the second study greatly reduced the cost of the procedures ($178 versus $728 if quarters had been used). Moreover, the tokens seemed to have some value to the riders, as 83% of the tokens were redeemed, 64% of them for additional bus rides.

Given the apparent success of these procedures, it is tempting to wonder whether they could be made even more economical. Recall that similar reinforcement procedures were quite successful in the early litter studies (for example, Burgess, Clark, & Hendee, 1971; Clark, Burgess, & Hendee, 1972) reviewed in Chapter 5. Later, reinforcement procedures for litter control were made more economical by reducing the number of rewards presented. A particularly clear example of this was the Kohlenberg and Phillips (1973) study, in which coupons good for Pepsis were awarded on the average to every seventh, tenth, or 20th person depositing trash in a designated container. The avowed purpose of not reinforcing every depositor was to reduce the overall cost of the procedure.

In a similar vein, Deslauriers and Everett (1977) attempted to improve the cost effectiveness of the procedures used by Everett and his colleagues in the 1974 study by awarding a token to every third person on the average and comparing the result with giving a reward to every person boarding the bus. After six weeks of baseline ridership data had been collected, the tokens were introduced. One was presented to every third person (on the average) boarding the bus during a 15-day experimental period. (Remember that we called this type of schedule a VP schedule in Chapter 3.) Large red stars were mounted on the front and sides of the bus during the experimental period each day (11 A.M.–2 P.M.). The tokens (pink wallet-sized cards) were handed out by an experimenter as people boarded the bus. Exchange sheets were posted on the bus telling patrons the exchange value of the tokens and the local merchants willing to redeem them. The probability of receiving a token for boarding the bus was posted in the advertising slots on the side of the bus and announced in newspaper ads three times each week.

After this 15-day period a token was dispensed to every rider for a period of ten days. This change in reinforcement probability was announced as before. Conditions were then returned to giving a token to every third person (on the average) for eight days, and finally tokens were discontinued altogether in a return-to-baseline phase.

During the baseline phase an average of 102.5 riders per day boarded the experimental bus. When a token was awarded to every third person during the first experimental phase, ridership increased to a mean of 113 per day. There was no further increase when every person was rewarded during the next experimental phase. However, when every third person was again rewarded in the fourth phase, ridership dropped to approximately 108 per day. Discontinuing tokens altogether in the final, return-to-baseline phase resulted in a drop to 71 riders per day.

These results show again the power of reinforcement procedures for increasing ridership on a public-bus system. More important, the direct comparison of the different reinforcement schedules allows an evaluation of the effects of procedures varying considerably in cost. As Deslauriers and Everett showed, giving a token to every third person (on the average) was as effective as giving a token to every person boarding the bus. These results are consistent with those of earlier littering studies showing that the density of reinforcement (and thus the cost) can be reduced significantly without impairing the effectiveness of reward-based solutions to environmental problems.

A few additional features of the Deslauriers and Everett study should be noted. As in earlier work (Everett et al., 1974), the tokens seemed valuable, since 82% were subsequently redeemed. Of these, 71% were spent on bus rides. The implication of this finding is that ridership on public-transportation systems might be readily increased by having drivers dispense tokens to boarding passengers on a variable basis. These tokens need only be good for additional rides and not for goods and services arranged with participating merchants. The cost of such simple procedures would certainly be minimal and might be outweighed by the additional revenues generated by the increase in ridership. Indeed, in the Deslauriers and Everett study the every-third-person schedule generated a 10% increase in ridership and thus, presumably, in revenue.

Actually, the 10% increase is conservative because it is based on ridership on the experimental bus only. An important feature of the study was that riders on two additional, control buses were monitored throughout all phases so that comparisons could be made not only for the data of the experimental bus but between them and those of buses not included in the experimental manipulations. The inclusion of these control buses turned out to be important because ridership on them showed a general decline throughout the different phases of the study. As the authors noted, this decline was probably the result of improved weather conditions and an increase in walking by persons who otherwise would be riding the bus. If one evaluates the *increase* in ridership on the experimental bus against its baseline levels only, an increase of 10% is found. However, the more appropriate comparison would be with the *decreases* in ridership on the control buses, since these reflect what would have happened on the experimental bus in the absence of the reinforcement procedures; that is, left to the effects of weather and other seasonal variations alone, ridership on the experimental bus should have decreased as it did on the controls. Token procedures prevented this decrease and actually produced a 10% gain. When compared with the controls, this ridership gain was 27%. These data highlight the importance of untreated controls in environmental research, a subject that will be discussed more thoroughly at the end of the chapter.

Finally, Deslauriers and Everett distributed questionnaires to the passengers during the baseline and token-to-every-person phases. In addition to questions dealing with occupation and origin, destination, length, and purpose of trip, the passengers were asked what other mode of transportation they would have used if they had not taken the bus. A similar questionnaire had been used by Everett and his colleagues in the 1974 study. In both studies a large percentage of the respondents indicated that they would have walked had they not taken the bus (for example, 73% in the later study). Only 20% said they would have taken a car. These procedures therefore appear to have little effect on the problem of automobile use, an issue to which we shall return later.

In a recent investigation the common practice of enticing riders to use the bus by having periods of free transit was experimentally evaluated. Everett, Deslauriers, Newsom, and Anderson (1978) compared the effects of three different ways of awarding free bus rides. Again, the system at The Pennsylvania State University provided the experimental setting. The researchers randomly selected 682 students from the university directory and mailed them free transit tokens according to three different procedures: (1) students in the noncontingent free-transit group ($n = 194$) received 12 tokens good for rides on any campus bus during a nine-day period. They were also told that they would receive an additional 12 tokens on the 11th day. (2) The students in the one-for-one contingent free-transit group ($n = 194$) similarly received 12 tokens but were told that for every token used during the nine-day period they would receive one token in the mail on the 11th day. (3) The students in the three-for-one contingent free-transit group ($n = 194$) were told that for every one of the 12 tokens they used during the nine-day period they would receive three tokens on the 11th day. The control students ($n = 100$) were merely telephoned on the tenth day and asked how many times they had ridden the bus during the previous nine-day period.

The number of rides taken by the students during the nine-day experimental period was the primary dependent variable. Since students had been randomly selected and assigned in equal numbers to the three experimental conditions, an equivalent number of rides per group would have been expected in the absence of any differential effect for the conditions. As it turned out, however, most rides were accumulated by the one-for-one contingent free-transit group ($n = 572$). The three-for-one and noncontingent free-transit groups accumulated 546 and 435 rides, respectively. Only 77 rides were taken by the students in the control condition.

In terms of rides per student, the one-for-one, three-for-one, noncontingent, and control groups yielded figures of 2.95, 2.81, 2.31, and .77, respectively. Thus, the two groups who received additional tokens for using the bus during the experimental period tended to ride more often than the group who received an additional 12 tokens whether they rode the bus or not. Moreover, all three experimental groups rode considerably more often than the controls, showing formally the effect of the free-transit procedures described earlier in the chapter. Finally, it does not appear to matter whether one or three tokens are given per ride, an important point worth considering when evaluating the cost of various free-transit approaches.

This is an interesting study that raises several issues. Since the students were required to write their names on the tokens, it was possible to determine whether rides were taken only by those actually selected for the study or whether some tokens may have been given to other students. Interestingly, 61%, 46%, and 52% of the riders in the noncontingent, one-for-one, and three-for-one groups, respectively, were students to whom tokens *had not* been mailed. Thus, a good deal of token trading was occurring. Since the greatest amount (61%) of trading was done by students in the noncontingent group, the authors concluded that students who knew they would receive additional tokens regardless of whether they rode the bus were especially likely to give away their original tokens.

These differences in token-trading frequencies are worth considering further. As might be expected, the total number of *different* riders varied across the experimental conditions. Since more tokens were given away, it is no great surprise to find that the noncontingent condition produced a larger number of different riders ($n = 188$) than the one-for-one ($n = 173$) and three-for-one ($n = 168$) contingent groups. Remember that the purpose of periodic free-transit programs appears to be to induce more people to ride the bus in order to learn of its benefits and thus continue riding when the free period ends. If so, then the more *different* riders a procedure produces, the better. Looked at in this way, the most effective condition might have been the noncontingent free-transit approach.

Even though overall ridership levels (total rides) were lowest for this condition, the total number of additional riders was 8.7% higher for it than its nearest competitor.

Unfortunately, the design of this study does not permit clear conclusions on the relative merits of ride-dependent and independent free transit. If the purpose of such programs is indeed to facilitate increased ridership, it is necessary to evaluate those increases *after* the program has been terminated. It is of no great moment to show an increase *during* periods of free transit unless one anticipates operating the system on such a basis permanently. Had data on overall ridership levels been collected after the experimental procedures employed by Everett and his colleagues had been terminated, different results might have been forthcoming. Hopefully, future studies will evaluate this important issue.

ALTERING THE USE OF AUTOMOBILES

As mentioned earlier, the increases in bus riding noted by Everett and his associates seemed to come primarily from persons who normally walk to their destination. Indeed, in the Deslauriers and Everett study (1977), only 20% of the riders said they normally would have taken a car. Although most efforts to increase the use of mass-transit systems seem designed to reduce the use of alternatives such as the private automobile, they are indirect efforts at best. We call them indirect because they do not deal with automobiles specifically. A few formal and informal efforts have dealt with automobile use directly, however.

As with the mass-transit studies, the best-known attempts to alter automobile use have been informal field studies conducted in and around major metropolitan areas. In each of these, the focus has been on increasing automobile efficiency by encouraging car pooling. For example, for several years toll-free passage has been provided during rush hours to cars crossing the San Francisco—Oakland Bay Bridge with three or more passengers. Similarly, one lane of a freeway serving Los Angeles was reserved for buses and for cars containing multiple occupants ("Diamonds Are Forever," 1976). As mentioned earlier, in Florida one lane of the South Dixie Highway near Miami was reserved for cars carrying two or more persons during rush hours (Rose & Hinds, 1976). A similar experiment on the Shirley Highway near Washington, D.C., reserved an express lane for buses and for cars carrying four or more persons (Everett, 1977). In Seattle, cars with three or more occupants are permitted to cross the Evergreen Point Floating Bridge at a fare of 10¢ instead of the normal 35¢ (T. W. Phillips, 1977).

In all of these informal studies, the strategy involves increasing the occurrence of one set of behaviors (car pooling) by making the alternative (solo driving) more difficult. The manipulation of response difficulty has been used in the solution of other environmental problems as well (see Hayes & Cone, 1977a). In the present examples the use of an automobile by one or two people is made more difficult than its use by three or more people. Another way of interpreting the tactic is that car pooling is made more reinforcing by making it faster and less expensive. The data on the success of these procedures are inconclusive at this point, however. In the Los Angeles freeway study, for example, car poolers saved about two minutes over a 12.5-mile stretch, but a 10% increase in accident frequencies was also reported. In the South Dixie Highway experiment an increase of 66% was noted (Rose & Hinds, 1976). If non-car poolers spend more time idling their car engines as they wait in traffic jams, the net effect on energy expenditures may be zero or even negative.

Further, various sneaky tactics have been employed to circumvent the experimental procedures. For example, enterprising students have hired themselves out as riders so that drivers could avail themselves of the faster lanes. Cars have also been observed carrying inflatable dummies and picking up people at bus stops. An added problem is enforcement of restricted access to the priority lanes. In this regard, Rose and Hinds reported an 8% violation frequency even with the use of six highway patrolmen for 5.5 miles of roadway. Obviously, further research on such things as establishing priority lanes is necessary before they can be regarded as useful additions to the collection of successful efforts at altering automobile use.

An innovative corporate program to induce employees to leave their automobiles at home has been tried out by the 3M Company in Minnesota (Everett, 1977). This "Commute-a-Van Program" was designed in the face of a need to provide a multimillion-dollar parking facility for employees. Rather than build the facility, 3M purchased 62 13-passenger vans and distributed them to 62 employees. These persons drive the vans and arrange for other employees to ride with them at a charge of 8¢ per mile. With eight persons accompanying the driver, the vans are operated at a break-even cost. For more than eight riders the driver earns a profit. In addition, the drivers are permitted (for a certain charge) to use the vans for personal transportation over and above the normal trips to work. It is not difficult to see the potential rewards of such a system for all the participants. The company benefits greatly, of course, by not having to build an expensive parking facility. It is tempting to suggest the arrangement of additional fiscal rewards, such as tax reductions over and above the business-expense write-offs, for companies developing such programs. After all, the potential reductions in energy use made possible by more efficient commuting would benefit all of us.

In addition to the corporate-level effort by 3M, reports of three formal, applied behavior-analytic investigations have been published that deal directly with the use of private automobiles by individuals (Foxx & Hake, 1977; Hake & Foxx, 1978; Hayward & Everett, 1976). In the first study university-student volunteers were assigned to either an experimental group ($n = 12$) or a contrast group ($n = 9$). Odometer readings served as the study's primary dependent variable. At the beginning the students' cars were checked to make sure the odometer was working. A reading was then recorded against which later driving could be measured. After approximately 35 days of baseline for the experimental group (28 days for the contrast group), a second reading was obtained, and miles-per-day figures were calculated for each student. Special precautions were taken to make sure that the odometers had not been tampered with and that students were not simply switching cars so that their own would show less mileage.

After the baseline period a rather complex reinforcement procedure was introduced for the experimental students. Included were personal "fuel conservation guides," which were given each participant. These listed mileage-reduction goals and the prizes that could be won for reductions of from 10% to 50%. For example, students reducing their mileage 10% below baseline were given $5. An additional $5 were added for each 10% reduction up to 50%. Persons reducing 20% or more were also offered a tour of a mental-health facility. Finally, various bonuses were given students achieving the greatest overall reductions. Three unannounced checks of odometer readings were conducted during the 28 days of the reinforcement period. These were accomplished by not telling the students a check was to be made until the day it was conducted. They were then asked what time they were leaving campus so an experimenter could arrange to meet them at the designated checkpoint.

During the experimental phase baseline conditions remained in effect for the contrast group. Their odometers were checked, but no effort was made to get them to reduce their driving. The last condition involved withdrawing the reinforcement procedures for the experimental group and returning to baseline, a phase lasting 14–16 days.

Results were reported separately for each student. Overall, the reinforcement procedures were shown to be effective. The experimental students reduced their driving from a mean of 36.1 miles per day during baseline to 27.6 miles per day when reinforced, a reduction of 24%. Contrast students actually increased their driving during the experimental period, from 32.1 to 35.0 miles per day (up 10%). When the reinforcement procedures were withdrawn during the return-to-baseline condition, the experimental students increased their driving once again, though not as much as in their previous baseline period (to 34.4 miles per day).

Though the reinforcement of reduced driving was effective, at least during the time the procedure was operating, the effects appear short-lived. Even so, however, of the nine experimental students who actually reduced their driving during the experimental phase, seven drove less in the final baseline phase than in the initial one. This is tentative support for the possibility that the experimental procedures produced some long-term effects in these students. A longer follow-up would be useful in future studies to document this possibility more fully.

No cost-effectiveness data are presented, so it is difficult to determine the practicality of the procedures employed. As the authors noted, however, the reinforcement condition involved numerous features—self-recording, daily feedback, reminders that someone was recording their driving, cash prizes, and a tour of a mental-health facility. Some of these components are obviously more expensive than others and might be eliminated in future studies evaluating the effectiveness of the separate parts of the Foxx and Hake package. The authors also discuss the feasibility of their procedures for large-scale implementation and provide suggestions in this regard.

In a follow-up study Hake and Foxx (1978) modified their earlier procedures to make them more feasible for large-scale use. College students were assigned to two groups: reinforcement and self-recording. As in the earlier study, miles driven per day served as the primary dependent variable. Several components of the reinforcement package used in the first study were evaluated more specifically in the second. Since some of the effects of the reinforcement procedures could have been due to the students' self-recording their mileage each day, this variable was isolated in the second study. Moreover, since the experimental group in the first study came from one of the authors' classes, his influence may have contributed to the effects of the reinforcement procedures. This "leader effect" was evaluated by selecting half of the reinforcement group from a class not taught by either of the authors.

The results again established the effectiveness of the reinforcement package. The students in the reinforcement group reduced their miles driven per day from a mean of 38.6 during baseline to 32.3 during the experimental phase, a reduction of 22.5%. Eight of the nine students in this group showed at least some reduction. The students in the self-recording group reduced their miles driven per day from a mean of 29.6 during baseline to 25.0 during the experimental phase, a reduction of 10.4%. Seven of the eight students in this group achieved reductions. The "leader" variable also appeared to play a part, since the four reinforcement-group students from the author's class showed a 40.3% reduction compared to that of only 8.2% for the five reinforcement students from another class.

An extremely worthwhile feature of the Hake and Foxx study was a subject-by-subject cost analysis comparing the value of the gasoline saved with that of the rewards dispensed. For the reinforcement group, a total of $79.97 in gasoline was saved ($8.88 per student), compared with a total reinforcer cost of $126 ($14 per student). As the authors noted, the prizes were too large to make the study economical, given the price of gasoline at that time. They suggested that future research could be more cost effective by restricting one's subjects to persons who drive a good deal and by arranging rewards to follow absolute rather than percentage reductions in miles driven relative to initial baseline levels. Of course, the gasoline figures do not tell the whole story, since they do not include the administrative costs of the procedures. Nonetheless, Hake and Foxx's subject-by-subject analysis should serve as a useful model for future research.

It has frequently been suggested that people waste energy-related natural resources because they have insufficient information about how much they are using. As the next chapter will show, increasing the availability of such information and noting its effects have been a common strategy of research in the energy-conservation area. Hayward and Everett (1976) attempted to evaluate the effects on automobile drivers as well. On the assumption that immediate con-

Your car costs you _____ ¢
for every mile you drive, as
calculated by the Federal
Highway Administration

So far this week your
car has been driven a
total of _____ miles,
at a total cost to
you of $ _____ .

You may
keep this
card and
show it to
others who
drive your
car.

**In the past _____ hours,
your car has been driven
_____ miles at a total
cost to you of: $ _____ .**

REMEMBER:
This card is intended to show you, the driver, how much your car costs you to drive. The figure shown
above represents what you have actually paid, whether by cash or credit, to drive your car the distance
indicated. This sum covers the costs of depreciation, maintenance, accessories, parts, tires, gas, oil,
garage, parking, tolls, insurance and State and Federal taxes. In addition, for every mile you drive, you
as a taxpayer must help to pay the costs of air pollution, congestion, highway construction and
maintenance, State and municipal police, and other car-related expenses. These costs have been added
on a per-mile basis.

Figure 9-1. Feedback on the operating, depreciation, and social costs of
driving a car. From *A Failure of Response Cost Feedback to Modify Car
Driving Behavior*, by S. C. Hayward and P. B. Everett. Paper presented at
the annual meeting of the Midwestern Association of Behavior Analysis,
Chicago, May, 1976. Used by permission.

sequences exert more control over behavior than delayed ones, Hayward and
Everett attempted to reduce driving by making information (feedback) about the
cost of automobile use more immediately available to drivers.

The experimenters randomly divided 90 persons commuting by car to a
large university into four groups: (1) operating-cost feedback—7¢ per mile; (2)
operating-cost and depreciation-cost feedback—15¢ per mile; (3) operating-cost,
depreciation-cost, and social-cost feedback—25¢ per mile; and (4) mileage feedback only. In an *ABA* design, miles driven per day during baseline *(A)*, feedback
(B), and return-to-baseline *(A)* phases served as the major dependent variable.
Attitudes toward automobile transportation were also assessed. Social costs were
"arbitrarily determined and were an attempt to represent items such as the costs of
air pollution, health decrements, and building facade decay" (Everett, 1977, pp.
12–13) induced by automobile emissions.

The number of miles driven was calculated for each subject each day and
multiplied by the relevant cost figures. This information was then written on a
5-inch by 8-inch card and placed on the windshield of each car. An example of
the card for operating-cost, depreciation-cost, and social-cost feedback is presented in Figure 9–1.

Unfortunately, no mileage reductions were produced by any of the four feedback conditions. Changes in attitudes did occur, however, with many participants voicing more negative views of the value of automobiles as a means of transportation. Moreover, the degree of change was correlated with the magnitude of the cost feedback such that those receiving the highest cost information changed their attitudes most.

Everett (1977) speculated that the failure to find effects may have been due to the abstract nature of the consequences manipulated. Although *feedback* about costs was made more immediately available to the participants in the study, the actual out-of-pocket expenditure of money was still delayed by the use of credit cards, annual or semiannual billing of insurance premiums, and so on. Everett wondered whether a meter installed in the car would be more effective. The driver might reduce mileage if required to drop a quarter in the meter every 2 miles in order to operate the vehicle.

Making the cost of various environmentally relevant behaviors more obvious seems an important approach in several areas. Its manipulation to effect reductions in residential electricity use will be discussed in the next chapter. Most of us are aware that the costs of numerous environmentally relevant behaviors are often long delayed or hidden. This is the result of a combination of numerous contemporary fiscal practices designed essentially to encourage consumption rather than conservation. Credit cards, installment plans, and infrequent billing (for instance, monthly, bimonthly, or even quarterly) by oil companies and public utilities are primary examples. With such billing practices the immediate reinforcing benefits of consumption are more powerful than the punishing effects of the delayed cost. Thus, the spend/conserve balance is tilted in favor of spending. We will have more to say on the relevance of free-enterprise marketing practices to environmental problems in the last section of the book.

REDUCING FUEL USAGE IN FLEET-OPERATED TRUCKS

In addition to the research just cited dealing with private automobiles, at least one research project has examined ways of increasing fuel conservation in a large fleet of corporate-owned trucks. The behavior of 195 drivers for a major textile company was the subject of studies by Runnion, Watson, and McWhorter (1978). These drivers as a group drove more than 6 million miles per year, with "intermill" drivers moving between 58 different company locations in three states and "long-line" drivers delivering freight in 32 states.

Three different dependent measures were used in the research. These were the miles per gallon obtained by both intermill drivers and long-line drivers and the percentage of fuel obtained by long-line drivers at company-owned outlets versus commercial ones. Since bulk-purchased fuel dispensed by company outlets was significantly less expensive than commercial fuel, the company was interested in increasing the use of its own outlets. However, our concern is with the first two measures of fuel actually used, regardless of its source.

In the first study, after a one-week baseline period, intermill drivers were informed by letter of the energy-saving program and given instructions on ways to drive more efficiently. Data on miles per gallon for the entire fleet and for each individual were posted weekly in the drivers' room at each terminal. In addition, drivers were sent letters praising improved performance, and informal social praise was provided by higher-level staff.

These conditions were in effect for one year, after which a second set of tactics was tried. These consisted of daily feedback letters, public posting of feedback by category of performance, and weekly drawings for items bearing the company's logo. Public posting involved listing the names of those achieving more than 6.0 miles per gallon. Every time a driver achieved 6.0 miles per gallon or more, one chance at the drawing was entered in his or her name. These procedures were in effect for an entire year, but the drawings and letters were used less and less frequently as the year progressed.

These efforts were associated with a 5.06% increase in miles per gallon during the first year over the baseline level. Actual miles per gallon averaged 6.02. During the second intervention year, miles per gallon averaged 4.18% over baseline, with the actual usage being 5.97.

The second study employed tactics similar to those of the first, except it was run with the long-line drivers, and a return-to-baseline condition was included in the second year. During the initial baseline week, miles per gallon averaged 4.8, rising to an average of 4.9 during the first intervention year. The first eight weeks of the second year were associated with an average of 5.01 miles per gallon, which dropped to 4.93 during the four-week return-to-baseline phase. Miles per gallon then rose to an average of 5.31 for the remainder of the second year. Thus, although efficiency increased only 2.08% in the first year, it jumped 8.96% in the second.

These may seem like small increases, but the company's fleet was so large that even fractional reductions in fuel use resulted in significant savings. During the second year of both studies, for example, enough money was saved to run the entire fleet for one month at no cost. Hopefully, future large-scale studies such as these will be conducted so that the reliability of the results can be demonstrated convincingly.

ISSUES IN ALTERING TRANSPORTATION BEHAVIOR

The Need to Study Additional Modes and Nonessential Uses

The studies we have described dealt with only a few major modes of conveyance. Obviously, numerous other forms of transportation will need careful and systematic study before we can adequately understand environmentally relevant movement of people and materials. As in other areas of environmental research, the various types of transportation behavior are not independent. Indeed, the interdependence of response alternatives may be even greater for transportation, since the use of one mode automatically excludes others. For example, the manipulation of private-automobile use produces concurrent changes in the use of other modes and vice versa.

Thus, in addition to automobiles and buses, other types of transportation will have to be studied if a comprehensive understanding of the relationship between environmental problems and the movement of people and materials is to be forthcoming. Additional forms of mass transit, especially planes and trains, should be investigated. Similarly, walking, bicycling, and the use of relatively efficient mopeds and motorcycles need study, with special attention given to ways of increasing the attractiveness of these alternatives.

Further, careful study of so-called nonessential recreational uses of transportation is needed. The proliferation of power boats, snowmobiles, and recreational vehicles continues in spite of greatly increased gasoline costs and governmental pleas for conservation. What variables control recreational transportation? Could it be reduced, as B. F. Skinner (1975) has suggested, by making the home environment more reinforcing? Could it be reduced by reinstating the tax for off-road uses of gasoline? Numerous additional variables could easily be listed that may have some effect. Presumably, a comprehensive national energy program would incorporate some of these in dealing specifically with recreational transportation.

Levels versus Patterns of Use

In addition to including other types of transportation, future research must consider dependent variables more carefully. In the mass-transit and private-automobile research conducted thus far, two aspects of use can be distinguished: level and pattern. As noted previously (Cone & Hayes, 1977), the transportation literature has generally concentrated on effecting changes in level of use; that is, efforts have been directed at increasing the number of persons riding buses (Everett et al., 1974) or at decreasing the number of miles driven in private automobiles (Foxx & Hake, 1977; Hake & Foxx, 1978). The distinction between levels and patterns of use is important in the energy-conservation area as well (see Chapter 10). Both transportation and power-generating systems have to plan for use at certain peak periods, when the maximum demand will be made on their services. As a result, a significant portion of each is unused a good deal of the time (that is, during nonpeak hours). If usage could be spread out more evenly, peak levels would be reduced, facilities would be used more efficiently, and less capacity would be required. Thus, fewer environmental resources would have to be expended.

As an example, consider travel to and from work. To accommodate large numbers of cars during the two major rush-hour periods each day, extensive freeway and bridge systems are needed. Similarly, mass-transit capacity must be large enough to handle rush-hour (peak) demand. If work-related travel could be spread more evenly throughout the day (for example, by staggering the hours of various industry groups), less capacity would be needed. Also, if geographic concentration of commercial enterprises could be reduced, less capacity would be needed.

The choice of dependent variables in studies of transportation behavior is related to whether levels or patterns of use are the targets (Cone & Hayes, 1977). With automobiles, for example, it makes sense to use miles driven per day (see, for example, Foxx & Hake, 1977; Hake & Foxx, 1978; Hayward & Everett, 1976) when overall reductions in level of use are desired. In such cases, concern is most clearly directed at conserving the natural resources necessary for the production of fuel. If concern is focused on the natural resources necessary for the production and maintenance of facilities supporting automobile use (roads, parking garages, and so forth), different dependent variables will be selected. Miles driven per day will be of less concern than a count of automobiles per geographic area, per unit of time, or both.

Whether patterns or levels of transportation use are the concern, however, future research should give more attention to dependent variables directly relevant to the objectives of each particular study. For example, if decreased use of automobiles is really the goal of free-mass-transit research, direct observation of automobile use should be included. If reduced consumption of gasoline is the target of a study on automobile use, measures of gasoline use would be more directly relevant than odometer readings of miles driven. Under such contingencies, participants might learn to cover the same number of miles in a more energy-efficient manner.

Similarly, the selection of one's independent variable will be controlled by decisions to change levels or patterns of use. If *levels* of automobile use are the focus, rewarding people for driving less makes sense (Foxx & Hake, 1977), as does the provision of feedback on miles driven and enhancing the immediacy of the costs involved (Hayward & Everett, 1976). If *patterns* of use are of more concern, stimulus conditions will have to be arranged to control the specific type of driving desired; that is, people will have to be rewarded for driving to particular places at particular times. Or the cost of driving to these places at these times might be manipulated. Higher bridge tolls and parking fees during peak hours and higher parking fees in densely populated downtown locations are examples.

The Need for Cost Analyses

Future research should also include careful cost analyses to permit adequate evaluations of the practical implications of findings. The token procedures of Everett and his colleagues would appear, superficially at least, to be cost effective. After all, a 27% increase in ridership was produced by awarding free tokens to every third passenger (Deslauriers & Everett, 1977). Presumably, these tokens did not cost the bus company anything. However, if all tokens were redeemed for bus rides, one-third of the passengers would now be riding for nothing. Thus, to break even on such a schedule, an increase in ridership of 33% would be needed.

Actually, a somewhat larger increase would be needed to break even, since the cost of producing the tokens would have to be recovered. Similar logic would apply in determining the break-even point for other token-reward schedules. Of course, costs to the transit authority could be reduced (or even eliminated) if one followed Everett's example of involving local merchants. If tokens were redeemable only for goods and services, then any increase in bus ridership should represent a net gain in revenue for the transit authority. The administrative cost of managing the token system would be higher, however, and might offset any gains; that is, additional staff and paperwork would be necessary for a system involving tokens redeemable for things other than more bus rides. Besides, it is not clear that merchants would support long-term, broad-scale programs.

Similar cost analyses need to be made of other suggestions for altering transportation behavior. Of course, it is unrealistic to demand exact figures for experimental procedures just being developed. However, as their effects are repeated in additional research, questions of cost and practicality become more reasonable.

Research Design

The studies cited in this chapter raise some interesting research-design questions that have general applicability to behavior-analytic solutions to environmental problems. The use of untreated controls in the Deslauriers and Everett study is a good example. A similar tactic was used in the Hayes, Johnson, and Cone (1975) litter study described in Chapter 5. Because Deslauriers and Everett included the two control buses, it was possible to show that the gains in ridership produced by the experimental bus were conservative; that is, when measured against its own baseline, an increase of only 10% was found. However, the use of the control buses showed what would have happened to ridership in the same time period if the token procedures had not been implemented. There was a general decline in ridership (apparently related to improved weather) during the time the experimental procedures were used that actually worked against them. The magnitude of this decrease was documented by the control buses. Comparing the data of the experimental bus against those for the control buses as well as against its own baseline permitted a more realistic evaluation of the effects of the token procedure (that is, a 27% increase rather than merely a 10% one).

This study nicely illustrates the need for behavior-analytic environmental researchers to be creative in their selection of research designs. Environmental problems are not likely to be stable over time. Although a problem will probably not change spontaneously just as the independent variable is being introduced or withdrawn, it is possible that steady changes throughout the study will work in the opposite direction of any improvements associated with that variable. The result might be an underestimation of the effects of one's experimental procedures. An overestimation might occur if the environmental change happens to be in the same direction as the effect of the independent variable. The use of designs with control groups helps guard against these problems. It is also possible to control for these gradual environmental changes in *ABA* designs without control groups by comparing data in the *B* phase with the average of those in both *A* phases (see Hake & Foxx, 1978).

Individual versus Group Contingencies

Another fascinating question raised by the research in this chapter is the arrangement of contingencies for individually identifiable subjects or for undifferentiated groups. In the Foxx and Hake (1977) study, for example, rewards were tailored to reductions in students' driving when measured against their own baseline. Thus, a 10% reduction earned the same reward for everyone, regardless of his or her initial level of driving. A similar, individually tailored reinforcement procedure was evaluated in an energy-reduction study (Hayes & Cone, 1977b) to be described in the next chapter. Such an approach allows rewards to be scaled to each subject's own levels of behavior. Presumably, such scaling results in a more effective procedure than one based on changes in group averages. For example, suppose Foxx and Hake had tied individual rewards to changes in the entire group. Thus, rather than being rewarded for reductions from his or her own baseline, each participant would receive a payoff only when the group as a whole showed a reduction. Such an interdependent, group-oriented contingency system (Litow & Pumroy, 1975) was used to reduce classroom noise (Schmidt & Ulrich, 1969) in a study described in Chapter 6. Indeed, group contingencies have been used frequently in behavior-analytic environmental research (McClelland & Cook, in press; Meyers, Artz, & Craighead, 1976; Witmer & Geller, 1976), but they have not been compared with individually arranged consequences. In fact, we are not aware of any such comparisons in applied behavior-analytic research generally. Although there are some environmental contexts in which individual contingencies are inappropriate (for example, master-metered apartment buildings), there are others in which either group or individual approaches could be taken, and it would be useful to know the comparative effectiveness of each.

Legislative and Technological Solutions

Legislative and technological solutions to transportation problems have been tried with some success. The effects of mandatory reductions in highway speed limits to 55 miles per hour are well-known. Moreover, federal standards for automobile fuel efficiency should continue to increase the miles per gallon obtainable by passenger cars. In addition, higher taxes on larger cars and increased gasoline taxes will probably produce some reductions in fuel consumption. Similarly, the engineering of smaller, more energy-efficient automobiles will bring about some savings, as will the building of larger, faster, more accessible mass-transit systems.

Neither legislative nor technological solutions to transportation problems are without their behavioral components, however. People must comply with changes in the law, and they must make use of new technology in order for environmental benefits to be forthcoming. Appropriate application of behavioral principles should facilitate the effects of legislative and technological change. In the last part of the book we will have more to say about the behavioral/legislative/technological relationship as it applies to numerous environmental problems.

The Need to Study Transportation Providers as Well as Users

Related to the above is the selection of the appropriate subjects for studies of change in transportation behavior. The research available to date has uniformly concerned users of transportation systems. Although at least legislative efforts have been directed at the builders of transportation systems, much more behavioral-science research is needed that addresses questions of how to get providers to alter their systems to be as energy efficient as possible. In addition to the building of fuel-efficient automobiles, buses, trains, and planes, research is needed on ways to get municipalities to use them. Moreover, numerous variables related to use should be studied, including scheduling, routing, efficient driving practices, and so on. Each of us has probably had the experience of passing long lines of buses with idling engines pumping pollutants into the air and using diesel fuel wastefully. Or we have seen the same bus at the same time each day with only one or two passengers aboard. These and numerous other practices could undoubtedly benefit from careful study by behavioral scientists.

SUMMARY

As research discussed in this chapter has shown, we are merely at the beginning of our efforts to understand how to move people and goods in fuel-efficient ways. The problems faced by researchers in this area are enormous, and large-scale, long-term, multidisciplinary studies will be required to solve them.

To date, public-transit authorities and municipalities have probably done more innovating than behavioral scientists have. They have manipulated fare structures primarily, but they have also tried to make mass transit more desirable by increasing its speed while simultaneously reducing the number of lanes available to automobiles. They have also rewarded car pooling by restricting the use of certain priority lanes to cars with multiple occupants.

In addition to these rather nonexperimental, informal efforts, we have described the work of a few applied behavior analysts who have systematically manipulated costs and rewards to note their effects on users. Several potentially promising beginnings have been made, and some have seemed close to being cost effective. Rewarding bus riders with tokens seems to increase ridership, and rewarding college students for driving fewer miles seems to decrease automobile use.

The studies available thus far are very preliminary, however, and much additional research is needed. Most of the procedures investigated to date have been evaluated over very short time periods and with groups that may not be very representative of the population at large. The effects have not been examined over long follow-up periods to determine their durability. In fact, the experimental phases of studies to date have been similarly short-lived, making it difficult to tell whether the innovative procedures would continue to be effective after their newness had worn off.

A number of issues were raised at the end of the chapter that need to be addressed in future research. Perhaps the most important of these is a more careful specification of a study's dependent variables. If increased bus riding is produced in order to reduce automobile driving, some data on automobile use should be collected. Everett and his colleagues have made this an obvious requirement in showing that most of their increases in bus ridership were produced by people who previously walked to their destination. If reduced driving is desirable because less gasoline will be used, some data on gas usage should be provided. The important issue of the timing of transportation behavior was also noted, since environmental resources could be conserved by leveling out the load on transportation systems.

Behavioral research in transportation is in its infancy. Hopefully, future scientists, such as readers of this book, will greatly enhance our knowledge in this area. Perhaps the projects in the next section will stimulate you to further research.

SUGGESTED PROJECTS

Reducing Automobile Use

This project is designed to show you how easily you can reduce your own driving or that of a family member by as much as 20% to 30%. It requires that you have access to a car of which you are the principal user. A motorcycle could also be used. If you are not the principal user of a car in your family, you can still carry out the project with someone who is. If you are the principal driver, the study will be self-administered. If someone else is, you can serve as the experimenter.

First, make sure the car's odometer is working properly. Then record the number of miles it shows and the date and time of the recording. Try to select a time for recording that you can use consistently from day to day. Next, prepare a graph on which to record the number of miles you drive each day. Your graph might look something like the one appearing in Figure 9–2. After reading your odometer at the same time each day, subtract the previous day's reading and record the miles driven on the graph. It is a good idea to keep a list of the mileage figures in a notebook somewhere as well.

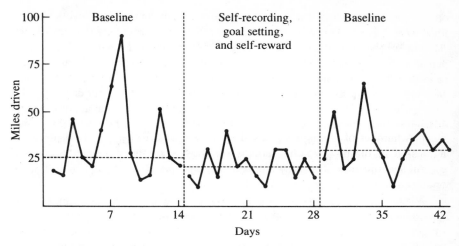

Figure 9–2. Fictitious data simulating the effects of a self-management procedure on self-recorded automobile driving.

After graphing your daily mileage for about two weeks, you should have a good baseline record of the amount of driving you do. Now draw a dashed vertical line on your graph after your last baseline point (as in Figure 9–2). Calculate the median miles per day you have driven during baseline. Any elementary-statistics book can be consulted for details on calculating a median. When you have it, draw a dashed horizontal line through your baseline data at a point representing the median. An example is provided in Figure 9–2.

Now you are ready for the intervention. We think you will find it easy to reduce your driving by 20% compared with your baseline, so that will be your driving-reduction goal. First, calculate 20% of your baseline median. Then subtract that value from the median to give you your goal. Now draw a dashed line horizontally across the graph from Day 14 to Day 28. That line appears in the intervention phase in Figure 9–2. You now have a visual representation of what you have to do to accomplish your goal. Since it represents a median reduction in the intervention phase of 20%, you must keep at least half of your daily mileage readings below that line. More than half will result in exceeding your goal.

For each day your mileage is at or below your goal, you should reward yourself. Select some object or activity that you enjoy and allow yourself access to it on these days. You might even scale your reward to the size of the reduction you accomplished that day. For example, each 5% or 10% below the baseline rate might be worth an additional 15 minutes of watching television, reading, and so on.

Another approach would be to accumulate points toward a big reward on the weekend. Each day below your goal line might be worth five points toward the total you have decided will qualify you to go out to dinner, to a movie, and so on. Or you might decide that a negative-reinforcement approach will work better. Each week, give $10 to someone with instructions to return it *only* if your driving stays at or below your goal for, say, four of the seven days. Otherwise, that person is to give the $10 to your *least* favorite charity or political party. This procedure has been found to be effective in getting people to study more, eat less, and change numerous other undesirable habits. Will it work for your driving?

After the 28th day you can stop trying to reach a certain goal and just go on driving as you were during the baseline condition. Continue recording and graphing your mileage daily, but do not reward yourself further. You may see a slight increase in driving in this second baseline phase. If so, it would appear at least tentatively that self-recording, self-reward, and a specific behavioral goal may be effective ways of reducing your driving.

There are other embellishments you might want to use to beef up the experimental procedures a bit. For example, you could post your graph in some conspicuous place in your home and explain to others living with you what you are doing. They can then watch your progress and apply appropriate social reinforcers or punishers as the data require.

Altering the Prevalence of Car Pooling

This activity will involve documenting and increasing the amount of car pooling that occurs at a large company, university, or other organization near you. You will need to define, measure, and increase the percentage of cars carrying multiple occupants to this organization each day. The project is outlined in the following steps.

Step 1: Select a site. Choose a major place of employment within your community that has fairly well-defined work hours and a large number of employees who drive to work. Students driving to a high school or college would also make good subjects. When you have selected a site and an observation time or times, try to pick an observation point from which you can clearly see most of the cars as they are parked.

Step 2: Define car pooling. We suggest that you define car pooling as the use of a single automobile by two or more persons for transportation to a location where all occupants get out and remain for an extended period. It is important to distinguish car pooling from cases in which one person is taken to work by another who then returns home with the car. That is why you should observe from a location near the parking lot.

Step 3: Collect baseline data. Having written a definition, decided on an observation period, and picked a location, you are ready to begin collecting data. You may want to do this each workday or every other workday, depending on your own schedule. It is best to use some procedure that yields a representative picture for all five days of the week, however. If you can observe only on certain days—say, Monday, Wednesday, and Friday—you will want to check an occasional Tuesday and Thursday to compare your data for representativeness. Perhaps you could train a friend to count on these days.

Keep track of all cars coming to your location. Record the number of persons who get out of each. Your dependent measure will be the percentage of cars involved in car pooling; that is, divide the number of such cars by the total number you observe. Record that percentage on a graph and watch for day-to-day, week-to-week variability.

It is a good idea to check on the accuracy of your recording. Human observers are usually less than 100% accurate even when counting and recording as obvious a variable as people getting out of parked cars. We suggest that you have a friend count the same cars and people as you do so you can compare your figures. Do this independently, however, so you will not bias each other's data. There are a variety of formulas for calculating interobserver agreement (see Wildman & Erickson, 1977), but a satisfactory one for your purposes is merely to divide the smaller total by the larger. Obviously, the more your counts agree, the closer your dividend will be to 1.0. If you find the agreement to be less than .75, you probably need to redefine car pooling or make sure that you are both observing the same cars at the same time.

After you have observed, recorded, and graphed for a number of days, your graph should begin to stabilize around some average figure. When this happens, you probably have a fairly accurate estimate of how much car pooling is occurring, and you are ready for the next step.

Step 4: Increase car pooling. Now that you have a good idea of the amount of car pooling occurring at your site, you are ready to intervene to try to increase it. There are a number of different things you could try at this point. We are not going to suggest a specific tactic, since the best approach will depend on your particular setting. You might consider placing fliers on the windshields of single-occupant cars urging car pooling. Or you might reward those already doing so with a flier thanking them for car pooling. Another approach would be to place a large sign near the parking lot urging people to car pool. Still another would be to place announcements in the local newspaper urging car pooling. Radio stations might donate a few announcements of a similar sort.

More involved approaches (and possibly more effective ones) would require the cooperation of the place of business you are monitoring. Since less parking space would be needed if more people came in fewer cars, the organization might be interested in helping with your project. Some car-pooling projects have used computerized lists of employees matched for home address and work schedule. These are made available to interested employees to make it easier for them to get in contact with others who may want to join a car pool. An easier approach might be to get the organization to arrange preferential parking for car poolers. Or car poolers might be allowed to leave a few minutes early or through a special, faster gate or lane. If your project is taking place at an organization that charges for parking, perhaps special, lower rates could be arranged for cars with multiple occupants.

Regardless of which approach you take, after introducing it, continue collecting data as you did during the baseline phase. When you notice clear and consistent changes in car pooling, you are ready for the next step.

Step 5: Return to baseline. To be sure that the changes in car pooling are related to your efforts, return conditions as nearly as possible to those existing during the baseline phase. Continue collecting data as you have all along. If you notice an obvious and consistent change in your data—that is, toward less car pooling—you can assume that your experimental procedure was effective. To make sure, go to the next step.

Step 6: Reintroduce your procedure. Put back in whatever you removed during Step 5. If it was truly affecting car pooling, you should once again see an increase as you continue to collect data. If car pooling increases once again, your project is a success. You are now ready for the last phase of the study.

Step 7: Turn the program over to others. Now that you have demonstrated an effective way to increase car pooling, your efforts should turn toward getting the organization to maintain the program on its own. Space limitations do not permit elaboration of all the fine points of doing so here. Suffice it to note that you want to phase yourself out of active project management and phase in responsible staff members of the organization. You should assume the role of consultant to them until they can manage the project completely on their own.

Chapter 10

RESIDENTIAL ENERGY CONSERVATION

Usually we have started our chapters with a short quote. This time we have one of our own anecdotes to relate. In one of our studies on energy conservation (which we will describe later), we attempted to reduce electricity consumption in a married-student housing complex. These apartments were rented, very cheaply, and utility costs were included in the rent. Our society's waste of energy can be illustrated by an incident that occurred while we were running this study. It was cold outside that day. All of the heaters in the apartments were undoubtedly going full blast. Strangely, however, the sound of an air conditioner came from one of the apartments in the complex. Upon further investigation, the reason became clear. One of the residents apparently did not like how warm his living room got from the stationary gas heater. Rather than turning down the heater, he had adjusted the temperature by simultaneously running the air conditioner!

The consumption of energy in the industrialized nations has reached levels that create many problems, given our current technology (Hubbert, 1974). The economic and environmental costs of the overconsumption of energy are reflected in resource shortages, inflation, geopolitical imbalances, air pollution, water pollution, oil spills, radioactive wastes, mine-acid drainage, destruction of wilderness areas, and other, similar difficulties.

These problems can be addressed in at least two major ways: (1) new sources of energy can be developed, particularly through the generation of new production technology (for example, in areas such as solar energy), or (2) our consumption of energy can be reduced. In the short term, conservation seems to be our best option. Put succinctly, the current energy crisis is largely a *behavioral* problem relating to energy-consumption behaviors (such as driving, cooking, turning up thermostats, buying energy-consuming devices) and energy-saving behaviors (such as installing insulation, turning off air conditioners, wearing sweaters indoors).

Portions of this chapter were taken from "Applied Behavior Analysis and the Solution of Environmental Problems," by J. D. Cone and S. C. Hayes. In I. Altman and J. F. Wohlwill (Eds.), *Human Behavior and Environment: Advances in Theory and Research*, Vol. 2. Copyright 1977 by Plenum Publishing Corporation. Used by permission.

Even if we had *unlimited* supplies of energy, conservation would still be a desirable goal. Without exception, all modes of energy generation create some pollution or disruption of the natural environment. Of course, these costs must be weighed against the benefits energy provides, but no method of power production is free of cost.

This chapter deals with the consumption of energy in residential settings. Other chapters have already addressed important energy-related problems, such as population control and transportation. Private residences use more than 20% of all the energy consumed in the United States, and a large part of this consumption is wasteful. Conservation efforts could reduce this waste, and the resulting cost to the environment, with no deleterious effect on the quality of living (Large, 1973).

To date there has been little apparent recognition of how sensitive energy-related behaviors are to control. Perhaps one reason is that powerful economic interests are served by the consumption of energy, especially power, oil, mining, nuclear, and coal companies. Analyses of the historical trends in energy consumption, production, and promotion (Federal Power Commission, 1970; J. C. Fisher, 1974) and of the contingencies controlling power production give little hope that extraordinary efforts to reduce consumption will be readily adopted by the power companies. Until recently, it was not uncommon, for instance, to see calls for increased consumption of electricity (see, for example, Gray, 1975). Further, more than 75% of the electrical-production capacity in the United States is owned by private interests, dependent upon making a profit (Farris & Sampson, 1973). Even publicly owned facilities are likely to attempt to sell more energy—or raise their prices—in order to retire bonds and so forth.

Winett (1976) has pointed out that the primary response to problems of supply, undoubtedly a real problem for many energy companies today, has been to increase prices and call for conservation in the media. As we will see later, educational campaigns of the sort typically promulgated by the power industry and the government are relatively ineffective. We will also show that merely increasing prices is a relatively inefficient method of reducing demand. For example, although the price of gasoline and other oil-related products soared in the middle and late 1970s, consumption—though initially decreasing—quickly returned to about normal (U.S. Bureau of the Census, 1976). Meanwhile, the profits of oil companies have risen enormously, and the problems of inflation and economic imbalances have grown worse due to the rising prices.

There is nothing sinister about the inertia shown by energy-related institutions in developing effective conservation programs. Throughout this book we have characterized environmentally relevant behaviors as natural phenomena that are sensitive to prevailing contingencies of reinforcement. The behavior of presidents of corporations is no less a part of the natural scheme of things than the behaviors we have examined in previous chapters. The proper response, as we will discuss further in the last chapter of this book, is not to blame these persons but to get about the business of devising systems that lead to different ends.

Behavioral scientists have gradually taken up the challenge of producing a behavioral technology adequate to the task of promoting energy conservation. Their research has avoided some of the systems-level problems by emphasizing programs that are suitable for the individual consumer. Several of these efforts, as we will show, seem quite promising.

As yet, the knowledge developed in this area has not had a substantial impact upon national energy policy. Politicians, economists, engineers, physicists, and others concerned with energy are unlikely to come into contact with this growing literature. If they do, they are unlikely to understand the methodology and principles you have become familiar with in reading this book. Agencies concerned with energy, such as the Federal Office of Energy, can be expected to view the involvement of psychologists and other behavioral scientists in the energy problem with some surprise. This attitude may explain some of the reported difficulties that behavioral scientists have had with federal agencies involved with energy conservation (Winett, 1976). This orientation seems gradually to be changing, but currently only a tiny fraction of the budget is earmarked for behavior experimentation. Nevertheless, substantial gains have been made, as you shall see.

ALTERING OVERALL ENERGY CONSUMPTION IN INDIVIDUAL RESIDENCES

Behavioral interventions in overall monthly energy use in private residences have been aimed at two dimensions of the consumption problem: patterns of consumption (peaking) and levels of consumption. The first has to do with the uneven demand for electrical power. During an average day the greatest use of electricity occurs at certain peak periods, usually between 8–11 A.M. and 5–9 P.M. A significant percentage of the power-generating capacity required for peak periods is idle during times of lower demand. Thus, if consumption patterns can be changed to more even demand requirements, smaller power plants could be constructed at less overall cost to the environment.

Patterns of Consumption (Peaking)

Kohlenberg, Phillips, and Proctor (1976) were among the first to try experimental modifications of patterns of electricity usage. They investigated the effects of incentives, information, and feedback on electrical-energy peaking in private residences. In this study a peak was defined as any excessive use of electricity by the subject family, regardless of the time of day. Using three volunteer families who had responded to an ad in an environmental newsletter, Kohlenberg and his associates first collected baseline data, then provided simple information. The information consisted of a description of the general relationship between peaking and the local environment (that is, the Pacific Northwest) as well as a listing of the normal wattage ratings of home appliances in terms of 100-watt equivalents. This information had no effect on peaking, so other procedures were tried. A feedback condition was implemented that consisted of the placement of a device in the house that turned on a light when a certain current level was exceeded. This continuous feedback produced a moderate reduction in peaking. After another baseline period an incentive-plus-feedback condition was presented, which contained several components: (1) The families were told about the overall effects of previous experimental conditions for the subjects as a whole. (2) They were asked to make a special effort to reduce peaking just "to show that it could be done." (3) They were offered substantial incentives for reduction (for example, double the monetary value of their power bill in return for a 100% reduction in peaking during the two weeks of the condition). (4) They were taught how to read the recording charts in the feedback device that had been placed in their homes, thereby allowing the families to monitor continuously the kilowatt-hours (kWhs) being consumed. The greatest impact occurred with this condition. Although Kohlenberg and his colleagues did not give the figures, the reductions in peaking appear from the graphs to have been approximately 30% and 65% of baseline for feedback and incentives plus feedback, respectively.

In terms of actual levels of energy consumption, reducing peaking may not be of much help, since the primary objective is to redistribute existing consumption more evenly throughout the day. Unfortunately, Kohlenberg and his associates did not report actual levels of electricity consumption for the three households in the various conditions, so it was not clear whether peaking reductions also reduced overall levels of consumption. Another problem with this study is the clarity of the conditions. Several variables were changed simultaneously in the incentive-plus-feedback condition, including demands to change, monetary incentives, and the type of feedback. These changes make the results of the study difficult to interpret, since we know little about the relative contributions of each of these components.

Zarling and Lloyd (1978) dealt with these problems in their study of peaks in residential energy consumption by four families. The conditions were baseline, written daily kilowatt-hour feedback (in which the families were told how much they consumed the previous day), and immediate feedback about peaking. The immediate peaking feedback was provided by a device that signaled, with a tone and a light, every time the household exceeded a 15-minute consumption criterion, which was based on baseline use. The results, in line with those of Kohlenberg and his colleagues, showed that immediate feedback on peaking was an effective technique for reducing peaks. Significantly, Zarling and Lloyd showed that reducing peaks through immediate feedback also reduced the overall level of consumption, and did so more effectively than daily kilowatt-hour feedback. Since power companies are often very much concerned with peaking (for economic reasons), this finding may provide an avenue whereby behavioral technology can be developed that benefits both the companies and the environment.

Overall Levels of Consumption

The great majority of behavioral studies in residential energy consumption have been designed to reduce overall levels of energy consumed in private residences rather than simply altering the pattern of use throughout the day. Many different approaches have been tried in these studies. We will break down these efforts into four major areas: informational appeals, feedback, rates, and incentives.

Information, appeals, and prompts. By far the most popular type of procedures we as a society use to foster conservation are antecedent procedures; that is, the occasion is (supposedly) set for energy conservation. For example, when the President calls for citizens to lower their winter thermostats, he is doing so in an attempt (presumably) to reduce energy usage. Despite the popularity of the procedure, there are few experimental data supporting its effectiveness or long-term practicality.

Heberlein (1975) examined the effects of three types of informational appeals on electricity consumption in an apartment complex. He surreptitiously monitored 84 apartments for 12 days and then divided the apartments into four groups: a control group and three experimental groups receiving different types of information. The types of information consisted of (1) a typical pamphlet containing energy-saving tips distributed by the local utility company; (2) an informational-appeal letter designed to accentuate the negative consequences, both personal and social, of excessive electricity consumption for the economy and the environment (the letter also emphasized the individual's personal responsibility for these effects); and (3) an informational condition designed to *increase* electricity consumption by emphasizing the benefits of consumption and claiming that any adverse effects could not be blamed on the individual consumer. Each form of information was presented in writing to each household with a reminder over the telephone. Note that these consumers did not know that they were participants in a study.

After the delivery of the information, the households were surreptitiously monitored for another 12 days. The results, a comparison of the before-and-after data, showed that *none* of the appeals had any effect at all on the consumers!

As it happened, the Arab oil boycott of 1973–1974 hit about one year later. The entire country was virtually saturated with mass-media appeals for energy conservation. Curious, Heberlein rechecked the energy consumption of the same apartments. The same meters were again read each day for 25 days. Depressingly, even this all-out media campaign was apparently not effective. Comparisons between the 25 days recorded during that period and those a year earlier showed no differences.

This latter part of the study constitutes a "natural experiment." In other words, conditions changed and naturally allowed for a comparison between two phases. As in all natural experiments, it is important to interpret the results with caution. Many things may have distinguished 1972–1973 from 1973–1974. Nevertheless, the results are very interesting. It would be difficult in an experiment to produce the flood of publicity and calls for conservation that accompanied the Arab oil embargo. Thus, it offered us a unique opportunity to assess the impact of informational appeals on energy consumption. The negative results should cause real concern about the value of informational appeals.

M. H. Palmer, Lloyd, and Lloyd (1978) examined the effects of two types of prompts on electricity consumption by four families. Prompts and appeals were in either the form of a daily written prompt (such as "Kill-a-watt. Conserve energy") or a letter from a government official urgently requesting conservation efforts. The experimenters also tested two feedback conditions, consisting of either a daily report of electricity consumed in kilowatt-hours (termed "consumption feedback") or a daily report of the cost of electricity consumed in dollars and cents, with a projected monthly bill based upon that rate of use ("monetary feedback").

The households in the study were selected from a Des Moines suburb. The first four families contacted agreed to participate and were selected as subjects. These families had their meters read at the same time each day. After baseline recordings experimental conditions were implemented in various orders for the four families. Thus, this experiment involved both the effect of feedback (to be considered in more detail later) and prompts and appeals.

Family A consumed 33 kWh per day during the initial baseline phase. Consumption decreased by 4 kWh per day when a monetary-feedback condition was introduced but returned to its original level when feedback was withdrawn. A combined-prompt condition (the daily prompts and the letter from the government) was followed by a 6-kWh reduction in consumption, which returned to its original level when the prompts were withdrawn. The results for this family provide support for monetary feedback as an effective intervention and also indicate that frequent prompting combined with a letter from a government official may reduce consumption, at least temporarily.

In Family B the initial baseline phase was followed by a government prompt, then daily prompts, then daily prompts plus consumption feedback, then baseline, and finally daily prompts plus consumption feedback. Family B consumed 22 kWh of electricity per day in the baseline period. That amount decreased by 4 kWh per day during the two prompting conditions. The addition of feedback to the prompts reduced the consumption rate by another 4 kWh per day. The rate increased by 5 kWh per day in the second baseline phase. It again went down by 4 kWh per day in the final combined-prompt-plus-feedback condition. Thus, the use of frequent prompts was apparently somewhat effective, especially when combined with feedback.

In Family C, after the initial baseline phase, the following phases were presented: government prompts, daily prompts, baseline, and consumption feedback. This procedure allowed for an evaluation of the two prompting conditions combined relative to baseline. As it happened, the data were such that no conclusions could be drawn. Prompts seemed to reduce consumption, but the consumption did not increase in the second baseline phase. The feedback condition produced no apparent effects.

The fourth family in this study was exposed only to feedback (which we will examine shortly), so those results will not be described. This study provides some limited evidence for the effectiveness of combined daily prompts and governmental prompts. Design difficulties preclude a statement on the effects of each prompting condition. The study used only a few subjects, and the interventions were in place for only short periods, so it should be interpreted cautiously. You can easily imagine that you might get tired of a note in your mailbox every day for years at a time! It would also be very difficult to set up such a program, so the usefulness of these data is somewhat limited.

Other studies (described in later sections) have similarly shown that informational appeals have relatively weak effects on overall residential energy consumption. The one study with somewhat contradictory data (M. H. Palmer et al., 1978) used repeated prompts over a short period. This does not mean that information is unimportant. We saw earlier (for example, in Chapter 7) that information and media appeals can influence environmentally relevant behavior. Indeed, we shall show later in this chapter that such procedures can sometimes influence energy-related behavior, but not typically at the global level assessed by these and similar studies.

Feedback. The term *feedback* is a general one that varies in its precise meaning from study to study. Procedurally, we are calling feedback any intervention in which consumers are told something about the amount of, cost of, or trends in their consumption. One good way to view it is that feedback procedures attempt to teach consumers to discern their own energy-consumption habits (for example, times when they are conserving versus times when they are wasting). Since there are long-term benefits to conserving, we may do more of it if we are merely made aware of when we *are* conserving.

In a way, most of us get some feedback every month or every two months when we receive our power bills. Unfortunately, this type of feedback is often not very effective in controlling consumption. There are, perhaps, several reasons for this ineffectiveness. Residential energy consumers receive greatly delayed feedback from their monthly bills. Further, the feedback supplied by bills is primarily in the form of the monetary value of the energy consumed that month. Some companies also provide cost-per-day figures. These figures are of questionable value because they are subject not only to the consumer's behavior but also to seasonal differences and rate changes. Kilowatt-hour figures are contained in the bill, but these are probably less comprehensible to the consumer and are also subject to seasonal fluctuations. Seasonal variations create real interpretive problems for the consumer. It may be difficult to know from one month to the next (or even one week to the next) what "normal" levels of energy consumption are. If it is unusually warm or cold, windy or calm, snowy or green, sunny or cloudy, energy consumption can be expected to be similarly "unusual." A last problem that limits the feedback value of a monthly bill is that people, quite simply, forget from one billing period to the next.

Several variables have been manipulated in experimental feedback systems in an effort to find ways to increase the effectiveness of the normal feedback most consumers receive in their bills. Before describing specific research, we will briefly mention the major feedback characteristics that have been studied thus far in programs designed to influence levels of energy consumption. These characteristics are the frequency, form, and source of the feedback.

The more frequent the feedback, the less of a delay there is between the consumption behavior and seeing its effects. Further, frequent feedback breaks the behavior into smaller units. In the feedback systems described earlier in the peaking section, feedback was immediate (and effective). The delay between behavior and its consequences has been shown to be an important variable in the control of behavior in applied settings (see, for example, Hall, Axelrod, Tyler, Grief, Jones, & Robertson, 1972) and has been thoroughly investigated as a basic matter (see Tarpy & Sawabini, 1974, for a review of this literature).

Unfortunately, it does not seem practical to attempt to increase the number of billing periods without a major advance in the technology of consumption monitoring. Presently, a meter reader must physically travel to the site of the consumption and read the metering device. The reader usually travels by car or light truck—an energy-intensive practice requiring a good deal of gas and oil. Greatly increased billing frequency (for example, weekly) could result in an increase in cost to the consumer that would wipe out any savings resulting from the procedure. Further, the increased use of gasoline as a result of the increased metering activity would diminish any environmental savings gleaned in energy conservation. A view of the overall effect of environmental interventions is important and should be kept in mind by behavioral researchers in the area. These difficulties notwithstanding, however, several researchers have provided very frequent feedback to consumers in just such a manner. Others have found more practical ways to increase feedback frequency.

As far as the form of the feedback is concerned, some feedback systems have used monetary feedback (for example, money saved); others have used kilowatt-hour feedback. Some studies have used percentage change; others have used simple arithmetic comparisons. Some have made comparisons to seasonally adjusted baselines; others have used no baseline whatsoever. All of these may be quite important differences even though all are called feedback.

Finally, most of the systems devised so far have used experimenters to read the meters. Some researchers, however, have taught the consumer to read the meter, thereby providing personal feedback through self-monitoring.

As we go through the feedback studies, note how they have varied these three dimensions of frequency, form, and source. Although little research has been done to vary these dimensions systematically within particular studies, they have been varied between studies. By considering their relative effects, some of the important dimensions of feedback can be discerned.

In one of the earliest such studies, Seaver and Patterson (1976) examined the impact of feedback and feedback plus social commendation on the consumption of home heating oil. A large pool of households (180) was randomly selected from a list of continuing accounts of a fuel-oil distributor and randomly assigned to one of three conditions: untreated control, feedback, and feedback plus commendation for reduction. The control group was not informed that their consumption was being monitored. The feedback group received a single slip in the mail indicating how much oil they had consumed during the delivery period (midwinter 1974), as compared to a similar period the previous year. The feedback-plus-commendation group received a feedback slip but were also sent a decal saying "We are saving oil" if their consumption was below normal. Thus, this study manipulated the *form* of feedback by comparing consumption to that of the previous year rather than simply telling consumers what had been consumed (as a utility bill does). The study also compared feedback of this type with and without a social consequence. Perhaps significantly, the decal, if put up in a visible place, may have also altered natural social consequences. Neighbors and others may have expected a good example from families displaying the decal. The feedback-plus-commendation group used significantly less oil in the delivery period after the feedback and commendation than either of the other two groups (about 10% less during the treatment phase). There was no statistically significant difference in oil usage between the control group and the feedback group.

This study shows that households that did not volunteer for a study on energy consumption were susceptible to behavioral procedures designed to reduce consumption levels. Further, a relatively inexpensive decal apparently had a substantial effect on consumption. But just adding a comparison to last year's consumption was apparently not very helpful. It cannot be said whether the social commendation worked because it was a reinforcer (a positive consequence of conservation) or because it was an important antecedent stimulus that changed the social structure surrounding the households. This distinction is important because if the commendation worked in the latter manner the effects might be stronger if the decal was sent to *all* families regardless of consumption. You can easily imagine that just displaying the decal would lead neighbors and others to ask what the families are doing to save oil. This, in turn, might lead them to attempt to practice what they preach.

There was a design problem with this study, however, that is important enough (and common enough) to warrant discussion. Although the consumption levels themselves yielded the results we have reported, the *change* in consumption from the 1973 baseline period showed a different effect due to the different baseline levels of the groups (see Cone, 1973, for an interesting discussion of this problem). As it happened, the random assignment between groups produced 1973 baseline levels that were highest for the feedback-plus-commendation group and lowest for the control group. Calculated on the basis of the phase means, the *percentage* changes [(1973 baseline means − 1974 treatment mean)/1973 baseline mean] were 9%, 17%, and 22% for the control, feedback, and feedback-plus-commendation groups, respectively. All three of the groups improved somewhat (perhaps due to weather changes), and the feedback group, when viewed in this manner, showed little difference from the feedback-plus-commendation group. Thus, perhaps the simple change in the form of feedback used in this study (comparing consumption to last year's) *did* have an effect.

Winett, Neale, Williams, Yokley, and Kauder (1978) studied the effects of individual and social feedback. The experimenters recruited 76 families door to door in three different residential areas. After baseline data were collected, group meetings were held in which the feedback procedures were explained. Three types of feedback were used: individual-household feedback, group-only feedback, and combined individual/group feedback. Each day the subjects received written feedback consisting of total kilowatt-hours consumed the preceding day (for the individual households, group of households, or both) and a percentage comparison with expected levels. The interventions were maintained over a five-week to six-week period, and the results were quite encouraging. All forms of feedback produced consumption decreases as compared to the fuel usage of a control group, which received no feedback. The greatest reductions (about 20%) were found with the combined individual/group feedback. Individual-only and group-only feedback produced reductions of 14% and 5%, respectively. Thus, it appears that it is helpful to know not only how *you* are doing but how well *others* in your neighborhood are doing in their efforts to conserve energy. Further, daily feedback decreased consumption.

A number of other studies (for example, Seligman & Darley, 1977) have also demonstrated the usefulness of daily feedback as a technique for controlling energy use. Unfortunately, as noted earlier, this is not a very practical procedure. Researchers have attempted to improve the practicality of feedback systems in one of two ways: by increasing the time period between feedbacks and by teaching consumers to monitor their own meters, so as to provide their own feedback (as frequently as they want).

Decreased frequency of feedback would be expected to produce rapid lessening of the effects found with daily feedback. Surprisingly, although the effects may be reduced, they are still clear. Bittle, Thaler, and Valesano (1978), for example, found a 24% reduction in consumption when weekly feedback was given. Even weekly feedback, however, may be too frequent, since it would require additional readings. Hayes and Cone (in press) carried this strategy one step further and used monthly feedback.

In the Hayes and Cone study, 40 subjects were selected (without their knowledge) from the account lists of a medium-sized New England utility company. The subjects were divided into two groups, a control group and a monthly-feedback group. The control group was not contacted at all throughout the study; their consumption records were simply passed on to the experimenters by the company. The monthly-feedback group received a letter from the utility, shortly

---

THIS IS NOT A BILL

Dear Consumer:

   With all the concern over energy conservation, we
thought you might like to know whether you are
consuming more or less electricity now than in previous
years. Based on our records for this address over the last
three years, your consumption of electricity this last month
was:

_____% below previous years. Congratulations! You are
      saving energy.

_____ % above previous years.

(For those of you who would like more detail, this last
month you consumed _____ kWh of electricity,
compared to the previous average of _____ kWh. At
today's prices, this means you saved/spent about an extra
$ _____ .)

Figure 10–1. A copy of the form letter sent to the subjects each month in
the Hayes and Cone study. Portions of the letter were blacked out, depending
upon whether the subject had saved electricity or not. From "The Reduction
of Residential Energy Consumption through Simple Monthly Feedback," by
S. C. Hayes and J. D. Cone. In *Journal of Applied Behavior Analysis,* in
press. Reprinted by permission of the Society for the Experimental Analysis
of Behavior, Inc.

after their usual bill, which simply stated whether the consumer had used more or
less than expected, based upon their consumption for that particular month in the
preceding three years. Actual kilowatt-hours (consumed and expected), percentage change from baseline, and money saved or wasted were also given (see
Figure 10–1). Note that all of this information is implicit in the normal monthly
bill but that making it explicit requires saving records for several years and doing
the calculations. Only the form, not the frequency, of the feedback is different.
With an *ABA* design the data showed a clear decrease in electricity consumption
for the feedback group during the feedback phase (see Figure 10–2). The effect
was maintained throughout a four-month intervention period. Withdrawal of the
feedback led to a return to higher levels of consumption.

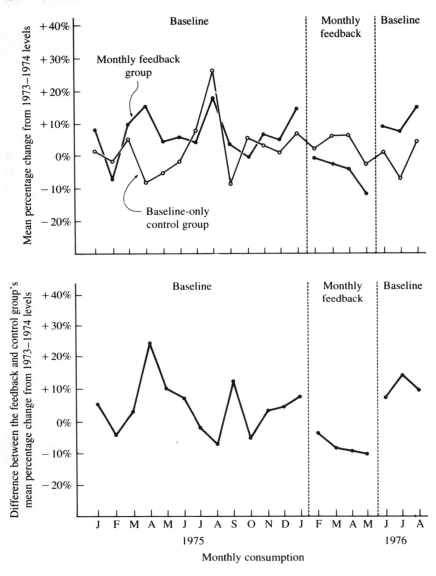

Figure 10–2. The upper half of this figure shows the mean percentage-change scores of the monthly-feedback and control groups in the baseline, monthly-feedback, and return-to-baseline phases. The lower half shows the difference between the percentage-change scores of the monthly-feedback group and the control group in the baseline, monthly-feedback, and baseline conditions. From "The Reduction of Residential Energy Consumption through Simple Monthly Feedback," by S. C. Hayes and J. D. Cone. In *Journal of Applied Behavior Analysis,* in press. Reprinted by permission of the Society for the Experimental Analysis of Behavior, Inc.

This study is quite encouraging for two reasons. First, it used a totally practical procedure. It relied only upon the usual readings taken by the power company. The calculations made could easily be done by a computer for a fraction of a cent per customer and simply included with the monthly bill. Second, these subjects were not volunteers; they were not even aware that they were participants in a study. Thus, these procedures may work with the general population.

The second strategy, teaching consumers to read their own meters, has been used in several studies. It was first tested, in a preliminary way, by Hayes (1977). Consumers were taught to read their meters and plot the figures on a form that automatically showed how much the bill would be if they continued consumption at that rate. Using a multiple baseline across subjects, Hayes found small but consistent decreases in consumption.

A more extensive study was conducted by Winett, Neale, and Grier (1979). They divided 71 nearly identical volunteer households living in townhouses into three groups: (1) self-monitoring, in which consumers were taught to read and plot their daily consumption; (2) daily kilowatt-hours and monetary feedback (provided by the experimenters); and (3) a no-treatment control group. In an *ABA* design daily feedback and monetary reward were shown to reduce consumption by 14%, but self-monitoring alone also produced a significant reduction—about 8%. Thus, it appears that self-monitoring may be a practical procedure for energy-use reduction.

Few studies have examined *why* feedback is effective when it is. At the beginning of this section, we presented one view: feedback is effective because it reduces the delay or makes clearer the relationship between behavior and significant consequences of that behavior. Becker (1978) has examined a related notion, that feedback is relevant only when you have a standard against which to evaluate the consequences. Thus, if you have *no* standard (that is, any consequence is as good as any other), feedback is irrelevant. Conversely, if you have no feedback (you do not know what, when, or to what degree you did what you did), then standards are irrelevant. You need both. Becker induced subjects to set high or low goals (standards) for conservation and gave some of them feedback (three times a week) but not the others. The results showed that only subjects with high standards *and* feedback consumed less than a control group. These results may explain some of the inconsistent findings in the various feedback studies. Feedback may work (or not) depending on the subjects' standards before the study even began. More basic research of this sort on the nature of feedback seems needed.

In summary, the feedback studies show that just knowing more about your own energy-consumption behavior often reduces consumption. This is so for volunteers and nonvolunteers; when feedback is given alone or with incentives; when it is given often or infrequently; when consumers themselves generate the feedback or when it is generated for them; and whether or not consumers actually pay their own power bills. Although we know little about the process through which feedback works, it seems to work best when we have some standard or goal against which to evaluate our performance.

Box 10–1. Subject Characteristics and Energy Conservation

Perhaps an additional way to encourage energy conservation is to gather together persons who naturally prefer energy-thrifty environments. We all know people who seem to be able to withstand a chilly room with little discomfort while others find it positively uncomfortable. Drawing on this notion, David Edwards, plant director for a small college in Maine, came up with a novel idea. He suggested that incoming students be asked whether they are cold-blooded or hot-blooded. All the students who reported being hot-blooded would then be placed in a dormitory where the thermostat was kept at a lower temperature. Whether this idea might actually work has not been tested, but using it certainly would give a whole new meaning to talk about the "hot-blooded males (or females) over in Dorm B"!

Energy rates and rate structures. Rate structures are currently arranged in most areas so that the cost of energy decreases as its use increases. Residential users, for example, may pay a higher cost per kilowatt-hour for the first 100 kWh than for subsequent consumption in the billing period. This type of rate structure has been termed a decreasing block rate (we will have more to say about this in Chapter 11). In this type of rate structure, residential consumers typically pay more per kilowatt-hour than industrial consumers, since the latter use far more electricity.

Other rate structures may hold some promise for the reduction of electricity consumption and are being implemented in some areas. One such rate is the flat rate. This plan would set a cost per kilowatt-hour that would apply to everybody, regardless of consumption levels.

Another proposal would adopt a progressive rate. The first few hundred kilowatt-hours of energy consumed each month would be very inexpensive, but the rate would increase steadily as consumption increased. This plan would provide protection to poor households. It is a reasonable proposal on the face of it and may reduce consumption. It could be subverted, however. Individual businesses could break their operations into several discrete units, each with its own energy account, thus decreasing the rate per kilowatt-hour. This type of rate plan is referred to by the industry as an inverted rate because it is the exact opposite of the current arrangement. It has been heavily criticized by the power industry ("Inverted Electric Rates," 1974). Although the cost of power production does not vary with the size of the consumer, it is argued that smaller customers require proportionately more expense in terms of delivery (for example, transmission lines), metering, and collection of bills than do larger customers and therefore should pay more.

In addition to changes in rate structure, some proposals have centered on the overall rate itself. The logic behind this approach is that conservation will come only when energy rates are increased to the point that it becomes economically important to conserve. Much of our national energy policy seems based upon this view (the deregulation of oil prices is an example).

Power companies are not eager to experiment in those areas, especially when the goal is decreased overall consumption (Kohlenberg, Barach, Martin, and Anschell, 1976; Winett, 1976). Regulatory boards, which might encourage such research, are not often known for their environmental concern. As Farris and Sampson (1973) point out rather gently: "Commissioners . . . have been known to move from government service into high positions in the industries which they have been regulating" (p. 66). Though regulatory boards are certainly most often honest and well-meaning, it is nevertheless true that an experimental approach to electricity consumption is unlikely to be adopted by such agencies.

This leaves us all in a difficult position. Due to the lack of experimentation, it is hard to know whether to support rate-structure changes. Most decisions are now guided by largely nonexperimental fields, such as economics. But it is one thing to *predict* that particular changes will yield benefits; it is another thing to *show* it.

In one of the few studies in this area, Kohlenberg and his associates (1976) conducted an interesting experiment on the effects of several different rates and rate structures on energy use. The study was conducted over a six-month period with nearly 200 consumers in Seattle. Three conditions were used. (1) In the rate-increase condition, subjects were required to pay 150% of their normal bill. (2) In the rate-structure condition a variable price per kilowatt-hour was used, dependent upon the amount of electrical-energy consumption. Some of the subjects in this condition experienced a steeply inverted rate structure (large increments in price per unit consumed as use increased), while other subjects experienced a relatively gradual inverted-rate structure. (3) In the feedback condition, subjects received weekly electricity-use reports. These included the amount and cost of energy consumed, a comparison to the previous week, and a comparison to the previous year. Seattle residents normally receive consumption feedback (from their power bills) once every two months. Due to the large amount of hydroelectric power generated in the area, electricity rates are among the lowest in the nation.

The results show that the subjects who were charged the higher rate decreased energy consumption by about 6% (a savings of 17 kWh each week). The rate-structure and feedback conditions did not significantly reduce electricity consumption. However, when feedback was combined with the higher rate structure, consumption dropped nearly 9%. Note that there were no reductions due to rate structure. Although such structures may be socially desirable (for example, so poor people can afford electricity), they apparently are not helpful in promoting conservation, according to this study. Another point: when rates were increased by 50%, consumption decreased only 6%. Since reductions of this level have often been reported with cheaper procedures, this seems to be an inefficient way to achieve conservation. Rate increases alone are surely not the best answer to our energy problems, although they may play a part.

Incentives. One of the most powerful but not necessarily most efficient techniques for promoting energy conservation is through experimental incentives— paying people for reducing their consumption. You might think (as many economists would; for example, see Winett, Kagel, Battalio, & Winkler, 1978) that this is essentially just the reverse of increasing rates and should produce similar results. But they do differ. It is one thing to pay more for consuming more. It is another actually to receive money for consuming less. You get clean feedback in experimental-incentive systems that you may miss in mere rate changes. As we just saw (Kohlenberg et al., 1976), feedback had an effect when added to rate increases.

In one of the first incentive studies, Winett and Nietzel (1975) examined the effects of information, feedback, and incentives on the overall levels of consumption of electricity and natural gas in private residences. The subjects were recruited in a manner somewhat similar to that used by Kohlenberg, Phillips, and Proctor (1976); subjects volunteered for the study in response to articles in the local newspaper. The households were randomly assigned to one of two conditions. One group of households ($n = 15$) received a "conservation manual" containing descriptions of energy-reduction techniques (that is, information) and a self-recording form with which to monitor weekly meter readings (that is, feedback). The other group of households ($n = 16$) received the manual and the recording forms but also received monetary payments for reducing their consumption of energy. Subjects who reduced their weekly energy use (an average of natural gas and electricity consumed) by 5%–10% below baseline levels received $2 per week; 11%–20% reductions yielded a $3 payment; and reductions of more than 20% earned $5. The household averaging the greatest reduction during the four weeks of the treatment condition received a bonus payment of $25, while the household with the next-greatest reduction earned $15. These interventions were presented in an *ABA* fashion in the two groups.

The data showed that the payment-plus-information-plus-feedback group averaged about 15% more electricity reduction than the information-plus-feedback group (natural-gas-consumption figures were about the same for the two groups). This difference was maintained somewhat during a two-week follow-up period but was not statistically significant. Thus, it appears that incentives (beyond those already in place in the form of the normal monthly bill) were an effective technique for energy conservation.

In a similar study Hayes and Cone (1977b) examined the effects of payments, feedback, and information on the electrical consumption of four apartments in a university housing complex. As in the Seaver and Patterson (1976) and Hayes and Cone (in press) studies, subject households were selected randomly and their electricity monitored before they were approached for cooperation.

The housing complex itself did not bill individual households for energy consumed, as you may remember from the anecdote at the beginning of this chapter. This circumstance is interesting from a theoretical point of view because it permitted an uncontaminated examination of the effects of payments, feedback, and information themselves rather than in combination with the natural ones involved in receiving a lower bill.

There were three major experimental conditions in the study: information, feedback, and payment. The information condition consisted of a poster that described ways to reduce the consumption of electricity and gave the amount of energy consumed per year (in terms of both kilowatt-hours and dollars and cents) by most common electrical devices (from Jurgen, 1974).

The feedback condition consisted of the daily distribution of a flier to each household containing the following information (in dollars and cents): (1) the amount of electricity consumed the previous day, (2) the amount of electricity consumed so far that week, (3) the amount of electricity that would be consumed for the week at that rate of consumption, and (4) the percentage above or below baseline level that the preceding figure represented (the baseline level used was the first baseline period of the study).

The payment condition consisted of cash payments to the household at the end of the week according to the percentage reduction in weekly electricity consumption as compared to the baseline level (note that this figure was the same as the fourth item on the feedback form). The original, or 100%-payment, schedule was as follows: a 10%–19% reduction earned a $3 payment; 20%–29% earned $6; 30%–39% earned $9; 40%–49% yielded $12; and 50% or more earned $15.

These payments were reduced later in the study, but the basic schedule remained the same; only the values of the payments themselves changed. A 50%-payment condition, for example, would yield $1.50 for a 10%–19% reduction, $3 for a 20%–29% reduction, and so on, up to a possible $7.50 for a reduction in consumption of 50% or more. Similarly, a 10%-payment condition would pay off at the rate of 30¢ for each successive 10% reduction, up to a maximum of $1.50 for a reduction of 50% or more.

After an initial ten-day to 13-day covert baseline period (in which the subjects did not know that they were being monitored), the families were asked to participate in the study. Four of the five households agreed to participate. The basic nature of the study was explained to them, and electricity consumption continued to be monitored daily over the next eight to 13 days without intervention so as to assess the reactive effects of monitoring itself. After this overt baseline period (with knowledge of recording), a 100%-payment condition was implemented across the four households.

Near the end of the sixth week, the four units were divided into two groups of two units each. The effects of feedback and payments were compared in one group of two units, while information and payments were compared in the other group.

The design was complicated, but a basic understanding can be had by examining the results, which are shown in Figures 10–3 and 10–4. Essentially, feedback was instituted, alone and in combination with payments, in Units 3 and

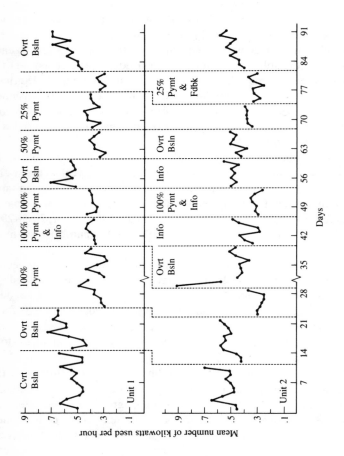

Figure 10–3. Kilowatt-hour values for Units 1 and 2 across the 91 days of the study. Abbreviations are: Cvrt = covert, Bsln = baseline, Ovrt = overt, Pymt = payment, Info = information, and Fdbk = feedback. The gap in the data between Days 31 and 32 was due to spring vacation at the university, during which most students leave town. From "Reducing Residential Electrical Energy Use: Payments, Information, and Feedback," by S. C. Hayes and J. D. Cone, *Journal of Applied Behavior Analysis*, 1977, *10*, 425–435. Copyright 1977 by the Society for the Experimental Analysis of Behavior, Inc. Reprinted by permission.

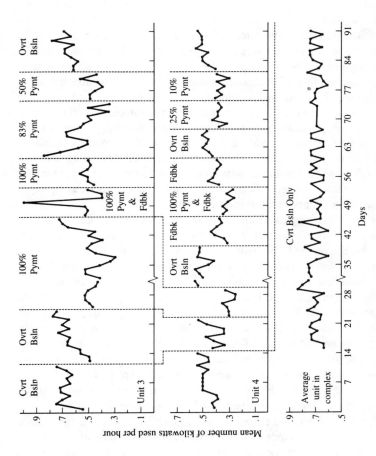

Figure 10–4. Kilowatt-hour values for Units 3 and 4 and for the average unit in the overall complex across the 91 days of the study. Abbreviations are: Cvrt = covert, Bsln = baseline, Ovrt = overt, Pymt = payment, Info = information, and Fdbk = feedback. The gap in the data between Days 31 and 32 was due to spring vacation at the university, during which most students leave town. From "Reducing Residential Electrical Energy Use: Payments, Information, and Feedback," by S. C. Hayes and J. D. Cone, *Journal of Applied Behavior Analysis,* 1977, *10,* 425–435. Copyright 1977 by the Society for the Experimental Analysis of Behavior, Inc. Reprinted by permission.

4, while information and information plus payments were compared in Units 1 and 2. Later in the study the relative effects of various levels of payments were compared, both alone and in combination with feedback.

The results showed that monitoring alone produced a small initial decrease in energy consumption, which returned to normal in a few days. Information alone also had the same effect. Feedback alone, however, resulted in stable though moderate reductions (about 17% below baseline levels). All reductions were calculated by the formula [(treatment − baseline)/baseline]. The 100%-payment condition was the most successful, producing a reduction of 34%, averaged across units. This effect was only slightly diminished by reducing the amount of the payments. There was no indication of an additive effect of payments and information; that is, the combined condition was no more effective than payments alone. The data on the additive effect of feedback and payments were unclear. In Unit 3 the data were so variable that a statement on the relative effectiveness of payments and payments plus feedback was impossible. In two other units (1 and 2), however, adding feedback to a 25%-payment condition seemed to result in a small decrease in consumption. Feedback may have only a small additive effect when combined with monetary consequences, or it may be that any additive effects are washed out by the floor effect produced by large monetary consequences for reductions in consumption.

This study is reassuring in a number of respects. It shows that monitoring itself is probably not an important variable in energy-consumption research. Further, as in the Seaver and Patterson (1976) and Hayes and Cone (in press) studies, randomly selected families produced results similar to those for the volunteer households used in other studies. One factor limiting the results of this study is that the apartments were heated by gas. Essentially, the electricity in these apartments was used for appliances and lighting. The results would probably have been less impressive if the heating were electric or if the size and design of the apartments had permitted more energy-consuming appliances.

Nevertheless, the results are significant. Recall that reductions in consumption were shown even with minimal payments, which were in fact below the value of the energy saved itself. Think about this for a moment, and you will see why this is important. These consumers did not pay their energy bills—the complex did. The complex could therefore save money by paying the residents a small bonus for conserving. Under at least some conditions, incentives may be both environmentally *and* economically desirable. We will have more to say about this later in the chapter.

The use of monetary incentives to reduce electricity consumption was also the subject of a study by Winett, Kaiser, and Haberkorn (1977). They divided 12 apartment units into two groups: experimental and control. After one week of baseline, the six experimental units were placed on a high-incentive system together with daily feedback and information on how to conserve energy. After one week, three of the experimental units were placed on a rebate schedule equal to 50% of the monetary value of any energy saved as compared to consumption during the high-rebate condition. The other three experimental units received no rebates. All six experimental units continued to receive feedback. After a week all six experimental units received feedback only.

The results of this study are a bit difficult to interpret because the phases were so short and there was high variability within experimental phases. The greatest difference between experimental and control units occurred during the condition of high rebates plus feedback and information. For the three experimental units that were placed on a reduced-rebate system, consumption was below that of the control units on five days but not on the other two days (when the temperature was highest). Feedback alone was not shown to be effective.

Winett, Kagel, Battalio, and Winkler (1978) compared two incentive systems, feedback, and information in 129 volunteer households. Four conditions were tested: (1) information about conservation, (2) information and weekly feedback, (3) a low incentive plus information and weekly feedback, and (4) a high incentive (up to 240% of the bill!) plus information and weekly feedback. The results showed a reduction (12%) only for the last condition.

Taken together, these studies show that incentives can have a strong effect on energy consumption. The reductions are only moderate in many of these studies, but even a moderate reduction could have a giant impact if implemented throughout the country. The global approach taken by these studies, however, has caused some researchers to wonder how consumers conserve energy; that is, specifically what do they do? The next section examines this question.

ALTERING SPECIFIC ENERGY-RELATED BEHAVIORS

Overall reductions in consumption must be the result of many specific behaviors (for example, turning down air conditioners, turning off lights). What are they? How do they change? Perhaps by concentrating on specific behaviors, some researchers believe, more effective programs can be developed and then implemented more broadly. Several researchers have attempted to do just that.

Wodarski (1975) presented the first such study. This study, admittedly a pilot project, was conducted in one household (two adults and two children). Index cards were taped to certain appliances, and the husband and wife were asked to record on the card when the particular appliance was turned on and off and the duration of its use. An *ABA* design was used, alternating baseline with a token-reinforcement procedure. During the token phases the couple earned points by using each appliance less than during baseline. At the end of each reinforcement period, the points could be traded for such backup rewards as a night out on the town.

The data indicated a clear effect of the token system on the use of the TV and radio, but no clear results were found for the use of the oven. This study should be regarded as a preliminary effort in a potentially worthwhile area, the analysis of individual consumption behaviors. Automatic-recording devices would be helpful in future efforts.

Another group of projects has examined procedures designed to get people to turn out lights. Lighting is a relatively minor part of our energy consumption, but it may be possible to develop procedures that work with lighting that could then be transferred to other, more important behaviors.

Winett (1977) examined this behavior in three college classrooms. Two of these rooms served as controls, while a third served as the experimental room. The rooms were observed while unoccupied once each day after 5 P.M. to see if the lights were on. After an initial baseline period a sign that had previously been placed on campus bulletin boards was placed over the light switches in the experimental room. The sign read "Every Little Light Lit Hurts; Please Turn Lights and Electrical Equipment Off When Not in Use." In the following weeks other signs were tried: a small sign reading "Turn This Light Off When Not in Use"; a large sign reading "Students and Faculty, Conserve Energy—Turn Out Lights after 5 P.M. or When No Class"; a small sign placed over the light switches and reading "Conserve Energy; Turn Out Lights after 5 P.M."; and another sign placed near the exit reading "Faculty and Students, Turn Out Lights after 5 P.M. or When No Class."

The results showed that the lights were on 78% of the days checked in the control rooms. The lights were on 95% of the time during baseline in the experimental room. The two nonspecific signs, which merely asked people to turn out the lights, had no effect. But when more specific information was added (turn out the lights *after 5 P.M.*), the lights were left on only about 40% of the time.

Delprato (1977) examined the effects of prompts on turning out the lights in men's rest rooms at a university. The intervention consisted primarily of a sign containing conservation information and asking that the lights be turned out. Reductions of more than 50% were found in the time that the lights were on. Luyben (1978) and Luyben and Luyben (1977) found similar results in college classrooms through the use of prompts.

It appears that prompts may be useful in the generation of specific, low-effort energy-conservation behaviors. However, it should be recognized that these studies were concerned with relatively trivial behaviors. Becker and Seligman (1978) examined the effect of a creative type of prompt on a more important behavior: air-conditioner usage. Heating and cooling account for the lion's share of home energy consumption, so anything that can influence these areas is bound to be important. Becker and Seligman thought that perhaps people leave their air conditioners on longer than they have to because they do not know that it has turned cool outside. They put together a device that blinked a light when the air conditioner was on and it was 68° F outside or cooler (at that temperature, consumers can cool their houses simply by opening the windows). The study showed that the device reduced electrical consumption by more than 15%. It would pay for itself, they said, in about two years.

REDUCING ENERGY CONSUMED IN MASTER-METERED HOUSING

So far, we have examined primarily the consumption of energy in private residential settings in which the household is individually metered and pays its own bills. But there are a number of settings in which residences are master metered (only one meter covers many residences)—for example, in dormitories, fraternity and sorority houses, and some apartment complexes. The procedures that worked or were practical in private residences may not work in these settings (and vice versa).

Newsom and Makranczy (1978) studied the effects of information, feedback, and incentives in several college dormitories housing more than 1500 students. Two types of programs were used, and the results were compared with data from control dorms. In one program a group contest was held. Dorms competed against each other for a cash prize to be awarded to the winning dorm. The cash went to the dorm treasury. In the raffle condition there was also competition between dorms, but the prize money went to an individual (determined by a raffle) in the winning dorm. Both of these procedures produced reductions in consumption, as compared to the control dorms (an average of about 5%). The total payments were $180, while the estimated savings were about $150. This is very close to a break-even point, so a school or apartment complex might economically establish a similar program.

Walker (1977) was able to devise an incentive program for master-metered apartment complexes that was cost effective. In this program, apartments were randomly checked to see whether the doors and windows were closed (unless the heater or air conditioner was turned off), and the thermostats were reasonably set (69° F for the heater and 74° F for the air conditioner). If these conditions were met, the resident received $5. The program was tested twice—once in the heating season and once in the cooling season—and yielded consumption reductions in the complex of 2.2% and 8.6%, respectively, as compared to a similar control apartment complex. The program cost about $200 a month in incentive payments, but it saved about $320 in electricity. Note that the thermostat settings used in this study are more liberal than those needed for comfort. Setting a slightly more conservative criterion might have produced even greater cost benefits for the owner of the complex.

One way to set up an incentive system for master-metered apartments is simply to share a certain percentage of energy savings with all the residents. This approach has been tested by Slavin and Wodarski (1977). In this system, consumers are given part (for example, 50% or 75%) of the savings they establish for natural gas or electricity. Consumers in these studies have also received informational material and periodic feedback (for example, every two to four weeks) about the group's consumption. One advantage of this approach is that it will be cost effective almost by definition. The benefits of any reduction over a sufficiently long period that can be shown to be the result of the incentive will be shared between the owner of the complex and the consumers.

The results of these studies have shown that such systems can influence energy consumption. Average reductions have ranged from 2% to 11% in the various apartment buildings studied. However, several subject variables may influence the effectiveness of the procedures, such as the types of appliances used or the size of the master-metered group.

Not all programs have used monetary incentives in master-metered buildings. Chandler, West, Anderson, Moore, and Hayes (1978) examined the effects of social feedback in several college dormitories. The feedback was of two types: (1) simple social feedback, in which the dormitory's percentage of energy use above or below baseline was displayed daily on graphs throughout the dorm, and (2) competitive social feedback, in which daily social feedback was given for the dorm itself *and* for a paired (competitor) dorm on campus. These two treatment procedures were alternated with periods of baseline.

The results showed that simple social feedback was not very effective in producing consumption reduction. However, competitive social feedback did influence consumption (about a 10% reduction). College dorms are often competing with each other in various arenas (such as intramural sports), so this competition may be a useful tool in energy-conservation programs. Whether competition would continue to be effective over the long term is unclear. There are some data suggesting that it might not be (McClelland & Cook, 1977).

McClelland and Belsten (1978) used a package of information, required group-discussion meetings, prompts (signs throughout the dorms), and monthly social feedback in a ten-week program in several college dormitories that housed almost 2000 students. The results showed more than a 10% reduction in consumption, as compared to expected levels of consumption based on baseline levels. In a subsequent study in the same dorms, a monetary incentive was added for some of the dorms, while others became control dorms. Further reductions of about 10% (compared to consumption in the control dorms) were found.

The studies reviewed in this section show that meaningful reductions in consumption can be achieved by relatively inexpensive interventions, even in very large groups. This conclusion is important primarily because these settings are ones in which behavioral technology is probably most likely to be widely and permanently implemented. Only in master-metered settings are the economic incentives likely to be large enough to promote immediate, widespread usage of the knowledge being developed in this area.

The energy studies reviewed comprise the largest and best-controlled body of research in behavioral approaches to environmental problems. There are, of course, many limitations to these efforts. Most of these studies have used volunteers, for example. Volunteers may differ in important ways from nonvolunteers. Fortunately, it appears that the two groups' actual energy consumption is similar (Hayes & Cone, in press), and some of these programs may be practical when set up totally on a volunteer basis. Others, however, would be important or practical only if widely implemented in nonvolunteer homes. It remains to be demonstrated that they will continue to be successful at that level. Many of the programs have also tended to be small-scale, short-term projects. These kinds of projects may be useful, but, ultimately, large-scale, long-term projects are also needed.

Few of the studies reviewed attempted a systematic variation of intervention programs along a conceptually important dimension. Thus, most of the conclusions about such questions as the important components of feedback have to be drawn by comparing several studies. This is a weak form of experimental comparison, and the comprehensiveness of the literature would probably increase faster if such comparisons could be made within studies. This is difficult, however. Energy consumption varies a great deal from time to time and from household to household. Accordingly, it is difficult to interpret small differences between groups. Given the fact that most households cannot conserve much energy beyond a certain point, it is difficult to achieve large enough differences to see the fine-grained effects of variables. One solution would be to conduct very, very large studies. Several of the recent studies have followed this strategy, especially those that have been supported by federal research grants.

One problem facing the area of energy control is the widespread sense of helplessness being generated by the ever-escalating cost of energy. As we will note in our last chapter, consumers are often aware that it is difficult to protect themselves from increased costs of natural resources. Indeed, conservation itself may actually raise the costs of energy by cutting into the revenues of energy concerns, necessitating a rise in prices.

One solution may be to test the psychological and behavioral impact of energy policy before it is implemented on a wide scale. The methodology presented in this chapter is fully adequate, at least theoretically, to the task of experimentally testing energy policy in this country. When the President advocates raising electricity rates or giving tax rebates to consumers who install insulation, it would be highly desirable to know with some certainty that these programs will work. Perhaps one of the main values of the research described in this chapter is not so much that it gives us an answer to energy conservation as that it does present a model for the evaluation and development of efforts in this area.

SUMMARY

Energy conservation is one of the major areas of research in behavioral solutions to environmental problems. The research done to date seems to show that information alone is rarely very effective in influencing energy-related behaviors. Feedback, in which consumers are told more about their energy-consuming behavior, is moderately effective in a number of settings and arrangements. Incentives are perhaps the most effective procedure yet identified, but it is difficult to establish a cost-effective and practical program (except in master-metered housing). The research done to date holds out the hope that energy policy might be better designed and tested so as to maximize its impact on us all.

SUGGESTED PROJECT

This project follows up on the study done by Seaver and Patterson (1976). In that study, consumers who reduced their consumption of fuel oil were given stickers that said "We are saving oil." It was shown that these consumers then reduced their consumption even further. Although the authors suggested that the effect was due to social commendation, it could also have been due to the fact that consumers who put up the stickers were then expected (for example, by neighbors) to reduce their consumption. Research in social psychology has long shown that people making such public commitments change their behavior to correspond with the commitment. For example, you would probably expect friends who had just claimed that they were really reducing their power consumption to set an example by turning out lights, turning down the thermostat, and so on. If they did not, you would probably give them a hard time!

In this study there will be three groups. You will first record the energy consumption of all three groups for a couple of weeks or more (they do not have to be volunteers; you might just read all the meters in an entire apartment complex, for example). Compare the amount consumed in the first part of the period to the last part. Then divide the entire group into those whose consumption went down from the first to the second part of the period and those whose consumption went up. Put one-third of each of these two groups into a control group. Now you have three groups: energy savers, energy consumers, and a control group made up of savers and consumers. Now send the savers and consumers each a sticker saying "We are saving electricity." Continue to record the consumption of all the households. If the sticker is really a reward, the savers should save even more; the consumers should consume even more. If, instead, the sticker works because those who put it up are making a public commitment, both savers and consumers should reduce their consumption relative to the control group.

Chapter 11

RESIDENTIAL
WATER
CONSERVATION

This country has an enormous supply of fresh pure water: the daily average rainfall is 4,200,000,000,000 gallons [Milne, 1976, p. 10].

For many years beyond A.D. 2000 total water shortages for the U.S. as a whole are highly improbable [Wolman, 1970, p. 47].

These opening quotes seem an unlikely beginning for a chapter on water conservation. Why bother? Even if existing water systems are operating at capacity, is not the solution merely to build more? After all, it would seem that there are untold reserves of water in more than sufficient quantity to serve a world population many times larger than its present size. Look at the oceans, the many lakes, the streams, and the rivers. Surely water from them can be captured for use. Is there really only a problem in the technology available to harness these sources?

We shall try to answer these questions in the present chapter after examining the overall world supply of water. We shall make the point that the important reasons for residential water conservation are not related to the amount of water involved but to the environmental costs related to its capture, transportation, purification, heating, and so on.

Since there has been no experimental behavioral-science work in water conservation, we will devote a good deal of discussion to the fascinating types of water-saving technology available and to some possible reasons that it has not been widely adopted. Finally, we include a section dealing with the types of experimental research that behavioral scientists could be doing in the area.

First, let us look more closely at the planet's water supply. It has been estimated that there are approximately 326 million cubic miles of water on earth (Milne, 1976, p. 25). Of this figure, 317 million cubic miles (97%) consist of salt water, leaving 9 million cubic miles of fresh water, presumably available for use. However, 7 million cubic miles of this water are locked up in polar ice and glaciers. Actually, only about 1 million cubic miles of fresh water are available for human consumption, or .3% of the earth's total! This is a very small fraction indeed. Because it is so large in absolute terms, however, the argument for water conservation is generally not based on a limited supply, as it has been with other natural resources.

A further look at how this usable water is actually distributed will be instructive in showing just what portion of the pie we will be dealing with in the rest of this chapter. As Milne (p. 25) has noted, human use of water falls into two major categories: (1) in-stream use, which does not remove water from its natural course, and (2) withdrawn water, which is water taken from its natural course and used before being returned. The bulk of withdrawn water is returned to nature without the need for any kind of treatment. Examples would be water used for agricultural irrigation and for watering lawns. Most water used in irrigation soaks into the ground or runs off, eventually returning to the natural water stream. Some evaporates, however, and its chemical state changes several times before it returns to the natural stream. Water that changes form or requires some type of treatment before being returned to nature is said to have been consumed (Milne, 1976, p. 26). Of the estimated 420 billion gallons of water withdrawn per day in the United States in 1975, 95 billion gallons per day were consumed, or about 23% (Murray & Reeves, 1977).

When consumed water is divided into various categories (for example, agricultural, municipal, steam electric, and so on), we find that the greatest portion goes to agriculture (85%), with something less than 5% going to residential users. With such a small percentage of our water being used in homes, why bother at all with residential water consumption? After all, if household consumption of fuel oil represented only 5% of the amount normally consumed, it is likely that conservation efforts would be directed toward larger users. Why not concentrate on agricultural uses of water?

The reason for residential water conservation rests less in the amount involved than in the environmental costs related to its capture, transportation, use, and disposal. Consider, for example, the obvious and not-so-obvious costs involved in the seemingly innocuous practice of providing a glass of ice water to every customer in a restaurant. In addition to the water in the glass, there are also the water in the ice and the water used to wash and rinse the glass. Then there is the electricity used to make the ice, to keep it frozen, and to operate the dishwasher. The soap used in the washing process has to be properly disposed of, as it may contain phosphates and other chemicals harmful to plant and animal life. Of course, this is just a superficial analysis of the environmental impact of a glass of ice water. There are undoubtedly additional factors not even touched on here.

Similar analyses could be applied to numerous other water-using practices, such as daily bathing or showering, car washing, lawn watering, and so on. The water required for each of the activities is only one of the factors that would be uncovered in a thorough ecological audit of the costs involved.

For example, consider how other utilities are affected by water use. According to Milne (1976), "domestic water heating alone consumes 4% of our total national energy budget" (p. 11). Thus, gas and electricity are closely tied to water use. Indeed, San Diego recently prohibited the installation of electric hot-water heaters in new residential construction. Alternative modes, such as solar systems, must be installed if natural gas cannot be used. Additionally, the energy cost to pump and otherwise transport water from one location to another is rapidly increasing. It is not widely appreciated that the use of more domestic water requires more sewage-treatment capacity, more storage, and the tapping of more remote, thus more costly, water sources. Better known is the potential environmental cost incurred when dams are built to store large quantities of water in reservoirs behind them. Perhaps the best example here is the Central Arizona Project embodied in proposed legislation calling for the construction of at least one large dam in the Grand Canyon (Soucie, 1968)! The idea so incensed environmentalists that they waged a successful campaign to prevent it.

Thus, the major reason for water conservation is not its scarcity but rather the environmental costs of supplying it. When viewed in this way, the importance of conserving water in residential settings is much greater than might be assumed from the small percentage of the total amount of water consumed.

Because the importance of water conservation is just beginning to be realized, no applied behavior-analytic work has been reported in the area. Thus, unlike earlier chapters, this one will focus more on the state of the physical technological art than on the behavioral.

MAJOR USES OF WATER IN THE HOME

If residential water conservation is to be encouraged, it is important to analyze the major ways water is used in a typical home. Amounts cited are somewhat arbitrary, because daily-consumption figures fluctuate widely from place to place and from one season to another. For example, Milne (1976) cites California Department of Water Resources data showing that consumption on the northern California coast averages about 153 gallons per person per day, but that consumption in the drier, southeastern portion of the state averages 410 gallons per person per day. Both these figures include nonresidential uses of water, however. (See Figure 11-1 for a representative breakdown of residential water use.)

Toilets consume the most of all water-using household appliances. The average toilet uses about 5.25 gallons per flush, or approximately 32 gallons per person per day. Showers are another big user, with about 4 gallons falling per minute of water flow. Thus, it is not surprising that numerous water-saving designs have been proposed for toilets over the years and that flow-limiting shower heads have also been appearing recently.

WATER-SAVING DEVICES

A great variety of water-conservation devices have been developed in the past few years. Since effective applied behavior-analytic solutions to water waste will undoubtedly benefit from the use of such devices, a few pages will be devoted to their description here. As noted in a recent Water Research Capsule Report of the Office of Water Research and Technology (U.S. Department of the

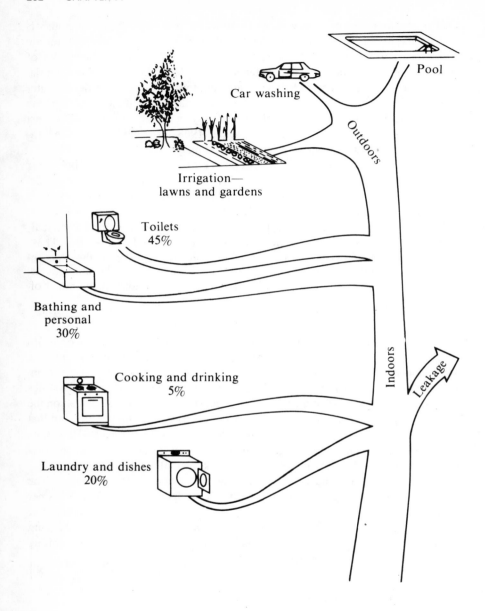

Figure 11-1. Typical distribution of residential water consumption. (Percentages shown are for indoor use only and constitute half of the total residential water use.) Adapted from *Residential Water Conservation,* by M. Milne. Davis, California: California Water Resources Center Report No. 35, 1976. Used by permission.

Interior, 1977), these devices really have three dimensions: they conserve water, they reduce waste flows, and they conserve energy. One example of their use that emphasizes the magnitude of the possible savings is a project carried out at The Pennsylvania State University. With the installation of $15,000 worth of water-saving devices, an estimated annual savings of $100,000 resulted. In an Environmèntal Protection Agency study of eight homes in San Diego, a $1 shower flow-control device was estimated to save $2.62 per year per home. Toilet inserts costing $4 each saved $6.30 per year per home, whereas toilets modified with a $5 device for different flush rates for solids and liquids saved $7.65 per year per home.

Water-Saving Toilets

A fascinating variety of water-saving toilets have been developed over centuries of experimenting with human-waste disposal. These vary greatly in cost, complexity, and amount of water saved. An extensive review and evaluation of these toilets is provided by Milne (1976). A few of the innovations described in his book will be discussed here to give some idea of the range of alternatives currently available.

Box 11–1. Did You Know?

The first water-using toilet was apparently patented in Great Britain by Alexander Cummings in 1775. Early models wasted a good deal of water, however, because no good system existed for controlling the amount that flowed in from an overhead tank. Indeed, early toilets were so wasteful of water that an Act of Parliament was needed to limit use to 2 gallons per flush.

It remained for Thomas Crapper to solve this problem in 1872. He invented the first valveless water-waste preventer that year, and his basic design is still used in toilets today. Many people give Crapper credit for inventing the toilet, but as R. Palmer (1973) has shown, that is not technically correct. This mistake is the reason that toilets are often referred to as crappers.

Toilet paper has a similarly interesting history. In the 1800s, people used little squares of paper, but earlier than that, the Romans used sponges on the ends of sticks (Milne, 1976). Various other approaches have been taken throughout history, with the 16th-century wealthy French using perfumed wool, and people of the Middle Ages relying on little balls of hay. The roll of toilet paper came along in 1880 (Milne, 1976).

Remember that the standard toilet in use in most U.S. homes uses anywhere from 5 to 7 gallons per flush. This figure (45% of all indoor water use) provides an appropriate baseline against which to compare suggested alternatives. One innovation that uses only 40%–50% as much water (thereby saving 22%–27% of total indoor water use) is the pressurized-tank toilet (Milne, 1976, pp. 191–193). Because water is introduced to the toilet bowl at a higher than usual pressure, less water is needed to flush and carry away the waste. The pressurized tank simply attaches to a regular toilet bowl, replacing the present tank. By using the pressure normally available in water-supply lines (35–120 psi), air is compressed by water entering the tank, thus avoiding the necessity of electrically operated compressors and minimizing the number of moving parts. The tank costs approximately $40–$50 and is easily installed on existing toilet bowls.

An interesting, more expensive alternative that uses no water at all is the freeze toilet (Milne, 1976, pp. 213–214). Basically, the toilet is a small freezer beneath a toilet seat. Wastes drop into a 6-gallon bag and are quickly frozen, thus preventing germs and odor. Heat from the small cooling compressor is transferred to the seat to minimize any discomfort to the user. The bag is removed when it is three-quarters full. The freezer toilet costs approximately $350 and requires some amount of electrical energy to run the cooler. However, since no conventional plumbing connections are necessary, significant cost offsets could be realized in new construction.

A last example of ecologically beneficial waste disposal is the composter toilet, which also uses no water at all. This model is often recommended by "back-to-the-earth eco-freaks" because of its environmentally sound way of handling not only toilet waste but kitchen garbage as well. Moreover, the humus produced can be used to enrich garden soil or lawns. The composter toilet is similar in design to the old country outhouse in that the toilet seat is located directly over a large tank in which the decomposition process occurs. Similarly, the kitchen garbage chute is directly over the tank. Peat mold, garden soil, and plant trimmings are introduced into the tank during its installation. These provide the basis for the decomposition of wastes. The entire process is automatic, resulting in about 3–10 gallons of humus per person per year. Appropriate venting removes odor and prevents dangerous gas build-up. The internal environment of the tank needs to be maintained at about 90° F for the bacteria to operate optimally, a problem in cold climates.

A more practical variant is the electrified composter toilet, which uses a stirrer to pump air into the waste and maintain an optimum composting temperature. More rapid decomposition occurs, permitting a much smaller tank. In fact, the entire toilet is only 21 inches wide, 27.5 inches high, and 30 inches long, compared to the 3-feet-wide, 5-feet-high, and 10-feet-long dimensions of the normal composter system. Of course, kitchen wastes are not included in the smaller version. Cost data are not readily available for the automated unit, but Milne (1976, p. 203) cites a figure of approximately $950 for the larger version (not delivered or installed). Again, as with the freeze toilet, some cost offsets could be realized if either version were included in new construction, since conventional plumbing would not be required.

These selected examples demonstrate that a variety of innovative water-saving alternatives are available for the largest single user inside the home. These vary greatly in cost and retrofitability, but, clearly, environmentally more beneficial toilets are within the grasp of most U.S. homeowners today.

In addition to buying completely redesigned toilets, it is now possible to purchase devices to modify already existing ones so they will use less water. Perhaps the best known is a dual or variable flush mechanism that allows the user to select the amount of water needed per flush. Thus, more would be used to dispose of solid than liquid wastes. A variety of these devices are available, each operating somewhat differently. They all have in common the requirement that the user control the amount of water used. Thus, the "flush-and-leave" feature of the modern bathroom is lost. This minor inconvenience aside, however, such devices save as much as 50% of the water normally used, permitting a very rapid recovery of their initial $5 cost.

Obviously, any reduction in toilet water use carries with it associated reductions in waste flow to septic systems and public sewers. Savings are immediately passed on to the conserving consumer in localities that tie monthly sewer rates to water use.

Other Water-Saving Devices

In addition to water-saving toilets, numerous innovations have recently been marketed for residential use. The flow-control device for showers mentioned earlier can save up to 60% of the water normally used, reducing the flow from 4 to 1.6 gallons per minute (U.S. Department of the Interior, 1977). Similar controls on faucets can reduce flow by 50%. Suds-saver cycles and variable water-level controls on clothes-washing machines can produce a 40% reduction in water use from the usual 50 or more gallons per cycle.

All of this suggests that the conservation-oriented consumer could save a good deal of water at relatively little initial expense with currently available technology. Specifically, with dual flush devices on toilets, water-flow restrictors in faucets and showers, and suds-saver and variable-level cycles on washing machines and dishwashers, daily use should drop from about 70 gallons to approximately 40 gallons per person per day. Without the laundry and dishwashing changes (relatively costly if new equipment is necessitated), a drop to about 45 gallons per day would still be realized. This would amount to a savings of roughly 36% of the water normally used inside the home.

Such a savings is rather remarkable considering the very small cost involved. With greater effort and expenditure, the amount of water actually consumed in a typical residence could be reduced to practically zero. For example, systems for recycling gray water (waste from baths and lavatories) have not even been mentioned. These are reviewed by Milne (1976), however, who shows them to be quite effective: "If all the grey water produced in the home could be gathered and reused up to 50% of the water used indoors could be saved"

(p. 309). Space limitations do not permit their detailed examination here, but, briefly, the systems involve running gray water through a filter and storing it for later use in toilet tanks or for outside irrigation. Most installations are not designed to return water to sufficient purity for drinking purposes.

In sum, the technology is available to support successful efforts at residential water conservation. However, the use of the technology in individual homes is not very widespread. There are a number of reasons for this state of affairs, many of which have parallels in other areas of environmental concern, especially energy consumption.

DETERRENTS TO RESIDENTIAL WATER CONSERVATION

In this section of the chapter, we will deal with some of the circumstances that impede the adoption of water-saving procedures in the United States. The discussion should be especially instructive because of the parallels with other areas just mentioned.

Billing Practices of Municipal Water Districts

There are numerous rate-setting practices used by residential water suppliers across the country. Among these are the set price, flat rate, decreasing block rate, increasing block rate, life-line rate, and peak-demand rate (Milne, 1976). The most common practice is to charge decreasing rates for additional increments of water use. With the *decreasing block-rate* structure, the first amount (block) of water—say, 500 gallons—is provided at the highest rate. The next block costs the consumer less per gallon; the next, less; and so on. This is a pricing strategy also commonly used by electric companies (see Chapter 10). The effect of this approach is that more water use leads to a higher utility bill, but it increases at a decreasing rate of cost per gallon.

The opposite practice is incorporated in the *increasing block-rate* pricing structure. Here the user pays one price for the first block of water, a higher price for the second, a higher for the third, and so on. It would not take a great deal of sophistication about behavioral principles to know which of these two tactics produces greater conservation (see Chan & Heare, 1975, cited in Milne, 1976).

Compare each of these with the *set-price* method, however, in which the consumer pays a set amount each month regardless of the water used. This tactic is used in cities that have no residential water meters. Although relatively rare (more than 90% of U.S. municipalities meter water use), there are still notable exceptions, including New York City and Sacramento. Obviously, either of the two previously mentioned systems would be more consistent with sound behavioral principles than the set-price method, which offers no direct financial consequence for varying one's use of water. Indeed, Robie (1975), in a comparison of per-capita daily consumption in metered and nonmetered cities, found rates of 185 and 330 gallons, respectively. In an earlier study water use decreased by nearly 50% when meters were introduced in Denver (Hanke & Boland, 1971). Unfortunately, the price was simultaneously increased, so it is difficult to know for certain that simply tying cost to use actually resulted in the decrease.

In the *flat-rate* pricing structure, each unit of water costs the same, regardless of the amount used. This is probably the most familiar pricing strategy, as it applies to many of our everyday purchases. For example, gasoline costs the same per gallon whether we buy 10 or 20. The consequence of using more water (or gasoline) under this structure is a proportionate increase in cost.

Recently there have been frequent references to the pricing of utilities, including water, on a *life-line* basis; that is, a certain amount necessary for survival would be provided at a low cost. Presumably, amounts beyond this would be billed at higher rates, making the system somewhat like that of the increasing block rate. As Milne (1976) notes, the "incentive to conserve" should be great as people try to reduce their overall consumption to stay within the amount provided at the initial low rate.

The last price structure, the *peak-demand* rate, deals explicitly with the issue of levels versus patterns of use already discussed in the previous two chapters. Just as with electrical-energy and public-transportation systems, excess capacity must be built into municipal water-supply systems to provide enough water to cover high-demand periods. Much of this capacity is unused (or at least underused) during nonpeak times. Peaks can be defined using various time intervals, but those most often used are hourly and seasonally. With electricity consumption the cost figures are often high enough to justify the expense of meters that cumulate kilowatt-hours used during different hours of the day. Thus, consumers can be charged a lower rate for nonpeak use, encouraging a shift to these times. For water use, however, it is not economically feasible at the present time to employ such meters. Instead, water rates can be adjusted on the basis of longer time periods, such as seasons of the year. Thus, higher rates could be charged during the peak summer period to discourage wasting water in outdoor irrigation activities and home swimming pools, in addition to encouraging conservation in normal indoor uses.

In sum, the prevalent practice of pricing water on a decreasing block basis is clearly not calculated to encourage conservation. Several of the alternatives mentioned would be superior in that regard, and the life-line approach has the added attraction of being more humane. Milne (1976) discusses a number of additional pricing tactics that might encourage conservation, including variable hookup fees for newly constructed houses, pricing discounts for houses outfitted with water-saving technology, direct subsidies, rebates, and modified taxation policies. Many of these suggestions are appropriate to consider with other utilities as well. Unfortunately, space limitations do not permit elaboration on them here.

One last point concerning the economics of water conservation is worth mentioning, however. That is the importance of considering the price elasticity of various forms of home water use. As Milne (1976, pp. 147–148) suggests, the demand for water used inside the home is rather inelastic; that is, relatively large increases in price will generally not lead to decreases in use. This is so because water is a necessity, and consumers cannot switch to readily available alternatives. Recent very large increases in the cost of gasoline showed a similar inelasticity of demand—at least during the short term. Consumers simply had no choice if the use of their automobile was a family economic and social necessity. Thus, simple, across-the-board, meat-ax solutions via price increases will not lead automatically to reductions in water use. A complex, carefully balanced approach using alternative pricing structures in combination with some of the other fiscal incentives described by Milne will doubtless be necessary if economic tactics are to have any effect on water-consuming behavior.

Knowledge of the Actual Costs of Water Use: Economic and Environmental

Another factor influencing the effort we make to conserve water is the amount of information we have concerning its cost. Pricing tactics have just been described. However, these do not assure us that the typical consumer knows anything about the money he or she spends on water each day. Moreover, there is probably even less information available to consumers about the environmental costs of unchecked increases in water use.

As suggested in our discussion of electricity consumption, it is difficult to be controlled by the price of a commodity when that price is unknown. In truth, the cost as a percentage of income is probably too small to exert much influence, particularly in view of water's necessity in a variety of household activities. Indeed, in a study conducted in New Hampshire (Andrews & Hammond, 1970), average annual household expenditures for water were in the neighborhood of $32–$42, or an average of .4% of total family income.

Although it may be difficult to get people excited about an amount comparable to what is commonly spent on stationery, knowledge of the costs of related utilities (for example, gas and electricity used to heat water) and more widespread environmental costs may exert more influence. Already, communities are placing moratoria on new development in some parts of the country, largely in response to overtaxed public services, including water supply and sewage treatment. The importance of slowing the burden on these utilities has led California to enact legislation (A.B. 1395) prohibiting the installation of toilets using more than 3.5 gallons per flush in new residential construction. The prohibition against electric hot-water heaters in San Diego has already been mentioned. Hopefully, local environmental costs of new water-treatment and sewage-treatment plants combined with the specter of huge dams in places like the Grand Canyon will be sufficiently visible and distasteful to cause greater individual water conservation. As noted in the previous chapter, there is some evidence that more explicit information or cost feedback exerts some control over energy use. Such data undoubtedly are part of the reason many electric and gas utilities are now including cost-per-day figures in their bills. Perhaps such figures would also affect water use to some extent.

Local Codes and State Laws and Regulations

The Los Angeles County Plumbing Code requires that toilets have a water-flushing capacity of at least 4 gallons (in obvious conflict with the state law just mentioned). The rationale for such a code in this and other communities is that enough water be used to assure that sewer systems do not become clogged. Other codes and regulations govern the recycling of gray water, the design of toilets, and the design and installation of complete home-plumbing systems. Many of these conflict with efforts to reduce water use. An obvious example would be the common practice of requiring new houses to be hooked into already existing sewers if the sewer line passes within a certain distance of the dwelling. Such requirements eliminate offsetting plumbing savings normally expected with the installation of such water-saving fixtures as composter toilets, even where other codes or laws do not prohibit these outright.

The complex of state laws, local ordinances, building codes, and union regulations that governs the way water is delivered to, used in, and carried away from residential dwellings will need thorough study before it can be redesigned for compatibility with environmental preservation.

Manufacturing Practices and Tradition

An efficient, highly organized, and centralized plumbing-wares industry has grown up in the United States that is designed to produce fixtures with certain generally accepted specifications. Naturally, just as in the automobile industry, change to newer, more environmentally protective product lines does not come quickly. Redesigning and retooling entire production systems in order to market new products are not something large manufacturers are going to take lightly. Nor are they likely to take the initiative in an area in which decades of familiarity and satisfaction with a particular fixture design will be associated with caution about new products. The risk to the manufacturers is clearly that their innovative, environmentally protective products will gather dust in suppliers' warehouses as customers stick with designs they know.

Recently there has been some movement toward change, however, and "now for the first time new plumbing fixtures that use less water are being marketed at prices that are competitive with traditional plumbing ware" (Milne, 1976, p. 14). To accelerate this activity, manufacturers are going to have to have increased pressure from consumers, legislative changes, and changes in municipal ordinances and local building codes.

Knowledge of Conservation Devices and Practices

A few short years ago, many of us were unaware of the significant difference we could produce in our heating bills by turning down the thermostat at night, by adding insulation to the attic, or by wrapping the hot-water heater in a fiberglass blanket. The energy crisis and ensuing mass-education campaigns have changed all that and left us better informed about energy-conservation techniques.

That early state of relative ignorance still characterizes our knowledge of water-conservation practices. It is probably safe to say that not many people know the significant amount of water used by various household appliances. Additionally, except for people living in regions recently experiencing serious drought, it is unlikely that many know that their water use could be reduced by 30%–40% through the installation of a few very inexpensive conservation devices. People in those areas experiencing recent drought know these things because local utilities waged extensive public-information campaigns. These mass-education programs paralleled more extensive ones following the 1973 oil embargo and were based on the common assumption that increased information about appliance water-usage rates and conservation practices would lead to the saving of natural resources. As the previous chapter showed, however, such information does not often lead very directly to reductions—at least in energy consumption. Perhaps a different effect would be experienced in the water-conservation area. It is unlikely, however, that public education alone will lead to significant changes in water consumption.

WHAT CAN BEHAVIOR ANALYSTS DO ABOUT WATER CONSERVATION?

The parallels between water use and electricity, gas, home heating oil, and gasoline use have been noted throughout this chapter. Even though we could find no formal behavior-analytic studies evaluating water-conservation approaches, perhaps some lessons could be learned from work in these related areas.

Educate Consumers

If the factors bearing on the use of available technology mentioned in the previous section are valid, it would make sense to direct our intervention efforts toward them. Indeed, the significance of each factor might be established by systematically varying it and noting changes in water use. For example, it is certainly a plausible *assumption* that more information about conservation devices and practices would lead to their greater use. Recall that a similar assumption was entertained at the beginning of Chapter 4 and that the remainder of that chapter was devoted to describing ways of testing its validity. Then, in Chapter 10, research was cited that actually tested the validity of this assumption as it applied to electricity use. Specifically, Hayes and Cone (1977b) found that merely educating consumers about the electricity-use rates of various appliances and about ways to conserve did not lead to reductions in electricity consumption.

The validity of the argument should not be accepted, however, before another difference between electricity and water consumption is considered. Behavior analysts began evaluating different approaches to electricity conservation only fairly recently. They have done so largely *in response to* greatly increased public awareness of the limits of the natural resources used to produce electricity and the cost of its production. When Hayes and Cone began "informing" their subjects of the use rates of various appliances, it is very likely that the subjects already had this information.

As suggested in the previous section, such widespread knowledge does not yet exist about water conservation. Thus, the provision of information might have greater effects. This might be so even though the economic incentive is clearly less powerful in the case of water.

In any event, this would be a logical and important area for behavior analysts to explore. It is even more important than in the case of electricity conservation because the value of mass-education approaches could be assessed *before* great sums of money were spent on them. This could easily be done in small, inexpensive pilot experiments of the type described in previous chapters.

Provide Feedback

Another line of research that has received a good deal of attention in the energy area is improved feedback to consumers about the amount and cost of their energy use. Unlike the rather disappointing effects of mass-education campaigns, feedback has been established as an effective controller of electricity consumption in residential settings. Perhaps feedback would affect water-conservation practices as well.

Of course, there is already naturally available feedback in the form of water bills. Unfortunately, these are often paid bimonthly or even quarterly and are thus likely to be too delayed and too infrequent to have much effect. In addition, the units reported on these bills are often unfamiliar to consumers (for example, cubic feet), making an easy translation from use to cost very improbable. These problems could be corrected if careful research showed frequency and form to be important variables in the billing process. Comparative bills could also be evaluated; that is, the effect of showing a consumer how much was used during a comparable period the previous year might be examined. Similarly, one could study the effect of showing the cumulative amount used and its cost so far for the year. Here again, the argument might be made that the cost of water is too minimal to allow these feedback variables to be effective. Whereas high energy bills could have served as an incentive to attend carefully to feedback in the electricity studies, the incentive simply is not there in the case of water.

There are several responses to this argument. First, although it is true that water bills are considerably lower than electricity bills, there are no data available on how high the bill must be before feedback is effective. Knowing more frequently the amount being used and its cost might cause reductions even if the cost is relatively low. Second, water bills could be increased by tying sewer charges to them. This is a common practice in many communities already. Third, water bills will get higher by themselves as new, more expensive purifying, pumping, and treatment plants are necessitated by increased water use and more rigorous regulatory policies.

Alter Rate Structures

Research should also be directed at the effect of the various billing structures described earlier. There is some evidence showing economies when communities switch from a flat rate to other structures (Hanke & Boland, 1971). However, there is no experimental research showing the effect of life-line billing or of the comparative value of this and other billing practices.

Behavioral scientists should also explore the interactive effects of type and frequency of feedback and billing structure. It is very unlikely that increasing feedback about use would have much effect under set-price billing practices. It might, however, under an increasing block-rate structure. Indeed, consumers might be quite affected if they knew that they had used 1000 gallons and that the next 500 were going to cost significantly more. What effect would stepped-up feedback have under a decreasing block-rate structure?

Of course, it is much easier to talk about taking an experimental approach to rate setting than it is actually to do it. The problems that social scientists encounter when trying to convince utility companies and commissions to evaluate their practices will be discussed in the last chapter of the book. Some progress is being made in this area, however, as shown by a recent evaluation of the practice of charging for directory assistance by the telephone company (McSweeny, 1978) and by electricity rate-structure evaluations by Kohlenberg, Barach, Martin, and Anschell (1976).

Instigate Legislative and Regulatory Changes

Two additional factors that affect the use of available water-saving technology are federal and state laws and manufacturing practices and tradition. Reductions in water use could be accomplished quite rapidly by laws, such as California's toilet bill, that prohibit the installation of inefficient appliances in newly constructed buildings. The job for the behavior analyst here is to effect change in the behavior of enough politicians to get such legislation enacted into law. More will be said on this approach in Chapter 13. Anticipating a bit, though, it may be that some of the earlier strategies will have to be successful before legislative solutions will be developed. For example, the public may have to become much more aware of the importance of conserving water and of the availability of water-saving technology before elected representatives will be influenced to pass appropriate legislation.

Evaluate Changes in Manufacturing Practices

Similarly, plumbing-wares manufacturers could readily promote the use of water-efficient appliances. They are not likely to, however, without some encouragement in the form of consumer pressure and legislative command. Perhaps behavior analysts could help manufacturers take a less reactionary stance by experimentally evaluating more efficient appliances. These evaluations would be designed to measure consumer reaction to the appliance with a view toward both its effectiveness and its eventual salability.

These are a few of the areas in which behavior-analytic involvement might facilitate the use of available water-saving technology. Numerous additional suggestions are offered by Milne (1976), including using customer rebates, encouraging large governmental agencies to model water-conservation practices and purchase only water-efficient appliances, prohibiting master metering in multiple-occupant dwellings, and encouraging water companies to track down unaccounted-for water losses (for example, via leaks) in their systems. Interested readers are urged to read Milne's very extensive suggestions for producing widespread savings in water use.

SUMMARY

This chapter is unlike previous ones in that no experimental evaluations of water-saving practices were presented. Until very recently, little or no concern has been focused on water conservation, and thus no experimental research has been done on the subject. The chapter made a case for the importance of water conservation not so much on the basis of the limited amount available but on the cost to the environment of its capture, treatment, transportation, use, and disposal.

We described the different ways in which the approximately 70 gallons of water per person per day are consumed in typical residences and noted that toilets are the biggest single user, averaging 5.25 gallons per flush. Various water-saving (or water-eliminating) toilet designs were described, as were numerous other commercially available water-saving devices. We noted that inexpensive, easily installed devices are presently available that would result in savings of 30%–40% in home water use.

We emphasized, however, that very little use has thus far been made of existing water-saving technology. Factors contributing to this limited use include the billing practices of water companies; the public's knowledge of the economic and environmental costs of water; laws, regulations, and local codes; manufacturing practices and tradition; and public awareness of the availability of conservation devices and practices.

Throughout the chapter we drew attention to the parallels between water conservation and previous discussions of energy use for residential and transportation purposes. The last section contained suggestions on things that might be done to encourage the adoption of water-saving technology and ways in which behavior analysts might evaluate them. We drew on approaches used in other areas, again because of the parallels just mentioned. We also pointed out that sufficient differences exist to suggest that some approaches (for example, mass education) might work for water conservation even though they have not proved effective in other areas (for example, electricity conservation).

SUGGESTED PROJECTS

Reducing Water Use at Home

This project involves the introduction and evaluation of concerted efforts to reduce water use in your own living situation.

Step 1. First, find your water meter and learn how to read it. You will need to get some baseline information about your current usage rates, so plan to read the meter about every three days and record your readings for several weeks. Plot the gallons (or cubic feet) used on a graph after each reading. If you read the meter after a set number of days each time, you can merely plot your data per two-day or three-day block. If the days between readings vary, you will have to convert to the figure for average use per day by subtracting the immediately previous reading from the present one and dividing by the number of days between them. Whichever method you use, be sure to examine your graph carefully as you plot each data point. Wait until the graph appears to be stable —that is, neither increasing nor decreasing consistently.

Step 2. Begin your conservation program. Up to now, you have merely been collecting baseline data while continuing to use water in your usual way. You should have made no deliberate effort to change this usage, concentrating instead on merely measuring it accurately. Design your own set of procedures to try to bring down your level of water use. If you live by yourself, it should be relatively easy to produce a change. If several other persons are using water measured by your meter, you should also involve them in the conservation program.

Since your individually tailored conservation program may be so successful you will want to patent it, be sure to write down each of the things you do to reduce water use. You should probably decide these ahead of time and make a list to follow during the intervention phase. Since at this point in the book you are already a sophisticated environmental-problem solver, we are not going to tell you what things to include in your water-conservation package. However, you might try turning off the shower while lathering up, taking shorter and fewer showers, flushing the toilet only to remove solid wastes and after every other urination, not running the water continuously while brushing your teeth, and washing clothes in larger batches.

Step 3. After you have implemented this package, continue to read your meter at the same frequency as during the baseline period. As you practice your water-saving activities consistently, you should begin to notice a decrease on your graph. Keep practicing conservation until a definite downward trend is evident on your graph.

Step 4. When the trend has been established, begin your withdrawal phase; that is, eliminate the special efforts you were making to conserve and simply return to your normal activities. Tell other participants that the project is over and they can resume life as usual. If the conservation package was what really produced the decrease noticed in the second phase, you should find the level of water use begin to increase once again.

Step 5. When an increasing trend is clearly evident, you may want to reinstate the package once again. Simply tell the others that water use has gotten out of hand and you need to return to the conservation practices. This would give you an *ABAB* design, in which the effects of your efforts in the initial intervention (or *B* phase) are replicated in the second.

Step 6. If time permits after you establish a decreasing trend once again in the second *B* phase, you may want to evaluate some of the components of your successful package. You can do this by eliminating one component and observing any changes in your data. Since daily fluctuations are likely to be fairly high, you may have to eliminate a significant behavior before any effect will be noted. Or you may want to group several practices and eliminate the entire group.

In any event, when you have discovered ways that effectively reduce water use for you, try making these practices a part of your daily routine. If you have been successful in getting others living with you to do the same things, your water usage should continue to decrease.

Community Conservation via Information and Feedback

The first water-conservation project was something you could design and initiate on your own. The next one requires you to expand your activities to include several different residential dwellings.

Step 1. Select six or more apartments or houses near yours that have outside water meters or ones that are easily accessible. Ask the occupants using these meters for permission to read them several times each week. Tell them that you are doing a class project involving meter reading and you need practice reading theirs.

Step 2. Read the meters and record and graph baseline data for each as described in the first project. After collecting stable baseline data, group the meters into pairs showing similar overall use, forming three pairs.

Step 3. Using a multiple-baseline design, introduce your intervention for one of the pairs. Keep recording baseline data on the others. Your intervention should consist of daily feedback about the amount of water used in the dwelling and written information on ways to conserve. You might consult the Hayes and Cone (1977b) study for specific suggestions on how to provide feedback and information.

In general, you will want some simple means of conveying daily-use rates to participants. You might simply jot this down on a 3-inch by 5-inch card and leave it in the mailbox each day. Your information might consist of a list of water-saving practices, such as those mentioned in the description of the first project, as well as data on the amount of water used in various appliances and activities. You might also provide descriptions of water-saving devices and addresses of nearby stores where they can be purchased. *Consumer Reports* and *Popular Science* may be good sources for ideas. It may take some time for complex procedures such as these to have an effect on water use, so be prepared to continue reading all meters for several weeks.

Step 4. When you detect a consistent downward trend in water use for the first pair, introduce the package to another pair and continue feedback to the first. The third pair of dwellings merely continues in baseline. When the second pair changes water use consistently, introduce the third group to the procedures.

Step 5. You may want to "block" your individual dwellings by twos and regraph your data using the mean of the two. This procedure may show clearer effects for your intervention, as it will eliminate some of the wide variability in meter readings from day to day. Your resulting graph will thus have three lines through the baseline and intervention phases instead of the original six.

The use of a multiple-baseline design in this case is appropriate because the independent variable is one that cannot easily be removed or withdrawn. Once you have given people information, it is difficult to take it back. Moreover, if they actually install water-saving devices, they are not likely to want to remove them just so you can show an experimental effect.

Step 6. Some caution should be exercised in conducting this project to make sure that your procedures are adequately evaluated. Be sure to get information from the participants about any planned trips away from home, any overnight visitors, or any unusually heavy water uses they may be anticipating. Also, be alert to the possible effects of changing seasons or sudden hot or cold spells. These could affect outside water use for irrigating, car washing, and so on. In general, it would be best to select participants who are not likely to use water outside their dwellings (for example, those living in apartment complexes).

Step 7. Finally, provide the results of your efforts to each of the participants. Show them graphs, tell them what was done, and find out from them how they went about saving water. This last step is very important. Often the participants themselves will suggest things that may never have occurred to you as the researcher. These may be valuable leads to examine in future studies.

PART V

PROMOTING THE USE OF BEHAVIORAL APPROACHES TO ENVIRONMENTAL PROBLEMS

Part I of the book laid out our biases concerning an effective behavioral-science contribution to solving environmental problems. Part II followed with the procedural tools for implementing solutions derived from these biases and the research armamentarium for evaluating the adequacy of the solutions. Parts III and IV provided examples of behavior-analytic approaches to a variety of problems, including those of aesthetics (litter and noise), health (population control), and resources (recycling, transportation, residential energy conservation, and residential water conservation). Thus, at this point the reader should have a pretty good idea of the basic orientation being espoused as well as the breadth of the problems that can be successfully attacked with it. In other words, the first four parts of the book have provided a summary of the accomplishments thus far and some appreciation for the potential that exists.

The last two chapters pull together the lessons of the previous ones, integrate the major trends, and suggest some issues that need to be addressed if the field is to continue to advance. Chapter 12 emphasizes the importance of establishing the generality of behavioral solutions. Throughout the book we have emphasized the importance of showing the relevance of proposed solutions to the behavioral principles enunciated in Chapter 3 and to their underlying conceptual/philosophical base, described in Chapters 1 and 2. The book has stressed that only by tying our activities to a consistent conceptual framework can we expect to develop a behavioral technology that is anything more than a bag of tricks, each having relevance to the solution of a single problem in a single locale at a single time. Only with this type of consistency can we hope to establish generally effective behavioral solutions. Chapter 12 outlines the types of generality we ought to be looking for and evaluates the progress we have made thus far.

In addition, Chapter 12 calls attention to the potential value of combining the active, direct behavior-analytic approach emphasized throughout the book with the less direct, reactive approach impugned in Chapter 2. The importance of developing strategies for preventing environmentally destructive behaviors from being acquired in the first place is also mentioned.

The last chapter deals with the need for a more macrosocietal view by behavior analysts concerned with the environment. Many effective solutions have been and will continue to be developed by adherents of this point of view. However, the impact of these solutions will be limited unless ways are found to implement and evaluate them on a much larger scale than has heretofore been possible. The need for a technology to influence the influential is nowhere more apparent than in efforts to get behavioral solutions to environmental problems implemented on a large scale. Chapter 13 offers suggestions for preparing behavioral scientists in ways that will maximize the impact of their contributions.

Chapter 12

THE GENERALITY OF BEHAVIORAL SOLUTIONS

Throughout this book we have given examples of behavioral solutions to environmental problems. We have shown ways to reduce litter on the ground, ways to reduce noise in public places, and ways to control population growth. We have also shown how to get people to recycle goods, use mass-transit systems more, and consume less water and energy.

As these problem areas have been discussed, you may have had questions about the solutions being suggested. It is fine, you say, to give children small amounts of money or trinkets for picking up trash, but how realistic is this as a long-term solution to problems of littering? Will it not be necessary to keep paying these kids if we want them to keep picking up trash? Besides, that tactic may work in public campgrounds in the Pacific Northwest, but will it also work in the littered urban environments of large cities? Will it work when the size of the problem is much greater than that dealt with in the experimental investigations described in this book?

You may also have wondered whether the procedures we have mentioned can actually be administered by persons who have not been trained as experimental social scientists. Just how much training and expertise are required to implement these various solutions? After all, some of them seem quite complicated.

These are important questions. Each of them deals with the overall issue of the general applicability and usefulness of behavior-analytic solutions to environmental problems. We have tried to answer these questions as we presented each of the various approaches. The answers are spread throughout the book, though, in a rather unsystematic way. Because of their importance, it seems appropriate to summarize some of the information pertaining to them in this chapter.

In addition to questions of general applicability, we will deal with other issues that have been raised concerning behavioral solutions to environmental problems. Criticisms of positive-reinforcement approaches will be mentioned and rebuttals offered. The relative merits of combining stimulus control and reinforcement procedures will be discussed. We will also return to the question of whether reactive studies have a place in the behavioral literature on environmental-problem solution and, if so, just what that place might be.

There are several intriguing logical difficulties in studying the overall generality of solutions to environmental problems. These will be dealt with in this chapter. Finally, we will call attention to a sorely neglected aspect of environmental problems, that of their prevention in the first place.

TYPES OF GENERALITY

Behavior analysts have always been concerned with the generality of changes they produce in behavior (see Baer, Wolf, & Risley, 1968; Cone, 1973; Stokes & Baer, 1977). Similarly, they are concerned with the generality of behavior-produced changes in the environment. Most often, generality is established through replication; that is, the procedures are tried again under different circumstances. If these circumstances are varied systematically, valuable information on generality is produced.

The types of generality of greatest concern to behavioral environmental-problem solvers are:

1. Whether the solution is durable—that is, whether it holds up over time.
2. Whether the solution can be implemented effectively by a variety of persons.
3. Whether the solution can be used successfully in different settings, locales, or environmental contexts.
4. Whether the success of the solution depends on the magnitude of the problem.
5. Whether the solution has implications for the solution of other kinds of environmental problems.

The application of behavioral principles in the environmental area is relatively new. As a result, researchers have been most concerned with demonstrating that their procedures work; that is, they have focused largely on the establishment of unequivocal relationships between their operations and changes in environmental characteristics. They have not dealt extensively with the generality of these relationships. Nonetheless, some evidence has been developed and will be reviewed in the following section.

EVIDENCE FOR THE GENERALITY OF BEHAVIORAL SOLUTIONS

Durability over Time

It is nice that behavioral solutions work to clean up a public campground, get people to use less electricity, reduce levels of noise, and recycle more aluminum cans. But how permanent are the environmental changes produced? How long does the campground stay clean? How long do people keep making successful efforts to reduce electricity use? How long will quiet prevail in a college dormitory? And how long will people keep taking cans to a recycling center?

Most of the studies cited in the preceding chapters were conducted over relatively short periods. Many relied on alternating environmental improvement and deterioration from phase to phase to demonstrate functional relationships between independent and dependent variables. In such studies the phases are often brief by necessity. For example, in trying to get more people to ride a public-bus system, Everett (1973) paid each boarding passenger a quarter. After an initial 20-day baseline phase, payments were introduced for three days, withdrawn for seven, and then reintroduced for one. Ridership changed radically across these different phases, showing increases of 149% and 180% during the two times that quarters were used. When paying people to ride was discontinued in the last phase, ridership returned to baseline levels. No permanent or even long-lasting change was produced in the environmentally relevant behavior being studied. Indeed, this research did not even address the issue of durability over time. It was limited simply to the question of whether the procedure would work.

It is generally characteristic of the research described in the preceding chapters that more concern was focused on whether procedures would work than on how long they would continue to be effective. Researchers have not yet attended to questions of "Fine, but for how long?" Consequently, we know next to nothing about the long-term durability of effects produced.

This is not a particularly startling state of affairs, and it is characteristic of the early stages of almost all new areas of scientific endeavor. One study cannot answer all questions, and it seems that priority in early research should be given to whether a procedure works at all. Once functional behavior/environment relationships have been established, issues of durability, effectiveness in other situations, and so on can be addressed.

In anticipation of the eventual conducting of long-term durability studies, several questions have been raised. Some people have questioned the practicality of reinforcement procedures that require payoffs to get an environmentally relevant behavior going. They claim that baseline/treatment/baseline studies adequately document the short-term nature of such tactics because, as in the Everett (1973) study just cited, behavior typically returns to baseline rates fairly soon after reinforcement is stopped. Thus, it would seem that the only way any degree of durability could be assured would be to continue payoffs indefinitely. This, it is claimed, would be highly impractical.

Such an argument is important and deserves to be taken seriously. Several comments seem to be in order. First, the issue of the permanence of environmental changes produced by rewards for increased environmentally protective behavior has not been explored thoroughly or systematically. Although it is true that studies using monetary consequences have shown rapid decreases in protective behavior when payments have been discontinued, usually such studies have terminated payments abruptly. The effects may have been different had the payments been phased out in a more gradual fashion. Indeed, Hayes and Cone (1977b) showed surprisingly durable effects when monetary reinforcers were reduced to as little as 25% of their original magnitude.

Second, the durability of the effects of a procedure does not seem appropriately evaluated in the absence of that procedure. In other words, the generality of effects over time refers to the consistency with which changed levels of environmentally relevant behaviors are maintained while the procedure is being used. This seems logically to be the case, since it is the basis on which other behavior-change strategies are introduced and evaluated. For example, consider the use of "Don't Walk on the Grass" signs. No one would expect to introduce these signs in an area, observe changes in lawn walking, remove the signs, and evaluate their long-term effectiveness on the basis of continued reductions in lawn walking! Instead, the signs would be reintroduced (or left in place initially), and their effects over time would be evaluated in their presence.

In another example, consider the introduction of laws against polluting, with stiff fines and imprisonment for their violation. Again no one would expect to introduce such laws for a time, observe their effects, and then repeal them to get evidence on the permanence of the effects. Generality over time would be evaluated while the laws were still on the books and penalties for their violation were still being assessed. Oddly, the same "in-place" logic does not seem to apply when positive consequences, particularly monetary ones, are used.

Another argument commonly raised about the use of positive consequences is their fiscal practicality. Critics wonder whether the effects of such procedures justify their cost. They point to the commonsense argument that utilities cannot afford to pay people *not* to use electricity. They also note that municipalities cannot afford to pay children to pick up trash (either monetarily or with small toys, badges, and other objects) or to pay people to ride buses.

In response to these observations, it is important to realize that, again, it is too soon to say just exactly what the expense of such procedures will be. Behavior analysts are beginning to be more complete in their accounting of the cost of different elements in their intervention packages but still have a long way to go. When they have attempted to "cost out" their procedures, however, the expense has compared favorably either with the currently used procedures (see, for example, Casey & Lloyd, 1977) or with the dollar value of the savings in energy produced (see, for example, Hayes & Cone, 1977b).

Moreover, whether utilities can afford to pay people for conservation depends greatly on how completely the environmental costs are audited. It may be that when a precise accounting of all energy-related environmental costs is available (especially those indirectly related to energy use, such as pollution, unreclaimed stripped land, off-site effects of energy production, and so forth), paying people not to consume will seem more realistic than it does now.

Implementability by Other Persons

Most of the behavioral research we have described can be thought of as pilot studies aimed at preliminary testing of the general feasibility of behavioral

approaches to environmental problems. As such, the studies have involved procedures put in place and operated by the researchers themselves. The ease
with which others could successfully replicate the procedures has not yet been addressed systematically.

There is some evidence that some of the solutions can be fairly easily
implemented, however. For one thing, the procedures have nearly always been
kept as simple and straightforward as possible. Giving children trinkets for
turning in trash, handing people 25¢ as they board a bus, and distributing fliers
announcing the hours and location of a recycling center are not particularly
complicated activities. Even the more involved tactics of providing daily kWh
feedback as a percentage of some baseline or expected usage and arranging
savings-bond programs for limiting family size are not all that complex to the
persons responsible for their implementation. Power-company personnel and
public-health officials are certainly trained well enough and have sufficient experience to handle the procedures successfully.

Additional evidence for the implementability of behavioral solutions by a
variety of different types of people comes from the fact that many of the procedures have been replicated by different researchers in vastly different geographic
locales. Littering research has been conducted in nearly all parts of the country,
for example, and it has involved everyone from trained research personnel to
those of the U.S. Forest Service and of commercial amusement parks and theaters. Similarly, the feedback procedures common in energy-conservation studies
have been implemented by psychologists, college students, and the staffs of
electrical-utility companies.

Thus, although no research has systematically addressed the issue of the
generality of behavioral solutions across a variety of implementers, there is some
limited evidence that is encouraging in this regard. As long as researchers continue to keep the procedures simple and continue to evaluate them in numerous
different studies, there is good reason to think that such solutions will get high
marks for this type of generality.

Implementability in Diverse Locales and Environmental Contexts

The behavioral research we have reviewed has been successfully applied in
vastly different geographic locales. For example, feedback has been shown to
produce energy conservation in Rhode Island, Kentucky, West Virginia, and
Washington, among other places. Litter has been successfully reduced in Seattle,
Kansas City, Philadelphia, Kalamazoo, and Morgantown, West Virginia.
Moreover, energy use has been reduced in individual homes, married-student
university apartments, and master-metered apartment buildings. Litter has been
reduced in city zoos, college cafeterias, U.S. forests, and federal prisons and on
highway roadsides and city sidewalks. As noted in Chapter 7, behaviorally based
birth-limiting procedures have been examined in widely diverse regions of the
world.

In general, solutions to the more widely researched problems (such as litter and energy) have shown satisfactory levels of cross-setting generality. Undoubtedly, behavioral solutions in other areas will show similar levels of generality as they are more extensively studied. Our evidence to date, however, is based on summarizing the results of numerous different projects carried out independently in diverse places. As with durability over time, no single study or program of research has yet looked systematically at the issue of cross-setting generality of behavioral solutions.

Generality across Different Problem Magnitudes

The research we have discussed has, admittedly, been somewhat limited in scope. The problems dealt with have deliberately been kept to a size manageable in experimental pilot research. We looked at lawn trampling in a very small, circumscribed area, not the entire college campus, for example. Litter has been cleaned up in certain clearly defined locations, but not in entire national parks or cities. Similarly, electricity use has been reduced in several homes or apartment buildings, but not in entire cities or states.

Nonetheless, though such large-scale projects have not been conducted, there has been sufficient variation in the size of those that have that we can get some idea of the likelihood that behavioral solutions are robust across different levels of magnitude. Moreover, the simplicity and nature of many of the solutions argue for their face validity in this regard. For example, in the Hayes, Johnson, and Cone (1975) study, which paid people who turned in marked items of litter, the target areas were deliberately kept small. This was done, as in most other studies, to make sure that accurate data could be obtained on the amount of litter on the ground. In large-scale applications of already proved procedures, however, this degree of accuracy would not be necessary. For example, rather than counting every piece of litter on the ground in a one-block-square area that completely defines the experimental space, counts would be made in randomly chosen blocks of an entire city.

There is another way of looking at problem magnitude, however, and that is in terms of severity. Regardless of whether one deals with one or two blocks or an entire city, one or two apartments or an entire residential area, and so forth, the severity of the problem may vary within the environmental area selected. For example, a city block may have an average of one piece of trash per square yard of sidewalk surface, or it may have 20. Residential energy consumers may use an average of 600 kWh of electricity per month, or they may use 1000. Does the effectiveness of behavioral solutions vary with the severity of the problem?

Again, this is a type of generality that has not been studied systematically. It is likely to be important, though, and should be given our attention. For example, consider the case of a terribly littered public campground. Initially, the reinforcement approach of Burgess and his colleagues (see Chapter 5) might be tried; that is, children using the campground might be offered small rewards for turning in trash they picked up in the area. Since there is a lot of trash at the start of the program, it should be easy for children to collect it and earn the reward. Indeed, counts of litter on the ground before and after the program is initiated might show that litter is quickly reduced by 75%. However, as more trash is picked up, it becomes more difficult for the children to find some to turn in for the reward. Thus, several things might happen. The difficulty in finding trash may lead to some children's dropping out of the program. Or interest in earning the reward may lead to bringing trash from other areas (or from trash barrels, automobile ashtrays, and so on). The importation of trash to earn rewards was documented in the Chapman and Risley (1974) study mentioned in Chapter 5.

In this example the initial effectiveness of the solution resulted in changes in the environment. These changes in turn lowered the effectiveness of the solution. Whereas trash on the ground may have been eliminated at a rate of 25% per day for the first three days, it then reached a plateau and remained relatively unchanged as children merely removed new trash thrown down since the previous day or turned in trash from other areas. To continue to be effective, the procedure would have to be changed to keep pace with the changes it is producing in the environment.

Examples from other areas are not difficult to develop. It is relatively easy to get the first 25%–30% reduction in electricity or water use. Once this reduction has been achieved, however, further reductions might necessitate different and/or more powerful procedures. Similarly, the elimination of 50% of the particulates from corporate smokestack emissions may be relatively easy. Producing greater reductions may require a level of technology and capital outlay not readily available.

Thus, some solutions to environmental problems may work at some levels of the problem and not at others. Because of this very real possibility, it will be important for researchers to specify initial environmental circumstances as clearly as they can; that is, initial problem levels or severity must be described in addition to the criteria for judging the problem solved. These descriptions must be standardized, so that different investigators can communicate clearly with one another. In this way the generality of various solutions will become established. As researchers apply the same procedures to different levels of the problem, they will obtain data supporting or refuting the general applicability of the procedures.

The Applicability of Solutions to Other Environmental Problems

A particular behavioral solution to a problem will be more useful to the extent that it can be applied successfully to other problem areas as well. For example, newspaper announcements of winners of weekly litter-pickup contests may increase the cleanliness of targeted urban areas. Would the same approach result in reductions in the energy used in residential dwellings?

We have shown examples throughout the book of similar procedures being applied successfully to different environmental problems. Paying people to turn in litter and paying people to use less electricity are but one example of the general applicability of one type of reinforcement approach. Antecedent-only, or discriminative-stimulus, procedures have also shown some generality in their application.

Although reinforcement and stimulus-control procedures can be given reasonably high marks for having general applicability across environmental problems, we should not be lulled into thinking that this type of generality will be automatically forthcoming for all or most behavioral solutions. A particular procedure is more likely to be generally useful to the extent that it emanates from an overall theoretical schema or conceptual viewpoint concerning behavior/environment relations. We have tried repeatedly to emphasize the conceptual underpinnings of what we have called environmentally relevant psychology for just this reason. It has consistently seemed to us that generating solutions from within a broad conceptual framework will result in a coherent, relatively well-integrated science of behavior/environment relations. Such an approach will avoid the bag-of-tricks appearance likely to characterize a literature containing numerous clever and effective solutions designed for specific problems of particular local concern. This parochial view of solving environmental problems is likely to result in solutions having limited implications for other problem areas.

TACTICAL CONSIDERATIONS IN BEHAVIORAL SOLUTIONS

Even though there has been no really systematic study of the generality of behavioral solutions, we have suggested that what evidence exists is definitely encouraging. In addition, the broad outlines of an effective technology are beginning to emerge.

Even at this early point it is probably safe to say that stimulus-control procedures have not been as effective as those altering the consequences provided for a behavior. The most effective, most generalizable forms of intervention are likely to be those using a combination of antecedent-stimulus and consequent-stimulus changes; that is, signs or messages urging people to respond in certain ways followed by rewards for doing so are likely to produce more change than using either approach by itself. Common sense would support this observation, and, indeed, this is really the tactic that behavior analysts use even though they may have focused attention on the reward process. A good example is the sign on the side of Deslauriers and Everett's (1977) experimental bus announcing that persons boarding the bus might receive tokens. It is quite common to communicate consequences to participants ahead of time (see, for example, Kohlenberg & Phillips, 1973; Powers, Osborne, & Anderson, 1973). In fact, it is only in studies designed to compare the two general approaches that the use of one without the other makes much sense. As an applied matter, a combination of antecedent and consequent approaches is nearly always going to be the tactic of choice.

Nonetheless, behavior analysts are likely to continue emphasizing one strategy over the other. Given its generally superior performance to date, the focus on consequent approaches will probably persist. If so, more cost-effective, less labor-intensive procedures should be examined. The remotely administrable reinforcement approach evaluated by Powers and his colleagues (1973) is a good example (see Chapter 5). Although most reinforcement tactics require the active presence of someone to administer the reward, these experimenters mailed theirs and did not need to be present at all. Hayes and his associates (1975) suggested that the marked-item procedure might be made automatic by developing large trash bins with sensing devices that would automatically detect marked items and dispense reinforcers to persons depositing litter.

The automation of reward procedures in other areas of environmental concern would be even simpler. For example, computers could automatically compare current use with that of a comparable earlier period and print commendatory statements or compute monetary rewards to be included on utility bills. Turnstiles or coin boxes on buses and subways could be programmed like slot machines to award free rides or tokens to patrons on a VP schedule. Noise-monitoring equipment could be similarly automated so that rewards are presented when selected levels of quiet have been reached. The point here is that we can easily find less expensive ways to use reward procedures that have been shown to be effective. In doing so, the generality of these solutions will be further established.

CONTRIBUTIONS OF REACTIVE RESEARCH TO BEHAVIORAL SOLUTIONS

To extend the usefulness of behavioral solutions, it has been suggested that "non-behavioral or 'reactive' studies" be used (Stokols, 1978). For example, the assessment of citizen attitudes about a particular environmental problem or context before intervening might lead to modifications in the intervention strategy that would enhance its effectiveness. Suppose you were interested in trying to get people to install variable-flush mechanisms on their toilets in order to conserve water. Suppose, further, that the persons you have earmarked for your water-conservation campaign think that less water per flush may lead to clogged sewer lines. You try unsuccessfully to get these people to install variable-flush mechanisms. Then someone casually mentions being concerned about clogging. You explain to that person that the reduced flow will pertain to liquid wastes only and that solids will still be transported with the same amount of water as before. The person utters "Ah ha!" and proceeds to install the device. Had you measured people's attitudes toward and/or knowledge about water-conservation practices *before* planning your intervention, you could have included an informational component to clear up any mistaken notions. Your participants then may have been more responsive.

Other examples of the advantages of combining behavior-analytic and reactive approaches are not difficult to generate. Imagine that you are planning to recruit children to participate in a campground litter-cleanup program that involves paying them 25¢ for every bag of litter turned in to you. How successful would you be if the parents of these children viewed such payments as bribery and refused to allow them to participate? Formal or informal assessment of parental attitudes ahead of time would undoubtedly lead to changes in the design of your procedure.

Finally, imagine that you are interested in evaluating behavioral approaches to improving the overall appearance of a small community. There may be numerous places to start—for example, litter on streets and sidewalks, abandoned automobiles, dilapidated houses, or unsightly signs protruding at random from places of business along the town's main street. Furthermore, there may not be much agreement among the townspeople about the seriousness of each of the problem areas. It may be that an evaluation of public attitudes would provide information that would determine which area to deal with first, how to modify your procedures to accommodate public opinion, and so on.

To be sure, these suggestions assume some relationship between attitudes about environmental circumstances and behavior in them. As was noted in Chapter 1, however, evidence is not awfully strong on this point. The data that are available have come primarily from correlational studies. But it is one thing to know that attitudes toward the Sierra Club predict willingness to support or join the club at a later time (Weigel, Vernon, & Tognacci, 1974). It is quite another to modify these attitudes and show differential rates of joining or to alter one's membership drive to accommodate differences in attitudes and show increased rates of joining. Similarly, it is one thing to show relationships among attitudes toward contraception and reported contraceptive use (Davidson & Jaccard, 1975) and quite another to change attitudes and show corresponding changes in use. In other words, before the value of a "transactional" (Stokols, 1978) approach to environment/behavior studies can be adequately determined, it will be necessary to conduct research showing functional relations between attitudes and behavior. Altering one and showing corresponding changes in the other under controlled circumstances would be most impressive. However, short of this, it would be useful to show that interventions specifically tailored to accommodate attitudes are more effective than those not similarly tailored.

In the interim, behavior analysts will probably want to concentrate their efforts on developing environmental interventions sufficiently powerful to override some of the effects of differences in populations. In other words, rather than spending their resources looking at behavioral/attitudinal interrelations as they affect the environment, behavior analysts may want to evaluate procedures that will work even if they are inconsistent with attitudes. An exaggerated example may make this point clearer. People might be willing to put variable-flush mechanisms on their toilets even if they believe the pipes will become clogged if they are paid $100 for doing so. Parenthetically, having installed the devices and not experienced clogging, the participants' attitude might then change to coincide with their new behavior; that is, behavior/attitude consistency might be produced by first changing behavior.

It is important to note, however, that it is the behavior and its functional relationship to the environment that are of paramount concern to the behavior analyst. Attitudes will be important only insofar as they have a functional relationship to environmental characteristics as well. Because attitudes tend to be relatively permanent, they do not lend themselves easily to the types of functional examination that behavior analysts are accustomed to doing; that is, they are difficult to evaluate in intrasubject designs, especially those of the *ABAB* variety. Since overt behavior having direct environmental impact is relatively easily examined in such controlled designs, that behavior rather than attitudes is likely to continue to receive the major share of the behavior analyst's attention.

PREVENTION OF THE DEVELOPMENT OF ENVIRONMENTALLY DESTRUCTIVE BEHAVIORAL REPERTOIRES

Throughout this book we have presented a rather simple-minded approach to the application of behavioral principles. Moreover, we have concentrated almost entirely on tackling the environment after a problem has been identified. Before a completely adequate science of behavior/environment interactions is available, however, behavior analysts will need to attend to ways of preventing environmental problems in the first place. Developing behavioral repertoires that include environmentally sound practices is an extremely important area of research that has been relatively ignored up to now. Indeed, very little is known about the teaching of such behavior. How, for example, are children taught not to litter? Is such teaching indeed a process of developing tolerance for mildly aversive immediate consequences in order to avoid seriously aversive ones at a later time?

To some extent the development of environmentally protective behavioral repertoires must rely on the establishment of rule-governed behavior. We have not dealt with this issue earlier, largely because it has been ignored in the literature. It is unavoidable, however, when issues of both the long-term durability of behavior change and environmental-problem prevention are being discussed. Since, for example, we cannot be present to reward people every time they dispose of trash appropriately, it would be more effective if they did so because they were "supposed to" than if they did it because they would receive an immediate reward. Doing things because one is supposed to or ought to is behavior that is under the control of rules. These rules are generally thought to have become influential as the result of a history of certain behavior/consequence relationships. If proper trash disposal pays off repeatedly in one's early childhood experience, one learns a generalized rule: "If this leads to good things, I ought to do it." This type of history results in the performance of acts in later life that do not appear to be under the control of any obvious environmental-stimulus change. They are, instead, under the control of one's reinforcement history or variables included therein. Research on the establishment of rule-governed environmentally relevant behavior in young children is needed to develop prevention strategies to complement the problem-solution tactics of behavior analysts in this area. Further, a full complement of preventive and ameliorative approaches will help establish the long-term durability of behavioral procedures. In the study of durability and the other forms of generality referred to earlier, an interesting problem confronts us, as the next section shows.

AN ECO-SYSTEMS PERSPECTIVE

As ecologists are given to reminding us, everything is indeed connected to everything else. Changing one aspect of the environment cannot help but change others whether we are aware of them or not. In a sense, then, it is meaningless to inquire whether a particular solution has generalized effects. That it does is an ecological truism that cannot be disputed. The more relevant question is not *whether* generalization has occurred but *what form* the generalization has taken. Have we unwittingly solved one problem at the expense of making others worse? Have we unwittingly benefited several aspects of the environment at which we were not even aiming?

As Willems (1974) has observed, behavior analysts could benefit from an eco-systems perspective. This is especially true of those attempting to solve environmental problems. Essentially, such a perspective means keeping a keen eye out for the numerous unplanned as well as planned changes produced by one's independent variable. Increasing the number of dependent measures in a study will help some here. Unfortunately, there are limits to every study, and every base will not be adequately covered. The best that we can hope for is that the ecological homily of connectedness will be considered by each investigator as studies are planned and conducted. If it is, at least gross oversights will be less likely in the future.

SUMMARY

This chapter has dealt with an issue that has traditionally concerned applied behavior analysts in all areas of endeavor: the generality of their solutions to social problems. We described five types of generalization of particular concern to environmental-problem solvers and briefly discussed evidence for each.

We noted that the most generally useful strategy thus far has been the reinforcement approach. Arranging positive consequences for engaging in environmentally protective behavior has been shown to be effective with a variety of problems. Criticisms of this approach in terms of its cost and the permanence of its effects were discussed, and logical problems with the "permanence" criticism were mentioned.

The most effective behavior-analytic solutions to environmental problems involve the combination of both antecedent and consequent approaches. In fact, it is extremely difficult to separate the two. As a practical matter, moreover, their separation is unnecessary and undesirable.

We next discussed the potential benefits of combining reactive and environmentally relevant approaches. Such a combination has a logical advantage, assuming some relationship between attitudes and other reactions *to* environmental circumstances and other behavior *in* them. Evidence for such relationships is scarce, however, and behavior analysts should develop procedures of sufficient power to override attitudinal and other reactions. Change in attitude might then follow the changed behavior.

Of course, more attention should be paid to the prevention of environmental problems in the first place. The study of rule-governed environmentally relevant behaviors in young children is important in developing prevention strategies. Long-term improvements in numerous environmental conditions will require basic changes in the ways we interact with them. Perhaps general environmental conscientiousness can be taught at an early age.

The last section of the chapter dealt with the logical problems posed by an eco-systems perspective. We noted that the entire question of this chapter should probably not be *whether* generalization has occurred but *what form* that generalization has taken.

Chapter 13

PROMOTING BEHAVIORAL-SCIENCE IMPACT THROUGH EXPERIMENTAL SOCIAL REFORM

The use of behavioral science, we have argued, is critical to the development of solutions to environmental problems. But we have a long way to go. You may have noticed that there are whole areas of environmental concern that have been touched upon only minimally or not at all in this book: air pollution, water pollution, pesticide use, nuclear radiation, endangerment of species—the list goes on and on. That is because we have tried to provide not so much a list of answers as a demonstration of the usefulness of behavioral science in the development of answers. Environmentally relevant psychology still has an enormous amount of work to do—truly, it has only just begun.

The development of behavioral technology will continue if the scientific community, and society more generally, can be convinced that physical technology alone cannot do the job because environmental problems are, in large part, *behavioral* problems: problems of life-style and habits, of ignorance and motivation.

It is perhaps understandable that most of the work to date has been done in areas in which the behaviors to be dealt with are those of the private individual. The list of environmental problems not addressed in detail in this book includes all of those problems that are thought to be the result of institutions in our society, such as business or government. It is hard to see how a private individual could significantly influence trends in the control of water pollution, for example. But if you give it a bit of thought, you may see ways in which even "institutional" problems are, in fact, behavioral problems. After all, institutions do not behave; people do. Presumably, the behavior of a city manager is just as understandable and potentially changeable as that of a lawn-trampling college student; the behavior of the president of a corporation is still the behavior of a *person*.

SYSTEMS-LEVEL CONTINGENCIES

Human behavior is a natural event. The behavior of societal institutions is the product of human behavior. Therefore, it should be possible to understand institutional actions using the same framework we have relied on throughout the preceding chapters. A systems-level problem is one in which the difficulty has to do with the interrelationship between persons or institutions, not simply single behaving individuals. Systems are known for their complexity. It is a truism that as you change one part of a system, you influence all parts of the system. Thus, it is very difficult to apply our framework at an empirical level. Nonetheless, it can be applied quite fruitfully at a conceptual level, as the following discussion may show. We will take a "systems look" at energy conservation.

Energy utilities are typically owned by stockholders. Although they are usually state-authorized monopolies, they are still considered free-enterprise companies. Investors expect these companies to make a profit. The company's president, vice-presidents, regional managers, salespeople, and the like are all hired, retained, and fired with an eye toward the monetary bottom line. Put another way, one of the most powerful reinforcers for these institutions is money.

Monetary gain for utilities depends upon many things: enough public good will to get rate increases through public utilities commissions; increasing or at least adequate production and distribution; effective management; reduction of costs. These are process goals, which have to be met on the way to the two ultimate outcome goals—for the individual in the company, success; for the company itself, profit.

Process goals (public good will, increasing production) are often in conflict with each other. For example, companies cannot currently afford open and vigorous campaigns to promote increased consumption of electricity. Public reaction would be swift and potentially devastating. At the least, such a campaign could limit future rate increases by turning public opinion against the company. At the worst, it could lead to the socialization of power production, one of the consequences these companies dread the most (see "Maine votes . . . ," 1973, for a particularly rabid attack on this possibility). Conversely, a company that takes serious and effective action to reduce energy consumption is in potential danger of having financial problems. Capital costs—for production and distribution systems—are not highly flexible. Suppose you buy a nuclear-power plant for $1 billion. The plant is built over a period of several years. It will meet expected energy needs in the next decade. The tremendous sums of money needed are borrowed and paid back over many years. For the first several years, of course, the plant itself is a real drain on resources. If consumption drops unexpectedly (or fails to grow at the predicted rate), the capital costs do not go away. The "mortgage" on the plant must still be paid.

An analogy would be buying an apartment house and then getting tenants for only half the apartments. The loan payments continue. In this case you could sell the apartment house. But who but an energy company would want a $1-billion nuclear-power plant?

When consumption drops too low, power companies have one main recourse available: rate increases. As we showed earlier, rate increases are not maximally effective consumption-control procedures, but they do increase company revenue. The net result of the double bind put on power companies is that they try to increase good will (for example, by advertisements calling for conservation) while maintaining adequate consumption at high rates.

Consumers are not unaware of these systems-level contingencies. In one of our projects (Hayes, 1977), we solicited volunteers for an energy study door to door. The reactions were quite instructive. About 10% of the households expressed this attitude: Why conserve? If too many people do it, they will just have to raise the rates, and we will all end up paying more for less. We had no real answer to that except to say that decreased consumption has other desirable effects, such as decreased pollution.

A similar example exists in the 1976–1977 California drought. When water supplies dropped perilously low, a tight conservation program was initiated. It worked, and worked well. Water consumption plummeted. The end result was that the public water companies could not meet their bond obligations due to the decreased revenue. The solution? A drought tax! Consumers were actually charged a tax because they cooperated in reducing their consumption! Consumers may be reluctant to cooperate in conservation efforts if they end up being hurt financially. It would have been better, for example, for the state to have covered the water bonds with general revenue rather than hit the consumer with a demoralizing specific tax on conservation efforts. The economic costs might have been similar in either case, but the negative psychological effect might have been less.

The California situation demonstrated another systems problem. When the goals for reduction in water consumption were set, they were set on the basis of individual consumption records (for example, reduce consumption by 10% over last year's). At first glance, this makes sense. After all, some families are big and some are small, and it would be difficult to equate water-consumption goals across households. But think about it for a minute. Suppose Family A is fanatical about conservation. Family B is wasteful. If each family has to reduce consumption by 10%, Family A may find it impossible, while Family B may readily comply. It will appear as though Family B is the conservation-minded one. In effect, Family A is being punished for having made consistent conservation efforts in the past. Again, consumers are aware of these relationships. If there are signs of scarcity or of impending rationing, consumption may actually increase as consumers jockey for position.

The solutions to many of these systems-level problems can come only from government. For example, only the government can devise ways to induce power companies to conserve. Power companies might be paid large rebates for achieving reductions in their sales of power. These rebates would offset their loss of revenues. The total benefit to society may justify such payments. You could conceive of the power companies as a large community of energy "households." Many of the techniques developed with homes might also apply at a systems level: public feedback (let the community know if the power company is selling more or less energy); competitive feedback (how is the rest of the country doing?); incentives (for example, tax breaks that would soften the economic impact of conservation); goal setting; and so on.

Not all action needs to be government based, however. Other systems-level problems can be addressed by the action of many individual consumers (for example, by bringing public pressure to bear on decisions). What seems important is that the behavioral realities of these problems be recognized. Much of the rhetoric over environmental problems casts people in roles as "good guys" and "bad guys": the company president is bad; the environmentalist is good. This type of argument is foolish and unnecessary. If there are problems, they are with the *system*, not the people; with the *behavior*, not the receptacle of that behavior. There is a common religious notion that relates to this: "hate the sin and love the sinner." Too much of the public debate about environmental problems is of the hate-the-sinner variety. Though it serves the purpose of giving vent to our frustrations, it delays ultimately effective action.

HOW CAN WE INFLUENCE SYSTEMS?

To date, almost nothing is known empirically about how people in institutions can be induced to behave in ways that foster environmental betterment. This is unfortunate because such information frequently seems critical to the success of behavioral technology. Perhaps you recall a study of ours described in Chapter 5 in which the patterns of walkers through a small university park were analyzed. From these data we made certain recommendations to the university personnel responsible for the park. The recommendations were only partially followed. We were disappointed. But after thinking about it for a while, you will see the inconsistencies in our attitude. We were not at all surprised when we found that energy consumers are not much influenced by educational material. After all, why should they be? Their behavior is presumably the result of existing contingencies; educational approaches may bear upon these in only a very limited way. Why, then, were we surprised when the designer did not respond to our data? They were just another type of information. He, too, was behaving as he did for a reason.

In order to implement some of our programs widely, we will have to learn more about how to influence the behavior of persons who are in positions of responsibility. This is easier said than done. But there may be ways. For example, suppose you find that a city manager is holding up action on a particular environmental issue. It would be tempting, but probably useless, to blame the person. A more effective response might be to organize a letter-writing campaign to bring public pressure to bear on the city manager's actions.

As of yet, behavioral scientists have not developed techniques that are easily applicable to the behavior of persons in politics or business. Virtually all the problems examined in this book in any detail are problems that can be studied with private individuals. This is fine, as far as it goes. But we recognize, and the field should recognize, that this leaves the field open to the valid criticism that it has failed to show success in influencing the sociopolitical behaviors that seem to have such a significant impact on many environmental problems. In fact, many of the most critical problems seem to be of this type.

This limitation is not unique to programs designed to solve environmental problems, of course. Political science, in general, has virtually no experimental base. It has only been fairly recently that political scientists have even begun to call for experimental research (see, for example, Laponce & Smoker, 1972; McConahay, 1973). Perhaps it is unfair to expect people interested in environmental problems to develop political-intervention techniques when these techniques have not been developed elsewhere. Nevertheless, this is one area we will need to address experimentally as time goes on.

In the meantime what can behavioral scientists do about systems-level problems? The main contributions that behavioral science has to make now are conceptual tools that make clearer the events influencing the behavior of individuals in the system. By analyzing these controlling events, the hope is that certain key areas may emerge. The right kind of leverage on the right persons in a system can influence the entire institution. What is currently *lacking* is the use of methodological tools to test these conceptualizations.

BEHAVIORAL EXPERIMENTATION: HOW, WHAT, AND WHY?

Part of the problem that behavioral scientists have in the political arena seems to be—at least at first glance—due to the experimental approach itself. People are not generally used to experimentation as a decision-making tool. The social programs implemented by political bodies are done so on the basis of belief more often than data. Politicians are put in the position of dispensing answers, not questions; of advancing programs, not experiments.

The public at large seems to share this attitude toward research. Clinicians often remark that clients seem to want the benefit of research ("Has this technique been thoroughly tested on people with my kind of problem?") without having to be involved themselves ("I don't want to be someone's guinea pig"). In other words, we value research outcomes while distrusting the process of research. Somehow, research carries with it the implication of needless manipulation, while social programs, no matter how ill planned or destructive, are supposedly being done with nothing but the best of intentions.

Behavioral scientists have long wondered why experimentation is not a more prominent part of social decision making. Calls have frequently been made for experimental social reform (for example, Fairweather, 1972) and the use of "natural experiments" (for example, Campbell, 1969; Snyder, 1962). Despite the resistance to it, some progress has been made toward fostering experimentation, as the next sections will show.

Small-Scale Demonstrations

One common tactic is to do enough pilot, or small-scale, work to be able to say with some certainty that a particular solution will work. The small-scale project may lead to a "foot in the door," so that answers can be given to politicians rather than questions. The hope is that, once in the door, the value of experimentation can gradually be taught.

Many of the studies described in this book are clearly projects of this type. Because of their limited magnitude, they are of little use in and of themselves. But they might be implemented more broadly, given enough support.

Simulations and Laboratory Analogues

Other strategies are possible, such as collecting data from games and computer simulations (see, for example, Coplin, 1968). The hope here is that we need not test complex and expensive interventions directly. Instead, we could examine the effects of various manipulations in the context of an analogue task. For example, we might set up a transportation game in which some players serve the role of community planners, others are bus riders, others are factory managers, and so on (see Everett, Studer, & Douglas, 1978). We could then examine the effects of changes in bus schedules or fares upon the selection of public transportation by game players. The problem with these studies, of course, is that they are so far from the real-life situation that there is plenty of room to draw incorrect conclusions. The value of simulations to the development of practical procedures in the environmental area is still unclear.

Experimental Social Reform

Another strategy is to encourage the small-scale testing of policy options in particular areas or with identifiable groups. This strategy is ideal if cooperation can be obtained because it essentially establishes experimentation as the method by which the correct policies will be chosen. One way that government has used this option is with "requests for proposals." These RFPs, as they are called, are issued by granting agencies when they would like research to be done on a particular question. In this way, government goes to the scientific community with requests for specific assistance in evaluating policies.

The above three methods of integrating research and policy formation can be thought of as some of the ways in which research feeds into the political process. It would be naive to suppose that research could or should be the only input into this process. Any policy will undoubtedly be strongly influenced by a host of factors, such as religious, cultural, ethical, political, economic, and so on. Research can tell us what *is*. It can even tell us what *should be,* if we first make the necessary value judgments. For example, a meaningful research question might be the following: "Assuming that we are willing to take any step short of violence to reduce the population, what would be the most effective procedure?" Research can never decide what the "proper" value judgments are, however. It cannot tell us whether we should value human life or environmental protection.

Social Reform as "Natural Experiments"

Although research cannot supply all of the information that must go into policy formulation, there is another sense in which research can contribute to policy. Rather than research's being an *input* to policy, there are times when research is an *output* of policy decisions. Probably one of the biggest contributions behavioral scientists could offer the decision making of societal institutions is through the dissemination of scientific methodology. Many of the decisions being made by government and business are at least potentially analyzable with little or no change of the plan of implementation at all. What is needed are sound, frequent measurements and a knowledge of design. For example, if a city tries out a new litter-control system and later drops the plan, the city has used a natural *ABA* design. If good measures of litter on the ground were collected frequently enough throughout, the data need only be analyzed with an eye toward this design. Time-series (intrasubject) methodology (Hersen and Barlow, 1976) is not well-known even in the behavioral sciences, much less in political bodies. If knowledge of it were more broadly available, there would be less resistance to research. After all, research is just a name for carefully evaluating our decisions. Good managers, politicians, and the like are doing time-series research all the time anyway, whether they know it or not.

WHAT DOES THE BEHAVIORAL SCIENTIST NEED?

A behavioral scientist possesses certain skills that can be used in the solution of environmental problems. Brief descriptions of these skills follow.

A Point of View

One of the dangers in technical development is that researchers may produce a mountain of techniques, facts, and procedures, each of which is relevant only to a particular problem in a particular setting at a particular time. We emphasized this point in the previous chapter. We need a set of principles to coordinate and systematize knowledge so as to make it teachable and understandable. We need a "language" to organize and help guide what we do. There are a number of language systems or scientific points of view that can be used, but we have emphasized an operant $S^D–R–S^R$ formulation because it seems to us that this language permits an analysis of a broad range of problems at a number of different levels. It is possible to use this formulation, for example, in sociology as well as psychology (see Burgess & Bushell, 1969), with individuals as well as entire governments. This flexibility is a major asset when attempting transdisciplinary research.

Scientific Methodology

Precise data collection and the creative use of experimental design are integral to the progress of environmentally relevant psychology.

A Direct Approach

Throughout this book we have tried to show the advantages of an active, direct approach to environmental problems. We have emphasized that there is a bottom line to research on environmental problems: the environmental problems themselves. Researchers ignore this fact at their peril, since environmental research that does not demonstrate environmental relevance of this sort is often of little use to anyone.

A Transdisciplinary View

Environmentally relevant psychology is not the domain of any one of the behavioral sciences. Sociologists, economists, political scientists, psychologists—all of these have a role. Throughout the book we have given examples of ways in which a transdisciplinary view is helpful. One aspect of the problem is less likely to be overemphasized or another ignored. For example, energy-conservation solutions that avoid the economic realities facing utility companies cannot hope to be successful. Population-control studies that avoid the sensitive political realities surrounding family planning are doomed to failure.

ISSUES IN THE PURSUIT OF BEHAVIORAL SOLUTIONS

Given the above qualities, a behavioral scientist should be ready to tackle environmental problems effectively. But there are many different ways to do so. There are different directions to take and roles to assume. At this point it is impossible to say which is right and which is wrong among these various alternatives. It is possible, however, to point to the issues involved.

The Level of Analysis

Certain problems are approachable at the level of the private individual. Others are not. Which level is the correct one depends upon the goal of the scientist and the nature of the problem, but clearly it is possible to attempt a solution at the incorrect level of analysis, only to be frustrated in the long run by the initial mistake.

Selecting Problems with Actual Environmental Relevance

It should be obvious that solutions to the wrong problems are no solutions at all. We have spoken at length about how too many behavioral scientists have studied problems that are only very indirectly related to environmental problems themselves. It is important that behavioral scientists carefully analyze the situation as it exists and determine what is actually causing the problem.

The Scope of the Study

There is a trade-off to be made between the study of problems on a large scale and on a small scale. Small-scale research, in which perhaps only a few persons are studied, has the advantages of increased control over events, more intensive analyses of the individual behavior, and, often, increased chances of concluding the experiment successfully and rapidly. However, the researcher may not know how to implement such studies broadly or what impact they would have. When these programs are expanded to a meaningful size, they may reveal significant flaws. Conversely, large-scale studies enable the researcher to examine the problem nearer the scale on which a program is eventually needed. Properly run, this type of study may increase the validity of the knowledge obtained. Yet the knowledge may be less intensive and facts may be missed at this scale that would be picked up in a smaller project. Further, large-scale studies are more difficult to run, and run well, and they take more time and more money. The scale of programs should be set at the size needed to gain useful information. Some programs can be done on a small scale with no loss of information. Others must be done on a large scale.

How Basic Should We Be?

One trend in the field is toward more and more work on developing successful techniques as opposed to advancing basic knowledge. This trend has caused some concern (Deitz, 1978; Hayes, Rincover, & Solnick, in press). The process of research has several natural steps: (1) a conceptual analysis of the problem, (2) a generation of an intervention based on that analysis, (3) a test of the intervention, and (4) an analysis of the effective components and parameters of the intervention. The concern is that we are concentrating too heavily on Steps 2 and 3. In particular, it has been shown that research involved in Step 4 is becoming less common (Hayes et al., in press). Such research is desirable because it helps develop our conceptualizations. Our techniques are built on a theoretical base. Researchers should not forget that there are many basic questions still to be answered. For example, many of the techniques described in this book have been based upon the notion of feedback. But what *is* feedback, and why does it work? We know very little about the answers to these questions. The term *feedback* is merely a descriptive one meaning many different things. If we knew *why* feedback works, we could devise programs to maximize these processes. Therefore, researchers should keep in mind the process questions (the "why" questions) even while asking the more immediate outcome questions (the "whether" questions).

What Should We Expect of Ourselves?

The special skills of behavioral scientists, to be used properly, require the support of many parts of society. Clearly, behavioral scientists cannot do the whole job. It is not necessary that behavioral scientists actually be the ones to run the on-line projects, that they actually be the ones to get these projects through legislatures. Rather, the researchers are needed to develop the solutions and to encourage their adoption.

In some scientific circles there is a support system that encourages the use of scientific discoveries. This system is not well established in environmentally relevant psychology. Accordingly, there is a tendency for us to be too critical of our own programs and to demand that they actually be shown to be successful when fully deployed. Going too far in this direction could bog down the whole field. The reason for this pressure is understandable. However, environmentally relevant psychology is trying to do for itself that which only societal support can do. Societal support will come only by developing it, not by circumventing it.

THE FUTURE OF ENVIRONMENTALLY RELEVANT PSYCHOLOGY

The future of environmentally relevant psychology is unclear but promising. It is a new area, and there are strong traditions that must be broken before it can be used fully. When the President decides to offer a tax incentive for such things as insulating homes, he is often doing so on the basis of belief, not experimental data. Massive, expensive attempts at behavioral manipulation are often entered into with little or no help from experimental behavioral scientists. Meanwhile, billions of dollars are earmarked for development and experimentation in physical technology. Perhaps the reason for this contradictory manner of treatment is that we are all dealing with behavioral influences every day. It is much easier for lay persons to see the value of experimentation in solar energy than in the processes of social influence. One is strange, the other familiar. We are much more likely to feel we know the answers to familiar questions. But feeling we know and knowing are two different things. The recent history of the United States is littered with the shattered remnants of social programs that failed to function properly, despite the efforts of all the experts who felt they knew the right answers. Perhaps it is time to try something different.

GLOSSARY

ABA design an intrasubject research design in which data are continuously collected during baseline *(A)*, intervention *(B)*, and return-to-baseline *(A)* phases.

analysis of variance a statistical procedure applied to data collected in an intersubject design to determine the magnitude of differences between two or more groups.

antilittering picking up litter or trash.

applied behavior analysis that branch of behavior analysis that deals with problems of social or clinical significance usually studied in their natural context.

area-specific free transit permitting rides on public conveyances without cost within certain limited geographic areas.

baseline the operant or naturally occurring frequency (latency, duration) of a behavior or environmental condition prior to trying to change it; the first phase in *ABA* and multiple-baseline designs.

behavior analysis the intensive study of the responding of individual organisms by systematically varying stimuli and noting changes in response.

behavioral ecology as used in this book, a term referring to the scientific study of the impact of human behavior on the environment.

behavioral technology see *technology, behavioral*.

BTU (British Thermal Unit) a measure of the heat energy value of fuels.

condom a thin sheath that is worn over the penis in order to prevent the emission of sperm into the vagina during intercourse.

consequation the deliberate programming of behavioral consequences.

consequence an event following a behavior.

contingency the relationship between an antecedent, response, and consequence.

control group subjects in a between-groups or intersubject research design who are not exposed to the independent variable, or experimental treatment. They serve as a baseline against which to compare the experimental group.

correlation coefficient an algebraic statistic measuring the extent to which two factors vary or change in related ways.

cost effectiveness a measurement of the relative cost needed to obtain a desired effect. A procedure is said to be cost effective if the value of its effects is greater than the cost of producing the effects.

cullet crushed used glass used to make new glass.

decibel (dB) a unit used to measure the perceived intensity of sound. A decibel is the logarithmic expression of the ratio between the sound pressure observed and the lowest audible sound pressure. This results in a measure in which each successive decibel is about equal to the smallest change in loudness a normal human ear can detect.

dependent variable the behavior to be changed in an experiment; changes in behavior that are said to depend on or be related to manipulations of the independent (experimental) variable.

discriminative stimulus an event regularly preceding a behavior that through consistent association with a given consequence reliably signals the organism that responding will lead to the consequence; S^D is the symbol used for a discriminative stimulus.

ecology a branch of science concerned with the interrelationship of organisms and their environment.

eco-systems perspective a point of view that stresses awareness of the far-reaching consequences of our acts throughout various parts of the environment.

empirical related to or based on experience.

environment the context (physical, behavioral, social, emotional) in which behavior occurs; the surrounds of an organism.

environmental psychology the study of relationships between behavior and the natural and built environments.

environmentally destructive behavior actions or responses leading to a reduction in the quality of the built or natural environment.

environmentally protective behavior actions or responses leading to an increase in the quality of the built or natural environment.

environmentally relevant behavior actions or responses related to the quality of the built or natural environment.

environmentally relevant psychology the study of behavior as it relates to the quality of the built or natural environment.

every-person (EP) schedule arranging a stimulus event to occur for each person who performs a particular act—for example, awarding tokens to each person boarding a bus.

experimental analysis of behavior that branch of behavior analysis that deals with basic behavioral processes, usually through studies in laboratory settings.

experimental group subjects in a between-groups or intersubject research design who are exposed to the independent variable, or experimental treatment. They are compared to the control, or untreated, subjects.

experimental replication showing the soundness of experimental results by doing the same (or nearly the same) experiment over again and seeing whether the same results are found.

extinction the process of returning a response to its original baseline level by no longer following it with a particular stimulus event.

factorial design an intersubject research design in which at least two variables (factors) are manipulated simultaneously, resulting in a minimum of four groups.

fading the gradual phasing out of a stimulus event, usually an antecedent or discriminative stimulus, so that the response will occur even in the absence of the event.

feedback information to a person about some aspect of his or her behavior; usually designed to increase or decrease the behavior.

fixed not changing; invariant.

fixed-interval (FI) schedule an arrangement in which a stimulus event occurs after the passage of a set amount of time since the last occurrence; an FI–10 schedule indicates that the event occurs every tenth unit of time (minutes, hours, and so on); compare *variable-interval schedule, fixed-ratio schedule,* and *variable-ratio schedule.*

fixed-person (FP) schedule arranging a stimulus event to occur every *n*th person in an invarying manner; for example, an FP–10 would mean that the event occurs every tenth person.

fixed-ratio (FR) schedule an arrangement in which a stimulus event occurs after the passage of a set number of responses since the last occurrence; the number of responses required for each occurrence of the stimulus determines the ratio: an FR–10 schedule indicates that the stimulus occurs after every tenth response; compare *fixed-interval schedule, variable-ratio schedule,* and *variable-interval schedule.*

functional relationship   exists when a change in one variable is associated with systematic changes in another.

group contingency   a contingency in which the behavior of an entire group is consequated, or the consequences apply to the entire group (or both).

independent variable   the experimental, or treatment, variable; that which is manipulated in order to observe its effects on other (dependent) variables.

interdependent group-oriented contingency system   arranging consequences for individual members of a group dependent upon changes in the entire group.

interobserver agreement   exists when two or more observers concur about an event.

intersubject design   a research design that relies on replicated differences between two or more subjects to demonstrate an experimental effect.

interval schedule   arranging stimulus events to occur according to the passage of a certain amount of time.

intrasubject design   a research design that relies on replicated differences within one subject or a group of subjects to demonstrate an experimental effect.

IUD (intrauterine device)   a small device, usually plastic, that prevents pregnancy when inserted in the uterus.

KAP studies   studies in population control for family planning in which subjects' *k*nowledge of, *a*ttitude toward, and *p*ractice of contraception are assessed by means of questionnaires.

Keep America Beautiful   "a national, nonprofit, nonpartisan public service organization working with citizen groups, governmental agencies, academic institutions and private industry to stimulate individual involvement in environmental improvement through education, communications, demonstrations and research" (KAB, 1976, p. 1).

kilowatt   1000 watts of electricity.

kilowatt-hours (kWh)   1 kilowatt-hour is equivalent to 1000 watts of electrical power consumed for one hour. A measure of electrical-power consumption across time.

law of effect   a response followed by a pleasant state of affairs is likely to be increased; one followed by an unpleasant or annoying state of affairs is likely to be decreased.

leachate   water that becomes acidic or contaminated by seeping through solid waste, such as that in landfills.

levels of use   the overall amount of a resource or commodity typically employed by a person; compare *patterns of use.*

littering   leaving an object in a place where it is unnatural, objectionable, and/or injurious.

marked-item technique   paying persons for returning, reporting, or picking up items that, unbeknown to the person, have been surreptitiously marked. Used to avoid program subversion in reinforcement schemes. (See Hayes, Johnson, & Cone, 1975.)

master metered   the monitoring of several households with a single meter, such as an electricity, water, or gas meter.

multiple-baseline design   an intrasubject research design in which baseline data are collected simultaneously on two or more behaviors or two or more persons at two or more times or at two or more places and the experimental (independent) variable is introduced sequentially to each.

noise   sound that produces undesirable or damaging psychological or physical effects.

operant behavior responding said to be largely under the control of the voluntary portion of the central nervous system; responding that operates on the environment and the future probability of which depends on the environmental changes it produces.

operational definition describing something in terms of the procedures used to measure it. For example, an operational definition of a chocolate cake is the recipe used to make it; environmental psychology is what environmental psychologists do; and so forth.

patterns of use variations in the amount of a commodity or resource used over a period of time; examples are gross variations in electricity and automobile use throughout the day.

payment-for-clean-yards approach arranging rewards to follow the removal of enough litter from an area that it can be regarded as litter free.

peaking a term that refers to the increased consumption ("peaks") of resources, such as electricity or water, during particular time periods.

person schedule arranging a stimulus event to occur on the basis of a number of persons performing a particular behavior. See *fixed-person schedule* and *every-person schedule;* compare with *interval* and *ratio schedules*.

physical technology see *technology, physical*.

pollution moving objects, materials, or substances from places where they are natural, unobjectionable, and/or harmless to places where they are unnatural, objectionable, and/or harmful.

preventive approaches behavioral solutions to environmental problems that emphasize changes in antecedent-stimulus events (for example, signs, mass-education campaigns) to get people to engage in environmentally protective behavior.

prompt a stimulus event occurring before a behavior and designed to facilitate the occurrence of the behavior.

punish to reduce the future probability of a behavior by actively changing stimulus conditions following that behavior.

punisher a stimulus event that, when it follows a behavior, reduces the future probability of that behavior.

punishment the act, process, or procedure of reducing the future probability of a behavior by following it with a punisher.

pyrolysis the degeneration of organic material through the application of heat in an oxygen-free environment. The process can be used to produce gas or oil from solid waste, though not yet at an economical scale.

ratio schedule arranging stimulus events to occur according to the passage of a certain number of responses since the last occurrence; the number of required responses for each occurrence determines the ratio.

reactive an approach to environment/behavior research that examines responses *to* an environmental circumstance rather than effects of the behavior *on* the environment.

recycling the reuse, recovery, reclamation, conversion, or remanufacture of resources in material goods.

reinforce to increase the future probability of a behavior by actively changing stimulus conditions following that behavior.

reinforcement, negative the process of increasing the future probability of a behavior by following it with the termination or removal of a stimulus event.

reinforcement, positive the process of increasing the future probability of a behavior by following it with the presentation of a stimulus event.

reinforcer a stimulus event that increases the future probability of a behavior it follows.

reinforcer, negative a stimulus event, the removal or avoidance of which increases behavior.

reinforcer, positive   a stimulus event, the presentation of which increases behavior preceding it.

remedial approaches   solutions or corrective actions taken for already existing environmental problems; compare with *preventive approaches*.

respondent behavior   responses said to be largely under the control of the autonomic nervous system. Their strength and probability of occurrence depend on antecedent-stimulus events. Withdrawing one's hand from a pinprick or a hot surface would be an example of respondent behavior. Compare with *operant behavior*.

retrofit   to go back and make a change in something after it has been produced—for example, to insulate a house that is 20 years old.

schedule of reinforcement (consequation)   a systematic arrangement of stimulus events following behavior so as to produce certain effects on that behavior; a specification of the relationship between behavior and consequences.

shaping   gradually changing the topography of a response until it closely resembles the target behavior; reinforcing closer and closer approximations of the target behavior.

social trap   a set of circumstances in which a person, an organization, or an entire society gets started behaving in a particular way that is difficult or impossible to change at a later time.

sound amplitude   the strength or intensity of a sound measured by the amount of pressure change (the amplitude of the sound wave). The amplitude of sound is perceived as loudness.

sound frequency   the number of complete cycles per second of a sound wave. The frequency of sound is perceived as pitch. The unit used to express frequency is hertz (Hz).

sound intensity   see *sound amplitude*.

sound wave   an alternation of positive and negative pressures produced by mechanical vibration that travels through a medium (for example, air or water) and is sensed by the ear.

source reduction   reduction of solid waste, before it enters the waste stream, by the manufacture and purchase of less resource-intensive goods or by increased durability or home reuse.

source separation   separating postconsumer waste at the source (that is, by the consumer) so that it can be readily recycled.

stimulus control   in a general sense, affecting behavior by environmental events; usually, affecting behavior by antecedent environmental events; bringing behavior under the control of discriminative stimuli.

technology   the art, craft, science, or skill of getting a particular thing done.

technology, behavioral   the use of behavioral-management procedures to get things done.

technology, physical   the use of physical or mechanical devices to get things done.

time-series design   a research arrangement in which measures are taken at several different times prior to and after the introduction of an experimental manipulation; the effects of the manipulation are gauged by changes in the data after it has been introduced.

token   a representative of another stimulus that exerts some consequential control over behavior. Behavior can be strengthened by following it with a token that can later be exchanged for something else (for example, food, money); behavior can be weakened by removing a token following it.

trash-buying approach   an antilitter strategy in which an area is cleaned of litter by rewarding persons who turn in trash collected from it.

tubal ligation   a sterilization operation on females that prevents the discharge of ova to the uterus.

variable   an event, occurrence, condition, or object that can have different values; experimental variables are those events and so forth that change in an experiment. See *dependent variable, independent variable*.

variable-interval (VI) schedule   an arrangement in which a stimulus event occurs following the first response after the passage of a certain amount of time on the average; a VI–10 schedule would mean that the event occurs after ten units of time (minutes, hours, and so on) on the average but sometimes occurs after the eighth, ninth, 11th, 12th unit, and so on; compare *fixed-interval schedule*.

variable-person (VP) schedule   an arrangement in which a stimulus event occurs every *n*th person on the average, or in a varying manner; a VP–10 schedule would be one in which the event occurs every tenth person on the average but sometimes occurs at the eighth, 12th, ninth, 11th person, and so forth; compare *fixed-person schedule*.

variable-ratio (VR) schedule   an arrangement in which a stimulus event occurs after the passage of a certain number of responses on the average since the last occurrence. The number of responses required for each occurrence varies around some average; a VR–10 schedule indicates that the event occurs after ten responses on the average but may occur after the eighth, 12th, ninth, 11th response, and so forth; compare *fixed-ratio schedule*.

vasectomy   a sterilization operation on males that prevents the discharge of sperm from the testes.

waste reduction   reducing the amount of waste that enters the solid-waste stream by reuse, increased durability, or production of less resource-intensive products.

watt   a measure of electrical power being used at the moment; a unit of power equal to the rate of work represented by a current of 1 ampere under a pressure of 1 volt.

withdrawal design   an intrasubject research arrangement in which baseline data are collected over several periods of time; an experimental variable is introduced while data continue to be collected, and the experimental variable is then removed while data continue to be collected. A minimum of three phases is used in such designs: *A* (baseline), *B* (experimental or intervention), and *A* (return to baseline). Evidence for an effect of the experimental variable comes from discontinuities in the data between the three phases.

REFERENCES

Adelman, I., & Morris, C. T. A quantitative study of social and political determinants of fertility. *Economic Development and Cultural Change,* 1966, *14,* 129–157.

Andrews, R. A., & Hammond, M. R. *Characteristics of household water consumption in three New Hampshire communities.* Durham, N.H.: Water Resources Research Center, University of New Hampshire, 1970.

Ayllon, T., Garber, S., & Pisor, K. The elimination of discipline problems through a combined school–home motivational system. *Behavior Therapy,* 1975, *6,* 616–626.

Azrin, N. H. Some effects of noise upon human behavior. *Journal of the Experimental Analysis of Behavior,* 1958, *1,* 183–200.

Bacon, A., Blount, R., Pickering, D., & Drabman, R. *An evaluation of three litter control procedures—Trash cans, paid workers, and the littery lottery in an institution for retarded citizens.* Unpublished manuscript, University of Mississippi, 1978.

Baer, D. M., Wolf, M. M., & Risley, T. R. Some current dimensions of applied behavior analysis. *Journal of Applied Behavior Analysis,* 1968, *1,* 91–97.

Baker, R. W., & Madell, T. O. A continued investigation of susceptibility to distraction in academically underachieving and achieving male college students. *Journal of Educational Psychology,* 1965, *56,* 254–258.

Balakrishnan, T. R., & Matthai, R. J. India: Evaluation of a publicity program on family planning. *Studies in Family Planning,* 1967, *1*(21), 5–8.

Baltes, M. M., & Hayward, S. C. Application and evaluation of strategies to reduce pollution: Behavioral control of littering in a football stadium. *Journal of Applied Psychology,* 1976, *61,* 501–506.

Barker, R. G. On the nature of the environment. *Journal of Social Issues,* 1963, *19,* 17–38.

Barker, R. G. *Ecological psychology: Concepts and methods for studying the environment of human behavior.* Stanford, Calif.: Stanford University Press, 1968.

Baron, R. A. *The tyranny of noise.* New York: St. Martin's Press, 1970.

Beales, P. H. *Noise, hearing, and deafness.* London: Michael Joseph, 1965.

Becker, L. J. Joint effect of feedback and goal setting on performance: A field study of residential energy conservation. *Journal of Applied Psychology,* 1978, *63,* 428–433.

Becker, L. J., & Seligman, C. Reducing air conditioning waste by signalling it is cool outside. *Personality and Social Psychology Bulletin,* 1978, *4,* 412–415.

Bell, P. A., Fisher, J. D., & Loomis, R. J. *Environmental psychology.* Philadelphia: Saunders, 1978.

Bergamasco, B., Benna, P., Furlan, P., & Gilli, M. Effects of urban traffic noise in relation to basic personality. *Acta Oto-Laryngologica Supplement*, 1976, No. 339, 37–38.

Bergamasco, B., Benna, P., & Gilli, M. Human sleep modifications induced by urban traffic noise. *Acta Oto-Laryngologica Supplement*, 1976, No. 339, 33–36.

Bergland, T. *Noise: The third pollution*. New York: Public Affairs Committee, 1970.

Berrien, F. K. The effects of noise. *Psychological Bulletin*, 1946, *43*, 141–161.

Berry, B. J., & Horton, F. E. *Urban environmental management*. Englewood Cliffs, N.J.: Prentice-Hall, 1974.

Bickman, L. Environmental attitudes and actions. *Journal of Social Psychology*, 1972, *87*, 323–324.

Bidwell, R. Recycling policy: An international perspective. In D. W. Pearce & I. Walter (Eds.), *Resource conservation: Social and economic dimensions of recycling*. New York: New York University Press, 1977.

Bingham, T. H. Allocative and distributive effects of a disposal charge on product packaging. In D. W. Pearce & I. Walter (Eds.), *Resource conservation: Social and economic dimensions of recycling*. New York: New York University Press, 1977.

Bittle, R. G., Thaler, G., & Valesano, R. *The effects of weekly cumulative cost feedback on residential electricity consumption*. Unpublished manuscript, 1978.

Black, T. R. L., & Harvey, P. D. A report on a contraceptive social marketing experiment in rural Kenya. *Studies in Family Planning*, 1976, *7*, 101–108.

Boggs, D. H., & Simon, J. R. Differential effects of noise on tasks of varying complexity. *Journal of Applied Psychology*, 1968, *52*, 148–153.

Bower, B. T. Economic dimensions of waste recycling and reuse: Some definitions, facts, and issues. In D. W. Pearce & I. Walter (Eds.), *Resource conservation: Social and economic dimensions of recycling*. New York: New York University Press, 1977.

Bragdon, C. R. *Noise pollution*. Philadelphia: University of Pennsylvania Press, 1971.

Brewer, D. W., & Briess, F. B. Industrial noise: Laryngeal considerations. *New York State Journal of Medicine*, 1960, *60*, 1737–1740.

Broadbent, D. E. Effects of noises of high and low frequency on behaviour. *Ergonomics*, 1957, *1*, 21.

Bruvold, W. H. Belief and behavior as determinants of environmental attitudes. *Environment and Behavior*, 1973, *5*, 202–218.

Burgess, R. L., & Bushell, D. *Behavioral sociology: The experimental analysis of social process*. New York: Columbia University Press, 1969.

Burgess, R. L., Clark, R. N., & Hendee, J. C. An experimental analysis of anti-litter procedures. *Journal of Applied Behavior Analysis*, 1971, *4*, 71–75.

Burgess, R. L., Clark, R. N., & Hendee, J. C. *Lessons learned from a summer-long attempt at litter control in a large developed campground*. Paper presented at the meeting of the American Psychological Association, New Orleans, September 1974.

Burns, W. *Noise and man*. Philadelphia: Lippincott, 1969.

Burns, W., & Littler, T. S. Chapter 17: Noise. In R. S. F. Schilling (Ed.), *Modern trends in occupational health*. London: Butterworth, 1960.

Byers, E. S., & Cone, J. D. Problem: How to reduce student litter. Solution: Use signs and a reward. *Food Management*, 1976, *11*, 65.

Campbell, D. T. Reforms as experiments. *American Psychologist*, 1969, *24*, 409–429.

Campbell, D. T., & Stanley, J. C. *Experimental and quasi-experimental designs for research*. Chicago: Rand McNally, 1966.

Canter, D., & Thorne, R. Attitudes to housing: A cross-cultural comparison. *Environment and Behavior*, 1972, *4*, 3–32.

Casey, L., & Lloyd, M. Cost and effectiveness of litter removal procedures in an amusement park. *Environment and Behavior*, 1977, *9*, 535–546.

Cernada, G. P. Direct mailings to promote family planning. *Studies in Family Planning,* 1970, *1*(53), 16–19.

Cernada, G., & Chow, L. P. The coupon system in an ongoing family planning program. *American Journal of Public Health,* 1969, *59,* 2199–2208.

Cernada, G. P., & Lu, L. P. The Kaohsiung study. *Studies in Family Planning,* 1972, *3*(8), 198–203.

Chan, M. L., & Heare, S. The cost-effectiveness of pricing schemes and water-saving devices, 1975. (Cited in Milne, 1976.)

Chandler, M., West, J., Anderson, N., Moore, J., & Hayes, S. C. *The effects of simple social and competitive social feedback on energy consumption in college dormitories.* Unpublished manuscript, 1978.

Chang, M. C., Cernada, G. P., & Sun, T. H. A field-worker incentive experimental study. *Studies in Family Planning,* 1972, *3,* 270–272.

Chapman, C., & Risley, T. R. Anti-litter procedures in an urban high-density area. *Journal of Applied Behavior Analysis,* 1974, *7,* 377–383.

Clark, R. N., Burgess, R. L., & Hendee, J. C. The development of anti-litter behavior in a forest campground. *Journal of Applied Behavior Analysis,* 1972, *5,* 1–5.

Clausen, J. A. Family structure, socialization and personality. In L. W. Hoffman & M. L. Hoffman (Eds.), *Review of child development research.* New York: Russell Sage Foundation, 1966.

Claussen, E. *Oregon's bottle bill.* Washington, D.C.: U.S. Environmental Protection Agency, 1973.

Collins, R. H. Gas recovery: National potential. *Proceedings of the Fourth National Congress on Waste Management Technology and Resource and Energy Recovery.* Washington, D.C.: U.S. Environmental Protection Agency, 1976.

Commoner, B. *The closing circle: Nature, man and technology.* New York: Knopf, 1972.

Cone, J. D. Assessing the effectiveness of programmed generalization. *Journal of Applied Behavior Analysis,* 1973, *6,* 713–716.

Cone, J. D., & Hawkins, R. P. (Eds.). *Behavioral assessment: New directions in clinical psychology.* New York: Brunner/Mazel, 1977.

Cone, J. D., & Hayes, S. C. *The submerged discipline of environmentally relevant psychology.* Paper presented at the meeting of the Midwestern Association of Behavior Analysis, Chicago, May 1976.

Cone, J. D., & Hayes, S. C. *Environmental psychology: Conceptual and methodological issues.* Paper presented at the American Psychological Association meeting, Washington, D.C., September 1976.

Cone, J. D., & Hayes, S. C. Applied behavior analysis and the solution of environmental problems. In I. Altman & J. F. Wohlwill (Eds.), *Human behavior and environment: Advances in theory and research* (Vol. 2). New York: Plenum, 1977.

Cone, J. D., & Parham, I. A. *Pollution by young children: Model and environmental effects.* Unpublished manuscript, 1973.

Cone, J. D., Parham, I. A., & Feirstein, D. B. *The effects of environmental cleanliness and model's behavior on littering in young children.* Paper presented at the meeting of the Eastern Psychological Association, Boston, April 1972.

Coplin, W. D. (Ed.). *Simulation in the study of politics.* Chicago: Markham, 1968.

Couch, J. V., Garber, T., & Karpus, L. Response maintenance and paper recycling. *Journal of Environmental Systems,* 1978, *8,* 127–137.

Craik, K. H. Environmental psychology. In *New directions in psychology* (Vol. 4). New York: Holt, Rinehart & Winston, 1970.

Cuca, R., & Pierce, C. S. Experimentation in family planning delivery systems: An overview. *Studies in Family Planning,* 1977, *8,* 302–310.

Cutright, P. Aid to families with dependent children, family allowances and illegitimacy. *Family Planning Perspectives,* 1970, *2*(4), 4–9.

David, H. P. Psychological studies in abortion. In J. T. Fawcett (Ed.), *Psychological perspectives on population*. New York: Basic Books, 1973.

Davidson, A. R., & Jaccard, J. J. Population psychology: A new look at an old problem. *Journal of Personality and Social Psychology*, 1975, *31*, 1073–1082.

Davis, K. The theory of change and response in modern demographic history. *Population Index*, 1963, *29*, 345–366.

Davis, K., & Blake, J. Social structure and fertility: An analytic framework. *Economic Development and Cultural Change*, 1956, *4*, 211–235.

Dehn, W. T. *Solving the abandoned car problem in small communities*. Washington, D.C.: U.S. Environmental Protection Agency, 1974.

Deitz, S. The current status of applied behavior analysis: Science versus technology. *American Psychologist*, 1978, *33*, 805–814.

Delprato, D. J. Prompting electrical energy conservation in commercial users. *Environment and Behavior*, 1977, *9*, 433–440.

Deslauriers, B. C., & Everett, P. B. Effects of intermittent and continuous token reinforcement on bus ridership. *Journal of Applied Psychology*, 1977, *62*, 369–375.

Diamonds are forever. *Time*, May 17, 1976, pp. 85–86.

Douvan, E., & Adelson, J. *The adolescent experience*. New York: Wiley, 1966.

Dow, T. E. Family size and family planning in Nairobi. *Demography*, 1967, *4*, 780–797.

Drabman, R., Spitalnik, R., & Spitalnik, K. Sociometric and disruptive behavior as a function of four types of token reinforcement programs. *Journal of Applied Behavior Analysis*, 1974, *7*, 93–101.

Dubey, D. C., & Choldin, H. M. Communication and diffusion of the IUCD: A case study in urban India. *Demography*, 1967, *4*, 601–614.

Duncan, R. C. An economic garbage collection and recycling service. *Compost Science: Journal of Waste Recycling*, 1976, *17*(1), 12–25.

Duncan, R. C. Private communication, July 28, 1978.

Eastman, W. F. First intercourse. *Sexual Behavior*, 1972, *2*, 22–27.

Edwards, A. L. *Statistical methods* (2nd ed.). New York: Holt, Rinehart & Winston, 1967.

Ehrlich, P. R. *The population bomb*. New York: Ballantine Books, 1968.

Ellery, M. D., Blampied, N. M., & Black, W. A. M. Reduction of disruptive behaviour in the classroom: Group and individual reinforcement contingencies compared. *New Zealand Journal of Educational Studies*, 1975, *10*, 59–65.

Enke, S. A rejoinder to comments on the superior effectiveness of vasectomy-bonus schemes. *Economic Development and Cultural Change*, 1961, *9*, 645–647.

Esler, A. Attitude change in an industrial hearing conservation program: Comparative effects of directives, educational presentations, and individual explanations as persuasive communications. *Occupational Health Nursing*, *26*, December 1978, 15–20.

Everett, P. B. *Use of the reinforcement procedure to increase bus ridership*. Paper presented at the meeting of the American Psychological Association, Montreal, August 1973.

Everett, P. B. *A behavior science approach to transportation systems management*. Unpublished manuscript, 1977.

Everett, P. B., Deslauriers, B. C., Newsom, T., & Anderson, V. B. The differential effect of two free ride dissemination procedures on bus ridership. *Transportation Research*, 1978, *12*, 1–6.

Everett, P. B., Hayward, S. C., & Meyers, A. W. The effects of a token reinforcement procedure on bus ridership. *Journal of Applied Behavior Analysis*, 1974, *7*, 1–9.

Everett, P. B., Studer, R. G., & Douglas, T. J. Gaming simulation to pretest operant-based community interventions: An urban transportation example. *American Journal of Community Psychology*, 1978, *6*, 327–338.

Fairweather, G. *Experimental social reform*. Morristown, N.J.: General Learning Press, 1972.

Farris, M. T., & Sampson, R. J. *Public utilities: Regulation, management, and ownership*. Boston: Houghton-Mifflin, 1973.

Fawcett, J. T. *Psychology and population: Behavioral research issues in fertility and family planning*. New York: The Population Council, 1970.

Fawcett, J. T., & Bornstein, M. H. Modernization, individual modernity, and fertility. In J. T. Fawcett (Ed.), *Psychological perspectives on population*. New York: Basic Books, 1973.

Fawcett, J. T., & Somboonsuk, A. Thailand: Using family planning acceptors to recruit new cases. *Studies in Family Planning*, 1969, *1*(39), 1–4.

Federal Energy Administration. *Project Independence report*. Washington, D.C.: U.S. Government Printing Office, November 1974.

Federal Power Commission. *Promotional activities of public utilities*. Washington, D.C.: U.S. Government Printing Office, 1970.

Ferster, C. B., & Skinner, B. F. *Schedules of reinforcement*. New York: Appleton-Century-Crofts, 1957.

Finnie, W. C. Field experiments in litter control. *Environment and Behavior*, 1973, *5*, 123–144.

Finnigan, O. D., & Sun, T. H. Planning, starting, and operating an educational incentives program. *Studies in Family Planning*, 1972, *3*, 1–7.

Fisher, J. C. *Energy crisis in perspective*. New York: Wiley, 1974.

Fisher, W. A., Fisher, J. D., & Byrne, D. Consumer reactions to contraceptive purchasing. *Personality and Social Psychology Bulletin*, 1977, *3*, 293–297.

Floyd, M. K. *A bibliography of noise*. Troy, N.Y.: Whitston, 1973 and following.

Fook-Kee, W., & Swee-Hock, S. Knowledge, attitudes, and practice of family planning in Singapore. *Studies in Family Planning*, 1975, *6*, 109–112.

Fourth Report to Congress: Resource recovery and waste reduction. Washington, D.C.: U.S. Environmental Protection Agency, 1977.

Foxx, R. M., & Hake, D. F. Gasoline conservation: A procedure for measuring and reducing the driving of college students. *Journal of Applied Behavior Analysis*, 1977, *10*, 61–74.

Franklin, W. E., Hunt, R. G., & Sharp, S. T. *Paper recycling: The art of the possible, 1970–1985*. Kansas City, Mo.: Midwest Research Institute, 1973.

Freedman, R., & Takeshita, J. Y. *Family planning in Taiwan*. Princeton, N.J.: Princeton University Press, 1969.

Gauging prices—and spending: Consumer Price Index. *Time*, March 13, 1978, p. 54.

Geller, E. S. Prompting anti-litter behaviors. *Proceedings of the 81st Annual Convention of the American Psychological Association*, 1973, *8*, 901–902.

Geller, E. S. Increasing desired waste disposals with instructions. *Man–Environment Systems*, 1975, *5*, 125–128.

Geller, E. S. Saving environmental resources through waste reduction and recycling: How the behavioral community psychologist can help. In G. L. Martin & J. G. Osborne (Eds.), *Helping in the community: Behavioral applications*. New York: Plenum, in press.

Geller, E. S. A behavioral analysis of a nationwide litter-control and resource-recovery program: The Clean Community System of Keep America Beautiful, Inc. In D. Glenwick & L. Jason (Eds.), *Behavioral community psychology: Progress and prospects*. Kalamazoo, Mich.: Behaviordelia, in press.

Geller, E. S., Bowen, S. P., & Chiang, R. N. S. *A community-based approach to promoting energy conservation*. Symposium presentation at the meeting of the American Psychological Association, Toronto, September 1978.

Geller, E. S., Chaffee, J. F., & Ingram, R. E. Promoting paper recycling on a university campus. *Journal of Environmental Systems*, 1975, *5*, 39–57.

Geller, E. S., Farris, J. C., & Post, D. S. Promoting a consumer behavior for pollution control. *Journal of Applied Behavior Analysis,* 1973, *6,* 367–376.

Geller, E. S., Witmer, J. F., & Orebaugh, A. L. Instructions as determinants of paper disposal behaviors. *Environment and Behavior,* 1976, *8,* 417–438.

Geller, E. S., Witmer, J. F., & Tuso, M. A. Environmental interventions for litter control. *Journal of Applied Psychology,* 1977, *62,* 344–351.

Geller, E. S., Wylie, R. G., & Farris, J. C. An attempt at applying prompting and reinforcement toward pollution control. *Proceedings of the 79th Annual Convention of the American Psychological Association,* 1971, *6,* 701–702.

George, E. I. Research on measurement of family size norms. In J. T. Fawcett (Ed.), *Psychological perspectives on population.* New York: Basic Books, 1973.

Glass, D. C., & Singer, J. E. *Urban stress: Experiments on noise and social stressors.* New York: Academic Press, 1972.

Government Accounting Office. *Conversion of urban waste to energy.* Washington, D.C.: U.S. Government Printing Office, 1979.

Grandy, G. S., Madsen, C. H., & Mersseman, L. M. D. The effects of individual and interdependent contingencies on inappropriate classroom behavior. *Psychology in the Schools,* 1973, *10,* 488–493.

Gray, J. E. Accelerating supply and use of electricity. *Public Utilities Fortnightly,* 1975, *95*(17), 12–24.

Greene, A. K. Bring 'em back, repack, and save. *Proceedings, 1975 Conference on Waste Reduction.* Washington, D.C.: U.S. Environmental Protection Agency, 1977.

Grobe, R. P., Pettibone, T. J., & Martin, D. W. Effects of lecturer pace on noise level in a university classroom. *Journal of Educational Research,* 1973, *67,* 73–75.

Grzona, A. G. An occupational health nurses' program. *Nursing Outlook,* 1961, *9,* 283–284.

Gudger, C. M., & Bailes, J. C. *The economic impact of Oregon's "bottle bill."* Corvallis, Ore.: Oregon State University Press, 1973.

Hake, D. F., & Foxx, R. M. Promoting gasoline conservation: The effects of reinforcement schedules, a leader and self-recording. *Behavior Modification,* 1978, *2,* 339–369.

Hall, R. V., Axelrod, S., Tyler, L., Grief, E., Jones, F. C., & Robertson, R. Modification of behavior problems in the home with a parent as observer and experimenter. *Journal of Applied Behavior Analysis,* 1972, *5,* 53–64.

Hamad, C. D., Bettinger, R., Cooper, D., & Semb, G. *Using behavioral procedures to establish an elementary school paper recycling program.* Unpublished manuscript, 1978.

Hamad, C. D., Cooper, D., & Semb, G. Resource recovery: Use of a group contingency to increase paper recycling in an elementary school. *Journal of Applied Psychology,* 1977, *62,* 768–772.

Hanke, S. H., & Boland, J. J. Water requirements or water demands? *Journal of the American Water Works Association,* 1971, *63*(11), 677–681.

Hansen, P. *Residential paper recovery: A municipal implementation guide.* Washington, D.C.: U.S. Environmental Protection Agency, 1975.

Hardin, G. The tragedy of the commons. *Science,* 1968, *162,* 1243–1248.

Harmon, B. The role of the personnel department in a hearing conservation program. *Personnel Journal,* 1974, *53,* 531–535.

Harris, V. W., & Sherman, J. A. Use and analysis of the "good behavior game" to reduce disruptive classroom behavior. *Journal of Applied Behavior Analysis,* 1973, *6,* 405–417.

Hayes, S. C. The effects of monthly feedback, rebate billing, and consumer directed feedback on the residential consumption of electricity (Doctoral dissertation, West Virginia University, 1977). *Dissertation Abstracts International,* 1977, *38B,* 2341. (University Microfilms No. 77–22,738)

Hayes, S. C., & Cone, J. D. Decelerating environmentally destructive lawnwalking. *Environment and Behavior,* 1977, *9,* 511–534. (a)

Hayes, S. C., & Cone, J. D. Reducing residential electrical energy use: Payments, information, and feedback. *Journal of Applied Behavior Analysis,* 1977, *10,* 425–435. (b)

Hayes, S. C., & Cone, J. D. The reduction of residential energy consumption through simple monthly feedback. *Journal of Applied Behavior Analysis,* in press.

Hayes, S. C., Johnson, V. S., & Cone, J. D. The marked item technique: A practical procedure for litter control. *Journal of Applied Behavior Analysis,* 1975, *8,* 381–386.

Hayes, S. C., Rincover, A., & Solnick, J. The technical drift of applied behavior analysis. *Journal of Applied Behavior Analysis,* in press.

Hays, W. L. *Statistics for psychologists.* New York: Holt, Rinehart & Winston, 1963.

Hayward, S. C., & Everett, P. B. *A failure of response cost feedback to modify car driving behavior.* Paper presented at the meeting of the Midwestern Association of Behavior Analysis, Chicago, May 1976.

Heberlein, T. A. Moral norms, threatened sanctions, and littering behavior (Doctoral dissertation, University of Wisconsin, 1971.) *Dissertation Abstracts International,* 1971, *32A,* 5906. (University Microfilms No. 72–02639)

Heberlein, T. A. Conservation information: The energy crisis and electricity consumption in an apartment complex. *Energy Systems and Policy,* 1975, *1,* 105–117.

Hersen, M., & Barlow, D. H. *Single case experimental designs.* New York: Pergamon Press, 1976.

Hoffman, L. W., & Hoffman, M. L. The value of children to parents. In J. T. Fawcett (Ed.), *Psychological perspectives on population.* New York: Basic Books, 1973.

Holland, H. H. Attenuation provided by fingers, palms, tragi, and VSIR ear plugs. *Journal of the Acoustical Society of America,* 1967, *41,* 1545.

Holland, J. G., & Skinner, B. F. *The analysis of behavior: A program for self-instruction.* New York: McGraw-Hill, 1961.

Horst, P. *Factor analysis of data matrices.* New York: Holt, Rinehart & Winston, 1965.

Hubbert, M. I. *U.S. energy resources.* Washington, D.C.: U.S. Government Printing Office, 1974.

Humphrey, C. R., Bord, R. J., Hammond, M. M., & Mann, S. H. Attitudes and conditions for cooperation in a paper recycling program. *Environment and Behavior,* 1977, *9,* 107–124.

Hunt, R. G., & Franklin, W. E. *Resource and environmental profile analysis of nine beverage container alternatives* (Vol. 1). Washington, D.C.: U.S. Environmental Protection Agency, 1974.

Hunt, R. G., Welch, R. O., Cross, J. A., & Woodall, A. E. *Resource and environmental profile analysis of nine beverage container alternatives* (Vol. 2). Washington, D.C.: U.S. Environmental Protection Agency, 1974.

Ingram, R. E., & Geller, E. S. A community-integrated, behavior modification approach to facilitating paper recycling. *JSAS Catalog of Selected Documents in Psychology,* 1975, *5,* 327. (Ms. No. 1097)

Inverted electric rates. *Public Service Magazine,* 1974, *69*(3), 16–19.

Jaffe, F. S. Estimating the need for subsidized family planning services. *Family Planning Perspectives,* 1971, *3,* 51–55.

Jaggi, B., & Westacott, G. Third world managers' attitudes toward pollution. Working paper 74-05. Binghamton, N.Y.: School of Management, State University of New York, Binghamton.

Jurgen, R. K. What to tell your neighbors. *IEEE Spectrum,* 1974 (June), 61–65.

Kagan, J. Waste: The problem that won't go away. *McCalls,* July 1977, p. 66.

Karen, R. L. *An introduction to behavior theory and its applications.* New York: Harper & Row, 1974.

Kazdin, A. E. Methodological and assessment considerations in evaluating reinforcement programs in applied settings. *Journal of Applied Behavior Analysis,* 1973, *6,* 517–531.

Kazdin, A. E. *Behavior modification in applied settings* (Rev. ed.). Homewood, Ill.: Dorsey Press, 1980.

Keep America Beautiful, Inc. *1976 Annual Review.* New York: Keep America Beautiful, 1976.

Keller, A. B., Sims, J. H., Henry, W. E., & Crawford, T. J. Psychological sources of "resistance" to family planning. *Merrill-Palmer Quarterly,* 1970, *16,* 286–302.

Kerbec, M. J. *Noise and hearing.* Arlington, Va.: Output Systems, 1972.

King, H. B. A more positive strategy. *Proceedings, 1975 Conference on Waste Reduction.* Washington, D.C.: U.S. Environmental Protection Agency, 1977.

Klinger, A. Abortion programs. In B. Berelson (Ed.), *Family planning and population programs.* Chicago: University of Chicago Press, 1966.

Klinger, A. Demographic aspects of abortion. In *International Population Conference* (Vol. 2). Liege: International Union for the Scientific Study of Population, 1971.

Knudson, V. O. Noise: The bane of hearing. *Noise Control,* 1955, *1,* 11.

Knutson, A. I. A new human life and abortion: Beliefs, ideal values, and value judgements. In J. T. Fawcett (Ed.), *Psychological perspectives on population.* New York: Basic Books, 1973.

Koffka, J. *Principles of Gestalt psychology.* New York: Harcourt Brace Jovanovich, 1935.

Kohlenberg, R. J., Barach, R., Martin, C., & Anschell, S. *Experimental analysis of the effects of price and feedback on residential electricity consumption.* Unpublished manuscript, 1976.

Kohlenberg, R., & Phillips, T. Reinforcement and rate of litter depositing. *Journal of Applied Behavior Analysis,* 1973, *6,* 391–396.

Kohlenberg, R. J., Phillips, T., & Proctor, W. A behavioral analysis of peaking in residential electricity energy consumption. *Journal of Applied Behavior Analysis,* 1976, *9,* 13–18.

Komarovsky, M. Functional analysis of sex roles. *American Sociological Review,* 1950, *15,* 508–516.

Kratochwill, T. R. Foundations of time-series research. In T. R. Kratochwill (Ed.), *Single subject research: Strategies for evaluating change.* New York: Academic Press, 1978.

Krishnakumar, S. Kerala's pioneering experiment in massive vasectomy camps. *Studies in Family Planning,* 1972, *3,* 177–185.

Krishnakumar, S. Ernakulam's third vasectomy campaign using the camp approach. *Studies in Family Planning,* 1974, *5,* 58–61.

Kryter, K. D. *The effects of noise on man.* New York: Academic Press, 1970.

Kulkarni, V. R. Wise men of Kuwar Khede. *Family Planning News,* 1969, *10,* 6.

Lahart, D. E., & Bailey, J. S. *The analysis and reduction of children's littering on a nature trail.* Unpublished manuscript, 1974.

Laponce, J. A., & Smoker, P. *Experimentation and simulation in political science.* Toronto: University of Toronto Press, 1972.

Large, D. B. (Ed.). *Hidden waste: Potentials for energy conservation.* Washington, D.C.: The Conservation Foundation, 1973.

Leitenberg, H. The use of single-case methodology in psychotherapy research. *Journal of Abnormal Psychology,* 1973, *82,* 87–101.

Levenson, H. Perception of environmental modifiability and involvement in antipollution activities. *The Journal of Psychology,* 1973, *84,* 237–239.

Levy, S. J. *Markets and technology for recovering energy from solid waste.* Washington, D.C.: U.S. Environmental Protection Agency, 1974.

Levy, S. J. *San Diego County demonstrates pyrolysis of solid waste.* Washington, D.C.: U.S. Environmental Protection Agency, 1975.

Lingle, S. A., & Holloway, J. R. Use of refuse derived solid fuel in electric utility boilers. *Proceedings of the Fifth National Congress on Waste Management Technology and Resource and Energy Recovery.* Washington, D.C.: U.S. Environmental Protection Agency, 1977.

Lipe, D. Incentives, fertility control, and research. *American Psychologist,* 1971, *26,* 617–625.

Lipscomb, D. M. *Noise: The unwanted sounds.* Chicago: Nelson-Hall, 1974.

Litow, L., & Pumroy, D. K. A brief review of classroom group-oriented contingencies. *Journal of Applied Behavior Analysis,* 1975, *8,* 341–347.

Lopata, M. Z. *Occupation: Housewife.* New York: Oxford University Press, 1971.

Loube, N. *Beverage containers: The Vermont experience.* Washington, D.C.: U.S. Environmental Protection Agency, 1976.

Lowe, R. A. *Energy conservation through improved solid waste management.* Washington, D.C.: U.S. Environmental Protection Agency, 1974.

Luyben, P. D. *Effects of informational and high and low salience prompts on energy conservation in college classrooms.* Unpublished manuscript, 1978.

Luyben, P. D., & Bailey, J. S. Newspaper recycling: The effects of rewards and proximity of containers. *Environment and Behavior,* 1979, *11,* 539–557.

Luyben, P. D., & Luyben, J. E. *Effects of a "presidential prompt" on energy conservation in college classrooms.* Unpublished manuscript, 1977.

Maas, R. B. Hearing protection in industry. *Nursing Outlook,* 1961, *9,* 281–283.

MacDonald, A. P. Internal–external locus of control and the practice of birth control. *Psychological Reports,* 1970, *21,* 206.

Madsen, C. H., Becker, W. C., & Thomas, D. R. Rules, praise and ignoring: Elements of elementary classroom control. *Journal of Applied Behavior Analysis,* 1968, *1,* 139–150.

Maine votes against public power. *Public Service Magazine,* 1973, *68,* No. 9–10, 36.

Maloney, M. P., & Ward, M. P. Ecology: Let's hear from the people. *American Psychologist,* 1973, *28,* 583–586.

McAllister, L. W., Stachowiak, J. G., Baer, D. M., & Conderman, L. The application of operant conditioning techniques in a secondary school classroom. *Journal of Applied Behavior Analysis,* 1969, *2,* 277–285.

McClelland, L., & Belsten, L. *Promoting energy conservation in university dormitories by physical, policy, and resident behavior changes.* Unpublished manuscript, 1978.

McClelland, L., & Cook, S. W. *Encouraging energy conservation as a social psychological problem: Consumption by tenants with "utilities included."* Paper presented at the meeting of the American Psychological Association, San Francisco, September 1977.

McClelland, L., & Cook, S. W. Promoting energy conservation in master-metered apartments through group financial incentives. *Journal of Applied Social Psychology,* in press.

McConahay, J. B. Experimental research. In J. N. Knutson (Ed.), *Handbook of political psychology.* San Francisco: Jossey-Bass, 1973.

McEwen, L. B. *Waste reduction and resource recovery activities: A nationwide survey.* Washington, D.C.: U.S. Environmental Protection Agency, 1977.

McGlotten, R. A labor viewpoint. *Proceedings, 1975 Conference on Waste Reduction.* Washington, D.C.: U.S. Environmental Protection Agency, 1977.

McLaughlin, T., & Malaby, J. Reducing and measuring inappropriate verbalizations in a token classroom. *Journal of Applied Behavior Analysis,* 1972, *5,* 329–333.

McSweeny, A. J. Effects of response cost on a million persons: Charging for directory assistance in Cincinnati. *Journal of Applied Behavior Analysis,* 1978, *11,* 47–51.

Meadows, D. H., Meadows, D. L., Randers, J., & Behrens, W. W. *The limits to growth.* New York: Universe Books, 1972.

Medland, M. B., & Stachnik, T. J. Good behavior game: A replication and systematic analysis. *Journal of Applied Behavior Analysis,* 1972, *5,* 45–51.

Melnick, W. Ear protectors. *Occupational Health Nursing,* 1969, *17,* 28–31.

Meyers, A. W., Artz, L. M., & Craighead, W. E. The effects of instructions, incentive, and feedback on a community problem: Dormitory noise. *Journal of Applied Behavior Analysis,* 1976, *9,* 445–457.

Millenson, J. R. *Principles of behavioral analysis.* New York: Macmillan, 1967.

Milne, M. *Residential water conservation* (Report No. 35). Davis, Calif.: California Water Resources Center, 1976.

Mischel, W. Theory and research on the antecedents of self-imposed delay of reward. In B. A. Maher (Ed.), *Progress in experimental personality research* (Vol. 3). New York: Academic Press, 1966.

Moore, B., & Holtzman, W. *Tomorrow's parents.* Austin, Texas: Hogg Foundation, 1965.

Mullins, C., & Perkin, G. The use of programmed instruction in family planning training programs: A preliminary report. *Studies in Family Planning,* 1969, *1*(37), 1–13.

Murray, C. R., & Reeves, E. B. *Estimated use of water in the United States in 1975* (Circular No. 765). Arlington, Va.: U.S. Geological Survey, 1977.

Newsom, T. J., & Makranczy, V. J. Reducing electricity consumption of residents living in mass-metered dormitory complexes. *Journal of Environmental Systems,* 1978, *1,* 215–236.

Nietzel, M. T., Winett, R. A., MacDonald, M. L., & Davidson, W. S. *Behavioral approaches to community psychology.* New York: Pergamon Press, 1977.

Nortman, D. Population and family planning programs. *Reports on Population/Family Planning,* 1971, *2,* 1–48.

Nunnally, J. C. *Psychometric theory.* New York: McGraw-Hill, 1967.

Osborne, J. G., & Powers, R. B. The current state of the art of litter control. In G. L. Martin & J. G. Osborne (Eds.), *Helping in the community: Behavioral applications.* New York: Plenum, in press.

Pacey, J. Methane gas in landfills: Liability or asset? *Proceedings of the Fourth National Congress on Waste Management and Technology and Resource and Energy Recovery.* Washington, D.C.: U.S. Environmental Protection Agency, 1976.

Page, T. Intertemporal and international aspects of virgin materials taxes. In D. W. Pearce & I. Walter (Eds.), *Resource conservation: Social and economic dimensions of recycling.* New York: New York University Press, 1977.

Pakter, J., & Nelson, F. Abortion in New York City: The first nine months. *Family Planning Perspectives,* 1971, *3*(3), 5–12.

Palmer, M. H., Lloyd, M. E., & Lloyd, K. E. An experimental analysis of electricity conservation procedures. *Journal of Applied Behavior Analysis,* 1978, *10,* 665–672.

Palmer, R. *The water closet.* Newton Abbott, Devon, England: David and Charles, 1973.

Passenger Transport, 1975, *33*(24), 2.

Paul, G. Behavior modification research: Design and tactics. In C. M. Franks (Ed.), *Behavior therapy: Appraisal and status.* New York: McGraw-Hill, 1969.

Pavlov, I. P. *Conditioned reflexes*. London: Oxford University Press, 1927.

Pearce, D. W., & Walter, I. (Eds.). *Resource conservation: Social and economic dimensions of recycling*. New York: New York University Press, 1977.

Perkin, G. W. Nonmonetary commodity incentives in family planning programs: A preliminary trial. *Studies in Family Planning*, 1970, *1*(57), 12–15.

Peterson, C. *Price comparison survey of beer and soft drinks in refillable and nonrefillable containers*. Washington, D.C.: U.S. Environmental Protection Agency, 1976.

Phillips, J. F., Silayan-Go, A., & Pal-Montano, A. An experiment with payment, quota, and clinic affiliation schemes for lay motivators in the Philippines. *Studies in Family Planning*, 1975, *6*, 326–334.

Phillips, T. W. *A review of experimental field studies involving the promotion of ecologically valid human behavior*. Unpublished manuscript, 1977.

Platt, J. Social traps. *American Psychologist*, 1973, *28*, 641–651.

Poffenberger, T. Motivational aspects of resistance to family planning in an Indian village. *Demography*, 1968, *5*, 757–766.

Pohlman, E. *Psychology of birth planning*. Cambridge, Mass.: Schenkman, 1969.

Pohlman, E. *How to kill population*. Philadelphia: Westminster Press, 1971.

Porapakkham, Y., Donaldson, P. J., & Svetsreni, T. Thailand's field-worker evaluation project. *Studies in Family Planning*, 1975, *6*, 201–204.

Powers, R. B., Osborne, J. G., & Anderson, E. G. Positive reinforcement of litter removal in the natural environment. *Journal of Applied Behavior Analysis*, 1973, *6*, 579–586.

Presser, H. B. Voluntary sterilization: A world view. *Reports on Population/Family Planning*, 1970, No. 5, 20–21.

Quigley, C. Our ecological crisis. *Current History*, 1970, *59*, 1–12.

Rachlin, H. and Green, L. Commitment, choice, and self-control. *Journal of the Experimental Analysis of Behavior*, 1972, *17*, 15–22.

Rainwater, L. *And the poor get children*. Chicago: Quadrangle Books, 1960.

Rainwater, L. *Family design: Marital sexuality, family size, and contraception*. Chicago: Aldine, 1965.

Reid, D. H., Luyben, P. L., Rawers, R. J., & Bailey, J. S. The effects of prompting and proximity of containers on newspaper recycling behavior. *Environment and Behavior*, 1976, *8*, 471–482.

Repetto, R. India: A case study of the Madras vasectomy program. *Studies in Family Planning*, 1968, *1*(31), 8–16.

Research Triangle Institute. *A national study of roadside litter* (prepared for Keep America Beautiful, Inc.). Research Triangle Park, N.C.: Research Triangle Institute, 1969.

Residential paper recovery: A community action program. Washington, D.C.: U.S. Environmental Protection Agency, 1977.

Resource Planning Associates. *Source separation: The community awareness program in Somerville and Marblehead, Massachusetts*. Washington, D.C.: U.S. Environmental Protection Agency, 1976.

Reynolds, G. S. *A primer of operant conditioning* (2nd ed.). Glenview, Ill.: Scott Foresman, 1975.

Rice, C. G., & Coles, R. Design factors and use of ear protection. *British Journal of Industrial Medicine*, 1966, *23*, 194–198.

Ridker, R. G. Synopsis of a proposal for a family planning bond. *Studies in Family Planning*, 1969, *1*(43), 11–16.

Ridker, R. Savings accounts for family planning: An illustration from the tea estates of India. *Studies in Family Planning*, 1971, *2*, 150–152.

Ridker, R. G., & Muscat, R. J. Incentives for family welfare and fertility reduction: An illustration for Malaysia. *Studies in Family Planning*, 1973, *4*, 1–11.

Robie, R. The tread of mighty armies. *Proceedings of the Second Annual Watercare Conference: Water Reclamation and Domestic Water Conservation.* San Jose, Calif.: California Association of Reclamation Entities of Water, 1975.

Rodda, M. *Noise in society.* London: Oliver and Boyd, 1967.

Rogers, E. M. Incentives in the diffusion of family planning innovations. *Studies in Family Planning,* 1971, *2,* 241–248.

Rogers-Warren, A., & Warren, S. F. (Eds.). *Ecological perspectives in behavior analysis.* Baltimore, Md.: University Park Press, 1977.

Rose, H. S., & Hinds, D. H. South Dixie Highway contraflow bus and carpool lane demonstration project. *Transportation Research Record,* 1976, No. 606, 18–22.

Ross, J. A., Germain, A., Forrest, J. E., & Van Ginneken, J. Findings from family planning research. *Reports on Population/Family Planning,* 1972, No. 12, 1–47.

Runnion, A., Watson, J. D., & McWhorter, J. Energy savings in interstate transportation through feedback and reinforcement. *Journal of Organizational Behavior Management,* 1978, *1,* 180–191.

Ruvin, H. The referendum in Dade County. *Proceedings, 1975 Conference on Waste Reduction.* Washington, D.C.: U.S. Environmental Protection Agency, 1977.

Sadd, W. Innovation versus regulation: Industry's view. *Proceedings, 1975 Conference on Waste Reduction.* Washington, D.C.: U.S. Environmental Protection Agency, 1977.

Schmidt, G. W., & Ulrich, R. E. Effects of group contingent events upon classroom noise. *Journal of Applied Behavior Analysis,* 1969, *2,* 171–179.

Schramm, W. Communication in family planning. *Reports on Population/Family Planning,* 1971, No. 7, 1–43.

Scott, C. E., Thomas, W. G., & Royster, L. H. Determination of in-use attenuation values for selected ear plugs. *Journal of the Acoustical Society of America,* 1973, *54,* 328.

Seaver, W. B., & Patterson, A. H. Decreasing fuel-oil consumption through feedback and social commendation. *Journal of Applied Behavior Analysis,* 1976, *9,* 147–152.

Seligman, C., & Darley, J. M. Feedback as a means of decreasing residential energy consumption. *Journal of Applied Psychology,* 1977, *62,* 363–368.

Seligman, C., Kriss, M., Darley, J. M., Fazio, R. H., Becker, L. J., & Pryor, J. B. Predicting residential energy consumption from homeowners' attitudes. Unpublished manuscript, Center for Environmental Study, Princeton University, 1977.

Shaw, E. A. G. Noise pollution: What can be done? *Physics Today,* 1975, *28,* 46–58.

Shearer, W. M. Acoustic threshold shift from power lawnmower noise. *Sound and Vibration,* 1968, *2,* 10.

Shuster, K. A. *Leachate damage assessment: An approach.* Washington, D.C.: U.S. Environmental Protection Agency, 1976.

Sidman, M. *Tactics of scientific research: Evaluating experimental data in psychology.* New York: Basic Books, 1960.

Silvermann, A., & Silvermann, A. *The case against having children.* New York: McKay, 1971.

Sirageldin, I., & Hopkins, S. Family planning programs: An economic approach. *Studies in Family Planning,* 1972, *3,* 17–24.

Skinner, B. F. *The behavior of organisms: An experimental analysis.* New York: Appleton-Century-Crofts, 1938.

Skinner, B. F. *Science and human behavior.* New York: Macmillan, 1953.

Skinner, B. F. *Verbal behavior.* New York: Appleton-Century-Crofts, 1957.

Skinner, B. F. Operant behavior. In W. H. Honig (Ed.), *Operant behavior: Areas of research and application.* New York: Appleton-Century-Crofts, 1966.

Skinner, B. F. *Walden Two revisited*. Paper presented at the meeting of the American Psychological Association, Chicago, September 1975.

Skinner, J. H. Effects of reuse and recycling of beverage containers. *Proceedings, 1975 Conference on Waste Reduction*. Washington, D.C.: U.S. Environmental Protection Agency, 1977. (a)

Skinner, J. H. Source reduction and separation: Impact on recovery facilities. *Proceedings of the Fifth National Congress on Waste Management Technology and Resource and Energy Recovery*. Washington, D.C.: U.S. Environmental Protection Agency, 1977. (b)

Slavin, R. E., & Wodarski, J. S. *Using group contingencies to reduce natural gas consumption in master-metered apartments*. Unpublished manuscript, 1977. Report No. 232, Center for Social Organization of Schools, The Johns Hopkins University, Baltimore, Md.

Slavin, R. E., Wodarski, J. S., & Blackburn, B. L. A group contingency for electricity conservation in master-metered apartments. *Journal of Applied Behavior Analysis*, in press.

Small, W. E. *Third pollution: The national problem of solid waste disposal*. New York: Praeger, 1971.

Smith, F. L. Pollution charges: The practical issues. In D. W. Pearce & I. Walter (Eds.), *Resource conservation: Social and economic dimensions of recycling*. New York: New York University Press, 1977.

Smith, M. B. A social–psychological view of fertility. In J. T. Fawcett (Ed.), *Psychological perspectives on population*. New York: Basic Books, 1973.

Snyder, R. C. Experimental techniques and political analysis: Some reflections in the context of concern over behavioral approaches. In J. C. Charlesworth (Ed.), *The limits of behavioralism in political science*. Philadelphia: American Academy of Political and Social Science, 1962.

Soucie, G. A. Reclamation or wrecklamation? In W. C. Kennard (Ed.), *Lectures on water conservation*. Storrs, Conn.: Institute of Water Resources, 1968.

Srinivasan, K., & Kachirayan, M. Vasectomy follow-up study: Findings and implications. *Gandhigram Institute of Rural Health and Family Planning Bulletin*, 1968, *3*, 13–32.

Stanford Research Institute. *Patterns of energy consumption in the United States*. Washington, D.C.: Office of Science and Technology, 1972.

Stokes, T. F., & Baer, D. M. An implicit technology of generalization. *Journal of Applied Behavior Analysis*, 1977, *10*, 349–367.

Stokols, D. Environmental psychology. In M. R. Rozenzweig & L. W. Porter (Eds.), *Annual Review of Psychology*, 1978, *29*, 253–295.

Stokols, D. In defense of the crowding construct. In A. Baum, J. E. Singer, & S. Valins (Eds), *Advances in environmental psychology*. Hillsdale, N.J.: Erlbaum, 1978.

Stokols, D., Rall, M., Pinner, B., & Schopler, J. Physical, social, and personal determinants of the perception of crowding. *Environment and Behavior*, 1973, *5*, 87–115.

Stone, R. B., Buchanan, C. C., & Steimle, F. W. *Scrap tires as artificial reefs*. Washington, D.C.: U.S. Environmental Protection Agency, 1974.

Strang, H. R., & George, J. R. Clowning around to stop clowning around: A brief report on an automated approach to monitor, record, and control classroom noise. *Journal of Applied Behavior Analysis*, 1975, *8*, 471–474.

Stuart, R. B., & Davis, B. *Slim chance in a fat world: Behavioral control of obesity*. Champaign, Ill.: Research Press, 1975.

Stuntz, M. S., & Hirst, E. *Energy conservation potential of urban mass transit: Conservation Paper No. 34*. Washington, D.C.: Office of Transportation Programs, Federal Energy Administration, 1976.

Stycos, J. M., & Back, K. W. *The control of human fertility in Jamaica*. Ithaca, N.Y.: Cornell University Press, 1964.

Stycos, J. M., & Marden, P. G. Honduras: Fertility and evaluation of family planning programs. *Studies in Family Planning*, 1970, *1*(57), 20–24.

Stycos, J. M., & Mundigo, A. Motivators versus messengers: A communications experiment in the Dominican Republic. *Studies in Family Planning*, 1974, *5*, 130–135.

Subcommittee on Transportation and Commerce, Committee on Interstate and Foreign Commerce, U.S. House of Representatives. *Materials relating to the Resource Conservation and Recovery Act of 1976*. Washington, D.C.: U.S. Government Printing Office, 1976.

Sun, T. H. Personal communication, 1975. Cited in R. Freedman and B. Berelson, The record of family planning programs. *Studies in Family Planning*, 1976, *7*, 1–40.

Sussman, D. B. *Baltimore demonstrates gas pyrolysis*. Washington, D.C.: U.S. Environmental Protection Agency, 1975.

Swee-Hock, S. Singapore: Resumption of rapid fertility decline in 1973. *Studies in Family Planning*, 1975, *6*, 166–169.

Tarpy, R. M., & Sawabini, F. L. Reinforcement delay: A selective review of the last decade. *Psychological Bulletin*, 1974, *81*, 984–997.

Taylor, G. H. R. Concerns of labor. *Proceedings, 1975 Conference on Waste Reduction*. Washington, D.C.: U.S. Environmental Protection Agency, 1977.

Thakor, V. H., & Patel, V. M. The Gujarat state massive vasectomy campaign. *Studies in Family Planning*, 1972, *3*, 186–192.

Thorndike, E. L. Animal intelligence: An experimental study of the associative processes in animals. *Psychological Review Monograph Supplement*, 1898, *2*(8).

Thurmann, A., & Miller, R. K. *Secrets of noise control* (2nd ed.). Atlanta: Fairmont Press, 1976.

Tietze, C. The demographic significance of legal abortion in Eastern Europe. *Demography*, 1964, *1*(1), 119–125.

Tognacci, L. N., Weigel, R. H., Widenn, M. F., & Vernon, D. A. Environmental quality: How universal is public concern? *Environment and Behavior*, 1972, *4*, 73–86.

Treadway, R. C., Gillespie, R. W., & Loghmani, M. The model family planning project in Isfahan, Iran. *Studies in Family Planning*, 1976, *7*, 308–321.

Treasure in the trash pile. *Forbes*, May 15, 1978, pp. 31–32.

Turner, R. K., Grace, R., & Pearce, D. W. The economics of waste paper recycling. In D. W. Pearce & I. Walter (Eds.), *Resource conservation: Social and economic dimensions of recycling*. New York: New York University Press, 1977.

Tuso, M. A., & Geller, E. S. Behavior analysis applied to environmental/ecological problems: A review. *Journal of Applied Behavior Analysis*, 1976, *9*, 526.

Udry, J. R. *The media and family planning*. Cambridge, Mass.: Ballinger, 1974.

U.S. Bureau of the Census. *Statistical abstract of the United States: 1976*. Washington, D.C.: U.S. Government Printing Office, 1976.

U.S. Department of the Interior. *Water conservation devices* (Water Research Capsule Report). Washington, D.C.: Office of Water Research and Technology, 1977.

Veatch, R. M. Governmental population incentives: Ethical issues at stake. *Studies in Family Planning*, 1977, *8*, 100–108.

Waggoner, D. *Oregon's bottle bill two years later*. Portland: Columbia Group Press, 1974.

Waggoner, D. The Oregon bottle bill—Facts and fantasies. *Environment Action Bulletin*, September 1976, 2–3.

Walker, J. M. *Energy demand behavior in a master metered apartment complex: An experimental analysis*. Unpublished manuscript, 1977.

Wang, C. M., & Chen, S. Y. Evaluation of the first year of the educational saving program in Taiwan. *Studies in Family Planning,* 1973, *4,* 157–161.

Ward, P. Deadly throwaways: Plastic six-pack binders and metal pull-tabs doom wildlife. *Defenders of Wildlife,* 1975, *50,* 206–213.

Ward, W. D. Auditory fatigue and masking. In J. Jergen (Ed.), *Modern developments in audiology.* New York: Academic Press, 1963.

Ward, W. D. A comparison of the effects of continuous, intermittent, and impulse noise. In D. Henderson, R. P. Hamerinik, D. S. Dosanjh, & J. H. Mills (Eds.), *Effects of noise on hearing.* New York: Raven Press, 1976.

Weigel, R. H., Vernon, D. T., & Tognacci, L. N. Specificity of the attitude as a determinant of attitude–behavior congruence. *Journal of Personality and Social Psychology,* 1974, *30,* 724–728.

Wendt, K. A. *Damming the solid waste stream: The beginning of source reduction in Minnesota.* Roseville, Minn.: Minnesota Pollution Control Agency, 1975.

Westerman, R. R. Waste management through product design: The case of automobile tires. *Proceedings, 1975 Conference on Waste Reduction.* Washington, D.C.: U.S. Environmental Protection Agency, 1977.

Westoff, C. F., Potter, R. G., & Sagi, P. C. *The third child.* Princeton, N.J.: Princeton University Press, 1963.

Westoff, C. F., Potter, R. G., Sagi, P. C., & Mishler, E. G. *Family growth in metropolitan America.* Princeton, N.J.: Princeton University Press, 1961.

What you can do to recycle more paper. Washington, D.C.: U.S. Environmental Protection Agency, 1975.

Whitfield, S. Noise on the ward at night. *Nursing Times,* 1975, *71,* 408–412.

Wicker, A. W. Attitudes versus actions: The relationship of verbal and overt behavioral responses to attitudinal objects. *Journal of Social Issues,* 1969, *25,* 41–78.

Wicker, A. W. Processes which mediate behavior–environment congruence. *Behavioral Science,* 1972, *17,* 265–277.

Wiggins, J. S. *Personality and prediction: Principles of personality assessment.* Reading, Mass.: Addison-Wesley, 1973.

Wildman, B. G., & Erickson, M. T. Methodological problems in behavioral observation. In J. D. Cone & R. P. Hawkins (Eds.), *Behavioral assessment: New directions in clinical psychology.* New York: Brunner/Mazel, 1977.

Willems, E. P. Behavioral technology and behavioral ecology. *Journal of Applied Behavior Analysis,* 1974, *7,* 151–165.

Wilson, C. W., & Hopkins, B. L. The effects of contingent music on the intensity of noise in junior high home economics classes. *Journal of Applied Behavior Analysis,* 1973, *6,* 269–275.

Winett, R. A. Efforts to disseminate a behavioral approach to energy conservation. *Professional Psychology,* 1976, *7,* 222–228.

Winett, R. A. Prompting turning out lights in unoccupied rooms. *Journal of Environmental Systems,* 1977, *1,* 237–241.

Winett, R. A., Kagel, J. H., Battalio, R. C., & Winkler, R. C. Effects of monetary rebates, feedback, and information on residential electricity conservation. *Journal of Applied Psychology,* 1978, *63*(1), 73–80.

Winett, R. A., Kaiser, S., & Haberkorn, G. The effects of monetary rebates and feedback on electricity conservation. *Journal of Environmental Systems,* 1977, *6,* 329–341.

Winett, R. A., Neale, M. S., & Grier, H. C. Effects of self-monitoring and feedback on residential electricity consumption. *Journal of Applied Behavior Analysis,* 1979, *12,* 173–184.

Winett, R. A., Neale, M. S., Williams, K., Yokley, J., & Kauder, H. *The effects of individual and group feedback on residential electricity consumption: Three replications.* Unpublished manuscript, 1978.

Winett, R. A., & Nietzel, M. Behavioral ecology: Contingency management of residential energy use. *American Journal of Community Psychology*, 1975, *3*, 123–133.

Winett, R. A., & Winkler, R. C. Current behavior modification in the classroom: Be still, be quiet, be docile. *Journal of Applied Behavior Analysis*, 1972, *5*, 499–504.

Witmer, J. F., & Geller, E. S. Facilitating paper recycling: Effects of prompts, raffles, and contests. *Journal of Applied Behavior Analysis*, 1976, *9*, 315–322.

Wodarski, J. S. *The reduction of electrical energy consumption: The application of behavioral analysis*. Paper presented at the meeting of the Association for the Advancement of Behavior Therapy, San Francisco, December 1975.

Wohlwill, J. F. The emerging discipline of environmental psychology. *American Psychologist*, 1970, *25*, 303–312.

Wohlwill, J. F. *A psychologist looks at land use*. Paper presented at a symposium, "Psychology and the Environment in the 1980's," University of Missouri, Columbia, Mo., December 2, 1975.

Wohlwill, J. F., & Carson, D. H. Epilog. In J. F. Wohlwill & D. H. Carson (Eds.), *Environment and the social sciences: Perspectives and applications*. Washington, D.C.: American Psychological Association, 1972.

Wolman, A. The metabolism of cities. *Cities*. New York: Knopf, 1970, pp. 156–174.

Wood, M. Quoted in "Boilermaker official stresses need for research in psychological impact of noise." *Noise Control Report*, 1973, *2*, 253.

Zane, T. L. *The effects of different litter control procedures on movie audiences*. Unpublished master's thesis, Western Michigan University, 1974.

Zarling, L. H., & Lloyd, K. E. *A behavioral analysis of feedback to electrical consumers*. Unpublished manuscript, 1978.

Zatuchni, G. I. *Post-partum family planning*. New York: McGraw-Hill, 1971.

Zelnick, M., & Kantner, J. F. The resolution of teenage first pregnancies. *Family Planning Perspectives*, 1974, *6*, 74.

Zifferblatt, S. M., & Hendricks, C. G. Applied behavioral analysis of societal problems: Population change, a case in point. *American Psychologist*, 1974, *29*, 750–761.

Zikmund, W., & Stanton, W. J. Recycling solid wastes: A channels of distribution problem. *Journal of Marketing*, 1972, *35*, 34–39.

AUTHOR INDEX

Adelman, I., 110
Adelson, J., 108
Altman, I., 173
Anderson, E. G., 60, 228
Anderson, N., 196
Anderson, V. B., 154
Andrews, R. A., 208
Anschell, S., 187, 212
Artz, L. M., 98, 166
Axelrod, S., 180
Ayllon, T., 98
Azrin, N. H., 89

Back, K. W., 118
Bacon, A., 68
Baer, D. M., 18, 35, 222
Bailes, J. C., 134
Bailey, J. S., 57, 146
Baker, R. W., 92
Baladrishnan, T. R., 117
Baltes, M. M., 58, 59, 61, 71
Barach, R., 187, 212
Barker, R. G., 3
Barlow, D. H., 43, 48, 63, 240
Baron, R. A., 89
Battalio, R. C., 188, 193
Beales, P. H., 91
Becker, L. J., 13, 35, 185, 194
Behrens, W. W., 3
Bell, P. A., 74
Belsten, L., 196
Benna, P., 91
Bergamasco, B., 91

Bergland, T., 89, 90
Berrien, F. K., 89
Bettinger, R., 146
Bickman, L., 13
Bidwell, R., 130, 132, 133
Bingham, T. H., 132
Bittle, R. G., 182
Black, T. R. L., 117
Black, W. A. M., 98
Blake, J., 111
Blampied, N. M., 98
Blount, R., 68
Boggs, D. H., 91
Boland, J. J., 207, 212
Bornstein, M. H., 111
Bower, B. T., 14, 131, 133
Bragdon, C. R., 90, 102
Brewer, D. W., 91
Briess, F. B., 91
Broadbent, D. E., 91
Buchanan, C. C., 147
Burgess, R. L., 55–58, 60, 71, 73, 134, 152, 226, 241
Burns, W., 90, 91
Bushell, D., 241
Byers, E. S., 69
Byrne, D., 113

Campbell, D. T., 238
Canter, D., 12
Carson, D. H., 19, 73
Casey, L., 63, 64, 71, 80, 224
Cernada, G. P., 115, 117, 118

Chaffee, J. F., 144
Chan, M. L., 206
Chandler, M., 196
Chang, M. C., 122
Chapman, C., 65–67, 71, 227
Chen, S. Y., 121
Chiang, R. N. S., 14
Choldin, H. M., 117
Chow, L. P., 115
Clark, R. N., 55, 56, 59, 60, 71, 72,
    134, 152
Clausen, J. A., 108
Claussen, E., 134
Coles, R., 100
Collins, R. H., 130, 140
Conderman, L., 35
Cone, J. D., 6, 9, 11, 12, 18, 33, 47, 50,
    55, 56, 65, 66, 69, 73, 75–79, 84,
    147, 156, 163–166, 173, 181–184,
    188, 190–192, 196, 211, 216,
    222–224, 226, 246
Cook, S. W., 166, 196
Cooper, D., 146
Coplin, W. D., 239
Couch, J. V., 145
Craighead, W. E., 98, 166
Craik, K. H., 3, 13
Crawford, T. J., 111
Cross, J. A., 134
Cuca, R., 116
Cutright, P., 114

Darley, J. M., 13, 182
David, H. P., 114
Davidson, A. R., 230
Davidson, W. S., 56
Davis, B., 30
Davis, K., 111, 114
Dehn, W. T., 147
Deitz, S., 242
Delprato, D. J., 194
Deslauriers, B. C., 33, 152–154, 156,
    164, 165, 228
Donaldson, P. J., 122
Douglas, T. J., 239

Douvan, E., 108
Dow, T. E., 113
Drabman, R., 68, 98
Dubey, D. C., 117
Duncan, R. C., 142, 144

Eastman, W. F., 114
Edwards, A. L., 38
Ehrlich, P. R., 3, 108
Ellery, M. D., 98
Enke, S., 121
Erickson, M. T., 171
Esler, A., 101
Everett, P. B., 33, 47, 48, 150–157,
    159, 161, 163–165, 168, 223, 228,
    239

Farris, J. C., 68, 135, 136
Farris, M. T., 174, 187
Fawcett, J. T., 110, 111, 118
Fazio, R. H., 13
Feirstein, D. B., 9, 55
Ferster, C. B., 31, 63
Finnie, W. C., 64, 65, 68, 69, 72, 75,
    81, 134
Finnigan, O. D., 121, 124
First, M., 141
Fisher, J. C., 174
Fisher, J. D., 74, 113
Fisher, W. A., 113
Floyd, M. K., 99
Fook-Kee, W., 120
Foxx, R. M., 157, 159, 163, 164, 166
Franklin, W. E., 128, 134, 135
Freedman, R., 117–119
Furlan, P., 91

Garber, S., 98, 145
Geller, E. S., 14, 56, 57, 65, 68–72, 81,
    127, 134–139, 141, 142, 144, 145,
    166

George, E. I., 20
George, J. R., 97
Gillespie, R. W., 122
Gillim, M., 91
Glass, D. C., 90, 91
Grace, R., 128
Grandy, G. S., 98
Gray, J. E., 174
Green, L., 7
Greene, A. K., 137
Grief, E., 180
Grobe, R. P., 97
Grzona, A. G., 101
Gudger, C. M., 134

Haberkorn, G., 193, 246
Hake, D. F., 157, 159, 163, 164, 166
Hall, R. V., 180
Hamad, C. D., 146
Hammond, M. R., 208
Hanke, S. H., 207, 212
Hansen, P., 142
Hardin, G., 7, 111
Harmon, B., 101
Harris, V. W., 98
Harvey, P. D., 117
Hawkins, R. P., 50
Hayes, S. C., 6, 11, 12, 18, 33, 47, 50,
    56, 66–68, 73, 76–81, 84, 147,
    156, 163–166, 173, 182–185, 188,
    190–192, 196, 211, 216, 223, 224,
    226, 229, 236, 242, 246
Hays, W. L., 38
Hayward, S. C., 47, 48, 58, 59, 61, 71,
    152, 157, 159, 160, 164
Heare, S., 206
Heberlein, T. A., 13, 65, 69, 177
Hendee, J. C., 55, 56, 60, 134, 152
Hendricks, C. G., 111, 123
Henry, W. E., 111
Hersen, M., 42, 48, 63, 240
Hinds, D. H., 151, 156, 157
Hirst, E., 150
Hoffman, L. W., 110, 113, 114
Hoffman, M. L., 110, 113, 114

Holland, H. H., 100
Holland, J. G., 26
Holloway, J. R., 140
Holtzman, W., 108
Hopkins, S., 95–97, 121
Horst, M. I., 40
Hubbert, M. I., 173
Hunt, R. G., 128, 134, 135

Ingram, R. E., 144, 145

Jaccard, J. J., 230
Jaffe, F. S., 118
Jaggi, B., 14
Johnson, V. S., 66, 147, 165, 226, 246
Jones, F. C., 180
Jurgen, R. K., 189

Kachirayan, M., 122
Kagan, J., 55
Kagel, J. H., 188, 193
Kaiser, S., 192
Kantner, J. F., 114
Karen, R. L., 30, 31
Karpus, L., 145
Kauder, H., 182
Kazdin, A. E., 42, 63, 81
Keller, A. B., 111
Kerbec, M. J., 91
King, H. B., 135, 138
Klinger, A., 114
Knudson, V. D., 89
Knutson, A. I., 114
Koffka, J., 3
Kohlenberg, R. J., 33, 62, 71, 175, 176,
    187, 212, 228
Komarovsky, M., 113
Kratochwill, T. R., 48
Krishnakumar, S., 124
Kriss, M., 13
Kryter, K. D., 90, 91
Kulkarni, V. R., 122

Lahart, D. E., 57
Laponce, J. A., 238
Large, D. B., 174
Leitenberg, H., 48
Levenson, H., 14
Levy, S. J., 139, 140
Lingle, S. A., 140
Lipe, D., 111
Lipscomb, D. M., 89, 90
Litow, L., 92, 166
Littler, T. S., 91
Lloyd, K. E., 176, 178
Lloyd, M. E., 63, 64, 71, 80, 178, 224
Loghmani, M., 122
Loomis, R. J., 74
Lopata, M. Z., 113
Loube, N., 134
Lowe, R. A., 139–141
Lu, L. P., 117, 118
Luyben, J. E., 194
Luyben, P. D., 146, 194

Maas, R. B., 101
MacDonald, A. P., 111
MacDonald, M. L., 56
Madell, T. D., 92
Madsen, C. H., 35, 98
Makranczy, V. J., 195
Malaby, J., 97
Maloney, M. P., 14
Marden, P. G., 117
Martin, G. L., 97, 187, 212
Matthai, R. J., 117
McAllister, L. W., 35
McClelland, L., 166, 196
McConahay, J. B., 238
McEwen, L. B., 134, 141
McGlotten, R., 135
McLaughlin, T., 97
McSweeny, A. J., 212
McWhorter, J., 161
Meadows, D. H., 3
Meadows, D. L., 3
Medland, M. B., 98
Melnick, W., 101
Mersseman, L. M. D., 98

Meyers, A. W., 47, 48, 98, 152, 166
Millenson, J. R., 26
Miller, R. K., 100
Milne, M., 199–209, 213
Mishler, E. G., 110
Moore, B., 108
Moore, J., 196
Morris, C. T., 110
Mullins, C., 118
Mundigo, A., 118
Murray, C. R., 200
Muscat, R. J., 121

Neale, M. S., 182
Nelson, F., 114
Newsom, T. J., 154, 195
Nietzel, M. T., 56, 72, 188
Nortman, D., 113
Nunnally, J. C., 38

Orebaugh, A. L., 68
Osborne, J. G., 55, 60, 228

Pacey, J., 130
Pakter, J., 114
Palmer, M. H., 178, 179
Palmer, R., 203
Pal-Montano, A., 123
Parham, I. A., 9, 55, 75
Patel, V. M., 121, 124
Patterson, A. H., 27, 181, 188, 192, 198
Paul, G., 42
Pavlov, I. P., 25
Pearce, D. W., 128, 132
Perkin, G. W., 118, 121
Peterson, C., 134, 135
Pettibone, T. J., 97
Phillips, J. F., 123
Phillips, T. W., 33, 62, 71, 152, 156,
    175, 188, 228
Pickering, D., 68
Pierce, C. S., 116

Pinner, B., 46
Pisor, K., 98
Platt, J., 7, 73
Poffenberger, T., 113
Pohlman, E., 107, 113, 116, 119, 121–122
Porapakkham, Y., 122
Post, D. S., 136
Potter, R. G., 110
Powers, R. B., 55, 60, 61, 71, 228, 229
Presser, H. B., 110, 119
Proctor, W., 175, 188
Pryor, J. B., 13
Pumroy, D. K., 92, 166

Quigley, C., 9

Rachlin, H., 7
Rainwater, L., 113
Rall, M., 46
Randers, J., 3
Rawers, R. J., 146
Reeves, E. B., 200
Reid, D. H., 146
Repetto, R., 122
Reynolds, G. S., 26
Rice, C. G., 100
Ridker, R. G., 121
Rincover, A., 242
Risley, T. R., 18, 65–67, 71, 222, 227
Robertson, R., 180
Robie, R., 206
Rodda, M., 89
Rogers, E. M., 121
Rose, H. S., 151, 156, 157
Royster, L. H., 100
Runnion, A., 161
Ruvin, H., 135, 138

Sadd, W., 138
Sagi, P. C., 110
Sampson, R. J., 174, 187

Sawabini, F. L., 180
Schmidt, G. W., 92, 93, 95, 97, 166
Schopler, J., 46
Schramm, W., 117
Scott, C. E., 100
Seaver, W. B., 27, 181, 188, 192, 198
Seligman, C., 13, 182, 194
Semb, G., 146
Sharp, S. T., 128
Shaw, E. A. G., 100
Shearer, W. M., 90
Sherman, J. A., 98
Shuster, K. A., 130
Sidman, M., 42
Silayan-Go, A., 123
Silvermann, A., 108
Simon, J. R., 91
Sims, J. H., 111
Singer, J. E., 90, 91
Sirageldin, I., 121
Skinner, B. F., 6, 21, 26, 31, 63, 134, 141, 163
Slavin, R. E., 195
Small, W. E., 127, 141
Smith, F. L., 132
Smith, M. B., 110
Smoker, P., 238
Snyder, R. C., 238
Solnick, J., 242
Somboonsuk, A., 118
Soucie, G. A., 201
Spitalnik, K., 98
Spitalnik, R., 98
Srinivasan, K., 122
Stachnik, T. J., 98
Stachowiak, J. G., 35
Stanton, W. J., 129
Steimle, F. W., 147
Stokes, T. F., 222
Stokols, D., 3, 14, 46, 111, 229, 230
Stone, R. B., 147
Strang, H. R., 97
Stuart, R. B., 30
Studer, R. G., 239
Stuntz, M. S., 150
Stycos, J. M., 117, 118
Sun, T. H., 121–122
Sussman, D. B., 139

Svetsreni, T., 122
Swee-Hock, S., 120

Takeshita, J. Y., 117–119
Tarpy, R. M., 180
Taylor, G. H. R., 138
Thakor, V. H., 121, 124
Thaler, G., 182
Thomas, D. R., 35, 100
Thorndike, E. L., 27
Thorne, R., 12
Thurmann, A., 100
Tietze, C., 114
Tognacci, L. N., 14, 230
Treadway, R. C., 122
Turner, R. K., 128
Tuso, M. A., 56, 65, 68, 69, 71
Tyler, L., 180

Udry, J. R., 117
Ulrich, R. E., 92, 93, 95, 97, 166

Valesano, R., 182
Veatch, R. M., 122
Vernon, D. T., 14, 230

Waggoner, D., 134
Walker, J. M., 195
Walter, I., 132
Wang, C. M., 121
Ward, M. P., 14
Ward, W. D., 91

Watson, J. D., 161
Weigel, R. H., 14, 230
Welch, R. O., 134
Wendt, K. A., 135
West, J., 196
Westacott, G., 14
Westerman, R. R., 138
Westoff, C. F., 110
Whitfield, S., 99
Wicker, A. W., 13
Widenn, M. F., 14
Wiggins, J. S., 38, 50
Wildman, B. G., 171
Willems, E. P., 19, 232
Williams, K., 182
Wilson, C. W., 95–97
Winett, R. A., 56, 94, 174, 175, 182,
    185, 187, 188, 192–194
Winkler, R. C., 94, 188, 193
Witmer, J. F., 65, 68, 144, 145, 166
Wodarski, J. S., 193, 195
Wohlwill, J. F., 3, 13, 19, 73, 173
Wolf, M. M., 18, 222
Wolman, A., 199
Wood, M., 90
Woodall, A. E., 134
Wylie, R. G., 68, 135

Yokley, J., 182

Zane, T. L., 57, 58, 60, 62, 71
Zarling, L. H., 176
Zatuchni, G. I., 118
Zelnick, M., 114
Zifferblatt, S. M., 111, 123
Zikmund, W., 129

SUBJECT INDEX

ABA, 48, 50

ABA design, 47, 77, 98, 122, 136, 145, 160, 183, 185, 188, 193

ABAB (C + B) design, 69

ABAB design, 47–48, 50, 93, 215
and ABA designs compared, 48
in litter studies, 56–57

ABAB intrasubject–withdrawal design, 83

ABABABA design, 61

ABACAD design, 63

Abortion, 114

Accelerative approach, 34–35

Accepter, 115, 118, 121–122
characteristic of, 119

Advertising campaign, 118

Aesthetic deterioration, 81

Aesthetic self-perpetuation, 74

Aesthetics, environmental, 15, 55

Air-conditioner usage, 194

Air pollution, 15, 18, 26, 160

Aluminum, 139

Amusement park, 64, 225

Analogue, laboratory, 239

Analogue research, 75

Analysis:
level of, 241
multiple-baseline, 49
parametric, 19

Analysis of a behavior, 18

Analysis of variance, 44–45

Analytic studies, 47

Antilitter, 31, 35

Antilitter behavior, 57

Antilittering, 8–9

Antilitter message, 57

Antilitter procedure, 59

Antilitter prompt, 69, 72

Apartment complex, 146, 195

Appalachian strip miner, 28

Appliance, water-efficient, 213

Applied behavior analysis, 42, 46, 55, 64

Applied behavior-analytic research, 48, 51, 63

Applied behavior-analytic solution, 73

Arab oil embargo, 177–178

Astronomy, 40

Attitude, 11, 13–14, 229–231, 233

Attitude/behavior interrelation, 230

Automatic procedure for reinforcing, 61

Automobiles, 4, 132, 138
abandoned, 147
altering the use of, 156, 163
cost of, 160
junked, 68
scrap, 131–132

Automobile use:
reducing, 166, 168
studies of, 156–157

Autonomic nervous system, 26

BA design, 64

BAB design, 95

BABA design, 147

Baltimore, 140

Bar press, 27

Barrenness, 113

Baseline, 50, 56, 60–63, 67

Baseline period, 48, 57

273

Baseline-to-experimental change, 50
Basic two-group true experiment, 43
BCACACDA design, 66
Behavior, 25, 26, 28
    directness of environmental relevance,
        11–15
    rule-governed, 231
Behavioral experimentation, how, what,
    and why, 238
Behavioral repertoire, environmentally
    destructive, 231
Behavioral scientists, skills needed by,
    240–241
Behavioral solutions, 222–225, 228
Behavioral technology, 19
Behavior analysts and water
    conservation, 210
Behavior-analytic environmental
    researcher, 165
Behavior-analytic solution, general
    applicability, 221
Behavior change, long-term durability of,
    231
Behavior-change strategies, effective, 34
Behavior studies, 14, 47
Bell, Alexander Graham, 87
Between-subject analyses, 42
Beverage container, 60, 72
Beverage-container litter, 134
Bicycling, 163
Big buck pass, 151
Bill, 179
Billing frequency, 180
Billing practice, 212
Billing practice of municipal water
    district, 206–207
Billing structure, effect of, 212
Biodegradable trash, 5
Birth rates, 110, 114–115
Black light, 68
Bottle bill, 134–135
Bottler, 134
Bottles, 60
Bribery, payment as, 230
Brightness standard, 133
Building heat, 140
Built environment, effect on behavior, 75
Bus, 47–48, 151–152, 154, 156, 165

California, 201, 208
California Department of Water
    Resources, 201
California drought, 236
California toilet bill, 212
California Water Resource Center, 202
Campground, 60
Cans, 134, 140, 142
Canvasser, India, 122
Capital cost, 235
Car-driving behavior, 160
Car pooling, 149, 156–157, 170–172
Cascade Mountain, 59
Cash payment, 121, 124, 132
Catalytic converters, 27
Causal relationships, 39–40, 42–43, 46,
    48, 50
Central Arizona Project, 201
Children:
    motivation for having, 121
    pleasure from having, 113
    value of having, 110
Classroom noise, 92–99, 194
Clean City Squares can, 65
Clean Community System (CCS), 70, 74
Coast Guard, 30, 33, 41
Collection center, 131
Columbia University, 76
Community-wide cleanup campaign, 70
Commute-a-van program, 157
Computer simulation, 239
Conception, 111
Congress, 139
Conjugate reinforcement, 32
Consequation, 31–32
Consequence, short-term, 7, 9
Consequence interval, 31
Consequence scheduling, 33
Consequences, use of, to control
        classroom noise, 92–94, 97
Conservation information, 194
Conservation tactic, 36
Consumer report, 216
Consumption, change in, 181
Consumption feedback, 178
Container option, environment cost, 134
Contingencies, individual versus group,
    166

Contingent music, effect of, 97
Continuous reinforcement, 31–32
Contraception, 119
    attitude toward, 230
    effects of, 111–114
Contraceptive approach, knowledge
    about, 117
Contraceptives, 30, 107–108, 111,
    113–114, 123
Control groups, 42–44, 46
Controls, 154, 165
Convenience store, 136
Conversion, 127
Corporate pollution of waterways, 73
Correlational studies, 37–41, 50–51
Cost accounting, 224
Cost analyses, 159, 164–165
Cost effectiveness, 60, 64, 81, 149, 152,
    158, 229
Cost feedback, 161, 209
Cotton, virgin, 133
Crapper, Thomas, 203
Crowding, 46
Cummings, Alexander, 203

Dallas, 151
Dams, 201
Death rates, 110, 115
Decelerative approach, 34–35
Decibel levels, 87–88
Decomposition, 204
Decreasing behavior, 28, 35
Decreasing block rate, 206–207, 212
Demand, method of reducing, 174
Demonstration, small-scale, 239
Dependent variable, 37–40, 42, 50–51,
    56, 62–63, 66–67
    in litter studies, 56, 61–62
    in mass transit studies, 155
Descriptive strategies, 40, 50
Designer as affected by data, 80–81
Designing environment, 74
Designs, 201
    intersubject, 19
    intrasubject, 19, 47–48, 60, 69
    multiple-baseline, 48, 50

Designs (continued)
    prior empirical evaluation, 79
    time-series, 48
    withdrawal, 47, 56
Des Moines, 178
Directory Assistance, charging for, 212
Discriminative stimulus, 6–7, 30
Disposal behavior, 62
Door-to-door canvassing, 124
Dormitory, 98, 144–145, 195–196
DRO, 93
Dual-flush device for toilet, 205
Dump, open, 130

Ear-protective devices, 100
Earth Day, 3
Eco-freak, 204
Ecological psychology, 4
Ecology, 43
Eco-systems perspective, 232–233
Educational bond program, 124
Educational setting, 92
Effect relationships, 42–43, 46, 48
Effects, replicated, 48
Eisenhower, Dwight D., 75–76
Electricity, 36–39, 41, 43, 46, 48–49
    conservation project, 198
    residential, 161
Electricity consumption, 50, 208
Electricity use, magnitude of reduction
    in, 227
Electric utility company, 43
Elementary school, 146
Energy conservation, 30, 159, 173–198
    in master-metered homes, 195–197
    need for, 173–175
    and prices, 174
    and psychologists, 175
    in residential settings, 173–198
Energy consumption, 18, 173–198
    in individual residence, 175
Energy crisis, 173
Energy policy, 175
Energy program, national, 163
Energy rate, 186

Energy use:
  altering overall levels, 177–193
  altering patterns of, 175–176
  and specific behaviors, 193–194
Energy utility, 235
Environment:
  clean versus littered, 75
  physical, 3
Environmental change, how permanent,
  222
Environmental cost of product, 131
Environmental design to perpetuate
  attractiveness, 74
Environmentally destructive behaviors,
  6, 10–11, 28–29
  examples of, 16–17
  prevention of, 231, 233
  relevance of, 11–15
Environmentally protective behaviors, 6,
  10–11, 34, 61, 74, 77, 79, 223
  examples of, 16–17
  relevance of, 11–15
Environmentally relevant behaviors, 5,
  25, 27–28, 30, 224
  cost of, 161
  directness of, 11–15
  long-lasting change in, 223–224
  types of, 11–18
Environmentally relevant movement, 162
Environmentally relevant psychology,
  5–6, 10, 15–21, 33, 47
  characteristics of, 18–21, 240–241
  a definition of, 18–21
  future of, 243
  importance of conceptual
    underpinning, 228
Environmental problems:
  dimensions of, 20
  parochial view of, 228
  stability over time, 165
  a taxonomy of, 15–16
Environmental programs, 19–20
Environmental protection, 40
Environmental Protection Agency, 29,
  203
Environmental psychology, dimensions
  of, 4

Environmental quality, 15
Environmental relevance, 241–242
  importance of demonstrating, 11–15,
    95
  need to demonstrate, 130
  presumed, 12
  types of, 15–18
Environmental structuring, temporary,
  75–76
Environment and behavior, 12
Environment study, 14
EPA, 4, 139, 142
Ernakulam District, 123
Europe, 140
  Eastern, 114
Evergreen Point Floating Bridge, 156
Every-person schedule, 32, 153
Experiment:
  basic two-group true, 43
  natural, 177, 238, 240
  true, 42–43, 46, 48
  two-group, 46
  two-group true, 44
Experimental effect, 44
Experimental group, 43
Experimental-group design, 44
Experimental-group studies, 46
Experimental manipulations, 18
Experimental manipulative research, 37
Experimental phase, 50, 60
Experimental social reform, 234, 239
Experimental strategies, 41
Experimental studies, 40, 51
Experimentation:
  role in policy making, 238–240
  scale of, 242
Extinction, 25, 29, 35

Factor analysis, 40
Factorial design, 44–46
Family, 108, 113
Family planning, 115–125
Federal Energy Administration, 149
Federal Office of Energy, 175

Federal standards for automobile fuel
    efficiency, 166
Feedback, 160–161, 164, 176, 178–183,
    185, 187–189, 192, 195
  competitive social, 196
  continuous, 176
  cost, 161
  daily, 182
  decreased frequency of, 182
  definition of, 179
  and energy consumption, 178–186
  form of the, 180
  frequent, 180
  how it works, 185
  individual-household, 182
  kilowatt hour, 180
  monetary, 178, 180
  monthly, 182
  peaking, 176
  and power bills, 179
  social, 196
  source of the, 180
  and standards, 185–193
  about water use, 211
  weekly, 182
  written daily kilowatt hour, 176
Feedback device, 175–176, 194
Ferrous metal, 139–140
Ferrous scrap, 131
Fertility, 111–114
Field worker, 118
55-miles-per-hour speed limit, 166
Fine, 29, 31, 33, 56, 73
Fixed-interval schedule, 31–32, 92
Fixed-person schedule, 32, 153
Fixed ratio, 32
Fixed-ratio schedule, 31
Flat rate, 206–207, 212
Fleet-operated trucks, 161
Florida, 156
Flotation tank, 139
Flow-control devices, 201, 205
Forest, national, 55
Forestry practice, 15
Form follows function, 75–76
Free-mass-transit research, 164
Free transit, 151, 154–156

Fuel, bulk-purchased, 161
Fuel conservation guide, 158
Fuel oil, consumption of, 198
Fuel usage, reducing, 161

Game, 239
Gas-mileage legislation, 138
Gasoline, 159
Gasoline use, 164
Generality, 22, 226
Generality of behavioral solution,
    221–222
Generalization, 233
Gestation, 114
Glass, 133, 139–142, 147
Government official, letter from, 178
Grand Canyon, 201, 208
Gray water, 205–206, 209
Green Canyon, 60
Group contingency, 92–94, 166
Group-incentive program, 122
Gujarat, India, 123

Hamburger coupon, effect of, 70
Handbill, 69
Health-related noise, 99
Health-related problems, 15
Hearing defects, 91
Hearing protection, 101
Heating oil, 181
Hertz, 86
Highway, 150
Highway litter, 55
Hospital noise, 99
Hot-water heater, electric, 200
Household appliances, 36, 194–195
Humus, 204

Illegitimate children, 114
Incentive program in population control,
    119

Incentives, 121, 122, 176, 195
    effects on energy, 188–193
    types of, 120–122
Incentive system, 139
Incineration, 130
Incinerator, water-wall, 140
Increasing behavior, 26, 35
Increasing block rate, 206, 212
Independent variables, 37–39, 42–48, 50
    interpretation of effects of, 42
India, 122–124
Individual versus group contingencies,
    166
Industrial waste, 9
Information, 175, 177, 179, 188, 192,
    194–195
    cost of water, 208
    effects on automobile use, 159–160
    ways to conserve water, 210, 216
Informational appeal, 177
Informational campaign in population
    control, 117–118
Information approach, water and
    electricity compared, 211
Infrasound, 86
Insulation, 4, 210
Interaction, 45
Intercourse variable, 111
Interdependent group-oriented
    contingency system, 166
Interior design, changing, 98–99
Intermill driver, 161
Intermittent-reinforcement schedule,
    31–33
Interobserver agreement, 81, 171
Intersubject design, 19, 37, 42–43
Intersubject study, 46
Interval scheduling, 31–33
Intrasubject approaches, 51
Intrasubject design for answering
    comparative questions, 63
Intrasubject designs, 19, 42, 47–48, 59
Intrasubject multiple-baseline design, 67
Intrasubject withdrawal design, 60, 66,
    69
Involuntary behavior, 26
Iowa, 63

Irrigation, 200
IUD, 113, 116–117, 119, 121

Japan, 114, 140
Junior Forest Ranger Badge, 60

Kansas City, Kansas, 66
KAP study, 115
Keep America Beautiful, Inc., 55–56,
    70–74, 80
Kennedy Youth Center, 66
Kentucky, 225
Kerala State in India, 123
Kilowatt hours, 50
Kitchen scrap, 142

Labor and noise, 90
Laboratory-analogue research on design,
    75
Landfill, 140
Land pollution, 15
Land reclamation, 15
Large-scale research, 242
Latin-square design, 136
Law enforcement, positive, 35
Law-enforcement agencies, 35
Lawnwalking, environmentally
    destructive, 76–79
Law of effect, 27
Leachate, 130
Leader effect, 159
Lecture, 97
Legislative changes, 212
Legislative solutions to transportation
    problem, 166
Levels versus patterns of use in
    transportation, 163–164
Life-line billing, 206, 212
Lighting, 194
Litter, 5, 8–9, 13, 30, 32–35, 55–73,
    75, 130
    beverage-container, 134

Litter *(continued)*
  in buildings, 68–69
  in clean versus dirty environments, 65,
    69, 71
  cost effectiveness of experimental
    program, 60, 63
  cost of cleaning up, 59–60
  deliberate planting of, 59–60
  ease of measuring, 55
  effects of verbal appeals to pick up,
    66–67, 71
  enforcing laws against, 73
  and environmental appearance, 75
  as a function of trash cans available, 65
  highway, 55, 64
  indigenous, 134
  large versus small items, 64, 66–67
  lottery, 61–62
  multiple-baseline analysis of, 67
  operational definition, 81
  payment for absence of, 66
  payment for turning in, 66
  percentage removed as dependent
    variable, 63
  preventive approaches, 71–73
  problem of, 55
  project to clean up, 83
  project to prevent, 81–83
  on sidewalk, 65
  in theaters and football stadiums, 56,
    58–59
  variable-person schedules in studies,
    62–63
Litter bag, 56–61, 64
Litterbugs, 57
Littering, 8–9, 28–30, 33, 50, 58–59
  as negatively reinforced, 73
  as operant behavior, 73
  operant conceptualization of, 55
  prompts to avoid, 68–69
  theoretical analysis of, 73
Litter-prevention tactic, 65
Litter problem, 63, 74
Litter with a built-in value, 60
Logan, Utah, 60
Logging practice, 130
Long-line driver, 161

Long-term positive consequence, 73
Los Angeles, 40, 156
Los Angeles County Plumbing Code, 209
Lottery, litter, 61–62
Loudness, 86, 89

Madison Avenue approach, 117
Magnetic separation, 140
Mailing, direct, 118
Maine, 134
Manipulative strategies, 41
Manufacturing or packaging,
    wastefulness in, 133
Manufacturing practice and tradition,
    209, 213
Manufacturing processes,
    environmentally undesirable, 131
Mapping function, 40
Marblehead, Massachusetts, 142
Marked-item technique, 67–68, 72, 147,
    229
Mass-education campaigns, 36
Mass-transit systems, 18, 150–151, 156,
    163, 166
Master metering, 195, 213
Mental health facility, 158
Metal, 141, 147
Meter:
  sound-level, 87
  water, 216
Meter reader, 180
Methane gas, 130, 140
Miami, 151, 156
Miles driven per day, 159–160, 164
Minnesota packaging law, 135
Mixed waste, 139–142
Mobile-home park, 146
Monetary incentive, 178, 192
Monsanto, 140
Monthly bill, 178–180
Morgantown, West Virginia, 66
Motivator, paid, 124
Multiple-baseline design, 48–50, 67, 95,
    185, 216
Municipal water district, billing practice
    of, 206–207

National forest, 55, 60
Natural experiment, 250
Natural gas, 7, 188
Negative consequence, informational
    appeal, 177
Negative correlation, 41
Negative reinforcement, 25, 35, 170
    of littering, 73
Negative reinforcer, 25, 28, 35
New England, 182
New York, 71
New York City, 55, 206
Noise, 15, 85–104, 166
Noise-control legislation, 101
Noise level:
    ambient, 97
    of cars, 102
    in college dormitory, 98
    factory with dangerous, 101
Noise pollution, 150
Noise reducers, 27
Nonlittering, 8–9
Nonreturnable beverage containers, 60,
    133–134, 138
Nonvolunteer, 196
North Carolina, 38
Nuclear power plant, 235

Odometer reading, 157–158, 164
Oil, 149–150
Operant behavior, 25–28, 35, 73
Operant paradigm, 6–7
Operationalization, 50
Operationalize, 37–38
Oregon, 72
Oregon bottle law, 134
Outdoor-recreation area, 59
Oven, 193
Overconsumption, 36
Overpopulation, 18

Pacific Northwest, 175, 221
Packaging, 133, 135, 137
Paper, 128–129, 141–142

Paper manufacturers, 131
Paper recycling, 128–129, 144–147
Paper stock, brightness of, 133
Park University, 77
Park ranger, 60
Pathways, 75–80, 83
Payment, 188–189, 192
    to conserve, 224
    durability of effect, 223–224
    phasing out, 223
Payment for clean yard, 66
Payment for volume, 66
Peak-demand metering, 206–207
Peaking, 175–176
Peak period, 163
Pennsylvania State University, 47,
    58–59, 151, 154, 203
Permanence criticism, logical problem
    with, 232
Person schedule, 33, 62, 152
Philadelphia, 65, 69
Physical environment, 3
Physical environmental problems, 6
Physical technology, 14, 19
Piecework, 32
Pilot research, 226
Pitch, 86
Pittsburgh, 151
Plumbing fixtures, 209
Plumbing wares industry, 209, 213
Policy formation, 239
Policy option, testing of, 239
Political-intervention technique, 238
Pollution, 9, 28–29, 31, 41, 55, 73
    air, 26
    defined, 9
    operant conceptualization of, 55
    water, 9
Pollution and resource depletion, 108
Polution behaviors, 9
Pollution control, 140
Pollution tax, 132
Popular Science, 216
Population, 38, 43–44
    psychological approach to, 110
    variable influencing, 110
Population as a problem, 107, 108

Population control, 107–126
 and educational bonds, 120, 124
 effects of religion on, 110–113
 and ethics, 108–110, 121–122, 124
 history of, 107
 and incentives, 119–124
 individual programs, 123
 informational campaign, 117–118
 large-scale programs, 123–124
 and monetary security, 113
 and motivation for children, 121
 and old age, 113
 research, 114–116
 service program in, 118–119
 views on, 110–114
Population density, psychological impact
  of, 110
Positive consequences, short-term, 7
Positive correlation, 38, 41
Positive reinforcement, 25, 27–28, 35
 criticism of, 221
 duration of its effect, 223–224
 fiscal practicality, 224
Positive reinforcers, 25, 27–29, 35
Postconsumer solid waste, 139
Posttest, 43–45
Power bill, 179
Power company, 187
Power production, 174, 186
Practical utility, 46
Pregnancy check, 115
Premise, 37–38, 41, 43, 50
President, 177, 197
Pretest, 43
Preventing environmental problem, 231
Prevention strategy, 232
Price elasticity, 207
Priority lane, 157, 167
Profit, 235
Programmed instruction, 44–45
Prompt, 57, 68, 177–178, 194, 224
Prompt-only approach, 70
Punishers, 25, 29–30, 35, 170
Punishing, 7, 34
Punishing effect of the delayed cost, 161
Punishment, 25, 28–31, 33, 35
Pyrolysis, 140

Questionnaire, 154

Radiation hazards, 15
Radio, 193
Radio campaign, 118
Radio for quiet, 95
Raffle, 195
Rainfall, daily average, 199
Rate-setting practice, 206
Rate structure, 186–187
 experimentally altering, 212
Ratio schedule, 31–33
Reactive research, 12–15, 74, 110, 229
 combined with behavior analytic,
   229–230, 233
 and noise, 85, 89–91
 in population control, 111
Rebate, customer, 213
Reclamation, 28, 127
Recovered material, advertising, 133
Recreational transportation, 163
Recyclable goods, collection and
   separation of, 131
Recycled products, 131, 133
Recycling, 6, 20, 26, 30, 60, 69,
   127–148
 bottles, 135–137
 cash payments, 137
 costs and benefits, 127–130
 definition of, 127
 factors inhibiting, 130–133
 in Oregon, 134–135
 prompts, 136
Recycling firm incentive, 132
Red Owl food store, 137
Reinforcement, 6–7, 27, 29–31, 34–35,
   161
 conjugate, 32
 effect depends on problem magnitude,
   227
 frequency of, 62
 negative, 25, 28, 170
 positive, 25, 27–28
 principle of, 27
 of reduced driving, 158

Reinforcement *(continued)*
  remotely administered, 229
  self, 170
  sensory, 97
Reinforcement density, 62–63, 153
Reinforcement history, 232
Reinforcement procedures, 61, 63, 166
Reinforcer, 34
  empirical definition of, 27
  negative, 25, 28
  positive, 25, 27–28
  social, 170
Religion, 113
Remanufacture, 127
Remotely administrable reinforcement,
    229
Remote-reinforcement procedure, 61, 71
Repeated measurement, 47
Replication, 48, 50
Representative, 38
Request for proposal, 239
Research, analytic, 18–19
  conceptually systematic, 19
  in environmental psychology, 11–21
  role in policy making, 238–240
  scale of, 242
  systems oriented, 19–20
  technologically precise, 19
  transdisciplinary, 241
  types of, 12–15
Research analogue, 75
Research design, 36, 44
  in transportation studies, 165
Research errors, 42
Research strategies, 36, 40
Reshelving tray, 69
Residential water conservation, 199, 206
Resource recovery, 133, 139–148
Resource-related problem, 18
Resources, 17
  consumption of nonrenewable, 18
  stream of, 131
Respondent behavior, 25–26, 35
Response difficulty, manipulation of, 156
Response interval, 31
Rest room, 194
Returnable bottle, 60, 134, 136–137
Returnable container, 135

Returnable goods, 133
Reusable goods, 133
Reusable product, 135
Reuse, 127
Reward procedures, 229
Rhode Island, 225
Rhythm method, 113
Richmond, Virginia, 64
River, 8
River polluter, 30
Rule-governed behavior, 231–232
Rush-hour demand, 163

Sacramento, California, 206
Sample, 38, 43
San Diego, California, 140, 200, 203,
    208
San Francisco–Oakland Bay Bridge, 156
Schedule effects, 63
Schedules, 31–33
Scientific methodology, 241
Scrubbers, 26
Seasonal variation, 179
Seattle, 59, 142, 156, 187, 225
Secondary-material firm, 132
Self-management procedure, 169
Self-monitoring, 180, 185
Self-recorded automobile driving, 169
Self-recording, 158–159
Self-reward, 170
Sensory stimulation, 97
Service program in population control,
    118–119
Set price, 206
Set-price billing, 212
Sexual intercourse, 111
Shirley Highway, 156
Short-term negative consequence, 73
Shower head, 201
Shredding waste, 139
Sierra Club, 230
Sign, nonspecific, 194
Signal-to-noise ratio, 90
Simulation, 239
Simulation study, value of, 149
Singapore, 120
Slot machine, 32

Small-scale resarch, 242
Smokestack emission, 227
Smokey the Bear patch, 60
Sneaky tactics, 157
Social commendation, 181
Social consequence, 181
Social cost, 160
Social interaction, 75
Socialization of power production, 235
Social Security, 113
Social traps, 7, 73
Social utility, 46
Society for the Experimental Analysis of
    Behavior, 48
Soil conservation, 18
Solar system, 200
Solid waste, 129, 131, 137–140
Solid-waste management, 74
Somerville, Massachusetts, 142
Sound, 85–104
    measurement of, 86–87
Source separation, 139, 141–147
South Dakota, 134
South Dixie Highway, 156–157
Speed limit, 166
Standards, 185
Stanford Research Institute, 150
State-authorized monopoly, 235
Statistical procedures, 45–56
Steam, 140
Steel, 131
Sterilization, 111, 113–114, 119, 121
    effect of religion on, 110
Sterilization camps, 123–124
Stimulus change, 30–31
Stimulus control, 30
Stimulus-control procedure, 228
St. Louis, 65, 141
Stockholder, 235
Subject withdrawal design, 62
Subsistence farmer, 113
Suds-saver cycle, 205
Supermarket, 136
Supreme Court, 114
Sweden, 132, 147
Swimming pool, 207
Systems, influence of, 237–238
Systems-level contingency, 234, 236

Taiwan, 117, 124
Tax, 163
Taxes, 166
Tax incentives, 8–9
Taxpayer, 55
Tax reduction, 157
Teacher reprimand, 94
Technical development, 240
Technological change, effects of, 167
Technology, 4
    behavioral, 5, 10, 19, 123
    physical, 4–5, 14, 19
    physical, in water conservation, 201
    water-saving, 199
Telephone company, 212
Temporary environmental structuring,
    75–76
Tests of statistical significance, 46
Theaters, 57–59, 68, 225
    littering in, 56–57, 62
Theory:
    need for solutions to be related to, 228
    role of, 19, 197, 240–243
Thermostat, 7
3 M Company, 195
Time-series design, 47–48
Tire scrap, 147
Toilet paper, history of, 203
Toilets, 201, 203–204, 213, 229
Token, 152–153, 155, 164–165
    for bus riding, 152–153, 228
    free, 47–48
    rewarding bus rider with, 167
Token system, 152
    administrative cost of, 165
Token trading, 155
Tone, 87
    pure, 90
Toxic substances, 15
Tragi, 100
Transactional, 230
Transdisciplinary research, 50, 241
Transportation, 149
    dependent and independent variables,
        163–164
    energy uses in, 150
    pattern or level of, 164
    recreational uses of, 163

Transportation behavior, 149
    additional research needed, 168
    issue in altering, 162
Transportation game, 239
Transportation provider, 149
    need to study, 167
Transportation system, 149, 167
Trash-buying approach, 67, 71
Trash importation, 66
Trial-and-error responding, 27
Tubal ligation, 113, 119, 123
TV, 193

Ultrasound, 86
United States, 108, 114–115, 117,
    119–120, 131, 133, 138, 140, 149,
    174, 200, 209, 243
U.S. Department of the Interior, 201, 205
U.S. Forest Service, 60, 225
Utility, 46

Value judgment, 239–240
Van pooling, 149, 157
Variable flush mechanism, 205, 229–230
Variable-interval schedule, 31–32
Variable-person schedule, 32, 62,
    152–153, 229
Variable-ratio schedule, 31–32
Vasectomies, 113, 115, 119, 121, 123
Vermont, 134
Vertical structure, 132
Vibration, 86
Virgin material, 131–132
Vocal appeal, 71
Voice-operated relay, 95
Volunteer, 196

Walt Disney, 57
Washington, D.C., 156
Waste:
    heat value of municipal, 141
    industrial, 9
    inorganic, 139

Waste disposal, 40–41, 130
    ecologically beneficial, 204
Waste disposal technology, 129
Wastefulness in manufacturing or
    packaging, 133
Wastepaper, 128, 131, 140–141, 144,
    147
Waste reduction, 133
    and behavioral technology, 133–137,
    139
    definition of, 133–134
    economic benefit, 138
    physical-technology approach, 147
Wastes, burying, 8
Water:
    categories of use, 200
    environmental cost of providing, 201
    gray, 205–206, 209
    knowledge of cost, 208
    major uses in home, 201–202, 213
    price elasticity–inelasticity, 207–208
    withdrawn, 200
    world supply of, 199
Water company rate-setting practice, 207
Water conservation, 199–201, 207, 210,
    214
Water-efficient appliance, 213
Water-flow restrictor, 205
Water pollution, 8–9, 15
Water Research and Technology, Office
    of, 201
Water-saving devices, 201, 203, 205,
    216
Water-saving technology, 199, 213
Water use, 214–215, 227
Water-waste preventer, valveless, 203
Waterway, 41
Wattage ratings, 38–39, 41, 43, 48–49
Welfare, 114
Wenatchee National Forest, 59
West Virginia, 225
West Virginia University, 69
Wild card bus, 151
Withdrawal design, 47, 56
Wood, 128
Woodland Park Zoo, 62
Wool, 133